Questions and Answers From the Bible

By
Les Feldick

About the Author...

"Study to show thyself approved unto God, a workman that needeth not to be ashamed, rightly dividing the word of truth."
 II Timothy, Chapter 2, Verse 15

Les Feldick is an Oklahoma rancher and has enjoyed that lifestyle for many years. Les and his wife, Iris, were married in 1953, and they have three grown children and six grandchildren.

What Les really likes is teaching the Bible. He has been teaching home-style Bible classes for over 30 years. His teaching is non-denominational, and his students come from diverse denominations and backgrounds. It was through one of these classes that a student helped open the door for his "Through the Bible" television program, which has been on the air for over 10 years.

Les has never had any formal Bible training. It is through the Holy Spirit that he is able to teach night after night, never using lesson plans or notes, and seemingly, never growing tired. Les teaches in five different cities each week.

Special note on how this book was assembled

The questions that are answered in this book were written by Paul Hartley, who also assembled the answers to the questions by gathering passages from Les Feldick's books which address each of the questions. Additional editing was then provided by some of Les Feldick's other Bible students. Care has been taken to confirm that the selected passages properly address each question for which they are provided as the answer. This process is explained here so that the readers will not think that Les Feldick provided each of these specific answers when asked each of these specific questions.

The exceptions to this process are those questions and answers in the section, "Answers from the Quarterly Newsletters". In those answers, Les has responded to specific questions that he has received from students.

This book also contains some notes of clarification provided by the students who assembled and edited this book. These notes are labeled as "Editor's Note:" so that the readers may clearly distinguish them from Les Feldick's commentary.

Effort has been taken to include enough surrounding text to preserve the context of the quoted passages. Never-the-less, readers are encouraged to study the books in order to more fully grasp the context. For this reason the book number, lesson number, and part number are given for each quoted passage.

Les Feldick Ministries

Copyright Policy

Part A — Beginning Faith — Page 2

Part B — Building Faith — Page 85

Part C — Complex Questions and Others — Page 165

Part D — The End Times — Page 249

Part E — Answers from the Quarterly Newsletters — Page 354

Part A - Beginning Faith

(1a) How do we know the Bible is really the inspired word of God ?

Editor's Note: Together, the two excerpts from Book 6 below, illustrate two key points. (1) The Bible contains prophecies of future events written hundreds (and sometimes even thousands) of years in advance which have been fulfilled and/or are still being fulfilled today. (2) God has a long-term prophetic plan for the nation of Israel which will be fulfilled. God has kept them alive as a nation, despite the efforts of many powerful nations to destroy them.

Book 6 LESSON TWO * PART III

Let's go back to Daniel Chapter 9. We'll see if we can finish down to verse 27 in this lesson, in order to validate this seven- year period of time as definitely in our future (not our future, because we're going to be gone, but in the future of the planet).

Daniel 9:24

"Seventy weeks are determined upon thy people and upon thy holy city, to finish the transgression, and to make an end of sins, and to make reconciliation for iniquity, and to bring in everlasting righteousness, and to seal up the vision and prophecy, and to anoint the most Holy."

That *"seventy weeks are determined upon thy people,...."* and that word 'weeks' here is used as we would use, 'dozen.' If I would say so many dozen, what would you automatically do? You would multiply it by 12. A week is always seven, and so seventy weeks of years is (a lot of the new translations have already calculated it for you and what have they got?) 490 years. *"**Four hundred and ninety years are determined upon thy people...**"* Daniel's people. And who are Daniel's people? The Jew - Israel. *"...and upon thy holy city, (Jerusalem) to finish the transgression, and to make an end of sins, and to make reconciliation for iniquity,..."* That all took place when? When Christ died on the Cross. And you remember several lessons ago this was one of the verses that we split with a parenthesis and a dash, because the next part of this verse is still future. It didn't happen at Christ's first coming. *"...**that is to bring in everlasting righteousness, and to seal up the vision and prophecy, and to anoint the most holy.**"* That hasn't happened yet. It will when He returns and sets up His kingdom, but it didn't happen at His first coming.

Come down through these next verses, but what you really figure out here that even though 490 years were in God's time table back here for the Nation of Israel, leading up to the rejection of The Messiah, would only total 483 years. Which means that there are seven years left that were not fulfilled at Christ's first coming.

Chronologists and archaeologists have teamed up and they have actually found the decree that Daniel mentions here, that gave the Jew permission to go back after their Temple had been destroyed by Nebuchadnezzar; it was dated, and from that date, it was March 14, 445 BC, up until Palm Sunday, **was exactly 483 years**. **That was fulfilled**. But, the prophecy said 490 years. And so that's why Bible scholars have sometime referred to the Tribulation as Daniel's 70th week. Sixty-nine of them were fulfilled at the Cross, but the 70th week, or that final seven years

2

is still unfulfilled. It's been pushed out into the future. Let's drop down to verse 27, it says, *"...And he* (the Anti-christ) *shall confirm the covenant with many for seven years."* Now, there is the triggering mechanism for the Tribulation!

Book 6 LESSON THREE * PART I

Turn to Matthew 24, for a quick review of our last lesson, where we left off with Jesus telling the Twelve the events of the Tribulation:

Matthew 24:15

"When ye therefore shall see the abomination of desolation, spoken of by Daniel the prophet, stand in the holy place, (whoso readeth, let him understand)."

He makes a tremendous statement that gives veracity to the Book of Daniel -- a book that has probably been under more attack by the scoffers and the liberals than any other book in The Bible, except maybe Genesis. But, here in Matthew 24, Jesus puts his stamp of approval upon the prophet Daniel. *"When ye therefore,..."* and remember He's talking to the Twelve; and so He is naturally talking primarily to the Jew. Never forget that this great Tribulation period, the seven years that is spoken of throughout all the Old Testament, is referred to here by Christ. And then, of course, the road map of it is in the Book of Revelation; that seven-year period is primarily, according to Jeremiah Chapter 30, Jacob's trouble. Which means it is primarily God dealing with the Nation of Israel after all these years of seemingly ignoring them, and yet not really. **Because always remember, one of the greatest miracles of the whole human race is the Nation of Israel. They should have been long gone, but here they are after over 4,000 years of history; and more than one government, more than one empire, more than one king has tried to obliterate them. And yet, here they are.**

I'm reminded of an anecdote I read years ago that during the time of Bismarck, I think it was, and the Prussian empire, he was an unbeliever and almost an agnostic, had one of his top gener-als who was a very devout believer. And so, one day as he was conducting his inspection, he came to this general and sneeringly said, **"General, tell me why do you still believe The Bible? Tell me in one or two words."** And the general, without a pause, said, **"Sir, the Jew."** And you see that is. The proof of this Book is the Nation of Israel. God is not through with them. He is still bringing them back to the land and that's why we're seeing this mass emigration into that little postage stamp piece of real estate, because God's getting ready to again pick up where He left off with His favored nation.

Now, here in Matthew 24, verse 15, He says to the Twelve, *"when ye therefore shall see the abomination of desolation spoken of by Daniel the prophet, stand in the holy place,* (that would be in the Temple) *whoso readeth, let him understand."* Let's go back to Daniel and pick up again those verses that Jesus was referring to, so we can tie it all together. Now, as I was driving up here for our lesson today, I was trying to sort things out in my own mind, because this is not just a short lesson, and we can go on to another subject some other time. We're trying to teach the whole scope of Scripture from Genesis through Revelation, and not in just bits and pieces; not as a shotgun approach, but we're trying to tie everything together. And I've known in my classes when people have gone through Genesis to Revelation four, five, six times with me; every time they will pick up things that they've never caught before. I used to apologize for reviewing, but I don't anymore, because every time I review, I know that somebody picks up a little bit that they've either forgotten, or they've never actually tied together. So, let's look at Daniel 9:24:

Daniel 9:24

> *"Seventy weeks are determined upon thy people and upon thy holy city, to finish the transgression, and to make an end of sins, and to make reconciliation for iniquity, and to bring in everlasting righteousness, and to seal up the vision and prophecy, and to anoint the most Holy."*

We're again dealing with the Nation of Israel; it's Old Testament, and some may say, "Wait a minute, you mean that the Old Testament isn't for us?" Of course it is! All Scripture is by inspiration and is profitable. So, we don't put lines through any of it. But, I maintain that you have to be aware to whom the particular passage was directed. And so, here again, Daniel makes it so plain that *"seventy weeks,"* or seventy weeks of years, or 490 years, *"are determined upon thy people."* God is speaking, of course, through the prophets. So, who are Daniel's people? Well, the Jew – Israel – the nation. *"and upon thy holy city,"* (Jerusalem), *"to finish the transgression and to make and end of sins, and to make reconciliation for iniquity."* Of course, that all took place at the Cross.

That's where sin was paid for, and all these things came to their culmination. But, on the other hand, there's still some time to go on after the Cross and the verse continues on, *"...to bring in everlasting righteousness, and to seal up the vision and prophecy, and to anoint the most Holy."* This is not an in depth study on prophecy; we're still going to go back to Genesis soon. But as I mentioned the last lesson, we've had so many requests to go back and spend a little time on end-time things, because we are getting so close to it all. And I agreed heartily, because, when I look at how long it's taken to go through the first 24 verses of Genesis, I'm honestly convinced that we won't be here long enough to finish the whole book. We'll be gone before it's all gone. So, we are just taking a brief overview.

Daniel 9:25,26

> *"Know therefore and understand, that from the going forth of the commandment to restore and to build Jerusalem unto Messiah the Prince shall be seven weeks, and threescore and two weeks; the street shall be built again, and the wall, even in troublous times: And after threescore and two weeks shall Messiah be cut off, but not for himself: and the people of the prince that shall come shall destroy the city and the sanctuary; and the end thereof shall be with a flood, and unto the end of the war desolations are determined."*

So then, here in verse 25 & 26, we see that these 490 years are broken down into a period that would be 483 years. Remember, that Abraham, the beginning of the Jewish nation, began about 2,000 BC. The Cross would be in the middle. Now, in this passage of Daniel, he is speaking of 483 years that would transpire from the decree from the king, which we find in Nehemiah 2. That decree was found to be dated in 445 BC. If I remember right, the date was March 14. All you have do is remember a scriptural year is 360 days, not 365. It's twelve months of 30 days, or 360 days. But you still have to compensate for those 5 days and leap years, so you just punch it out in your calculator, even with our present day calendar, from 445 BC, archaeologists have found this. It's not just pulled out of a hat. From 445 BC until the year of the Crucifixion, as I calculate it, comes to within about one year. And there can easily be that much difference in calendarization and so forth. So always remember that the Scripture is so accurate. **Nothing is guesswork.** And if there is a discrepancy, it is ours, not God's.

So, anyway, Daniel has determined that there would be 483 years from that decree of Nehemiah 2 until the Crucifixion. But, the total years that God was going to deal with Israel was 490. So, if 483 took place up to the Cross, that means there is seven years left. And consequently, most Bible scholars, and those who do a lot of writing, will refer to the seven-year period as Daniel's seventieth week. **Sixty-nine were fulfilled at the Cross. God's clock stopped,** and the last seven years are still ahead of us. They still have to be fulfilled. Now, then, as you go into verse 26, it speaks of a coming prince. *"After the threescore and two weeks shall Messiah be cut off* (at the Crucifixion), *but not for himself,"* He didn't die because of anything He had done. He died for us, "and the people," (now here's where you have watch carefully as you read), *"...the people of the prince that shall come,..."* Now, the prince that shall come is a small letter "p," and is the reference to what we call the Anti-christ. Christ is the Prince and He would be capitalized.

But, this prince is a small letter, and it's a reference to the counterfeit christ, the Anti-christ, and it's the people out of which he will one day come that will destroy the Temple. And we know that was done by the Roman general, Titus, in 70 AD. So, that verse tells us at the time of the Anti-christ's appearance, he will have to come out of the geographical area that comprises the ancient Roman empire. And it's coming to pass right before our eyes. It's basically the European Community, which by the end of this year, they hope to be able to call a Federation of Europe, or a United States of Europe. And so, the geographical part of it is already in place; that somewhere out of that revived Roman empire this prince will make his appearance.

Book 10 LESSON ONE * PART I

Editor's Note: These next two sections explain how the various books of prophecy written hundreds of years apart fit perfectly together, and play a critical part in the interpretation of each other. This is even more amazing when one considers that the writers of Scripture often did not understand the meaning of these things when they wrote them.

NEBUCHADNEZZAR AND DREAM (DANIEL 3)

We trust that as you study with us that you will find it to be as thrilling and understanding to you as it is in our classes. We have no ax to grind; we're an informal Bible study and we don't try to twist peoples arms into thinking one way or another. We just like to open the Scriptures and help people see what **The Book** really says. So many of us have been bound by tradition, and if there is any word in the Scripture that is condemned, it is tradition. We must be careful that we don't find ourselves locked into a tradition that is not necessarily in line with **The Book.** So this is our only goal; and that is to help folks see what the Bible really says.

This Book is so gloriously supernaturally put together so that there is no possible way that human hands could have done it. For example, there are three books of Prophecy written by Jews of course. But all written outside the land of Israel. Daniel, which we will be looking at, is one of them. **Daniel is writing from Babylon,** while he is captive there under King Nebuchadnezzar. The second one is the Book of Ezekiel which was also written from captivity in the next empire, as **Ezekiel writes from Persia**. And the third one is the last Book of the Bible, the Book of Revelation, written by **John from the Isle of Patmos,** which is in the Aegean Sea, between Turkey and Greece. Now those three Books of Prophecy also are unique in that all three write in symbolism.

Just stop and think about it. Ezekiel uses for example, The Dry Bones, The Stick, and the Fiery Wheel. All those are symbolism, but they have a literal truth. Now we come into the Book of Daniel and we will see this Great Image, with a head of gold, and a chest of silver, a belly of brass and on down its body. It's a symbolism of all the great empires that would be coming down through history. And then when you get to the Book of Revelation written by John, most people are afraid to even study the Book of Revelation. They can't understand it. And therefore won't even read it, simply because it is in symbolic language. But you see all those symbolisms are all interpreted by Scripture itself, in one place or another. And all you have to do is search the Scriptures and these things begin to fall into place.

Editor's Note: The prophecy in Daniel chapter 2 of the Great Image with the head of gold, mentioned above, foretold the fall of the great kingdom of Babylon and the future rise of the great kingdoms of Medo-Persia, Greece, and Rome. This teaching is not included in detail here due to its length, but a related prophecy from Daniel chapter 8 is explained below. Readers are encouraged to see Book 10 where the prophecy of the Great Image is explained in detail.

Book 6 LESSON TWO * PART II

Daniel 12:1,2

"And at that time shall Michael stand up, the great prince which standeth for the children of thy people: and there shall be a time of trouble, such as never was since there was a nation even

to that same time: and at that time thy people shall be delivered, every one that shall be found written in the book. And many of them that sleep in the dust of the earth shall awake, some to everlasting life, and some to shame and everlasting contempt."

The previous 11 chapters have been an out-laying of prophecy. In fact, **Daniel and Revelation just fit together hand in glove.** You can't study Revelation without studying Daniel and vise versa. So, now, as you come into the last chapter of this great book of prophecy, Daniel writes this: *"..and at that time shall Michael stand up, that great prince which standeth for the children* (Israel), *and there shall be a time of trouble such as never was since there was a nation even to that same time; and at that time thy people* (Israel, the Jews) *shall be delivered, every one that shall be found written in the book."* Now, this is what Paul refers to in Romans as that remnant. *"...And many of them that sleep in the dust of the earth,..."* In other words, they have died and they've reverted back to the dust. *"...many of then shall awake,..."* and here we have a parallel with John's Gospel, Chapter 5, *"...some to everlasting life and some to shame and everlasting contempt...."* Again, you've got the believer and the unbeliever listed here. Now let's skip over to verse 8:

Daniel 12:8,9
"And I heard, but I understood not: then said I, 'O my Lord, what shall be the end of these things?' And he said, 'Go thy way, Daniel, for the words are closed up and sealed till the time of the end.'"

Daniel is saying that he heard but he understood not. Now, I've always maintained, as I've taught the Old Testament, **that all Scripture is inspired of God.** Peter says so clearly that prophecy came not in the old time by will of man; and, you remember, I ridiculed the concept several months ago, of these things having originated around the camp fire and then just having been handed down as legend. That's not what our Bible is at all. **Our Bible is the very inspiration of the Spirit of God and as Peter says, that these holy men of God wrote as they were moved along by the Spirit.** Now under those circumstances, do you think they understood everything they wrote? Why, no way! And here it's so plainly.

Look what Daniel says, after writing this great book of end-time prophecy (and he's writing it 2500 years before it happens). And look what he says in verse 8. *"And I heard,..."* He realized what he had been writing, but look at what he says next. *"...I understood not* (!)," He didn't understand what he was writing. *"And I said, 'O my Lord, what shall be the end of these things?'"* Now, that much he could comprehend. There were some terrible times coming upon this planet. But he couldn't understand it. And so he said, *"'what shall be the end of these things.'"* And The Lord said, *"'...go thy way, Daniel, for the words are closed up and sealed till the time of the end."*

I always like to look back and read about men from years ago. You will find that it wasn't until near the turn of the century that men began to get a comprehension of prophecy. Before that, there was not a clear cut teaching of how these things were going to unfold. And that's exactly what God told Daniel. It wasn't for men to understand until we get close to the end times. And now, every week, it is so much easier to understand. I know, 20 years ago, when I'd teach the Book of Revelation, it was hard to get people to understand what it was saying. Now, I can teach the Book of Revelation and people are almost running ahead of me with current events and news.

Book 11 LESSON ONE * PART I

Editor's Note: This next section shows that Daniel wrote about the rise and fall of various empires hundreds of years before they came into existence, and history shows these prophecies were fulfilled.

2 Peter 1:21
"For the prophecy came not in old time by the will of man (but here is how it came about. The word "holy" means set apart. Holy men of God spake, not as they dreamed it up, not as they had remembered what they heard around a camp fire, or what had been handed down from genera-tion to generation)*: but these holy men of God spake as they were moved by the Holy Ghost."*

What is this saying? Everyone of us will meet someone once in a while who will say, "I don't see how you can believe all that stuff. After all, why do you think the Bible is more right in what it teaches than the Koran or the book of Mormon?" or anything else that they may say is their guideline for doctrine. I'll tell you why. There is not another book written that makes prophetic statements like our Bible does. Hundreds, even thousands of years before they happen and they all come true. What hasn't come true, will!

This is our reason for teaching prophecy. It is to show beyond a shadow of a doubt that this Book is the Word of God. And it's prophecy that has been spoken, and fulfilled to the last jot and tittle as much of the Old Testament already has been. We have no reason to doubt that the rest of it will be. Because the same God that fulfilled the first ninety percent of prophecy, is the God that's going to finish the last ten percent. All of that is just to show why we like to spend as much time in prophecy as we do.

The main reason we are studying prophecy now, is, as we come through the Old Testament, we reach to Daniel. Let's go back to the Book of Daniel now to Chapter 8, which we skipped when we came through. But, you remember on our sojourn up through the Scriptures, starting with Genesis, we have just come right on up, unfolding our timeline, and, consequently, since Daniel is in captivity under the Babylonian empire we stopped there in our progressive revelations. But, of course, Daniel is a book of prophecy. And so, he is dealing almost entirely in his whole book with events that would happen to the Gentile world. Now, back here in Chapter 8, let me show you how accurate prophecy has been. It's already been fulfilled as you will notice starting with verse 1:

Daniel 8:1
"In the third year of the reign of king Belshazzar a vision appeared unto me, even unto me Daniel, after that which appeared unto me at the first."

And he goes on to say that he saw a vision way out there in Shushan, which was the capital of the Medes and Persian empire on the Tigris River. In this vision he's going to see the unfolding of the rather immediate history (not the long term).

Daniel 8:3
"Then I lifted up mine eyes, and saw, and, behold, there stood before the river a ram which had two horns: and the two horns were high; but one was higher than the other, and the higher came up last."

Everyone envisions some horrible looking creature with a horrible looking pair of horns. Let's go back to a statement I made several weeks ago. Three books of our Bible were written outside of the land of Israel. All three of them are mostly prophetic, and all three of them deal primarily with Gentile prophecy. Daniel is one of them. He writes from Shushan on the Tigris river; Ezekiel is another, he also writes from captivity; and the third Book is Revelation, when John, the Revelator, wrote from the Isle of Patmos in exile. None of those three books were written in Israel. However, they were all written by Jews, and all three wrote in symbolism. The symbolism here is that the ram was indicative of the Medes and Persian empire. In fact, their coins had the ram's head on them. The crown of the Medes and Persians had the likeness of a ram. And so, there's no doubt from history and archaeology, that Daniel is seeing the vision concerning the empire of which he was a part, and that was the Medes and Persians represented by the two horns.

The horns in Scripture always refer to kings or the top guy in control. Try to remember that, because when you get to the Book of Revelation, you are going to see this leader with ten horns. And that simply means a government with ten distinctive heads or presidents, or kings. The Medes and Persians are the two kings. One of them is the father of Cyrus. He was the one horn, but his son Cyrus became so much greater, and pushed the empire out further, that Daniel sees it as the greater of the two horns. And that's all they are, two kings, the father and son. Now, as the Medes and Persians began to expand out their empire, they enveloped the land of Israel, and they took the city of Jerusalem. Then they went down into Egypt. And then they went around the Mediterranean Sea, and started overrunning what is present day Turkey - and they were headed toward Europe. But Daniel sees something that's going to stop this Medes and Persian Empire. Verse 4:

Daniel 8:4

"I saw the ram pushing westward, and northward, and southward; so that no beasts might stand before him, neither was there any that could deliver out of his hand; but he did according to his will, and became great." They were the greatest empire on the earth at that time.

Daniel 8:5

"And as I was considering, behold, an he goat came from the west on the face of the whole earth (they're in the Middle East. The Medes and Persians are coming from the east, in the area of the Tigris and Euphrates Rivers. They are moving around the north side of the Mediterranean Sea, and here comes a power from the west to meet them head on. It's a he-goat, and we know from archaeology that the Grecian Empire emblem was the goat. It was on their coins and other emblems. They recognized them as the he-goat. So this he-goat came from the west*), and touched not the ground: and the goat had a notable horn* (One. What was Alexander the Great? - a conqueror of one (not a consortium like the Medes and Persians). He alone arose from the Grecian Empire.) *between his eyes."*

Daniel 8:6

"And he came to the ram that had two horns, which I had seen standing before the river, and ran unto him in the fury of his power."

Let's break that verse down. ***"And he came to the ram"*** (now what do you have? Do you have a fight between two animals? No, you have a fight between two empires. So, the Grecian Empire is going to run head-on into the Medes' and Persians' Empire. And of course we know from history who won? The Greeks did. Alexander overran the Medes' and Persians' Empire, and ruled the greatest empire on earth by the time he was 33 years old. And he was also known in history as a general who conquered swiftly. He would move his armies with speed such that the then-known world knew nothing of. He would take chances, and was almost reckless in the chances that he would take. But he always seemed to come out on top. He never really lost an army.

So it was unique to Alexander the Great's military campaign. I think the word that shows that in verse 6 that many of us might miss is "ran:" but as this he-goat came he **"ran;"** see the indication of his swiftness and speed? ***"...and ran unto him in the fury of his power."*** Now, people read this and all they picture is a couple of animals in a wild animal fight of some kind - all it is, is two empires. Now you say, "Where do you get it?" Well, just move across the page to verse 20. And as I have said so often, Scripture always does it's own interpreting.

Daniel 8:20,21

"The ram which thou sawest having two horns are the kings of Media and Persia. And the rough goat is the king of Grecia (it's plain isn't it?)*: and the great horn that is between his eyes is the first king* (Alexander the Great)*."*

Daniel 8:22

"Now that being broken (you know what happened to him - he died; probably of alcoholism. He was only 33 years old. The great empire that Alexander the Great set up so swiftly, was immediately divided between four of his Generals. And so the empire became a quadrangle. It was no longer "one."), *whereas four stood up for it, four kingdoms shall stand up out of the nation, but not in his power."* In other words, no longer an Alexander.

Daniel 8:23

"And in the latter time of their kingdom (these four generals), *when the transgressors are come to the full, a king of fierce countenance, and understanding dark sentences, shall stand up."*

This is an interesting little quirk of Scripture and prophecy. The little king, spoken of here as being so fierce and powerful, on the pages of secular history wasn't enough to amount to a paragraph. But he was a king who went down to Jerusalem and utterly persecuted, and put under tremendous pressure, the people of Israel. So, in God's plan of things, he becomes a prime player. But other than that, he is only a little blip on the radar of history. Let's look at this man because he is a picture, or a type of the last man of fierce countenance. He is a picture of the Anti-christ. So this is the only way we can look at the description of this Antiochus The Great. The very same descriptive words connected to him are also descriptive of this Man of Sin. I'm going to wind up with the biblical description of this world ruler that is coming on the scene (we think before much longer). Let's look at verse 24, still speaking of Antiochus The Great, in history shortly following Daniel's vision:

Daniel 8:24

"And his power shall be mighty, but not by his own power: and he shall destroy wonderfully (in other words, beyond human comprehension the things that he would do.), *and he shall prosper, and practise, and shall destroy the mighty and the holy people."* See, he came down and persecuted the Nation of Israel.

Daniel 8:25

"And through his policy also he shall cause craft to prosper in his hand (in other words he's going to be successful in his little era of history)*; and he shall magnify himself in his heart* (this is all indicative of what the Anti-christ is going to be like thousands of years later)*, and by peace shall destroy many* (in other words he's going to be a political manipulator, and we are going to see that in a little bit. How the man Anti-christ is going to have such charisma, he's going to have the world just really licking out of his hands, because of his charismatic personality. And this fellow was able to do the same thing): *he shall also stand up against the Prince of princes* (now that's capitalized, so he's actually going to stand up in the face of God, and try to fight against Him)*; but he shall be broken without hand."*

Book 4 LESSON TWO * PART II

Editor's Note: This section illustrates that the writings of the Old Testament fit perfectly with the writings of the New Testament. And as we saw above, the writers of Scripture often did not understand the meaning of these things when they wrote them. Added to this is that fact that the Bible was written down by many different men living at different times who could not have collaborated to write this incredibly intricate Book.

Go, if you will, to Matthew 28. In our last chapter we showed that Jesus definitely referred to Himself as the `I AM,' or the Jehovah of the Old Testament account. In Matthew 28 He alludes to this title, The Most High, by virtue of what He says in verse 18:

Matthew 28:18
"And Jesus came and spake unto them, saying, `All power is given unto me in heaven and in earth.'" He is the possessor of Heaven and earth. He is not only the Jehovah, but He is the El Elyon.

Before we go back to Genesis 14, I want to explain my ridiculous illustration. Repeatedly I will read or hear `so-called' theologians (I use the term loosely - not all of them, but too many of them) who will refer to the Bible as nothing but a compilation of Jewish myth and legends. I remember reading one who said that all this `stuff' (as he put it) in the Old Testament began as the ancient Jews sat around their campfire and exchanged stories; that after several generations someone got the idea they should be writing this stuff down. Result? The Old Testament. That's just as absurd as the illustration I gave you. When seminaries and educated men with degrees who have written their dissertations, make a statement like that, it is just as absurd as the jeweler saying there is no difference between a multi-thousand dollar Swiss watch and a $5.00 alarm clock. It is just as ridiculous.

I remember a few years ago reading that the president of one of our more well-known seminaries made the statement that the account of Moses and the burning bush was just a figment of some good Jew's imagination. I don't know that he has ever retracted his statement. That's absurd! Hopefully, I have shown you how the Bible is so meticulously put together that the theme is never lost. It comes all the way through from start to finish. Everything is in its rightful place. How in the world could 44 men, living over a period of 2000 years, do that without the super-natural? They couldn't.

What I try to emphasize is that you and I can rest on this Book. It is letter perfect (in the original). I realize that all we have are translations and there have been some slight errors in translation. But God has so brooded over His Word that He hasn't allowed any gross error to come in, not even in our translations, so that we can rest on this as the inspired God-breathed, Word of God. When we can just believe it without doubting, whether it is the account of the creation, the Flood, the call of Abraham, the Covenant with the Nation of Israel, the Gospel of the Cross, the writings of Paul or the Book of Revelation, what do we say? - It is the Word of God! It is miraculous from start to finish and we have no room for doubt.

Here is another good example of what I am talking about. Clear back in 2000 BC when no one in Scripture had any idea of God the Son going to a Roman Cross to purchase mankind's redemption. Oh, it was there in latent terms as in Genesis 3:15 where the seed of the woman would crush the head of the serpent. Now we know what He was talking about, but they didn't. Even the writers of Scripture didn't understand these things. But God so put all these things into His Word, that it fully assures us that He knew everything from start to finish before it ever happened.

In the middle of Genesis 14:18 we find that Melchizedek brought to Abram bread and wine. They certainly used bread in the worship in the tabernacle - the table of shewbread. The wave offering was the sheaf of grain. Another time they would have drink offerings of wine and they would pour that out, but never was bread and wine associated in combination throughout the Old Testament economy. In the Age of Grace, what does the bread and wine speak of? The Lord's Supper; the Communion Table. . The only way we can really identify that is to go back to Matthew's Gospel where we have The Lord's Supper. Jesus instituted The Lord's Supper at the Last Supper, at the Passover.

Matthew 26:20
"Now when the even was come, he sat down with the twelve."

Matthew 26:26,27
"And as they were eating, Jesus took bread, and blessed it, and brake it, and gave it to the disciples, and said, `Take, eat; this is my body.' And he took the cup, and gave thanks, and gave it to them, saying, `Drink ye all of it;'"

I'd like to ask a question. Did the disciples understand what all of this stood for? They didn't have the foggiest notion. They followed His directions, but there is no explanation by The Lord Jesus, or even by the writer of this Gospel account, that they had any idea what He was doing. So, we have to wait until we come to the writings of the Apostle Paul. Now we understand what it was all for. Turn with me to I Corinthians, Chapter 11. Here, again, is progressive revelation. The eleven there at the night of the Passover didn't understand it. Jesus didn't explain it; it wasn't time yet. The Lord's Table of the bread and the cup is a memorial of His death, and on the night of the Last Supper His death hadn't taken place yet.

I Corinthians 11:23-26
"For I have received of the Lord that which also I delivered unto you, That the Lord Jesus, the same night in which he was betrayed, took bread: And when he had given thanks, he brake it,

*and said, `Take, eat; this is my body, which is broken for you: this do in remembrance of me.'
After the same manner also he took the cup, when he had supped, saying, `This cup is the new
testament in my blood: this do ye, as oft as ye drink it, in remembrance of me.'"* Verse 26 gives
us the explanation. *"For as often as ye eat this bread, and drink this cup, ye do shew the Lords
death till he come.'"*

This is the purpose of The Lord's Supper. It is remembering what Christ accomplished on the
Cross; that just as in ignominy and shame His Body was broken, the bread is broken. The pouring out of His Blood is, of course, in the cup. Back in Genesis we have the picture of His death,
burial and Resurrection, but that's all. All of this is to reassure us that the Word of God is so true.
It is so supernatural.

Book 4 LESSON TWO * PART III

When educated men, theologians, (that's what they claim to be) take the Bible and say it is nothing more than a bunch of Jewish legend and myth; or, as others have said, there may be some
of the Word of God in it, but not all of it is; as soon as you take out part of it you would lose
the fabric of this beautiful thread-work that goes all through Scripture. The main reason for my
teaching throughout the last few lessons, is to show that this Book is so supernaturally woven
together, we never have to doubt that it is the Word of God. I'll admit that all we have today are
translations. The King James (I still like it) is a translation. When I say the Word of God is letter
perfect and word perfect, I am referring to the original manuscripts before anyone ever touched
them. Portions of every book of the Old Testament were found in the Dead Sea Scrolls; the Book
of Isaiah being almost totally intact. Those are the oldest copies of the Word of God that man
has come up with so far.

When they translated the Book of Isaiah out of the Dead Sea Scrolls, the King James Version
was almost letter perfect. This is when I was assured that I would stay with the King James
Version. Even after all the translations and copying, we have a Bible that is nearly error free.
Sometimes I'll say I think the King James translators could have used this word or that word,
but for the most part it is so accurate that we can just rest upon it.

(2a) What are the attributes of God ?

Book 1 LESSON ONE * PART II

"In the beginning, God created the heavens and the earth."
"In the beginning ..." We really don't know just when that was. Evolutionists say the earth is millions of years old while Creationists believe it to be only a few thousand years old, but nobody
really knows for sure. Whenever it was, however, we know that "in the beginning" it was God at
work. There is no use trying to put a time frame on it because the Bible doesn't tell us.

Even in the New Testament in John 1:1 it only says *"In the beginning ..."* When the beginning was, time-wise, is not really vital for us to know. But the next word - "God" - Oh, how important that one is!

Mankind's, and especially the church's concept of God, it's attitude toward God is very superficial. You've all heard such terms as "The Man upstairs," or said something like "Somebody up there is watching over me." But God is so immense, so powerful, so wonderful, that we have nothing with which to compare Him.

The only way to get a true picture of Him is from His Word. From there we can draw attributes ... concepts, ideas, pictures of Him that are true.

Attributes of God

1. God is Sovereign. He is absolute. Psalm 8:4 says *"What is man, that Thou are mindful of him? and the son of man, that Thou visitest him?"* See also Romans 9:19-21. Everything that comes into being is a result of the sovereign choice and creation of God. Consequently, we should never question God, "Why did you make me as I am?" You are God's unique creation. We live and move under a Sovereign God.

2. God is Grace and Love. God's attitude toward even the worst of sinners is that He wants to save him. See Romans 5:8-11, 20-21.

3. God is Infinite. He is without end - without limit. Scientists tell us that the universe is expanding outward at a tremendous speed, but God is always beyond it. The universe will never go beyond our infinite God.

4. God is Omnipresent. God is everywhere, always present. The Psalmist said,"... *if I make my bed in hell, behold, Thou art there."* See Psalm 139:7-17.

5. God is Omniscient. He is all-knowing. There is not, or was not, or will never be a time when God had to seek advice or to consult someone or some source outside Himself, or study something out. Certainly within the Godhead there was counsel, but it was immediate, there was no debate among the Father, Son and Holy Spirit.

6. God is self-existent. He has no beginning, He has no end.

In Genesis 1:1, "God" refers to the Trinity - God the Father, God the Son, and God the Holy Spirit. This Triune God is Spirit, invisible, intangible - He is unable to be comprehended with the senses of man. But in Col. 1:15, speaking of Jesus, it says, *"Who is the image of the invisible God, ..."* God became visible in the flesh; He became touchable.

(3a) Why did God create us?

Book 21 LESSON THREE * PART III

Ephesians 3:10,11
"To the intent that now (after the finished work of the Cross and the revelation of this great

Gospel of Grace) *unto the principalities and powers in heavenly places might be known by the church* (the true believers) *the manifold wisdom of God, According to the eternal purpose which he purposed in Christ Jesus our Lord:"*

Why did God do it all? You know I've had questions come in over the phone such as, "Well if God knew that the world was going to end up in such a mess, and that men would rebel so, then why did He ever make them in the first place?" Well it all boils down to that question we've had since we were kids. Who am I, where did I come from, and why am I here. Why are we here? We're objects of God love. Now to be an object of love, what does the giver expect in return? Love, and that's why He made the human race. Angels couldn't respond, and so He made the human race with that indwelling attribute of will to either respond to His love or to reject it. And so that's why He had to bring Satan on the scene so we could exercise that choice, otherwise there would be no will exercised. So the whole program of the human race was that God could have prepared people to fellowship with. And to return or extend His love to them that had responded of their own free will to His love. And that's why we are here, and that's why the vast majority of mankind are given the free option to reject it if they want to. Remember, God doesn't want someone in His Heaven if they can't respond to His love. But to those who respond to His love, He's prepared things like what Paul says:

I Corinthians 2:9
"But as it is written, `Eye hath not seen, nor ear heard, neither have entered into the heart of man, the things which God hath prepared for them that love him.'"

Oh listen, the world out there I know thinks that we're a bunch of kooks, and fanatic nuts, and I know they do. And I just tell them, "Hey, live it for 70 or 80 years." So what. But I've got an eternity of the things that will make the best this earth can offer seem like an old pig pen by comparison. But you see they can't understand that we have simply responded to an extended love, and that's why He went to the Cross; it was love. Now what was the final eternal purpose? Paul doesn't really tell us here in Ephesians Chapter 3, but if you will come on over to II Timothy Chapter 1 we will find out.

II Timothy 1:7,8
"For God hath not given us the spirit of fear; but of power, and of love, and of a sound mind (the world may think we're nuts, but God knows better). *Be not thou therefore ashamed of the testimony of our Lord, nor of me his prisoner: but be thou partaker of the afflictions of the gospel according to the power of God;"*

Now listen what kind of power are we talking about? We're talking about the kind of power that can fling the stars, planets, sun and the moon into orbit without the benefit of a rocket or computers, and they never bump into one another, they're all out there in perfect synchronization. That's the kind of power we're talking about. I mean it's mind boggling. Now reading on.

II Timothy 1:9
"Who hath saved us, and called us with an holy calling, not according to our works (see how The Bible put down works for Salvation?), *but according to his own purpose..."*

You know back in the Book of Acts, Peter makes it so evident that before anything was ever created the Triune God had a meeting in eternity past, not that they had to sit around the table and banter it back and forth, but nevertheless the Trinity got together and agreed on creation, on mankind, knowing that he would sin, and they set up the plan of Salvation out of which the Son would come down and die, and be raised from the dead. That's all part of this eternal purpose that God implemented before anything was ever created. Now finishing that verse.

II Timothy 1:9
"Who hath saved us, and called us with an holy calling, not according to our works, but according to his own purpose and grace, which was given us in Christ Jesus before the world began,"

Isn't that glorious? I mean this is past human understanding, you and I are here today as recipients of His grace, but God knew about us way, way back before anything was created. We're not an accident in time, we are according to His divine and eternal purpose. Now let's return to Romans Chapter 5 again for a few moments. Remember verse 1 says, we have this peace that passeth all understanding. Peace with God. How many people have to lay their head on the pillow at night and toss and turn until their guilt complex runs rough shod over them. They know they're not at peace with maybe fellow men or maybe with government and certainly not with God. But the believer can put his head on the pillow and be at perfect peace with his Maker. Know that the work of the Cross has settled everything. Know that all these promises are true if we believe them. We rest on them. Now verse 2:

Romans 5:2
"By whom also we have access (how?) *by faith into this grace wherein we stand, and rejoice in hope of the glory of God.."*

In other words God's unmerited favor has just opened the windows of Heaven, and made it accessible to every human being anywhere and everywhere. But there has to be a door of access, and what is it? **"FAITH!"** Remember when we first started our series of lessons on Romans. I gave many of the things that God did the moment we believed. He sanctified us, He forgave us, He justified us, He glorified us, He baptized us into the Body, and on and on we went. And I said about everyone of them - **"did you feel it when it happened? Could you see it when it happened? Could your neighbors see it when it happened?"** So how do we know these things happened? The Book says so! And that's faith! Everything becomes a reality then by faith.

(4a) Is an unbeliever an enemy of God ?

Book 23 LESSON ONE * PART III

But we have to be aware, for the most part, the world today is totally unconcerned about things of the Spirit. They're more concerned with how much salary they can make, how big their home is, and how many cars they can drive. There is nothing wrong with those things in their rightful place, but when they become first priority, blinding them to spiritual truths, they're going to be awfully sorry someday. They are going to wish they would have had their priorities straight.

Romans 8:6
"For to be carnally minded is death (spiritual death, and eternal doom without end)*; but to be spiritually minded is life and peace."*
And what kind of life? The eternal life of God Himself has now become part and parcel of every one of us who believes, and it's going to carry throughout all eternity. We can't comprehend that, at least I can't, anymore than I can comprehend the outer edges of space; it is beyond us. When I read some of these things it just boggles my mind. I was reading an article that someone gave me the other night. To show the eternalness and the infiniteness of God, our sun in the solar system is so huge that it would take a million and three hundred thousand of our planet earth just to equal the size of it. Now, that's beyond my understanding, and then the star Centaurus out there is so much bigger again than our sun that it would take several hundred thousand of our sun to equal the size of it. That's the infinite God! That's eternity! And that's where we're headed. So we're dealing with eternal things that are without dimensions, that are beyond human comprehension. And what little we **do** comprehend, we appropriate how? By faith!

I've stressed over the years this is not some far out kooky stuff that some Jew sat by his camp fire and dreamed up. No, No. Because there is so much of prophecy in this Book that foretold events hundreds, and thousands of years in advance, and it's all come true. Everything that hasn't come true yet - we can already see the handwriting on the wall, that it's about to. If that much is true, then why can't it all be true? Well, it is. So when we contemplate these things, we just rest on The Word of God as absolute, it's true, and as sure as anything can be, and we can rest on it.

This next verse throws a curve at most people. And this is another thing that would be hard to comprehend if The Book didn't say it.

Romans 8:7
"Because the carnal mind (anyone who is still under the control of old Adam. Someone who has never had the power of the Gospel operate in their life, he is still the carnal mind, and that mind) *is enmity against God;..."*

You talk to good people here in Oklahoma or anywhere else you can think of, and they'll say,

"Well, no, I don't hate God. I love God, I believe in Him, I'm not His enemy." Oh, no, The Book says they are, and The Book doesn't lie. Now, how can The Book say that when people say the opposite. Because you see their old Adamic nature is still a rebel, and that's what people have to be convinced of. Their old Adamic nature is a natural born rebel against the things of God. And if you're a rebel, then you're an enemy! There are many of us that use the expression, **"With friends like that, who needs enemies?"** Well, it's the same way with God. A lot of these people who claim to be His friend, hey, He can't call them His friends. They're His enemy. Why? Because they're in that state of mind that is rebellious. They're not going to do what God says to do. They're not going to admit that they're a sinner. They're not going to admit that they have a spiritual lacking. Well, what is that? That's rebellion. And when you're a rebel, then you're an enemy, and it's that simple. Now, reading on:

Romans 8:7
"Because the carnal mind is enmity against God (now the next part of that verse is shocking)*: for it* (the Adamic mind) *is not subject to the law of God, neither indeed can be."*

That's scary isn't it? Do you know what I always think of when I read that? I think it's amazing that man is as civilized as he is. I really do. Because the unsaved person is not subject to the law of God. God doesn't expect the unbeliever to keep His law. God doesn't expect the unbeliever to be a good person, because God sees down in his nature that he's anything but good. Let's go back to where we were several months ago in Romans Chapter 3, and let's start at verse 10.

Romans 3:10-12
"As it is written, `There is none righteous, no, not one: There is none that understandeth (that is in that old Adamic nature)*, there is none that seeketh after God. They are all gone out of the way, they are together become unprofitable; there is none that doeth good, no, not one.'"*
And you see people won't agree to that, and will say, "Now wait a minute that's not me. I do a lot of good. I'm a good citizen, I contribute to a lot of charity." But you see that's not what God is looking at. He's looking at the heart. He's looking at their old Adamic carnal mind.

Romans 3:13-18
"Their throat is an open sepulchre (that's an open grave, there's nothing pretty about that)*; with their tongues they have used deceit* (we see this in our government and everything else)*; the poison of asps is under their lips: Whose mouth is full of cursing and bitterness: Their feet are swift to shed blood* (I don't even listen to the news much anymore, because of all the murders, and why? Because that's the Adamic nature see? And he's being turned loose more and more)*; Destruction and misery are in their ways* (you don't believe that? You haven't see the news in Bosnia lately)*: And the way of peace have they not know: There is no fear of God before their eyes."*

Why not? Because they have no comprehension of Who God is. They have no real comprehension of the power that He can employ, they ignore Him, and push Him out of their thinking. That's exactly what Paul is talking about in Romans 8:7. Let's look at it again.

Romans 8:7
"Because the carnal mind is enmity against God: for it is not subject to the law of God, neither indeed can be."

Now, that's hard to swallow isn't it? That mankind is not subject to the law of God, and can't be? That's what it says, and it means exactly what it says. And here's the problem with the Christian community even in our present time now. We would like to think that maybe we could legislate some decent morality, and cause people to stop all of these murders, and stop the teenage pregnancy, to stop drug additions, but you can't. We've seen that in the drug war, they can't stop the drugs, and they'll never stop the drugs until people stop wanting to use them. See? When people stop using drugs then the whole business will fall apart. Even back in the days of prohibition we had the same thing. They could pass a law prohibiting the sale of whisky, but did it stop? No. Because people still wanted it, and as long as someone wants it someone will produce it. That's human nature. And even though the laws of God are clear, and precise, mankind totally rejects them. Verse 8, and here's a conclusive thought: if this is the state of mankind which is lost; if this is the way people are when they are outside of the *Gospel*, outside of being positionally *"in Christ,"* then:

Romans 8:8
"So then they that are in the flesh cannot please God."
One of the absolutes of Scripture is in Hebrews Chapter 11, the great faith chapter:

Hebrews 11:6
"But without faith it is impossible to please him;..." (God)
And so the unbeliever who is an enemy of God is an enemy simply because he has does not have faith.

Book 41 LESSON ONE * PART II

Romans 8:8
"So then they that are in the flesh cannot please God."
But do they like to pray? Oh you bet they do. My when they've got a need, they pray. Well do you think God is interested in their prayers? No, because they're enemies. He's not going to answer the prayer request of an enemy, as they're not His children. I've always made the statement - yes, when a lost person cries out for salvation, God hears him. Absolutely He does! Before he even calls the Book of Isaiah says. But in everyday, mundane things when the lost person prays, God doesn't hear him, he's an enemy.

You know I've used the illustration that if your neighbor's kid comes to you and says, "I want a new bike, will you get me one?" I think it would be a rare individual that would say, "well come on son, I'll buy you one." No, rather we'll usually say, "Well that's your dad's job, that's not my responsibility to buy you a bicycle." And the reason we won't buy one is he's not our kid. Well you see that's just normal. That's not being mean spirited or anything like that, but just simple good economics. You can't buy bikes for all the kids up and down the block. Now God doesn't treat the human race much differently. If there is no love for Him and they're His enemies, He's not going hear their prayers, until of course they call for salvation, and then He becomes the God of EVERYTHING! Looking at verse 8 again.

Romans 8:8
"So then they that are in the flesh cannot please God."
Then for sake of time come on down to verse 13, and this will wind up this little dissertation of people who are still in the flesh, who have never been saved.

Romans 8:13a
"For if ye live after the flesh, (the things of this world is your concern, and you have no concept of eternity) *ye shall die:…"*
You know Iris and I travel and see the highways packed with people and we can't help but wonder, "How many of these people that we're meeting on these freeways and highways ever for a moment consider eternity?" How many ever stop to think of something of the Spiritual? For the most part I don't believe it ever enters their mind. Now I hope I'm wrong, but I don't believe it does. They're so wrapped up in the things of this world. So this is their future, that if all their living for is the flesh, these homes, cars, and credit card bills that are beyond their budget, and all the pressures of the world, they've got no time for God, and the Spiritual things and Paul says if that's you lifestyle, "ye shall die spiritually. You have no hope for eternal life." But verse 13 continuing is the flip side.

Romans 8:13b
"… but if ye through the Spirit do mortify the deeds of the body, ye shall live."

So it becomes then an option. Are you going to live for the flesh and die for eternity, or are you going to live Spiritually here and maybe miss out on a few of the things that the world thinks they have to have, and live eternally? That's quite an option, but it's mankind's choice.

(5a) What is faith ?

Book 20 LESSON TWO * PART I

II Peter 3:15a
"And account (or understand) *that the longsuffering of our Lord is salvation;…"*

That's the whole theme of this Book from the time man is created, and falls in Genesis Chapter 3, all the way to the end of this Book. It is a Book that is trying to bring about the salvation of a fallen human race. The whole theme of this Book! And in that regard you can find Christ in one form or another on almost every page from cover to cover. Because this is God's main concern that the human race can find salvation, that's why He has done so much. Verse 15 again:

II Peter 3:15,16
"And account that the longsuffering of our Lord is salvation even as our beloved brother Paul also according to the wisdom given unto him hath written unto you; As also in all his epistles, speaking in them of these things (what things? Salvation, and all that attends it)*; in which are some things hard to be understood,..."*

Get back into Peter's shoes. Peter was steeped in Judaism, steeped in legalism, steeped in Temple worship, steeped in all the Covenant promises coming out of the Old Testament for the Nation of Israel. Then for him to all of a sudden have to admit that God was not dealing anymore with the Nation of Israel on the Covenant promises, but instead, He is out to bring Salvation to the whole human race. That was unthinkable for him (reference Galatians 2:7-9). So Peter has a hard time with Paul's Gospel, and I know he did. And even here at the close of his life, he's still hedging just a little bit.

II Peter 3:16b
"...which they that are unlearned and unstable wrest (or twist)*, as they do also the other scriptures, unto their own destruction."*

You know I pointed out to the class last night, how many times can you take a rank liberal, or someone from a different religion all together, and they can speak of the Lord, and the Holy Spirit, and make you think that they know what they are talking about, and they know nothing. But they use all the right words, and that's what Peter means here, that they twist the Scripture to their own destruction. Let's go back to Romans Chapter 1, verse 16 again:

Romans 1:16a
"For I am not ashamed of the gospel of Christ: for it is the power of God unto salvation to every one that believeth;..."

Most people think it says to everyone that repents, is baptized and joins the church, but it doesn't. Or to everyone that does good. Or to everyone that keeps the commandments. You see, it doesn't say any of those things, but only to everyone that believeth the Gospel. Now why do I stress that from program to program? Let's go for a moment to the Book of Hebrews Chapter 11:6 We haven't looked at this verse in a long time. If only humanity could understand this. But the majority completely ignore it. They walk it underfoot:

Hebrews 11:6
"But without faith it is impossible to please him (God)*;..."*

So what does God look for first and foremost? Faith! And when God doesn't see faith there is nothing that He can do. You can go all the way back to Cain and Abel, and I imagine that Cain was probably a better guy than Abel was. He probably had a more noble personality, and a harder worker, but what was his problem? No Faith! He didn't believe what God said. Abel did! Esau and Jacob are another perfect example. Esau was probably a better man than Jacob, so far as worldly views were concerned, but why couldn't God use Esau? No Faith! He didn't believe a thing concerning what God had said. The Nation of Israel, what was God's constant controversy with that nation? They wouldn't believe Him. After all that He had done on their behalf, and the visible manifestation of His power, yet they just couldn't believe. He said, "Why didn't they enter into their rest? Because of unbelief!" What's the problem with the world tonight? It certainly isn't the lack of technology, or education and intelligence, and the ability to read. What's the problem then? They can't believe it when they read it, or hear it. No Faith! And when there is no faith, you cannot even get close to pleasing God! It's impossible. Back to Romans once again.

Romans 1:16b
"...to the Jew first, and also to the Greek."

Now naturally, when Paul began his ministry back in the Book of Acts, we found that everywhere he went, he went to the Jew first in the synagogues. It was a logical place to start. Because after all, Israel had been the Covenant people of God, they had been steeped in the Word of God. They were the very writers of this Book, and so it was very logical that was the place to start. But after about thirty-some years, and they continued to reject it, Paul comes to that final statement, and says, "From henceforth we go to the Gentiles." And so for the past 1900 + years, this precious Gospel has been going primarily to the Gentiles, but it's still open to a Jew. However, he now is going to have to come the same way we do because Paul says over and over in the Book of Romans that there is no difference.

I've told my classes over and over that we know that from the very beginning of His dealing with the Nation of Israel, God called out Abraham, Isaac, and Jacob, and the first thing He let them know was that He was going to set the Nation apart. They were to be a sanctified, set apart nation of people. You get into the Exodus with the Nation preparing to come out of Egypt, and the first three plagues also came upon Israel along with the Egyptians. But after that, He put a division between Israel and Egypt where none of the plagues could touch Israel. And He did that to prove His power. And so He put that division between them. And that was the beginning then of this great separation that God put between the Jew and the Gentile. And this continued all the way up through the Old Testament. He was dealing primarily with those Covenant people, the Nation of Israel. But they were 'stiff-necked' (as the Scriptures called them), they were steeped in unbelief, and finally God had to let the Temple be destroyed in 70 AD Then the Nation was dispersed, the land was emptied of them.

And that brings a thought today. Why can't our politicians seem to understand that Palestine has always been the home of the Jew? They sure don't act like they understand. They act as if the Jew is the impostor, the carpetbagger, the squatter. That's the way they treat the Jew today. That's his home land, and you can't take that away from him. But God providentially uprooted them, because of their unbelief; but at the same time that He uprooted them, what did He promise them? That He would bring them back again. All the Old Testament screams of that. And we should be aware it, that indeed God is still going deal with His national people of Israel.

Romans 1:17
"For therein (that refers to the word `salvation' in verse 16) *is the righteousness of God revealed from faith to faith: as it is written* (And then quoting from Hab. 2:4, we find), `The just shall live by faith.'"

Martin Luther finally came to this conclusion. He was cloistered in a Catholic monastery, and then all of a sudden the light shone in, and what did Martin Luther conclude? *"The just shall live by faith."* Not by works, not by religion, or ritual, but by faith. So that became his great theme of the Reformation. I think Christianity has come close to losing it again. We are all wrapped up in works, and materialism, and do this and do that. We have a program for everything. We are losing the whole idea that the just shall live by faith. And if you have heard me teach for a period of time, you know that I have a clear cut definition of the word faith. And what is it? "Taking God at His Word." That is all faith is! Let's go back to the Book of Hebrews and look at the Scripture's own definition of The Word. Turn to Chapter 11, the great faith chapter.

Hebrews 11:1-3
"NOW faith is the substance (it's the very core, it's the epitome) *of things hoped for, the evidence of things not seen* (things you can't touch and see). *For by it the elders* (Old Testament saints) *obtained a good report. Through faith* (by taking God at His word) *we understand* (and know) *that the worlds were framed by the word of God, so that things which are seen were not made of things which do appear. "* We are dealing with the invisible, and the only way we can comprehend the invisible is how? By faith!

Book 9 LESSON ONE * PART II

Romans 3:23
"For all have sinned, and come short of the glory of God; " Every human being, going all the way back to what man? Adam. We have all sinned - Jew and Gentile.

Romans 3:24

"Being justified freely by his grace through the redemption that is in Christ Jesus: Now verse 25, here is the verse I want:

Romans 3:25

"Whom God hath set forth (watch your grammar here. Who is the Whom referring to? Christ Jesus in verse 24. So it's Christ Jesus that God hath set forth) *to be a propitiation* (propitiation is a great big word that people just stumble over and hope they don't have to deal with it again. But it is not that kind of a word. It is, in my line of thinking, the most inclusive one word in the whole New Testament. Christ is our propitiation. And how does he become your propitiation? By Faith! He becomes our propitiation) *through faith in his blood* (not His life. Not His three years of exemplar miracle working and so forth. He can only become the propitiation through faith in His blood, whereby he can), *declare his righteousness* (not yours or mine) *for the remission of sins that are past, through the forbearance of God:"* And then I love verse 26:

Romans 3:26

"To declare, I say, at this time his righteousness: (Who's righteousness? Christ the propitiator) *that he* (Christ) *might be just* (what does <u>just</u> mean in plain English? Fair) *and the justifier of him* (that repents and is baptized? No, that is not what is says. It says) *which believeth in Jesus."* And what is believing? Faith. And what is faith? It is believing. You see, you can't escape it.

Book 28 LESSON TWO * PART I

I Corinthians 13:5

"(Love) Doth not behave itself unseemly, seeketh not her own, is not easily provoked, (Now that doesn't mean it can never be provoked, but it's not easily provoked) *thinketh no evil;* (True love can think no evil. That's quite a statement isn't it? Now verse 6.

I Corinthians 13:6-8a

"(Love) Rejoiceth not in iniquity, but rejoiceth in the truth; (Love) *Beareth all things, believeth all things,* (Remember faith is the other word for believeth, so our faith is based on love. The whole crux of the work of the Cross was the love of God, that He showered on mankind when He sent the best that heaven had to the Cross of Calvary. So far as Christ is concerned, God's wrath was poured upon Him while He hung there, but as God's wrath was poured on Christ the love of God was shed abroad on the human race.) *hopeth all things, endureth all things."* Then verse 8a: "Love never faileth:...."
Love will never let us down.

(6a) Who is the Lord Jesus Christ ?

Book 30 LESSON THREE * PART II

Now there is another point. You have no idea how many people are asking the question, "Well, Who is Christ?" A lot of people are confused. Some have the idea that Christ never really amounted to anything until He was born at Bethlehem. They do not have the understanding that Jesus of Nazareth was the manifestation in the flesh of the Creator God of Genesis 1:1. I show that when we teach the Book of Genesis that Christ, as we know Him in the New Testament, was the Creator of the Old Testament.

John 1:1-3
"In the beginning was the Word, and the Word was with God, and the Word was God. The same was in the beginning with God. All things were made by him; and without him was not any thing made that was made."

John 1:14a
"And the Word was made flesh, and dwelt among us,...."
As I explained to a person yesterday morning on the phone, and this very concept that we talked about in our last lesson. that when Christ died He paid the sin debt of every human being from Adam until the end of time. He could have never done that if He had not been the God of glory. So Jesus is the fleshly manifestation and is the image of that invisible eternal God. Turn with me for a moment to the Book of Colossians in Chapter 1. And let's see how this fits so beautifully with what the Holy Spirit inspires the apostle to write back in the letter to the Corinthians.

Colossians 1:15
"Who *(speaking of the Son in verse 13, and who has redeemed us in verse 14 through His Blood.)* is the image *(or visible manifestation)* of the invisible God, the first born of every creature:"

So you see this is what we have to take by faith. I know I can't prove this in a laboratory experiment, but the Scriptures says it. And by faith we believe it, that God the Triune, God the Father, God the Son and God the Holy Spirit were invisible. But God the Son stepped out of that invisible Godhead and became the visible manifestation of the whole. And that's Christ, that's The Lord Jesus of Nazareth. Do you see that? Now verse 16, and here we find that Paul, by inspiration of the Holy Spirit, attributes The Lord Jesus with the Creation.

Colossians 1:16
"For by him (Son in verse 13) *were all things created, that are in heaven, and that are in earth, visible and invisible, whether they be thrones, or dominions, or principalities, or powers;* (that even goes into realm of Satan and his powers) *all things were created by him, and for him."*

So that's why I say He is the same God in Colossians as He is in Genesis. The only difference is He has now taken on human flesh, human appearance. He is the image of the invisible God. I had a whole living room full of people about 25 years ago the first time I taught this. And when I just laid this out so clearly that Jesus of the Cross was the same God Who created everything in Genesis 1:1 it just blew their minds. And these people had been in church all their life, but they had never seen that before. And that's what we have to understand that Jesus of Nazareth was same God of Genesis 1:1, the only difference being He had now been manifested in the flesh. And that's why when we put our faith and trust in what He has accomplished, then we're not just talking about some Jew who grew up in a carpenter shop. But rather we're talking about the Creator Himself Who has taken it upon Himself the very work of redemption.

JEHOVAH
Let's pick up right where we left off in Genesis 2:4:
"These are the generations of the heavens and of the earth when they were created, in the day that the LORD GOD made the earth and the heavens."

As we noted last time, all through Genesis 1 the term "God" is used to refer to the Triune God, Father, Son and Holy Spirit. Beginning in Chapter 2, however, we have a new name of Deity - "LORD GOD" - or Jehovah God. You are all probably familiar with the term "JEHOVAH" because it is used often in the Old Testament. This term is very important, for it brings the Name of God from the Old Testament through the New Testament where Jesus personally comes to earth in the flesh. The word "JEHOVAH" is made up of two Hebrew words, "Jahweh" and "Havah." "Jahweh" is the word for "I AM." Remember Moses' experience in the wilderness with the burning bush? (See Exodus 3:6,13-14.)
"I AM THAT I AM ... thus shalt thou say unto the children of Israel, `I AM has sent me to you.'"
"Jahweh," then is the eternal, pre-existent, "I AM." The word "Havah" means "to be revealed," and is a continuing action verb, or means "to continually be being revealed." Jehovah, therefore, means "the Eternal, Pre-existent I AM Who is to be more and more (continually) revealed to mankind."

As we go further in the Scriptures, we will find that various extensions are added to the word "Jehovah" to give more definition and understanding to our concept of God. For instance, "Jehovah-Joshua" would mean "the eternal, pre-existent I AM who is to be more and more revealed to mankind as the "Savior." ("Joshua" means "Savior"). In the New Testament, then, we find the name "Jesus." This is the Greek equivalent to the Hebrew "Jehovah-Joshua" or "God the Savior." (See Matthew 1:21). So, the Word of God from Genesis to Revelation, gives us a continuing revelation of the eternal "I AM."

Think about it. First the LORD GOD walked with Adam in the garden in the cool of the day; then He revealed Himself to Abraham (see Genesis 18) and when Abraham prepared the meal, the Jehovah of the Old Testament actually sat down and partook of it.

Now, in order to show that with Adam on the scene, the Eternal, Pre-Existent "I AM" is God the Son, and is going to be the One Who is to be more and more revealed as we come up through the human experience, turn to Exodus 3. Here God revealing Himself to Moses in the burning bush - not in physical form as before, but by means of a human voice. The Lord speaks to Moses, telling him that he's standing on holy ground and instructing him to remove his shoes. Then in verse 13: "*Moses said unto God, 'Behold, when I come unto the children of Israel, and shall say unto them, `The God of your fathers has sent me unto you;' and they shall say to me, `What is His name?' What shall I say unto them?*"

Notice right at the beginning, that even though Jehovah, God the Son, has been separated out of the Godhead as a unique Person, yet He is still one with the Godhead, He is still God!

Remember that Moses had lived in Egypt for the first 40 years of his life. He knew and understood the thinking or mentality of both the Egyptians and the Israeli who had been in bondage there for nearly 400 years. Egypt had many "gods," and each one of them had a special name; and Moses knew that when he told them that God had sent him, they would ask him, "What is His name?" - which one sent you to us? Therefore, he asked God for His Name. In verse 14 God gives the answer: "*And God said unto Moses, `I AM THAT I AM:' and he said, `Thus shalt thou say unto the children of Israel, I AM hath sent me unto you.*"

It is this same "*I AM*" that we discussed before and the Old Testament will continue to refer to Him as JEHOVAH. In fact, in Exodus 6:2,3 God says, "*And God spake unto Moses, and said unto him, I am the LORD;*" Remember that `LORD' can be inter-changed with JEHOVAH; "*And I appeared unto Abraham, unto Isaac, and unto Jacob, by the name of God Almighty, but by my name JEHOVAH was I not known to them.*"

When theologians say that Jesus didn't claim to be God and that they don't believe in His Deity, see what they have to do to Scripture? They have to throw it out! Look at John 8:52-58. The Pharisees are testing Jesus in these verses, trying to drive Him into a corner. Whenever He said or implied that He was God, or the Son of God, to them it was pure blasphemy, and that's why they were trying to get Him to say in no uncertain terms that He was the God of Abraham. Then, they thought they would have just cause to put Him to death! As far as they were concerned, that was as blasphemous as one could get!
"*Then said the Jews unto him, Now we know that thou hast a devil. Abraham is dead, and the prophets; and thou sayest, If a man keep my saying, he shall never taste of death. Art thou greater than our father Abraham, which is dead? and the prophets are dead: whom makest thou thyself?*" Talk about a caustic reply. Look at Jesus' answer to them:
"*Jesus answered, If I honour myself, my honour is nothing: it is my Father that honoureth me; of whom ye say, that he is your God: Yet ye have not known him; but I know him: and if I should say, I know him not, I shall be a liar like unto you: but I know him, and keep his saying. Your father Abraham rejoiced to see my day: and he saw it, and was glad.*"

Remember as we discussed earlier that it is recorded in Genesis 18 that Abraham prepared a meal and God sat and ate with him and pledged His covenant with Abraham. So Abraham knew all about the Messiah's coming some day to the sons of Israel. Jesus rightly said, "Abraham rejoiced to see My day." But look at the Jews' reply in verse 57: "Then said the Jews unto him, *'Thou art not yet fifty years old, and hast thou seen Abraham?'*" In the "timeline" illustration at the beginning of this book, we indicated that Abraham had lived about 2000 BC, so the Jews here are aghast that Jesus, who was only about 30 years old, would say that he had seen Abraham! But Jesus' answer is beautiful and straight to the point; verse 58:
"Jesus said unto them, `Verily, verily, I say unto you, Before Abraham was, I am.'"

Jesus claims His Old Testament identity, I AM. He is stating that He is the eternal, pre-existent I AM who would be more and more revealed to humankind. We've seen how He was revealed in various ways to various Old Testament people, and here we see Him revealed in the New Testament as the Son of God, born of Mary in the flesh, presenting himself to the nation of Israel. He goes to the cross and rises from the dead and again reveals Himself unto His followers for 40 days - but in His post-resurrection form He is again different than He was before the Cross, because now He is in His resurrected, glorified body - the body fashioned as ours one day will be. It was a further revelation!

As we look deeper into the New Testament, we find the Apostles, Peter and Paul beginning to reveal Jesus as the "God of all grace" (I Pet. 5:10), and as the Lord Jesus Who loved us and died for us, and gave Himself for us (Gal. 1:4, I Tim. 2:6; Titus 2:14); all further revelations of the very person of Christ Who so loved us and had such compassion for us that He would even go to the Cross for us to purchase our redemption (Heb. 12:2).

And then, what is the name of the final book of the Bible? The Book of Revelation! It's a misnomer to call it "The Revelation of St. John the Divine," for it is actually "The Revelation of Jesus Christ" Himself, and within its pages we see Jesus coming in the clouds of glory to be the King of Kings and Lord of Lords. Do you see the constant revealing of Jesus through the Scriptures? As we study through the Word of God, we see more and more of Who Jesus is!

(7a) Why did Adam and Eve eat the forbidden fruit ?

Book 1 LESSON ONE * PART IV

Soon in our studies we'll be coming to Genesis 3:1-6. We'll see Eve in the garden. She has everything she could possibly want: a perfect home, a perfect husband, a perfect environment. And what does Satan tempt her with? "If you'll eat the forbidden fruit, you'll be `like God.'" And she falls for it!

Book 1 LESSON Three * PART III

We've seen in earlier lessons that God extended His love to the human race and expected or wanted our love in return. Knowing that we (his future bride) were in bondage to a cruel master (Satan), Jesus was willing (like the Hebrew slave-husband in verses 5 and 6 of Exodus 21) to come in the form of a man in order to win our freedom through His death on the Cross. And there has never been a more cruel or vicious form of death ever devised by man than death by crucifixion! Jesus was willing to suffer and go through that for us. He didn't have to - it was His choice because of His great love for us. Go back to Genesis 3:6. Adam loved his Creator; but he loved his beautiful helpmeet more, and he thought he was about to lose her. So he had to choose, and he decided he'd rather eat the forbidden fruit and violate the Word of God than lose her and remain obedient.

..... And that's what he did - he ate the fruit that she offered him. Immediately upon his taking that first bite of the fruit of the tree of the knowledge of good and evil, the process of death began not only in him, but in the entire creation. Immediately, he lost communion and fellowship with his Creator. Immediately, his soul, (his mind, will and emotions) took on the sin nature - a rebellious attitude toward God. We're not sinners because we've sinned, we're sinners because we're children of Adam.

LESSON Three * PART IV
RESULT OF ADAM'S SIN

Let's begin again at Genesis 3:6. As we closed last week, we saw that Adam had just eaten of the fruit of the tree of the knowledge of good and evil. Paul, writing to Timothy, said that Adam was not deceived as Eve had been, but he knew exactly what he was doing and what the consequences would be.

I Timothy 2:13,14:
"For Adam was first formed, then Eve. And Adam was not deceived, but the woman being deceived was in the transgression."

Adam had to make a choice between obeying his Creator and losing his beautiful helpmeet, or disobeying his Creator and remaining with the woman. After contemplation, the last few words of Genesis 3:6 tell the whole story, "He did eat."

The moment he ate, a lot of things began to happen. It's necessary for us to clarify this point, because some preachers, teachers and theologians teach that there wasn't an original sin or fall, and our only problem is with the sins we commit personally.

However, Paul writing in this "Age of Grace" or Church age to the brethren in Rome who were primarily Gentiles, declares with certainty that there was an original sin. Turn to

Romans 5:12:
"Wherefore, as by one man sin entered into the world, and death by sin; and so death passed upon all men, for that all have sinned:"

Before Adam ate, nothing died - there was neither sin nor death on this lovely earth home God had created for His man. But both sin and death entered this world with Adam's fall. Death came upon all by his sin.

(8a) Why did the Lord Jesus Christ give Himself to die for us?

Book 23 LESSON THREE * PART II

ROMANS 8:31-39
Now, we only covered two verses in our last lesson, and we're still in verse 32, and I can't emphasize enough that everything that God now has done, and is doing on our behalf, is based on that finished work of the Cross, where God did not even spare His Son. Why? So that He could purchase mankind back to Himself. Now, the first thing we may wonder if we're not taught in these things is, Well, why does God have to do this? He's Sovereign, and He could do any way He wanted, but you see God never goes against His own principals. God is Holy, God is righteous, God is Omnipotent, He is full of all knowledge. And so He knows what has to be done to reconcile fallen man back to Himself. And so in His knowledge, and understanding He is the One Who determined that it had to be the sacrificial death of Himself on our behalf.

Book 22 LESSON ONE * PART IV

Romans 5:15,16
  "But not as the offence, so also is the free gift. For if through the offence of one many be dead, much more the grace of God, and the gift by grace, which is by one man, Jesus Christ, hath abounded unto many (in other words all that will believe)."
  "And not as it was by one that sinned, so is the gift (in other words, as Adam plunged the human race into condemnation with his act of sin, so Christ has lifted the human race, by virtue of death on the Cross): *for the judgment was by one to condemnation* (every one is under that condemnation), *but the free gift is of many offences unto justification."*

And like I've said in the last three lessons, Paul is just hammering this theme of justification home. I don't want anyone who has heard me teach these first few chapters of Romans ever forget this word **"Justification."** This is what we are, we're justified by a judicial decree of the Almighty God Himself, that since we have believed the Gospel for our Salvation, then He can restore us back as Adam was before he fell. Of course we're still going to sin, and He has made

31

compensation for all of that by virtue of His Advocacy at the Father's right hand. Now let's move on into verse 17.

Romans 5:17a
"For if by one man's offence (Adam's) *death reigned* (as a king) *by one* (because of Adam); *much more..."*

Do you see how Paul is constantly driving home the Grace of God, which is going to compensate for the fall of Adam, is greater than anything Adam did? And this is what we have to understand, that, yes, it seems like God is severe in condemning everyone who was born out of Adam's race, but yet He's not severe because He's made the way back for every human being without lifting a finger. If God would makes us do something almost impossible for our Salvation then that would be different, but He doesn't. He just lays it right out in front of every human being. You know when I teach John Chapter 10 the good shepherd chapter, I always ask where is the door to that sheep fold? Is it up on some cliff? Is it across the ocean? No it's on ground level, it's where anybody can walk through it. It's accessible for anyone to go into the door of the sheep fold. So Salvation is not something that people have to obtain or work for or grasp at, but rather it's right in front of every human being. Now reading on.

Romans 5:17
"For if by one man's offence death reigned by one; much more they which receive abundance of grace and of the gift of righteousness shall reign (not like old death does, but now we're going to reign forever) *in life by one, Jesus Christ."*

Not because of what I do, but because of what He accomplished. So as Adam was the federal head of the human race, and he plunged everyone into a place of condemnation, the second Adam, Jesus Christ has accomplished everything that is necessary to bring fallen man back to Himself. The only difference is now there has to be an exercise of will. Now I know there is a lot of controversy of how much will is exercised in Salvation, and how much of it is in election. But nevertheless, I sort of bring the two extremes to the middle, and granted, God has to open our eyes, and hearts. But on the other hand man has the prerogative to reject it. And I think that is what will be so hard on lost people when they go through all eternity regretting their rejection of God's opportunity.

Now verse 18. Notice that verse starts out with ***"Therefore."*** When Paul uses 'therefore' and 'wherefore,' just go back and see what he has said. This is so heavy and important that it's just repeated over and over for about two or three chapters. That means God wants us to get it straight. Yet Salvation can be by nothing that man can do, but it's all been accomplished by the work of the Cross, and He is just in being the Justifier of those who believe. He's not cutting corners. God isn't winking at man's sins. He has paid the total price for it so now He can be just in justifying the unbeliever.

Romans 5:18

"Therefore as by the offence of one judgment came upon all men to condemnation; even so by the righteousness of one (this constantly brings the two into play) *the free gift came upon all men unto justification of life."*

Book 22 LESSON TWO * PART III

Now let's get down to the subject at hand, and that would be in Romans Chapter 6, and this whole idea of overcoming the old sin nature, old Adam, and to enter into this new life which, of course, is what Christianity is all about. Christianity is not a religion, it's not just something that we work for, it is something that is all accomplished by the Grace of God and by His power, and that alone. Now let's review verse 6 and come right on into verse 7.

Romans 6:6a

"Knowing this, that our old man (the old nature) *is crucified* (put to death)....:

Let's stop and qualify. When Adam and Eve were in the Garden of Eden, and God had made only one stipulation, one responsibility, and that was not to eat of that one tree, God said:

Genesis 2:16,17

"And the LORD God commanded the man, saying, 'Of every tree of the garden thou mayest freely eat: But of the tree of the knowledge of good and evil, thou shalt not eat of it: for in the day that thou eatest thereof thou shalt surely die.'"

Now I call that the very first fundamental law in Scripture. Then it's repeated in Ezekiel.

Ezekiel 18:4

"Behold, all souls are mine; as the soul of the father, so also the soul of the son is mine: the soul that sinneth, it shall die." Then Paul in that classic third Chapter of Romans tells us:

Romans 3:23

"For all have sinned, and come short of the glory of God;"

And so God has mandated that as soon as Adam sinned, and as soon as every son of Adam has sinned, what has to be the result? Death! And there is no getting around it. The soul that sinneth has to die. It's a command of God, but God gave mankind what we call a loophole. Yes we have to die, but we do not have to die in ourselves, we can take Christ's death as our substitution. And so this is the whole concept then of Salvation, and that is, yes, we have to die because we're sinners, but if we will just simply believe the Gospel, then Christ's death takes our place. That's what we call the substitutionary death of Christ. He took my place, and He took yours. So that's why Paul has to teach that the old Adam has to be crucified, he has to be put to death because he's a sinner. Now let's read on.

Romans 6:7

"For he that is dead is freed from sin (or old Adam)*."*

I used to have two judges in my classes years ago, and one of them has since passed away, and when we would come to something like this, then naturally it always helped to get the feedback from somebody who has firsthand knowledge on these things. And when we would come to this idea that old Adam had to die in order to be broken from any relationship in the future, then I would use the analogy, especially with one of these judges in the class, by saying, "Now look, you have someone up for murder, and you've gone all the way through the trial process, and it's evident that he was guilty. In fact, you can almost bet that the jury is going to vote to put him to death, but what if about a week before it's all over the guy dies? He's dead, then what?" Well, you all know how those judges answered. The trial's over. It's all done, because you don't try a dead man. Even though he was as guilty as can be there is nothing you can do once he dies. Well, it's the same way with regard to old Adam, the only way we can separate ourselves from that old Adamic nature is to put old Adam to death. And the moment that he dies, he loses that control over us. Have you got the picture? And that's exactly what verse 7 is saying.

Romans 6:7

"For he that is dead (been crucified) *is now freed from sin* (old Adam)*."*

And until old Adam is put to death, he reigns as a king. Now verse 8, so Paul is building all of this for our own information to increase our faith of where we are as believers.

Romans 6:8

"Now if we be dead with Christ (if we have identified with that death then that's when we died, and that all comes by faith when we believe the Gospel)*, we believe that we shall also live with him:"*

Book 28   LESSON TWO * PART I

I Corinthians 13:6-8a

"(Love) *Rejoiceth not in iniquity, but rejoiceth in the truth;* (Love) *Beareth all things, believeth all things,* (Remember faith is the other word for believeth, so our faith is based on love. The whole crux of the work of the Cross was the love of God, that He showered on mankind when He sent the best that heaven had to the Cross of Calvary. So far as Christ is concerned, God's wrath was poured upon Him while He hung there, but as God's wrath was poured on Christ the love of God was shed abroad on the human race.) *hopeth all things, endureth all things."* Then verse 8a: "Love never faileth:...."
Love will never let us down.

Editor's Note: For further insight into this question, see the answer to the question, "Why did God require a blood sacrifice?", which is explained later in this book.

(9a) What is the only way to be saved during this present age of grace ?

Book 20 LESSON ONE * PART IV

Now let's look at the Gospel as outlined in I Corinthians Chapter 15, and beginning with verse 1. I never tire of repeating it, and I hope you never get tired of hearing it.

I Corinthians 15:1
"MOREOVER, brethren, I declare unto you the gospel which I preached unto you, which also ye have received, and wherein ye stand;"

"...wherein ye stand" is a positional term. That's why he writes in another place that we are not to be blown about with every wind of doctrine. Some people are so shallow in their understanding of Scriptures, that they see someone on television or someone can come to their door and they have a good line, and a nice approach, and they fall for it. We are supposed to be so well versed in the Scriptures that something like that won't happen. We are to be like an anchor, steadfast, immovable. Now verse 2.

I Corinthians 15:2,3
"By which also ye are saved (it's only by this Gospel that you are saved. It's not by something else), if ye keep in memory what I preached unto you, unless ye have believed in vain." And now here comes Paul's Gospel in verse 3:
"For I delivered unto you first of all that which I also received (here he's talking about what we saw in Galatians in our last lesson, how that by revelation, "He made known unto me," Paul says. This is what the Lord revealed to him. We will find that Paul's Gospel is not based on the Judaistic Law, or just on the fact that Christ was the Messiah of Israel, but it's that The Messiah of Israel, The Son of God, died on that Roman Cross, shed His Blood, was buried and rose again, and here it is), how that Christ died for our sins according to the scriptures;" This was in the Old Testament. It was all in the pre-eternal mind of God, that all of this would fall into place.

I Corinthians 15:4-6a
"And that he was buried, and that he rose again the third day according to the scriptures." That's the Gospel! And to prove that Christ rose from the dead we see in verse 5 and 6 the following.
"And that he was seen of Cephas, then of the twelve: After that, he was seen of above five hundred brethren at once;..."

Paul tells us that he also saw Him in person. Paul knew that He was alive. Now back to Romans 1:16. That's The Gospel – that Christ died for the sins of the world. And that's what Paul expressly desires to get across to people. It's so hard for people to comprehend that this is all they have to do. **Just believe the Gospel for Salvation**. If you really believe He will save you. Now you know that I'm not an easy believer. You know that. I'm not just talking about making a mental acknowledgment and you're all right. No, **what I'm talking about is a Holy Spirit driven belief, that my eternal destiny is based on what He did for me on that Cross.** And we will be seeing more and more of that, especially when we get into Romans Chapter 6, where Paul just begins to draw that simple analogy of a little seed that's planted in the ground, but before that plant can come forth, and bring forth fruit it must die first. So the whole analogy is that, **"When Christ died, we died. When He was buried, we were buried. When He arose from the dead, we also arose out of deadness in the old Adamic sin nature to a new life."** Verse 16 again:

Romans 1:16

"For I am not ashamed of the gospel of Christ: for it (The Gospel, not our works, or denomination, not anything that we can do, but rather The Gospel) *is the power of God unto salvation..."*

One of the newer translations waters this down by using the word 'salvation' as a better way to heaven. Salvation is much more than a better way to heaven. Salvation is that all inclusive work of God on our behalf, whereby we are forgiven: He justifies us, He sanctifies us, He glorifies us, He baptizes us into the Body, He seals us with the Holy Spirit, He fills us with the Holy Spirit, and on and on you can go in all that was accomplished on your behalf by an act of God instantly the moment you believe. And you're not going to necessarily feel any of those things, but they have happened to you if you were genuine in your belief. But how do I know that these things have happened to me? The Book says so. And that's where faith comes in. That's what The Book means when it says we are saved by faith and are to live and walk by faith. Taking God at His Word. So, you just simply have to know what The Book says. When you come to Salvation, and say, "I don't understand this or feel any different," remember The Book says that it has happened. And that is what God is pleased by. Remember Hebrews 11:6:

Hebrews 11:6a

"But without faith it is impossible to please him:..."

You should be able to say, **"Yes, I know that I'm forgiven,"** not because I'm so perfect, or any better than anybody else, but simply because I believe what this Book says!** I can't make it any plainer than that. So when an individual realizes that he's in the cesspool of sin, in that old slave market, and there is no hope of getting out, unless the power of God takes him out; God pulls him out of that deadness in sin, and gives him new life, sets his feet as the Scriptures say, ***"On a Rock,"*** and does all these things for him. That's what believing does! After that, you become a totally new person in your outlook on life, in your desires, and you don't work for that. Remember, you won't become a mature Christian overnight. It's going to take time. The Christian life is like coming into physical life. We come into the Christian life as a babe in Christ, just an infant that needs tender loving care. An infant that needs nourishment, and protection. That's what a new believer is.

But God doesn't expect a new believer to stay a babe in Christ. He expects them to begin to grow in Grace, and knowledge and wisdom. To grow in a new lifestyle. Over the years I've told my classes the basic fundamental aspect of a Christian life, the part that will immediately become visible to our friends and relatives, and yes, the whole community; a true born again child of God is going to be a good citizen. Have you ever thought of that? When we are a practicing believer, we will be a good citizen. In other words, you won't find a true child of God giving the police department fits. Now there may be isolated instances, that's always a possibility. But the basic believer will be a good citizen, and a good parent. He will be a good grandparent. He will be a good child. He will be a good teenager. Now that doesn't mean we are perfect. Nevertheless, we will be the kind of person that will enhance society. If you could have a community of 100% born again believers, then you would have a pretty decent place to live.

I'm not saying that it would be perfect. It's just like the local church, no church is perfect. I said on this program once, if it was perfect I'd like to find it, but I wouldn't dare join it because it would be no longer perfect. But, for the most part, God's power unto salvation has imparted all these things on our behalf and they will make us different. That doesn't give us the right to walk around like we are perfect, or better than everybody else. But what we have is an imputed position that God has accomplished on our behalf. We will look at that more in depth later in Chapter 3.

Romans 1:16b
"...for it is the power of God unto salvation to every one that believeth; to the Jew first and also to the Greek."

I said at the close of the last lesson that there were many things in there that normally people would think should be. Over the years, I have taught to be aware of what is **not** in Scripture that many of us think **should be**. Well, here is a good one. Let me read this verse the way a lot of people think it should have been written. **This is just an example: "For it is the power of God unto salvation to every one that repents, and is baptized, joins the church, gives ten percent of his income, does good works, and believes."** But it doesn't say that does it? There are a lot of these things that people just automatically think are requirements for Salvation, and they're not! They are all right in their rightful place **after** Salvation. **But so far as our salvation is concerned it's based totally upon our faith in the Gospel, and what God has said concerning the finished work of the Cross.**

(10a) How were people saved in Old Testament times ?

Book 33 LESSON 2 * PART II

Now in our last lesson we were looking at the fact that Abraham was justified by faith + nothing! I can't emphasize that enough, although I should be known for that by now. Our salvation rests on nothing that we can do in the flesh, but it is all resting on the finished work of the Cross through His death, burial, and resurrection, and now we appropriate it by faith. Then after we have received salvation, then yes we move into an area of service and what ever you put on it.

But not for salvation. Now in verse 7 Paul continues on with Abraham as his theme.

Galatians 3:7
"Know ye therefore that they which are of faith, (in other words those of us who have entered into a salvation experience by faith only) *the same are the children* (or the sons) *of Abraham."*

Now I've got to stop there for a while. How many people have come up to me and said, "Well we've always been told that when we became a Christian we became a Jew." And I always tell them, I don't know who told you that but they are way out in left field, because a Jew is a Jew by virtue of, first and foremost, his birth, his genetics, his blood line, and the keeping of the Law. But a Gentile is a Gentile of the Gentiles, and if you've had salvation then you are simply a Gentile sinner saved by Grace, and not a Jew. Then they point to this verse we have just read. **"But the Bible says, we are children of Abraham."** Well you've got to realize what the Bible is saying, and not take it out of context. What the Bible is really saying here in verse 7

Galatians 3:7b
"...they which are of faith, (way) *the same are the children of Abraham."*

We have entered in the faith way + nothing the same way that Abraham did, and so consequently we are spiritually now connected to this man Abraham. Now to follow that up we've again got to go all the way back to Genesis. I'm sorry. I hadn't planned on doing this but we must. So let's turn to chapter 13, and there are some interesting words in this passage. Now of course this is the chapter after the Abrahamic Covenant was given so he's already on covenant ground, he already has all these promises. Now look what God says to Abraham.

Genesis 13:16a
"And I will make thy seed..."
Or your off spring. Also here is another little quirk of Hebrew. You have to discern from the context whether the word *seed* is singular and speaking of Christ or whether it's plural and speaking of the whole Nation of Israel. Now that takes some doing I know, and I know when we taught Genesis I gave the example even in our English language. You can have 12 sheep over there, and 1 over here, but what do you call them? Sheep. It's the same way with the Hebrew word that pertains to the word *seed*. It can be plural, but the same identical word can be singular, so you must use your where with all to determine from the text is it speaking singular, and the Messiah, or it is speaking plural the children of Israel. Well this one is plural.

Genesis 13:16
"And I will make thy seed (the off spring) *as the dust of the earth:..."*
Now what's dust? Is it earthly or heavenly? Well it's earthly. So his earthly progeny would be as

the numbers of the sand of the sea. In other words the Nation of Israel would be in terminology of course that is comparative. Compared to the rest of the nations of the ancient world were by far more in number. Now turn the page to Genesis chapter 15, and verse 5. And now look what God promises.

Genesis 15:5
"And he brought him forth abroad, and said, Look now toward heaven, and (count or) *tell the stars, if thou be able to number them: and he said unto him, So shall thy seed be."*

Now what was God doing? Playing games? No. God in His infinite Sovereign Grace was promising Abraham 2 different groups of people that would be connected to him. Now naturally the dust of the earth was his earthly offspring who came by the sons of Abraham, Isaac and Jacob. Now when God brings him out and tells him to look toward the heavens, now God is talking about a heavenly connection. Most of you have been hearing me teach long enough to know that we have two concepts in Scripture, **"The earthly people Israel and The heavenly people who are the Church."** All right. Abraham is being promised a connection to both of them. He will have an earthly progeny which was the children of Israel, but he's also going to have a heavenly progeny which are those who have entered in like he did by faith, and faith alone.

So now you have this two fold promise the Nation of Israel which would be earthly, but also a group out there some place who would be connected to him only in the realm of the spiritual. Now I think that I've already made my point as you come back to the Book of Galatians. Let me put something on the board, and maybe it will help a little bit. **On the time line we have Abraham back here 2000 years before Christ. Also on this time line we have the finished work of the Cross at Calvary, and then here you and I stand in this interval from the time of the early Acts, and I think especially with Paul's ministry, and the Body of Christ is being called out.**

All right I think I've already made my point. How do we become members of the Body of Christ that is being called out? By faith + nothing! Abraham became the Friend of God and his righteousness because of his faith + nothing also! And this was done just by believing what God said. Now if you were in an algebra class what would I be able to say? There's an equality. Right? This is equal to this. Why? Because Abraham received eternal life the same way the Church age believer does, we all came in the same way. Now to make my point, how did people back here from Adam, Abel, Seth, Noah, and all the way up to Abraham, how did they come into a right relationship with God, faith + nothing? No way, but rather it was faith + sacrifice. **They couldn't approach God without the sacrifice. Coming up to the Cross even in Christ's earthly ministry, did Jesus ever teach the concept of a salvation by faith and faith alone. No. What were they to do? They were still to be adherence to the Law of Moses, they also had the added responsibility of repentance and water baptism, + their faith.** But faith alone wouldn't cut it. Even in the early chapters of Acts, it wasn't just faith and faith alone. They had to repent and be baptized, and that was a requirement. It wasn't just empty words, but a requirement.

But then along comes the apostle Paul with faith + nothing, and this is why he had so much opposition. And that's why I imagine out there at least silently I've also got that opposition. I don't hear it personally, but I know it's out there. **"Les you make it too simple! You've got to repent and be baptized."** And I've even had people call and say, **"Well we've always been told that you have to repent, be baptized, and speak in tongues before we're saved."** *Well that's not faith + nothing, that's faith + something.* OK now what's my point?

That just as surely as Abraham was saved by faith + nothing when he believed God when He told him to go to a land that He would show him. We, in the Body of Christ, are saved by faith + nothing when we believe God when he tells us to believe the Gospel for salvation in I Corinthians 15:1-4. So by the basis of faith + nothing Abraham had imputed righteousness, you and I as members of the Body of Christ have also imputed righteousness, and that makes us just like Abraham. Does that make sense? No one else in all of God's economy had that privilege. Let me show you in the Book of Hebrews. Maybe that will make my point. Chapter 11 - the great faith chapter. It goes clear back to Genesis chapter 4.

Hebrews 11:4
"By faith Abel (believed God? No. He offered. He did something) *offered unto God a more excellent sacrifice than Cain, by which he obtained witness that he was righteous, God testifying of his gifts: and by it he being dead yet speaketh."* By faith, primarily, but it was faith plus. Now you come all the way down to verse 7.

Hebrews 11:7
"By faith Noah, being warned of God of things not seen as yet, moved with fear (and what did he do?) *prepared an ark to the saving of his house; by the which he condemned the world and became heir of the righteousness which is by faith."*

He did something. Now, let me ask you. If Noah would have stood out there in the Middle East and said, "All right God, I believe you that a flood is coming," and never built an ark, what would have happened? He would have gotten washed away along with the rest of them. But along with his faith that a flood was coming, what did he do? He built an ark. And all the rest of the way up through Scripture, all those great men of God, Jacob, Isaac, David and all the rest. They were men of faith, but faith alone? No! Faith plus Temple worship, plus Law keeping, plus this, plus that. Am I making my point? **But Abraham never made a sacrifice until years later. He did not do anything he just simply believed God. God saw that man's faith and He imputed** righteousness to him. **And so it is with us. Without out doing a thing, we just simply say, "Yes Lord, I believe it, that you died for me, that you were raised in resurrection power, with all my heart."** And that's all God is looking for.

(11a) What are the attributes of Satan ?

Editor's Note: The following teachings show that Satan is "an angelic personality with tremendous power", "god of this world", the "Master Counterfeiter" that can appear as the "angel of light". He is "a liar, and the father of it". He controls "demons and evil spirits", and "his (Satan's) ministers are also be transformed as the ministers of righteousness". (That is, Satan's ministers can appear as ministers of God). "We know he has the power of the universe at his disposal with only the sovereign power of God to control him!"

Book 2 LESSON TWO * PART III

Satan, Paul tells us, can transform himself into an angel of light (II Cor. 11:14).
Don't just delegate Satan to some little monkey in a funny red suit with a tail and horns and a pitchfork! That is not the Biblical picture of Satan. He is an angelic personality with tremendous power. The Apostle Paul tells us that Satan can transform himself into an "Angel of Light." We know he has the power of the universe at his disposal with only the sovereign power of God to control him! So this Cainitic civilization is going to be driven by the powers of Satan and not by the powers of God.

Book 1 LESSON TWO * PART I

Genesis 1:28
"And God blessed them, and said unto them (that is Adam and Eve, although Eve hasn't been created, she is still in Adam. So He is addressing them both.), `Be fruitful, and multiply, and replenish the earth, and subdue it: and have* (what?) *dominion...'"*

In other words Adam was to have rule over the whole creation under God. He had total dominion. He was going to be literally God's second in command. When Adam sinned, what happened to that role as having dominion? He lost it. He dropped the ball. Who picked it up? Satan did. From that time on Scripture makes it so abundantly clear, who is the god of this world tonight? Satan is. Another Scripture says, "The world lieth in the lap of the wicked one." Satan is the god of this world. Everything that mankind accomplishes, whether it's good, beautiful, ugly, or bad, who has prompted it? Satan has. God is not in the business of a material world. And so the world is truly in the lap of that wicked one. Satan has total dominion. Let me show you another good example. Go to Matthew Chapter 4 if you doubt me. Here we have the temptation. And Satan is trying every ploy, trying to get Jesus to bow down to him.

Book 1 LESSON Three * PART III

Matthew 4:8-9

"Again, the devil taketh him up into an exceeding high mountain, and sheweth him all the kingdoms of the world, and the glory of them; And saith unto him, 'All these things will give thee, if thou wilt fall down and worship me.' Then saith Jesus unto him, 'Get thee hence, Satan: for it is written, "Thou shalt worship the Lord thy God, and him only shalt thou serve."'"

This was the time of the Roman Empire, an empire that governed everything from the British Isles on the north and west to the Ganges River in India on the East. In essence, Satan says "Everything you can see or think of as far as material possessions are concerned can be yours, Jesus, if you'll just fall down and worship me. I'll give them all to you." Remember, Scripture teaches that Satan is the God of this World, and this passage really confirms it. If these kingdoms had not been his to give, this would not have been a temptation to Jesus for He would have known that. But at that time they did belong to Satan - he just didn't know that Jesus would possess all of them, not by bowing down to him then, but later, by right of conquest, after completing His work on the Cross and defeating him totally at the resurrection. Satan didn't know that one day Jesus will return as King of Kings and Lord of Lords!

Book 2 LESSON THREE * PART I

Even though Cain had turned his back on God and was out of the presence of God, he did have a motivating power. When Cain pushed God out of his life, the power of Satan entered in. You can't create a vacuum. There is no such thing as having absolutely no spiritual influence in one's life. If God is pushed out, Satan is going to come in! Just because we speak of Satan as being evil, and representative of wickedness, he doesn't always do awful things. He is very well qualified to promote good, even beautiful things in order to accomplish his purpose. When Paul said that Satan could transform himself into an angel of light, Paul was explaining that Satan is the "Master Counterfeiter!" He is a counterfeit of God at every opportunity. If he can make something look like an original, he'll do it.

When the U.S. government hires people to work in the Treasury Department, particularly in the area of counterfeit, they don't show them lots of counterfeit bills. Instead, for six months those people study nothing but legitimate American currency. The idea is that if they know meticulously how the original looks, when they see something that is counterfeit, they'll recognize it immediately. That's what we as believers must do with the Scriptures - be so profound in our knowledge of the Scriptures that when the cults come along, or when people come to our doors with something less than the truth, we'll recognize it immediately as a counterfeit. Because Satan, the "master counterfeiter" is so capable of making his fake look like the original, we must know the genuine article so we can recognize the difference.

Book 34 LESSON ONE * PART II

Romans 3:20b
"...for by the law is the knowledge of sin."

All the Law can show mankind is their sinfulness, not their salvation. Isn't it amazing how Satan can totally counterfeit the issue? Now today, Satan has convinced millions, probably billions, that if they do the best they can, if they keep the Law, at least as much as possible, somehow they'll make it. They've got that idea and it's just stuck in their craw and they refuse to see what the Book says. The Book says they're never going to make it. Because by the keeping of the Law, is no flesh justified. But we have to experience that price of redemption, which is by having our faith in that shed Blood of Calvary.

Book 36 LESSON TWO * PART I

John 8:44b
"...for he (Satan) *is a liar, and the father of it."* Now let's see what Satan says to the woman. Turn with me to Genesis 3 and verse 4 and following.

Genesis 3:4-5
"And the serpent said unto the woman, Ye shall not surely die: 5. For God doth know (doesn't that sound like the false teachers of today using the Scriptures? Oh they give credit to the Holy Spirit, and make it sounds so official, but it's just as much the power of Satan as this was. So Satan can say) *that in the day ye eat thereof, then your eyes shall be opened, and ye shall be as gods,* (small "g" of course) *knowing good and evil."* Now is that what God had said? Come back to chapter 2 again for a moment, we've got to compare Scripture with Scripture. God is speaking.

Genesis 2:17a
"But of the tree of the knowledge of good and evil, thou shalt not eat of it:..."
See that's exactly what God called that tree. Do you see how meticulous Satan can be when he gets ready to deceive somebody? Oh he didn't goof it up, but rather Satan said it to Eve just exactly the way God said it. Now coming back to chapter 3 and verse 5

Book 34 LESSON TWO * PART IV

Galatians 5:8
"This persuasion (to come away from Paul's Gospel of Grace) *cometh not of him that calleth you."*

Who called them? The Holy Sprit of God. Well if the Holy Spirit did not lead them away then

43

what spirit did? The evil spirit. Remember we've only got two spirits in the world. It's either of the Holy Spirit or of the satanic evil spirit. Let's go back to John's little epistles. I don't like to say anything unless I can show it from the Book. Go back to I John Chapter 4, and this is what the world is up against tonight just as much as when Paul wrote to the Galatians. The human race hasn't changed one iota, not one bit.

I John 4:1
"Beloved, believe not every spirit, but try the spirits whether they are of God: because many false prophets are gone out into the world." And then you come on down to verse 3.

I John 4:3
"And every spirit that confesseth not that Jesus Christ is come in the flesh is not of God: and this is that spirit of anti-christ, whereof ye have heard that it should come; and even now already is it in the world."

So what are we up against? The two spirits. It's either of the Holy Spirit or of the evil spirit. Now of course Satan has his demons, but nevertheless it's going to originate in the satanic powers, and this is what the world is up against. I mean it's up against everything that Satan can throw at them. You know I always remind people, don't get the idea that all Satan can promote is what we call skid row behavior. Satan will promote the most beautiful things, Satan will promote that which we think is culture and enlightening as long as he can keep people from the truth. He doesn't care what he uses as long as people fall for it. With Satan the end always justifies the means. Satan will use good things but it will be of the evil spirit rather than the Holy Spirit that is speaking.

Book 37 Lesson Three • Part II

Exodus 7:10-12
"And Moses and Aaron went in unto Pharaoh, and they did so as the LORD had commanded: (the Lord is in full control) *and Aaron* (with the Lord's instructions) *cast down his rod before Pharaoh, and before his servants, and it became a serpent. 11. Then Pharaoh also called the wise men and the sorcerers:* (these are Satan emissaries) *now the magicians of Egypt, they also did in like manner with their enchantments. 12. For they cast down every man his rod, and they became serpents:* (where are they getting their power? From Satan, and his evil spirits. Now here is the comforting part of this whole passage) *but Aaron's rod swallowed up their rods."*

Which of course shows us that God was still supreme. But never fail to understand that the spirits of the Satanic powers are real, and numerous, and it's up to us to determine which spirit are we dealing with. Now I'm comfortable with the fact that as believers, the satanic spirits cannot have any kind of control over us, because our Spirit power is sufficient to withstand all the powers of the evil one. But we have to understand that they are there, and we have to deal with them. In fact jumping ahead a little bit in Ephesians let's look for a moment at chapter 6, and maybe this will make my point. This tells us that the satanic powers are out there.

Ephesians 6:11
"Put on the whole armour of God, that ye may be able to stand against the wiles of the devil."
Now the Scripture could just as well have said it the other way around.

"Put on the whole armour of God, so that you can stand for God." But the Scriptures don't say that. Instead it tells us to prepare for our adversary. Then go into verse 12, and here's the reason we're to put on that armour.

Ephesians 6:12
"For we wrestle not against flesh and blood, but against principalities, against powers, against the rulers of the darkness of this world, against spiritual wickedness in high places."

Do you see how plain that is? Now these are all spirit powers that you and I have to discern, "The only one we should be directed by is the One and only Spirit that has anything to do with us, which of course is the Holy Spirit."

Book 38 Lesson Two • Part I

Ephesians 4:27
"Neither give place to the devil."
In general terms how much print does Paul give to Satan? Very little. He'll just make a statement about Satan here and there, and we're going to look at a couple of them here in a bit. Turn with me to II Corinthians chapter 4, verse 3. Now these aren't the only two instances, but this is the way it usually pops up. The reason I want to take time to do this is because we see so much lately of where the so called Christian community is being admonished to war against Satan. We have to fight against Satan, we have to do things against Satan, but Paul doesn't teach that. Paul recognizes his power, but he doesn't spend long verses at a time telling us how to fight a war against Satan.

Now we'll see this a little bit in Ephesians chapter 6, but all he does is let's us know that he's there. Paul's emphasis is not Satan, but rather is the Christ of glory. And when Christ rules our life, and when He's in control, Satan can't touch us, and we don't have to worry all that much about fighting against Satan if we center on Christ and His work of the cross. And I think for this reason Paul doesn't give a lot of ink to Satan.

II Corinthians 4:3-4
"But if our gospel be hid, it is hid to them that are lost: 4. In whom (the lost of this world) *the god of this world hath blinded the minds of them which believe not, lest the light of the glorious*

gospel of Christ, who is the image of God, should shine unto them."

Now for goodness sakes who's the god of this world? Well Satan is. See how subtle Paul puts this in here? He could have just came right out and said, "Satan had done it." But he doesn't, but rather he gives him another term, *"the god of this world hath blinded the minds of them which believe not."* Now still in II Corinthians, turn over to chapter 11.

II Corinthians 11:13-14

"For such are false apostles, deceitful workers, transforming themselves into the apostles of Christ. 14. And no marvel; (don't let this surprise you) *for Satan himself is transformed into an angel of light."*

Do you see that? Oh he's the god of this world back here in the earlier verses, and keeps people blind from the truth, but many times he blinds people with his light. And it's a counterfeit light, and people are so gullible and will say, "Oh that must be the work of the Spirit." But you see it isn't. but rather it's the work of the evil spirit, it's the work of Satan the counterfeit, the impostor, the deceitful individual. So keep these things in mind, *"for Satan himself is transformed into an angel of light."* Now look at verse 15.

II Corinthians 11:15a

"Therefore (since Satan can do this, and we know he does) *it is no great thing if his ministers also* (human being that he's using) *be transformed as the ministers of righteousness;..."*

That's what they try to tell people that they're the ministers of righteousness, but Paul tells us they're emissaries of Satan. So what do we have to know? The truth from the false! And the only way we can do that is just keep our nose in the Book, and when we do that then the Holy Spirit will certainly do His part to be able to keep us discerning truth from error.

(12a) What are the three temptations ?

Book 15 LESSON ONE * PART II

I Corinthians 15:45,46

"And so it is written, `The first man Adam was made a living soul; the last Adam was made a quickening (or life giving) *spirit.'" "Howbeit that was not first which is spiritual, but that which is natural; and afterward that which is spiritual."*

I have stressed over the years that all through Scripture this is the process - first the natural, and then the spiritual. For example, Adam the natural and then the second Adam which is Christ. Cain the natural and then Abel the spiritual. Esau the natural and then Jacob the spiritual. Another one is King Saul the natural, and King David the spiritual. This goes all the way through Scripture. You can even take it into the end-time in the final seven years. First we have the Anti-christ then we have Christ. **In our own experience we come on life's scene as natural, and then when we experience salvation we become spiritual.** It is just a fact of Scripture. And so Paul makes that point in verse 46. Let's read it again:

I Corinthians 15:46,47
"Howbeit that was not first which is spiritual, but that which is natural; and afterward that which is spiritual." "The first man is of the earth, earthy (God made him from the elements of the dust)*: the second man is the Lord from heaven."*

So as Adam is the federal head of the human race in Genesis, now Christ is the response to that Federal head, because Adam fell. That is the whole understanding that when Adam fell, there had to be some way of restoring that headship. And the second Adam, Who is Christ, was the One Who would restore. I can't prove this from Scripture, but I like to think that Adam, before he sinned, had a body identical to Christ's in His earthly appearance. Maybe you have never thought of that before. But you see Adam, before he sinned, was incorruptible. He could have lived forever if he had not fallen. Christ of course as we saw from the temptations did not fall. And as they laid His body in the tomb, did it begin to decay? No, because it was incorruptible. And it never started the decaying process. So always hold those two in contrast.

Adam, the Federal head of the human race, was given dominion over everything that God had created. It was his to rule and reign over. That is what the word `dominion' meant. And yet Satan came on the scene, with one little temptation, and Adam with all of that power at his disposal; beautiful circumstances; nothing to be desired; it was all there for him; yet he fell.
Now in contrast, here comes Christ in His earthly ministry, not as the royal King as yet (although He is presenting Himself as the King), but He is coming more as a lowly servant, riding upon a foal of an ass. This is what confounded the Jews. They were looking for Someone to come riding on a white steed like a Roman General or Emperor. Jesus epitomized the servant when He washed the disciples' feet. And that is why they couldn't understand how this One, Who was the very Creator of the universe; The One Who had come to be the King of Kings not only of Israel, but of the whole planet could get down on His knees and wash the disciples' feet. And now at His temptations He comes under wilderness circumstances. Whereas Adam had it all, Christ, as the Spiritual, comes under those adverse conditions but did not succumb as Adam did. All the areas of temptations are covered that you and I as believers face even in the twentieth century. In those three temptations Christ suffered the attacks of Satan that cover everything that Satan can throw at us. And let's look at them here in this passage in I John Chapter 2:

I John 2:15
"Love not the world, neither the things that are in the world. If any man love the world, the love of the Father is not in him."

The Greek word for this word **"world"** here is Kosmos, from which we now get the word

`Cosmos.' Add a few letters on to it and you get Cosmopolitan. And what is a Cosmopolitan? The dictionary gives a very simple definition. **A Cosmopolitan is a citizen of the world.** Think about that. So what is the world as this text uses it? This whole world system: economic, politics, entertainment, pleasures, the good as well as the bad things. That is all wrapped up in this word, **"world."** That doesn't mean that you can't enjoy the good things, and have a nice home, or have a good living. But it's like the Scripture says in *I Timothy 6:10, "For the love of money is the root of all evil:..."* Remember **money** isn't, **but the love of money is!** **Loving** money is what makes people become corrupt in order to get it. It's the same way with the world. Don't love the world or it will grab you, and you can't let go. This is what the things of the world try to do, and when that happens you will become part of the world and your Christian witness will be destroyed. Verse 16:

I John 2:16
"For all that is in the world (this world system)*, the lust of the flesh* (what was Christ's first temptation? Bread, because He was hungry. So He suffered the lust of the flesh)*, and the lust of the eyes, and the pride of life, is not of the Father, but is of the world."*

Now in applying this verse to the temptation of Christ, the first one we discussed is obvious. That was the lust of the flesh. He was hungry. The second one was the appeal to the eye because of that vast crowd that would witness His miraculous plunge from the pinnacle of the Temple. But the third one is when Satan says, **"I'll give you power over all these Kingdoms."** What did that appeal to? His pride. That what makes some politicians what they are - people who quest for power. It feeds the ego and pride. Applying this to Eve, what was the first part of Satan's appeal to Eve? Look at the fruit, its good to eat. It was appealing to the eye. But the basis of the whole temptation was, **"You can be like God!" And we call that the lie.**

Now to be like God, what would that give her? Power and Pride. And it is the same way for you and I tonight. Let's look at another Scripture, Hebrews Chapter 4. I've had people ask me after a class, **"How in the world can the Scriptures say that Jesus tasted of every temptation that I'm faced with. He couldn't have."** Remember, not each individual one, but in the categories He did. Because you can place every temptation that befalls you and I into these three same categories. It will always be the **"lust of the flesh," "lust of the eye,"** or **"pride of life."**

Hebrew 4:14,15
"Seeing then that we have a great high priest, that is passed into the heavens, Jesus the Son of God, let us hold fast our profession (because He's there!)*. For we have not an high priest* (Christ) *which cannot be touched with the feeling of our infirmities* (but rather we do have a High Priest Who **can** be touched with the feeling of our infirmities)*; but was in all points tempted like as we are, ye without sin."* Let's look at one more verse in I Corinthians Chapter 10. I hope you are seeing how all of this fits together.

I Corinthians 10:13

"There hath no temptation taken you but such as is common to man (you can't say, `I'm in a unique position, no one has ever been faced with this before - Christ was!): *but God is faithful, who will not suffer you to be tempted above that ye are able; but will with the temptation* (Satan is going to hit us) *also make a way to escape, that ye may be able to bear it."* Now that's a promise. If we look for the situation to get out of temptation you can, because God has made all the provisions to escape. It's based on the fact of Christ own experience.

(13a) What are the two kinds of death mentioned in the Bible ?

Book 1 LESSON Three * PART IV

Let's look at and define what we mean by death. There are two kinds of death mentioned in the Bible:

1. Physical Death - separation of the soul and spirit from the physical body. In teaching the Scriptures, most preaching emphasis is placed upon "saving the soul." But God is just as interested in the body as He is in the spirit and soul of man. God deals with us as whole people, not just with our spiritual side. If you search the Word from Genesis to Revelation, you'll not find any reference to a man accomplishing anything separated from his body. Even in the life to come, God has promised us a new "glorified" body.
God has also instilled within us a desire to live. Even when we are ready for death and looking forward to it, we fight against it.

2. Spiritual Death - Separation from God for eternity, also known as, "the second death." A thinking individual will have the same apprehension of a spiritual separation from God as he has of the physical separation of the spirit and soul from the body. (At least he should have)! Romans 5:14 says,
"Nevertheless death reigned from Adam to Moses, even over them that had not sinned after the similitude of Adam's transgression, who is the figure of him that was to come."

Adam as the Federal Head of the Human Race, sinned and caused death to come to the entire human race. In the same way the "Second Adam" or Christ, by virtue of His death and resurrection was able to impart life to all. This was a Sovereign act of the Sovereign God to restore the human race to fellowship with Himself, but it's not automatic - each man must make the individual choice to receive it.

In Ephesians 2:1-7, Paul is writing to encourage the believers at Ephesus as well as all future generations of believers. Look especially at verse 5: *"Even when we were dead in sins, (God) hath quickened us together with Christ (by grace ye are saved);"*

We, who were dead in sin by virtue of being children of disobedience (Adam), God chose to make alive in Christ Jesus! Let's go back to Genesis and compare Genesis 3:7 with Genesis 2:25. Immediately after Adam ate:

"And the eyes of them both were opened, and they knew that they were naked; and they sewed fig leaves together, and made themselves aprons."

They immediately recognized their nakedness. But, in 2:25:

"And they were both naked, the man and his wife, and were not ashamed."

What a difference! With one act of disobedience, they changed from childlike innocence to sinful self-consciousness and shame. Where once they could walk even in God's presence, now they attempted to cover themselves, and even ran and hid from His presence.

Notice that God did not instruct them to make the aprons of fig leaves to cover themselves. Something else prompted them to do that. This is what we call the energy of the flesh ... man doing what he can do.

Look at Proverbs 14:12. This is an excellent passage to memorize, because it is so appropriate under so many different circumstances.

"There is a way which seemeth right unto a man, but the end thereof are the ways of death."

Since Adam's sin, mankind has been trying to rationalize his actions; trying to see "just how can I get around this?"

Adam and Eve knew that God would soon be down to walk with them in the garden, and they rationalized that maybe they could cover themselves with fig leaves and God wouldn't notice their nakedness. People are still trying to do the same thing today.

If you ask people this question, "If you were to die today, on what basis do you think God should let you into heaven?" You'll get as many different answers as you have people to ask.

Look at other world religions. The people who followed them work hard to do "What seems right to them," but to Holy God, it's futility.

The term "religion" is used usually in a bad sense in the Bible. It refers to mankind's attempt to reach and merit favor with God. True Christianity, on the other hand, is God reaching down to unworthy, sinful man, offering His mercy, grace and love.

Man, on his own, can never merit favor with God; rather he must be seen in light of what God has done for him in Christ Jesus. In Genesis 3:7, we've seen that Adam and Eve dealt with the physical aspects of their problem when they made the fig leaf aprons. They couldn't, however, deal with the spiritual aspects of their dilemma. In verse 8, they hide. The leaf aprons just won't cut it. They are ashamed and afraid, and they hide from the face of God. Mankind has not

changed one bit over the years; they still try to hide from God. John 3:19 says,
"And this is the condemnation, that light is come into the world, and men love darkness rather than light, because their deeds were evil."

Confrontation with Holy God brings fear to the hearts of sinful men, and they run and hide. Verse 20 reads:
"For everyone that doeth evil hateth the light, neither cometh to the light, lest his deeds should be reproved."

No sinner ever goes looking for God - God always looks for the sinner!! Praise God!

(14a) Where do we go when we die ?

Book 14 LESSON ONE * PART IV

Revelation 20:13
"And the sea gave up the dead which were in it; and death and hell delivered up the dead which were in them (now watch that language. Hell is going to give up those that are in it)*: and they were judged every man according to their works."* And then those who had been occupying hell...

Revelation 20:14
"And death and hell were cast into the lake of fire (do you see the difference between those two places? Death and hell is the place of the unbeliever who has died and is waiting for this Great White Throne judgment. He waiting for the resurrection out of hell, only to go to something far worse, which is of course the lake of fire. And the Bible calls this); **This is the second death."** They died physically and now they die spiritually. The definition of death is: for the physical, it's the separation of the spirit from the body. For the spirit realm, death is the separation from God. It's an eternal separation. Now look at the difference between hell and the lake of fire.

First, we have to go back to some the scriptural descriptions of these things. Where is hell? And what is it comprised of? Let's go back to Matthew Chapter 12. This is from the Lord's own lips. The scribes and Pharisees are dealing with Jesus, and Jesus says:

Matthew 12:39
"But he answered and said unto them, `An evil and adulterous generation seeketh after a sign; and there shall no sign be given to it, but the sign of the prophet Jonas:'"
There is a lot more in this verse than I have time to comment on. But I will say it refutes those who say that Jonah was an imagination, or a myth. Jesus gives perfect credit to him. Now verse 40:

Matthew 12:40

"For as Jonas was three days and three nights in the whale's belly; so shall the Son of man be three days and three nights (where?) in the heart of the earth."

We know that when the thief on the Cross turned to Jesus and said, ***"Remember me when thou comest into thy Kingdom."*** Jesus' answered, ***"Today thou shalt be with me in paradise."*** But here Jesus says **that in those three days and three nights, He's going to be in the center of the earth."** He went down into what? The Apostle's creed says that, **"Jesus died, was buried and descended into hell."** I've had so many people say to me, **"You mean Jesus actually went to hell?"** Well, yes and no. And here's the reason. We have three words in Scripture that all speak of the same place. Down in the `center of the earth' is what Jesus' own words were. And down there is what we call in Hebrew Sheol, In the Greek it's called Hades. And in English it's called hell. All three pertain to this center-most part of the earth. Go to Luke Chapter 16. The only way you can put these things together is to compare Scripture with Scripture. They are all in here, but you've got to look for it.

Now here in Luke 16, we have the account of the rich man and Lazarus. And we won't take it verse by verse for sake of time. Most of you have heard sermons on this or at least you can remember when you did. How that Abraham and Lazarus were there in Paradise, but the rich man was in torment. Let's come down to verse 22 and 23:

Luke 16:22,23

"And it came to pass, that the beggar (Lazarus) *died, and was carried by the angels into Abraham's bosom: the rich man also died, and was buried; And in hell he lift up his eyes, being in torments, and seeth Abraham afar off, and Lazarus in his bosom."*

This is just one instance where this took place. It didn't happen routinely, but the Lord presents this one instance for our benefit.

Luke 16:24

"And he (the rich man) *cried and said, `Father Abraham, have mercy on me, and send Lazarus, that he may dip the tip of his finger in water, and cool my tongue; for I am tormented in this flame.'"*

We know that he's not there bodily, He will have that reserved body in the lake of fire, but here in hell he's there only in the realm of the soul and spirit. But soul and spirit are so intrinsically involved with the body. And I always like to give this illustration: my wife is a nurse and she has told me (and I have read and you have heard) where an amputee comes into the hospital and experiences pain in the leg that is no longer there. They call it **"phantom pain."** They have been so used to that leg, that even though it's gone they still feel the pain that would be in it. And I bring that into this setting. The soul and spirit are so intertwined with the body of our make up, that even though the rich man's body was in the grave upon the surface, yet the soul and spirit were suffering as if it were bodily suffering. So he was tormented and was in thirst.

Abraham responds and says:

Luke 16:25
"But Abraham said, `Son, remember that thou in thy lifetime receivedst thy good things, and likewise Lazarus evil things: but now he is comforted, and thou art tormented.'"

Luke 16:26
"And beside all of this (even if I would want to come)*, between us and you there is a great gulf fixed: so that they which would pass from hence to you cannot; neither can they pass to us, that would come from thence."*

So what do we have? We've got hell, or hades, or however you want to define it, but Abraham defines it as a great gulf fixed. Now on one side was torment, no doubt about it. But on the other side was Paradise. We know that before the Cross, all the way from Adam, that men lived and died. Even the believers died with the two exceptions (and I'm always pointing out that God is God and He can make His exceptions). But there were only two that did not die and go down into Paradise, rather, they went up. They were Enoch and Elijah. Now those were God's exceptions. Other than those two, the rest of the believers of the Old Testament could not go to Heaven. They had to go down to Paradise, because the atoning blood of Christ is the only thing that removes the stain of sin. Animals' blood couldn't. So these Old Testament believers were saved for eternity, but they were not ready for God's presence, because their sins had not been atoned for by the blood of Christ. So they went down to Paradise.

On the other hand, the lost from Cain till even today are going down into hell as we understand it, but into the torment side. When the thief was told by Jesus, **"Today shalt thou be with me in paradise,"** Christ was speaking of what He said in Matthew **about the center part of the earth.** Remember Christ said that, I didn't. That He would be three days and three nights in the center part of the earth. Now the Apostle Paul, the Apostle to the Gentiles, puts his stamp of approval on all of this in the Book of Ephesians, and that is why I find it so comfortable and easy to teach. And here it comes out in such plain language. This isn't gobbledy-gook, or something that takes a theologian's degree to understand. Just take it for what it says;

Ephesians 4:7
"But unto every one of us is given grace according to the measure of the gift of Christ."

Ephesians 4:8
" Wherefore he saith, When he ascended up on high (as he did in John Chapter 20:17. That's when I think Christ took all of these that were in Paradise with Him)*, he led captivity captive, and gave gifts unto men."* Watch the term `captivity and captive.' Now verse 9:

Ephesians 4:9,10
"(Now that he ascended (in other words He went up), *what is it but that he also* (what?) *descended first into* (where?) *the lower parts of the earth?* He went down into the Paradise side of hell or Hades, where Abraham and the Old Testament saints were.
He that descended is the same also that ascended up far above all heavens, that he might fill all things.)"

Now putting it in just plain visual perspective, the following happens. From the Cross, He and the thief went down into the Paradise side of Sheol, Hades, or hell. But on the Resurrection morning, when He told Mary in *John 20:17 "...Touch me not.; for I am not yet ascended to my Father:..."* I think right here is where Christ emptied the Paradise side and took those Old Testament believers with Him. And where is Paradise today? It's up in Heaven! Paul teaches in *II Corinthians 5:8 "...rather to be absent from the body, and to be present with the Lord."* We don't go down into the heart of the earth! We go immediately up into the presence of the Lord, because that is where Paradise is now located. The Old Testament tells us that hell, the place of torment, is enlarged. In other words, after Paradise was removed that whole area has now become then, totally the place of torment. So when an unbeliever dies today, that unbeliever still goes down to this place of torment.

Now here we are at the end of the thousand years reign and rule of Christ and we are at the Great White Throne. It's up in space somewhere. It's not on the earth, because the earth has fled away. So now in the resurrection of the unjust, they are brought back bodily because that's what resurrection denotes. Now, back to Revelation 20. Here the lost stand before the Lord, Who in their case is the Judge, and not the Savior. As Judge, He shows them their record, and there will be degrees of punishment. Jesus made that so plain, when He said to the people of Capernaum in Matthew 11, the following:

Matthew 11:23,24
"And thou, Capernaum, which art exalted unto heaven, shalt be brought down to hell: for if the mighty works, which have been done in thee, had been done in Sodom, it would have remained until this day. But I say unto you, `That it shall be more tolerable for the land of Sodom in the day of judgment, than for thee.'" So He makes it very plain that the people of Capernaum would suffer more in their eternal doom, than the horrible people of Sodom.
In verse 14 of Revelation Chapter 20 we find:

Revelation 20:14,15
"And death and hell were cast into the lake of fire. This is the second death. And whosoever was not found written in the book of life was cast into the lake of fire."
I don't care if people don't like to preach this subject any more, the Book stills says it. And there are groups who try to make believe that a God of love couldn't do this. But I've shown you that God's love was so great at the Cross that there is no room for removing the eternal doom of the

lost person. Now then the lake of fire, where is it? Well, who knows? We know it must be in space and not on the earth. And with the reading I do, it could even be a black hole in space, A black hole is a place where time is nothing. I also read at one time they thought that because of its tremendous specific gravity it is tremendously dense. And there is intense heat, even though it's intense darkness, with a feeling of constantly falling. Anyway, that's the thoughts of our people who study space. I'm just throwing that out as a possibility. I'm not saying it is, but we do know the lake of fire is eternal, without end and the lost will spend forever there. And the sad part is, they didn't have to go there. That's going to be awful. To think they missed glory because they didn't believe the Gospel, as simple as it is. It's sobering, as much as we would love to see the Lord come today, the only thing that tempers my enthusiasm is the fact that maybe today and tomorrow a few will still be saved and escape all of this. But it behooves us to be mindful that the eternal doom of the lost is something beyond our comprehension.

(15a) Will people that are not saved be judged for their sins?

Book 6 LESSON ONE * PART IV

Revelation 19:11,12
" And I saw heaven opened, and behold a white horse; and he that sat upon him was called Faithful and True, and in righteousness he doth judge and make war. His eyes were as a flame of fire, and on his head were many crowns; and he had a name written, that no man knew, but he himself."

"His eyes were as..." what? *"...a flame of fire,..."* Now, it doesn't say they were a flame of fire, but they are just like flames of fire. In other words, they will be so penetrating, there will be nothing that can escape them. Nothing can be hidden from them; it will all be revealed. Now, let's come back to 1 Corinthians. This is the language that Paul is using. We will come before the **Bema Seat** (now here is where I have to make a qualification, the lost people from Cain until the very end of time as we know it, they of course will appear before the Great White Throne. And it's only for the lost, there will be no believers at the Great White Throne. Here Christ will be the judge and will judge the lost of all ages).

In John's Gospel, Chapter 5, Jesus taught so plainly, that there will be two resurrections. The resurrection of the just, and the resurrection of the unjust. In other words, the unbeliever is also going to be resurrected out of Hell before the Great White Throne, and he will appear there bodily in a newly resurrected body, but it will be a body fit not for glory and not for Heaven; but a body fit for the eternal lake of fire. It will be a body that will have many of the same appetites of this one, but without any hope of ever satisfying it. And so, that's why the Scriptures said to let the drunkard be drunken still, and let the whoremonger continue on with those appetites, for they will never be satisfied. They will also have an eternity of regret. Remember, nobody goes before the Great White Throne except **those who choose to go there. Salvation has been**

offered to all people (everyone; red, yellow, black, and white; rich, poor; it doesn't make any difference). But, if they reject it, they are going to end up at the Great White Throne.

Book 14 LESSON ONE * PART IV

But now coming back to the Great White Throne in Revelation 20:12
Revelation 20:12
"And I saw the dead (of all ages), *small and great, stand before God* (in their resurrected bodies);..."*

Their bodies won't be glorious like ours. But theirs will be fit for the lake of fire. Remember, their bodies will not be consumed or burned up, but their bodies will be tormented forever and ever. They will have all of their senses and feelings. As awful as it is, and it is awful, that's why most people have quit talking about it. But that still doesn't take it out of Scripture. Don't forget, the finished work of the Cross has made it possible for **every human being** to escape this lake of fire judgment. They will realize when they stand before God they made their choice for this punishment. We look at certain aspects of human history, and say they never had a chance, they never heard. Well, they must have had some kind of chance; otherwise God would not tells us in the Book of **Romans 1:18:20 "...so that they are without excuse."** And they **are** without excuse! I think that will be part of their torment of that final doom - that constant regret that they are there, and they didn't have to be.

As I teach John's Gospel, Chapter 10, about the Shepherd and the sheep fold, I always point out where the door is into the sheepfold. It's not somewhere that is inaccessible, or unreachable, but right at ground level. **Right smack in front of every human being as they sojourn through this life.** And so God is absolutely just and fair, that when people have trampled under foot what He suffered and died for, then He doesn't have to show mercy, and He won't. This is going to be a place of judgment and it's going to be awful. When people say that you and I as believers will sit and watch this Great White Throne judgment take place they don't know what they are talking about. That would be horror of horrors. We wouldn't want to see the lost stand there and hear their doom prescribed. And I'm glad we won't. Now finishing verse 12:

Revelation 20:12b
"... and the books (plural) *were opened, and another book* (singular) *was opened, which is the book of life: and the dead were judged out of those things which were written in the books, according to their works."*

Now the Book of Life is going to show them that their name is not there. There are two views on this. Some maintain that every person's name is in the Book of Life, and if they die without salvation then their name is blotted out. The other view is that when people are saved and experience salvation, their name is placed in the Book of Life. And there are Scripture verses for both approaches. **But regardless, at the Great White Throne they are going to see their name is not there.** They will have no argument. God brings up their record. I know God has no problem keeping a record of every human being that ever walked the face of the earth. I know He will have the record, and it will be completely accurate.

Revelation 20:13
"And the sea gave up the dead which were in it; and death and hell delivered up the dead which were in them (now watch that language. Hell is going to give up those that are in it)*: and they were judged every man according to their works."* And then those who had been occupying hell...

Revelation 20:14
"And death and hell were cast into the lake of fire (do you see the difference between those two places? Death and hell is the place of the unbeliever who has died and is waiting for this Great White Throne judgment. He waiting for the resurrection out of hell, only to go to something far worse, which is of course the lake of fire. And the Bible calls this); *This is the second death."* They died physically and now they die spiritually. The definition of death is: for the physical, it's the separation of the spirit from the body. For the spirit realm, death is the separation from God. It's an eternal separation.

(16a) Will people that are saved be judged for their sins ?

Book 14 LESSON ONE * PART I

SALVATION: HELL VERSUS LAKE OF FIRE:
NEW HEAVEN AND EARTH

We were talking about believers coming up before the judgment seat of Christ, the Bema seat. Bema is simply the Greek word for judgment seat. It came from the Olympics - the seat of the judges. I stressed in our last lesson it's a seat of judging not for Heaven or hell, but rather for what rewards we will receive. This will only be for believers and the Body of Christ who one day will come before the Bema Seat for rewards. We will definitely get rewards based on our Christian walk in this life here on earth. Of course, the rewards are going to come to their fruition primarily in the Kingdom economy. When the Kingdom finally comes on the earth and becomes active, Christ will be King of Kings and Lord of Lords, the world wide Ruler, and we will be ruling and reigning with Him.

Now here is where the reward aspect comes in, as we reign and rule with Him, our level of responsibility is going to be based on our faithfulness here. And that is why it behooves us as believers to labor, to work, and serve for the rewards we will use in the Kingdom Age. I think most people would rather be active as opposed to being inactive and sitting on the sideline. I know I would. I couldn't stand sitting on the sidelines.

Book 13 LESSON THREE * PART IV

II Corinthians 5:10a
"For we (believers) *must all appear before the judgment seat of Christ;..."*

I think that word 'judgment' is an unfortunate translation in our King James, because the word here in the Greek is Bema. It was the Bema seat. Paul took that from the Olympics. Paul made many references to the Olympic games. So the Bema seat at an Olympic game was the place of the judges. As you watch a tennis match on television they have judges who sit on the line of the tennis court, and it's up to the them to determine if a shot has gone in or is out of bounds. Now in so many cases you could say the judge is sitting on the Bema seat. They are sitting on the seat of a judge.

Now as Paul uses this analogy then, the Bema Seat, on which Christ will be sitting as the Judge, is not to determine heaven or hell. It's not to judge us for our sins, because the believers sins have already been judged totally and completely at the Cross. We will never again have to face our sins. Now this doesn't give license, not by any stretch of the imagination. We won't come before the Bema Seat shaking in our boots wondering if we are going to make it or not. I had a gentleman in one of my classes share with me not too long ago that his father-in-law, I believe, was getting rather elderly, and had come to spend the remainder of his life with his daughter. The gentleman relating the story said, "Les would you believe that this fellow was a highly thought of well-known evangelist in his denomination. And yet I can still hear the old fellow as he walked across our living room bemoaning to himself, 'Will I go to heaven when I die.'" Here he had been preaching to thousands of people throughout his lifetime, yet he didn't have an assurance of where he would spend eternity. Isn't that sad? There are multitudes like that. They profess salvation, and say, "Oh, yes, I believe in Christ," But then they turn right around and think they have to work, work, work, hoping that somehow they can still make it. This is not the Gospel of Grace that the Apostle Paul preached. The Gospel of Grace says that Christ releases the power of salvation at our believing (and when I say believing I'm not just talking a mental accent. I'm talking about a genuine Holy Spirit opening of the heart, and we can without any reservation say, "I know that Christ died my death. I know that He rose from the dead, and that He had power to overcome sin and Satan."). That's the kind of faith God is looking for. When He sees it, our sins are judged, and we are cleansed of them. Then He seals us, and sets us on our way working, and serving Him. As a believer, the whole concept here is that we live a life well-pleasing now as a child, with the idea of gaining a reward for meritorious service. Finishing verse 10, we must all appear before the Bema Seat:

II Corinthians 5:10b
"... that every one (believers) *may receive the things done in his body* (while we as believers in

this life), *according to that he hath done, whether it be good or bad."*

So we will stand before Him to see if we are going to receive a reward. Let's follow that back to I Corinthians Chapter 3. Here again the Apostle is writing to the Gentiles of Corinth, so basically he is writing to you and I. Again he uses the pronoun 'we.'

I Corinthians 3:9
"For we are laborers together with God (now he points the finger at the believer and says)*: ye are God's husbandry, ye are God's building."* You are something that God is working on.

I Corinthians 3:10
"According to the grace of God which is given unto me (Paul is speaking in reference to his own ministry)*, as a wise masterbuilder, I have laid the foundation* (Paul is speaking about a building situation)*, and another buildeth thereon. But let every man take heed how he buildeth thereupon."*

In other words the foundation is there. And that is the basis for any kind of a building. But now comes all the various workers that are going to put their little bit into this building. Now verse 11. Notice Paul doesn't claim to be the foundation:

I Corinthians 3:11
"For other foundation can no man lay than that is laid, which is Jesus Christ."

He is the basic foundation of all our works. And you can't begin to build on that foundation until you have experienced His salvation. There is no such thing as working for that. But after God has imparted salvation and the power of God has been released into our very existence, then He expects us to serve him. That doesn't mean we have to be a Billy Graham, or go to the foreign mission field, or have to be teachers or something like that, but in Romans 12, we've got all these areas of service that believers can fill. I've told my classes, over the years, every single believer has at least one gift that can be used in God's service. Many times people are exercising their gift and seeing all the fruits of it and they come to me and say, "Well, Les, I wish I had a gift." You've got a gift and you're using it! Just keep on doing what you are doing, whatever it may be. People who are elderly and can't get out and do much anymore, they can serve the Lord in just prayer alone! Prayer changes things. Older people could literally turn a nation around if they would pray. Others may have accumulated enough wealth that they can judiciously give and further God's work.

Now, I don't buy this thing of, "I'll just put it out there and God's knows my heart." No, God has given every individual intelligence and discernment. You give where God directs you and give where it will be honoring to Him. Don't just throw it out there someplace and think, "Well, this is good enough. I've given in the right attitude." No, you are to be judicious even in your giving. There's all kinds of places and ways to serve God. Ministering to the poor and sick are two ways. These are gifts of serving. Now, as we serve, come to verse 12:

I Corinthians 3:12
"Now if any man build upon this foundation gold, silver, precious stones, wood hay, stubble;"
As we enter into this life of the Christian walk or service, God provides opportunity for six building materials. Wood, hay and stubble; gold, silver and precious stones. Those are the ones that are available. Now, of course, a lot of believers never get anything more than wood, hay and stubble. That's as far as they ever get. But you see, others will get out and put forth some effort and energy and they're going to drum up some gold, silver and precious stones. Here's the way you have to look at these six materials; which ones can withstand the flames of the judgment fire? I'm not talking about Hellfire, I'm talking about the Judge's eyes. He's going to have eyes of fire that are going to penetrate our works at the Bema Seat. Which ones are going to survive those flaming eyes. Well, not the wood, hay and stubble because that's going to go up in a puff of smoke. It's the gold, silver and precious stones, whatever that may be. In other words, the things that have lasting value. The things that have really made a difference, maybe in your home, in the community, in your church, or whatever. That's the gold, silver and precious stones. Now let's read on again in verse 13:

I Corinthians 3:13
"Every man's work (it's the masculine gender, but includes everyone as a believer. Not for salvation) *shall be made manifest* (like being put under a spotlight. As we come before the Bema Seat to see what our rewards are going to be, we are put in the spotlight. Then the penetrating eyes of Christ will burn off the draught showing if you have gold, silver or precious stones left)*: for the day shall declare it, because it shall be revealed by fire; and the fire shall try every man's work of what sort it is."*

I Corinthians 3:14
"If any man's work abide (survives His scrutiny) *which he hath built thereupon, he shall receive* (not salvation, but) *a reward."*

I know a lot of people are turned off by the concept of rewards, but it's very scriptural. The Scripture maintains that you and I are literally to work for rewards. Verse 15, but:

I Corinthians 3:15
"If any man's work shall be burned (that has no reference to hell. That just simply says that if all we have is hay, wood, or stubble ... we didn't do things for the right reason for example. And the Lord looks at it, and our works shall be burned up and disappear)*, he shall suffer loss* (not his salvation, but of his reward)*: but he himself shall be saved; yet so as by fire."*
This person will be there, but he will not have earned the reward. Now let's go over to Chapter 9. Here Paul is again going to use one of his many allusions to the Olympics. Paul must have truly

loved the Olympics. Here he's writing to you and I, the believers:

I Corinthians 9:24,25
"Know ye not that they which run in a race run all (they all take off at the starting gun. But how many receive the prize?)*, but one receiveth the prize?* (now who determines the winners? Judges who sit on the Bema Seat) *so run, that ye may obtain."*

"And every man that striveth for the mastery is temperate in all things (what's he talking about? Their training period, while they were getting ready for the race. They maintained good diet, exercise, and they didn't overdo anything. The Scripture says, "that in all things be temperate." We wouldn't have so many of these health problems if people were just temperate). *Now they* (these athletes) *do it to obtain a corruptible crown* (you know what corruptible means, it doesn't last)*; but we an incorruptible."*

Paul says, **"We don't run and work for something that is going to pass off the scene in short order. But ours is what? Incorruptible!"** And even though Christianity has been on the scene almost 2000 years, the rewards that those early believers earned are still there. They are still waiting, and when we get there our rewards will be there also. Have you stopped to think about God's rewarding for the believer at the Bema Seat, at the end. We don't receive rewards as we come along. And do you know why? Because the next generation will benefit from everything that you and I do in the Lord's service (if this world keeps going). The same is true for the wicked person. His activity is going to effect people of the next generation, and generations to come.

Sometimes I think of that dear old Pastor that first asked me to teach in Sunday School. Do you know that someday, whatever I've been able to accomplish is also going to go to his credit. And someday down the road, people whose lives I have touched, whatever they do, is one day, going to come to my credit. And so it is with every believer. And that's why it will all come at the end. And now, I'd like to give this illustration. If you throw a pretty good sized rock into the middle of a fairly large pond of water, how far do the effects go? To every inch of shore line! And so it is with the believer. Everything we do will ripple out and have an effect on more and more people. Now verse 26: The Apostle
Paul then says:

I Corinthians 9:26
"I therefore so run (that I may win the prize.)*,..."*

(17a) When did God lose the human race?

Book 6 LESSON ONE * PART II

"Being justified...." Justification is that judicial act of God. Now, when I use the word 'judicial,' I mean like a judge on the bench hands down a decree. **Justification** is when God, The Judge, judicially declares the sinner (that person who recognizes that they are undone and are under the control of old Adam) to be **just as if he had never sinned.** That's beyond our comprehension. Even after we've been justified, we still are prone to fall and sin, yet what does God tell us? He says we are justified! He sees us as if we had never sinned! We'll never have to come before the judgment seat of Christ, as believers, and have to answer for our sins. **Never! Our sins are forgiven. They are under the Blood. Christ took care of it and we will never have to stand before Him with sin on our back.** Our sins are buried in the deepest sea and God has put up a sign which says, **"No Fishing!"** He has completely removed them. They are not going to come back and plague us. **That's** being justified.

Let's continue in verse 24: *"...freely* (without a cause...and how did God do it?) *by his grace* (unmerited favor) *through the redemption...."* I think you all know what the word 'redemption' refers to: losing something and buying it back. And it's a Scriptural term. When did God lose the human race? When Adam sinned. We're all in Adam, remember? It was there God lost us. So now, what does He have to do? Buy us back with a price. Satan is a hard task master; he won't let go of us easily. And this is the whole idea of redemption -- that God has to buy us back for Himself because He lost us in Adam. The word redemption here, especially in Romans, goes back to the Roman slave market in particular, for a beautiful illustration. The Greek word is **Agorazo.** We're not going to be concerned with that word so much, but we're talking about a slave market.

Just like in today's stock market, there were certain terms back then that applied only to the slave market. And these were the three that were usually exercised by wealthy Romans who would go down to the slave market and just spend the day. It was a good past-time for them to go down and buy a slave and leave it in the market. And, when they left that slave in the market (much like a stock trader today can buy stocks in the morning on the board of trade or stock exchange and, if at one o'clock in the afternoon, the market has jumped a couple of points, he can resell that same stock), if the price went up, they could sell the same slave that same day.

Well, the Romans could actually do that with slaves. But, the one we're most concerned with here in Scripture is the term **Exagorazo.** Now the term **'ex'** always means out. So, in this case, they could buy a slave, take it out of the market and take it home, thereby becoming that slave's owner. Then, they could exercise the third part with regard to slaves -- they could **'Lutroo' him,** or **set him free.** So, with that background, let's look at this verse. Here, the Roman legions have just come down from barbarian Gaul in Northern Europe. And they've got this teenage lad who has probably been beaten and dragged several hundred miles - and here he is in the slave market. But this rich, benevolent Roman sees this young man and sees something in him of worth. So, what does he do? He buys him; and instead of leaving him in the market to trade again, he takes him home, cleans him up and gives him light duty.

This young man has never lived so sumptuously, although he is a slave. And then, one day, this Roman master calls this young man into his office and says, "You've been an ideal slave and I'm going to now give you your freedom. I have paid for your citizenship. You are free to go wherever you want to go. You are a Roman citizen." What do you suppose that young man would say considering the fact that slaves who were not fortunate enough to be bought, were thrown to the lions in the coliseum? He would probably say, "Master, there's no way that I could do that after all that you have done for me. You bought me out of that awful slave market. You've put me in new clothes, you've cleaned me up and you've given me the best of duty. Master, I love you, and I will never leave you. I'm going to serve you all the rest of my life."

Now, doesn't that say it all? **That is what God rightfully expects from every child that He has saved.** He has taken us out of the slave market of Satan; He has broken the bonds of sin. He has cleaned us up and given us a whole new outlook on life. He has given us the Holy Spirit and all the promises of eternity to come. So, what should be our logical reaction? **"Lord, you've done so much for me. The least I can do is serve you and be your faithful bond-slave."**

Editor's Note: Later in this book, under the question, "How was Lord Jesus Christ born without sin?", Les explains why the human race did not come under sin by virtue of Eve, even though she had eaten the forbidden fruit first. Sin came upon the whole human race by way of Adam's sin.

(18a) What is the one reason God sends someone to Hell ?

Book 30 LESSON THREE * PART I

II Corinthians 4:3a
"If our gospel be hid..." (or veiled)
Something is over it so that hearts cannot comprehend it. What has to happen? Well someone has to remove the veil, and in this case who is holding the veil in place? Satan is, as we'll see in the next verse.

II Corinthians 4:4a
"In whom the god of this world..." (Satan)
A lot of people don't like to talk about Satan. They think of him as a cartoon character in a red underwear suit, and a pitchfork with some horns on his head, but listen, that's not the Satan in The Bible. The Satan of The Bible is a powerful being. Paul says in another place that he can

transform himself into an angel of light. So this is what Satan is doing so expeditiously today. Satan is constantly confusing the issue with his seeming light, but remember it's Satan who -

II Corinthians 4:4b
"...hath blinded the minds of them which (will not repent and be baptized? Notice it doesn't say that. So what is God's controversy? They won't believe. They) *believe not,..."*

It's not that we have to repent, it's not that we have run down some aisle in repentance. But rather what does God demand for salvation in this day of Grace? That we believe the Gospel. Now is a mighty good time to look at the Gospel of salvation that saves us and places us into the Body of Christ. Jerry Pool isn't here with us today, but if he was here he'd be winking at me, and I know what he'd be saying. So turn back with me to I Corinthians Chapter 15. And bless his heart, Jerry started coming to my classes about 16 years ago and I guess one of the first Thursday nights he attended I must have struck a cord with these first 4 verses in I Corinthians, **"The Gospel!"** There is no clearer place in the whole Bible where the Gospel is laid out in full. This beats John 3:16 a hundred miles. Now I have nothing against John 3:16, but John 3:16 can't even come close to what Paul writes here. Remember any time that Paul makes a reference to the Gospel in any of his epistles it's always this one. All right verse 1:

I Corinthians 15:1,2
"Moreover, brethren, I declare unto you the gospel (absolutely. Today there is only one Gospel of Grace.) *which I preached unto you, which also ye have received, and wherein ye stand;* (that was all it took. When they believed the Gospel then God literally moved heaven and earth to bring that person to place of enlightenment. And as soon as we believe the Gospel this Book begins to open up to understanding. And it begins to make sense) *By which also ye are saved,* (it's by this Gospel and this Gospel only that we're saved. I don't care if it was in Corinth or any other area of the world, whether it was back in 50 AD or in the present year it makes no difference because this is the Gospel that saves lost people.) *if ye keep in memory what I preached unto you, unless ye have believed in vain."*

Paul is saying, **"Don't believe the wrong thing for salvation."** Listen God is meticulous. Again this same Jerry had been to a funeral of a dear friend, a good person, and I'll never forget the look on Jerry's face when he said, "Les is there any chance that God might compromise this a little bit and let this person in?" No way! Because God is not a compromiser. **God has made the plan of salvation so simple, and plain that He is not going to let someone slip in a side door, and say, "Well I thought..."** You see that's what Cain did. I always have to go back to Cain and Abel because they were so typical. Abel did just exactly what God said to do. Abel believed what God said and he acted on it. But old Cain rationalized, and said, "Yeah but I think that if I do this and if I come on with all of this effort then God will accept me." **But did He? No!** I've often said that Cain was probably a better person than Abel. It wouldn't surprise me a bit. Because Cain tried, but what was his problem? Cain didn't believe what God said.

And it's the same way today. If people are going to somehow or other connive around this simple Gospel, then I don't believe that God is going to accept them. Now I don't know hearts, and I never pretend to, but I have to go by what The Book says, and The Book says that this is the Gospel by which people are saved. Here it is in verse 3 and 4.

I Corinthians 15:3,4
"For I delivered unto you first of all that which I also received, (now here we come back to the revelation that Paul received from the ascended Lord, and not from Christ's earthly ministry. Christ had the finished work of the Cross now behind Him. So this is what was revealed by the ascended Lord for us to believe for salvation) *how that Christ died for our sins according to the scriptures;* (This was in that whole preordained plan of the ages that Christ would go to the Cross) *And that he was buried, and that he rose again the third day according to the scriptures;"*

Now folks that's the Gospel that you **must believe in your heart for salvation**. And isn't it so simple. Oh there is no string attached, there is no prescribed ritual, there is no particular way that you have to do this. You can believe it at the kitchen sink, you can believe it driving down the road, you can believe it when you wake up in the middle of the night. You can say, **"Yes I see it. For me there is only one remedy, and that is that Christ died for my sins, and He arose from the dead!"** Then God does all the rest. God saves us. God sets our feet on a Rock, and He begins to open up the Scriptures, and then we begin to comprehend the truth of The Bible from cover to cover. Now this isn't going to happen all at once, but salvation happens all at once. I told a class many years ago that **salvation is not a process, but rather salvation is an event. Salvation is an instantaneous event. Christian growth is a process. Bible understanding is a process, but salvation is a one time event.** And what an event to be translated from darkness to light! To know your sins have been forgiven, and to know that you're justified! And all this happens instantaneously.

I noticed in my studies of this past week that in all of Paul's letters that we never have to beg God to forgive us of our sins. Think about that. And yet for most people who are putting out the plan of salvation they say, "You have to ask God to forgive you of your sins, you have to repent." Well I can't find any of this in Paul's letter to the Church Age believers. It's not in here, but rather my Bible tells me that when Christ died the death of the Cross, He took on Himself not just the sins of those who are saved, but rather He took on the sins of every human being that has ever lived or will ever live. And when He took every human being's sin then He could cry to the Father, "Those sins are forgiven," All of those sins are buried in the deepest sea, never, never to be brought before us again. So even when lost people slip out of this life into eternity, their sins are already forgiven. But they had not believed unto Salvation. Now when we get into Chapter 5 of II Corinthians we're going to find the word "Reconciliation" and the same thing applies. Every human being that has ever lived has now been reconciled to God by virtue of the work of the Cross.

But now I have to clarify that don't I? I think this will be a good illustration. Those guys in Congress who hold the money bags, and can hand it out by the billions. For a particular program they can appropriate millions of dollars, but that money stays in that account until somebody out there starts drawing on that account. Am I right? Is that government process? You know it is. All right the money is already appropriated, but it won't do a nickels worth of good until somebody draws on it and puts it to use. Now that is God! At the Cross God paid the payment for every person's sins. He paid their eternal doom, He did everything that needed to be done. So now all that lost people have to do is draw on that account. And how do they do that? By simply believing the Gospel for their salvation. But the reason they will never enjoy all the ramifications of that finished work is that they are never going to draw on it by believing. They will never exercise the faith that God demands. Now isn't that sad? You know I think when people go to the Lake of Fire for all eternity, they won't be going there for all their sins. They're not going there because of the drunkenness, and adultery and whatever you want to call sin. **They're going there because of their unbelief!** And if I'm not remembered for anything else I want to be remembered for that. That lost humanity is going to their eternal doom for only one reason, and that is they refuse to believe that everything is already done. And isn't that sad. And who is keeping them from seeing all of this? The powers of Satan as we see in II Corinthians 4:4:

II Corinthians 4:4a
"In whom the god of this world hath blinded the minds of them which believe not,..."
And how does Satan do it? I think his favorite choice today is to keep people so busy. Everybody is so busy. Our kids are all involved in sports from the time they get old enough to walk. And so it is a constant bombarding of our time with everything except the things that count. And so I believe this is Satan's biggest instrument. And there is nothing wrong with a lot of those things. There's nothing wrong with kids playing T-Ball, or basketball; but what's it doing? It's keeping their minds so occupied that they never have time to think in terms of the spiritual. Oh, the old Devil loves it when we're preoccupied. The more he can keep people in programs, and the more he can keep people with their eyes on material things the more old Satan can say, **"I've got them veiled, I'm keeping them blinded, and I'm the winner.**

(19a) How can God Who is a God of love and mercy possibly consign people someday to that awful Lake of Fire?

Book 21 LESSON ONE * PART II

Isaiah 61:10
"I will greatly rejoice in the LORD, my soul shall be joyful in my God (why is Isaiah filled with joy?)*; for he hath clothed me with the garments of salvation, he hath covered me with the robe of righteousness,"*

You see the whole purpose of God giving us this Book is to bring us to the point of Salvation.

Every human being has to reach that point if they're going to escape God's wrath. And God is going to do everything that He can to keep every person from falling under that condemnation. And God has done that, and He's made it so available. You know I've had people ask in my classes more than once, **"How can God Who is a God of love and mercy possibly consign people someday to that awful Lake of Fire?** Listen it will be easy, and I mean that. It's going to be easy, because He's done everything that could possibly be done to keep them from it. He's given us The Word, He's given us men who are willing to preach and teach it so we can understand that all we have to do is **"BELIEVE"! Faith plus nothing!** See there is no energy involved in believing, it's just accepting what God has said. No questions asked, but people don't want to do that. They simply don't want to believe what God has said concerning Salvation.

Romans 1:16
16For I am not ashamed of the gospel of Christ: for it is the power of God unto salvation to every one that believeth; to the Jew first, and also to the Greek.

I Corinthians 15:1-4
1Moreover, brethren, I declare unto you the gospel which I preached unto you, which also ye have received, and wherein ye stand; 2By which also ye are saved, if ye keep in memory what I preached unto you, unless ye have believed in vain. 3For I delivered unto you first of all that which I also received, how that Christ died for our sins according to the scriptures; 4And that he was buried, and that he rose again the third day according to the scriptures:

Romans 10:9-10
9That if thou shalt confess with thy mouth the Lord Jesus, and shalt believe in thine heart that God hath raised him from the dead, thou shalt be saved. 10For with the heart man believeth unto righteousness; and with the mouth confession is made unto salvation.

I Thessalonians 4:14
14For if we believe that Jesus died and rose again, even so them also which sleep in Jesus will God bring with him

There are so many more scriptures that Paul uses to show us Salvation. And when we do believe like Isaiah, then immediately because these two imperatives have now been fulfilled, what happens? He has clothed me with the garments of Salvation, and covered me with a robe of righteousness.

Book 14 LESSON ONE * PART IV

Revelation 20:14,15
"And death and hell were cast into the lake of fire. This is the second death. And whosoever was

not found written in the book of life was cast into the lake of fire."

I don't care if people don't like to preach this subject any more, the Book stills says it. And there are groups who try to make believe that a God of love couldn't do this. But I've shown you that God's love was so great at the Cross that there is no room for removing the eternal doom of the lost person.

(20a) What else does the Bible say about atheists and non-believers ?

Book 9 LESSON TWO * PART IV

What is the basic difference between believing in God and believing God? It is all the difference in the world. See you can believe in God, and I suppose that 95% of Americans say, "I believe in God." The other 5% say they don't, but way down deep when the deathbed comes they do. I do not believe there is an absolute atheist. To believe in God is one thing. To believe God: that enters into faith; that implies that God has said something. And as soon as God said something and we believe it, then it is faith. For example, He tells us (in I Corinthians 15:1-4) that for our salvation we are to believe that Christ died for us, was buried, and rose from the grave, and that he did that for you and me. Now that is faith.

Book 20 LESSON THREE * PART I

Titus 2:11
"For the grace of God that bringeth salvation hath (already) *appeared to all men."*
Now granted, when Paul wrote, the Roman Empire comprised ninety percent of the then-known world. But they had all heard. I think Paul is going all the way back to the flood. When Noah and his three sons and their wives came off the ark, they all had a knowledge of God. But what happened? Within a generation or two they began to do what Romans 1:18 says. They began to hold down the truth. They stood on it, and kept it underfoot. Remember all the revelation that God had given mankind, beginning with Adam. Deep in the heart of every human being, even in that Adamic nature, is the knowledge that there is a God. I've had people tell me they are atheists, but that's just an excuse. They're trying to convince themselves they are, but down deep within each atheist is the knowledge of God. So I maintain there is no such thing as an atheist. They all know there is that nagging desire to fill the vacuum that God placed in mankind when He created them. In history and archaeology you will never find a group or a tribe of people that did not have a worship of some sort. And always associated with a blood sacrifice. They're going to have that need for a blood sacrifice, and it all goes back to the way God created mankind. So man has that knowledge that there is a Creator. Now verse 21: the reason they are without excuse is:

Romans 1:21

"Because that, when they knew God, they glorified him not as God, neither were thankful; but became vain in their imaginations (Solomon said, "Vanity, vanity, all is vanity." What was he talking about? Humanism! When they leave God out of their thinking, then it's empty)*, and their foolish heart was darkened."*

Book 38 Lesson Three • Part II

Ephesians 5:15b

"...not as fools, but as wise." Now we all have our own idea of the definition of a fool, but I always have to use the Scripture for the best definition. So let's go back and look at it in Psalm chapter 14.

Psalms 14:1a

"The fool hath said in his heart, There is no God..." Now most Bibles will have the *"There is"* italicized, which means that it's been added to hopefully clarify it, but in this case they didn't do this verse any good at all by adding those two words. I like the way it read just by leaving it the way it was intended.

Psalms 14:1a

"The fool hath said in his heart, no, God...."
Not that there is no God, because I don't think there's a person alive that can honestly say that. Now there are some who try to claim they're atheists, but way down deep inside of them, when the death angel comes knocking on their door, they're suddenly going to realize too late, that there is a God, and that there is an eternity. So I don't like to look at this verse in that light, but rather if you'll put a comma after the word no, the fool says no to God. Do you see that? The fool says, No, God, I'm not going to do what you tell me, I'm not going to believe what you say. Now that's a fool! Now as soon as you get the concept that the fool is the person who says no to God, he's the man who is then destitute of faith.

So the definition of a fool then is actually a person who is destitute of faith, and we've had examples in the Scriptures of such people. Cain was the first one. The guy was destitute of faith, and consequently he didn't bring the kind of sacrifice that God had told him to bring, because he didn't believe what God had said, he rationalized. The next one we come to early on in Scripture is Ishmael. Ishmael was not a man of faith. He went and did just exactly opposite of what God, through his father Abraham had said, "Not to marry Canaanites," so he went and did it anyway. He showed the fact that he was destitute of faith because he said no to God.

(21a) How does the Bible describe the eternal heaven and earth ?

Editor's Note: Chronologically according to the Bible, the rapture will occur, then the 7 year tribulation. Then Christ will return to defeat Satan and rule for 1000 years. Then the eternal heaven and earth will be created as described below.

Book 14 LESSON TWO * PART II

Revelation 21:1a
"AND I saw a new heaven and a new earth:..."

I try to get people to ask themselves questions as they study their Bibles. This verse should stir a question. What happened to the old ones? Scripture has the answer. Go to II Peter 3:10. I feel these verses in II Peter give us the reason for Revelation Chapter 21:

II Peter 3:10
"But the day of the Lord (remember this term, *"...the day of the Lord"* actually begins with the onset of the Tribulation and runs all the way through the thousand-year reign of Christ in the Kingdom) *will come as a thief in the night* (it will catch the world by surprise. Notice there is a semicolon at the end of night. Many times a punctuation mark in the Scripture will skip hundreds or thousands of years. That's the case here)*; in the which the heavens shall pass away with a great noise, and the elements shall melt with fervent heat, the earth also and the works that are therein shall be burned up."*

I like Peter who, though an uneducated fisherman with no degree in science, uses the very terms that scientists use today. We speak of this earth made up of elements. The various elements and fervent heat in verse 10, spoken of in verse 11 as dissolving, is another science term. These are the exact words that Peter uses with regard to this planet, *"the earth also and the works that are therein shall be burned up."* I see no room here for leaving even the core of the earth.

II Peter 3:11
"Seeing then that all these things (what things? Everything that makes up the planet. I don't know if this will include the solar system or not. Our solar system is just a pin-point compared to all of outer space. My pastor made an analogy in a sermon which I liked. He said if man could launch a rocket, pointing it to outer space, and even if he could get it going 186,000 miles per second (the speed of light), at any given point in time will it stick into the ceiling of outer space? I'd never thought of that. Naturally the answer is "no." If it did, there would have to be something on the other side. This is completely beyond our imagination - the vastness of space; that something going at the speed of light can keep on going forever. But, as far as space goes, God is always beyond it. The infinity of God and space is mind boggling. But we know that "these things" applies to all that makes up our planet) *shall be dissolved, what manner of persons ought ye to be in all holy conversation and godliness,"*

Peter is saying, "Since you dealing with this kind of God, who is man to even attempt to reject

Him." But we also know that throughout human history the largest percentage of men have kept God out of their life. I try not to get on a stump and start preaching, but I get so alarmed that our younger generation seems to have no concept of God, of eternity, or things that are spiritual. They're living for the here and now. They're living for the gratification of the flesh, with no concept of the Scriptures. It just scares me. On the other hand we have to understand that all of this is getting ready for these end-time events, when the Anti-Christ will appear. These kids in our so-called "Christian America" have no concept of what's coming. Being ignorant of the Scripture, when they hear this charismatic individual promising peace and prosperity, they will fall for him hook, line, and sinker. Back to Revelation 21. As this planet has been plagued with the curse and sin for so long, we find that it is totally dissolved. Then the following:

Revelation 21:1
"AND I saw a new heaven and a new earth: for the first heaven and the first earth were passed away (gone!)*; and there was no more sea."*

Because the earth here has passed away, that's the reason Hell has to be emptied out. Most people don't think of these things. Hell as we know it is, at this moment, in the very center of this earth. But since this earth is going to blow up and be completely destroyed (as we saw in II Peter Chapter 3), even the inhabitants of Hell must be removed. In order for this to happen, Christ will resurrect the lost bodily out of Hell to stand before the Great White Throne. Then this old planet can be destroyed. Now for the exciting part:

Revelation 21:2
"And I John saw the holy city, new Jerusalem (the one for all eternity)*, coming down from God out of heaven, prepared as a bride adorned for her husband."* Remember in John Chapter 14?

John 14:2
In my Father's house are many mansions: if it were not so, I would have told you. I go to prepare a place for you."

I don't know if Jesus had the new Jerusalem in mind here, but we know that God has this glorious abode that we'll enjoy for all eternity. He'll still have a thousand years to work on it if He needs that much time. It will be beyond our comprehension. Now verse 3:

Revelation 21:3
"And I heard a great voice out of heaven saying, `Behold, the tabernacle of God is with men, and he will dwell with them, and they shall be his people, and God himself shall be with them, and be their God.'"

When this happens, God is going to be in the very present (not in a distant place where we have to take Him by faith). And eternity being what eternity is, it is in another dimension that you and I can't comprehend. Even though there will be billions in eternity, each one of us will know God as personally as we do our own parent. That is one of the unique qualities of the eternal. Now verse 4:

Revelation 21:4-6
"And God shall wipe away all tears from their eyes (this is what makes Heaven the Heaven as we think of it)*; and there shall be no more death, neither sorrow, nor crying, neither shall there be any more pain: for the former things are passed away.* I like to tie tears, death, sorrow, and pain to this earth. That is part of the curse and the earth today! *And he that sat upon the throne said, 'Behold, I make all things new.' And he said unto me, 'Write: for these words are true and faithful.' And he said unto me, 'It is done, I am the Alpha and Omega* (only one Person in the Godhead says that. It's Christ. So the Lord Jesus refers to Himself as)*, the beginning and the end. I will give unto him that is athirst of the fountain of the water of life freely.'"* That's the eternal part again.

Revelation 21:7,8
"He that overcometh shall inherit all things; and I will be his God, and he shall be my son." In verse 8 we have a reminder from God of those who will not be in this eternal state with us.

"But the fearful, and unbelieving, and the abominable, and murderers, and whoremongers, and sorcerers, and idolaters, and all liars, shall have their part in the lake which burneth with fire and brimstone: which is the second death." The final separation from God.

Revelation 21:9-11
"And there came unto me one of the seven angels which had the seven vials full of the seven last plagues (of the Tribulation)*, and talked with me saying, Come hither, I will shew thee the bride, the Lamb's wife."* These are terms of position, not communal living. This bride is the new Jerusalem descending out of Heaven.
"And he carried me away in the spirit to a great and high mountain, and shewed me that great city, the holy Jerusalem, descending out of heaven from God. Having the glory of God: and her light was like unto a stone most precious, even like a jasper stone, clear as crystal;"

I won't read all the descriptions (which are completely beyond our comprehension). With the gem stones and jewels that will make up this city (it isn't just going to be gold), it's going to be everything that we think of as wealth and beauty.

Revelation 21:12-15
"And had a wall great and high, and had twelve gates, and at the gates twelve angels, and names written thereon, which are the names of the twelve tribes of the children of Israel: On the east

three gates; on the north three gates; on the south three gates; and on the west three gates. And the wall of the city had twelve foundations, and in them the names of the twelve apostles (Peter and the eleven) *of the Lamb. And he that talked with me had a golden reed to measure the city, and the gates thereof, and the wall thereof."* Now in verse 16, he brings it into language we kind of understand.

Revelation 21:16

"And the city lieth foursquare (it won't be so many miles wide and long, as our cities are today, but rather long, wide, and high - actually a cube. Some feel it might be a pyramid, but I doubt that; I think it will be a cube)*, and the length is as large as the breadth: and he measured the city with the reed, twelve thousand furlongs. The length and the breadth and the height of it are equal."*

So we have a cube that is 1500 miles in each direction, plus 1500 miles high. That is from New York City to Denver to Mexico City. From Mexico City into the South Atlantic Ocean and back to New York City. That would be a 1500 mile square. And this city goes up 1500 miles. What's another reason we'll need a new earth? Well, that city could never rest on the earth we have now. The curvature of the earth would fall away from it, and most of the city would be setting out there like birds' wings. I think this new earth will be so big, that even a city this size won't go beyond the curvature. Get your calculators out and tell me how large this new earth will have to be for this city to sit on it. And there will be billions in glory. I think most Bible believers agree that infants and little children under the age of accountability are going to be in glory.

Looking back through human history, what percentage of infants got beyond infancy? Take the third world tonight and think of the millions of infants that die before they are even a year old. They will all be in glory as adults. That makes me think this new earth will be so huge and beautiful that no one is going to be crowded. Remember, this 1500-mile city is just our apartments so to speak. And as you come down through the text, we find there is going to be food production. I think there will be all the aspects of the thousand-year Kingdom reign. I feel there will be an animal Kingdom, and birds. There won't be a sea, so there might not be fish. I think it will be an extension of the Kingdom economy, except on a greater and grander scale. God is preparing this that we might have pleasures evermore. Not pleasures as the world thinks of pleasure, but as God thinks of pleasure. I don't know what that will be but I know one thing (knowing God as I do), He can't make a mistake. It's going to be glorious. To think that man will turn his back on all of this for seemingly 10 or 15 years of a so-called "good time."

Put it this way. Show me a person who "lives in the fast lane" (we see this constantly with entertainers, etc.). How long can their body take it? Only a few years. They burn themselves out for just a few years of "pleasure." And they have turned their back on an eternity of real pleasure! Isn't it foolish? But mankind can't get these concepts straight. They think in terms of living their own life and having a good time for three-score years and ten, not worrying about what comes after that. I look at it the other way around. I'm not that concerned about this three score and ten; I'm more concerned about the billions of years ahead of us. Now, let's move on.

Revelation 21:19,20

"And the foundations of the wall of the city were garnished with all manner of precious stones. The first foundation was jasper; the second, sapphire; the third a chalcedony; the fourth, an emerald; The fifth, sardonyx; the sixth sardius; the seventh chrysolite; the eight, beryl; the ninth, a topaz; the tenth, a chrysoprasus; the eleventh, a jacinth; the twelfth, an amethyst." Such beautiful gem stones! These foundations are going to be garnished with them. And then verse 21. This would make any bride's mouth water.

Revelation 21:21

"And the twelve gates were twelve pearls, every several gate was of one pearl" (the Bible says it. Women have gone to great lengths to possess the biggest pearl in the world, but here we will have gates made of a single pearl): *and the street of the city was pure gold, as it were transparent glass."* This is where songwriters have picked up that we will tread the streets of gold. But this is our prospect. Since God is present with us there is not need for a place to worship.

Revelation 21:22,23

"And I saw no temple therein: for the Lord God Almighty and the Lamb are the temple of it. And the city had no need of the sun (that doesn't mean there won't be a sun. Because when you get into Chapter 22 the sun is mentioned again. But there won't be a need for the sun), *neither of the moon, to shine in it; for the glory of God did lighten it, and the Lamb is the light thereof."*

Revelation 21:24

"And the (what's the next word? Please underline it) *nations* (Remember, the Kingdom economy will slip right into eternity, except on a new Heaven and earth. We have nations in the Kingdom and we'll have nations in eternity. The Kingdom will be forever and ever) *of them which are saved shall walk in the light of it: and the kings of the earth do bring their glory and honour into it."* It appears there will be nations with sub-governments under the headship of God (which comes back to the promise to you and I as believers). We will reign and rule with Him.

Revelation 21:25-27

"And the gates of it shall not be shut at all by day: for there shall be no night there. And they shall bring the glory and honour of the nations into it. And there shall in no wise enter into it any thing that defileth, neither whatsoever worketh abomination, or maketh a lie: but they which are written in the Lamb's book of life."

(22a) How should we pray ?

Book 38 Lesson Two • Part IV

When people today call or write about prayer this is the first place that I take them. These are absolutely the best verses on prayer.

Philippians 4:6a
"Be careful (or worry) *for nothing;..."*
You've seen these little wall plaques that say, "why worry when you can pray." Well there's more to that than meets the eye. We're not supposed to worry. Now we can be concerned. I think everyone of us have concerns, and we have that right to have those concerns, but we're not to fret and worry.

Philippians 4:6b
"... but in every thing by prayer and supplication with thanksgiving...."
It doesn't do you any good to petition God if you forget to thank Him for it in advance as you pray.. Thanking God is the criteria, that's the modus operandi for prayer. Make it with thanksgiving.

Philippians 4:6b
"...let your requests be made known unto God...."
He isn't limiting your request. It can be anything as long as it's in Godly reason of course, but let your requests be made known unto God. Here we can come, and ask with thanksgiving, **but God may say,** *No!* **He may say,** *no not right now, maybe later.* **He may say,** *Yes.* But regardless how He answers in verse 6, you've already got the answer in verse 7. We've got the answer to our prayers here in verse 7, and what is it?

Philippines 4:7
"And the peace of God, (no matter how God answers our request) *which passeth all under-standing, shall keep your hearts and minds through Christ Jesus."*

Do you see why we don't have to worry about anything? It's because we have that peace of God, and that's what keeps us. I know that's beyond human understanding. I know we're all human and we do worry and fret, and get overly concerned, and yet I think most of us have to admit that through all of our tight spots, we came through it with God's help. Now that's where we have it over on the world. God never promises us that we're going to go through life without problems. We're going to have just as many problems as many in the world around us, but what's the difference? **We have God with us in our problems, we have Him to take us through and we can rest assure in that.**

Another Scripture comes to mind in Psalms chapter 37. Now this is from David even under the Law, but I can still go back and use it in application, and it's a beautiful couple of verses. This passage fits right along this same line of thinking. The peace that passeth all understanding will keep our heart and minds through Christ Jesus. Now let's look what David writes, and let's start with verse 5. My what a promise.

Psalms 37:5
"Commit thy way unto the LORD trust also in him; and he shall bring it to pass"

Maybe not in our timing, but in His. Isn't that a promise? My I've gone through trying times myself, and I just about wear that verse out. But do you know what it means to commit something? It means you take it to God and leave it with Him. I think I've given this example before. Regardless what you think of the Post Office, I think most of you just go and drop your letter in the mail slot. Do you go home and for the next week fret and worry whether it got to it's destination or not? No. Because as soon as you dropped that letter, what did you do? You committed it to the Postal Service to take care of it. You don't go home and lose sleep over worrying if the letter got there. Because you're assuming that it will. You committed it, and you let it go at that. Now this is what verse 5 means.

Psalms 37:5
"Commit thy way unto the LORD; trust also in him; and he shall bring it to pass."

When you have a need, a problem, or concern, you simply commit it to the Lord. You take it to Him, and you leave it there, you don't hang on to it. If you hang onto that letter, it never will get down into the mail, because you've still got it. But if you let it go then it's committed. The other verse I like here in this chapter is verse 7.

Psalms 37:7a
"Rest in the LORD,..."
Do you know what it means to rest? It means to relax. Turn those concerns over to Him, don't hang on to your problems. But rather *"Rest in the Lord."*

Psalms 37:7b
"...and wait patiently for him:
See, we're in a society of instant gratification. Give it to me now Lord, I'm in a hurry! No we have to learn to *"wait patiently for him."*

Psalms 37:7b
"...fret not thyself because of him who prospereth in his way, because of the man who bringeth wicked devices to pass."

Boy we see that every day don't we? We look at the young ungodly world around us, and all their prosperity, and wealth, and wonder, "Why?" Don't worry about that, because those are things that are in God's hand. **But our responsibility is to commit our way unto the Lord, trust in Him and let Him bring it to pass in His own time**. Some times it takes a lot longer than we think. It may take years, but God will do it in His own time.

Book 40 Lesson Three • Part III

Colossians 1:12
"Giving thanks unto the Father, which hath made us meet (or prepared us) *to be partakers of the inheritance of the saints in light:"*

Now let's look at giving thanks to the Father. I've had several questions lately, it's funny how they sort of come in groups, and the question is, "Is it appropriate to pray to the Father in this age of Grace? Well I taught it on television, and had forgotten when I taught it but I found it the other day, so I'm going to have you turn back to Ephesians chapter 5, because maybe some of you or some of the listening audience wonder about praying to the Father, as the Lord's prayer instructs us to do. Yes that has not changed. This is as clear cut an answer as you can get.

Ephesians 5:20
"Giving thanks always for all things unto God and the Father in the name of our Lord Jesus Christ:"

Isn't that exactly how we do it? So it's still appropriate today, yes we do pray to the Father, and we do all in the name then of the Lord Jesus Christ, and we're going to see that relationship in the Trinity in little later verses, but for now come back again to Colossians chapter 1. So Paul as he prays to the Father in the name of the Lord Jesus Christ he has thanked God, the Father that He took these Colossians out of paganism, out of darkness, out of the chains of the satanic powers and translated them into the heavenly kingdom. **Now what's happened to the Colossians has happened to us. We too have been translated from a position in darkness, and we are now citizens of the heavenly kingdom.** Now Paul does not make a big a do about our kingdom relationship, because after all that's primarily associated with the nation of Israel.

Book 41 LESSON THREE * PART IV

Colossians 3:17
"And whatsoever ye do in word or deed, do all in the name of the Lord Jesus, giving thanks to God and the Father by him."

Now there's the process again, as Paul also gave it in Ephesians on how we're to pray. I still have people ask, "Are we still supposed to pray in the name of Jesus?" Absolutely! Come back with me to Ephesians chapter 5. You'll see this is plain English, this is the process.

Ephesians 5:20
"Giving thanks always for all things unto God and the Father (how?) *in the name of our Lord Jesus Christ;"*

Now that's the Scriptural instructions, and Paul says the same thing here in Colossians. Now looking at Colossians again.

Colossians 3:17
"And whatsoever ye do in word or deed, do all in the name of the Lord Jesus, giving thanks to God and the Father by him."

By the Lord Jesus, because after all He's the One that's at the right hand of the Father, He's the One that's the advocate, He's the One that is the intercessor, and it only makes common sense. In fact another verse comes to mind in I Timothy chapter 2. Again it's a good admonition for all of us.

I Timothy 2:1-5
"I exhort therefore, that, first of all, supplications, prayers, intercessions, and giving of thanks, be made for all men; 2. For kings, (our government) **and for all that are in authority, that we may lead a quiet and peaceable life in all godliness and honestly. 3. For this is good and acceptable in the sight of God our Saviour. 4. Who will have all men to be saved, and to come unto the knowledge of truth. 5. For there is one God, and one mediator between God and men, the man Christ Jesus;"**

Oh aren't you glad you don't have to go through a priest, or a religion, but you have clear access into the throne room.

Book 30 LESSON TWO * PART I

II Corinthians 1:11
"Ye also helping together by prayer for us, that for the gift bestowed upon us by the means of many persons thanks may be given by many on our behalf." In other words Paul then, and like we do today, realized what really sustained him in his ministry. The prayers of the saints! Never fail to pray for one another. Pray for us, and others in the ministry that God is using to reach hearts. Remember prayer changes things.

Book 41 LESSON TWO * PART I

Colossians 2:13
"And you, being dead in your sins (absolutely, we were as under the control of the old nature, our spirit was completely of fellowship with God and so that's what Paul says we were in the

world. We were dead in sin) *and the uncircumcision of your flesh* (by virtue of being Gentiles) *but hath he* (God) *quickened* (has regenerated our spirit. He has crucified old Adams and has given us a new nature. A new divine nature) *together with him, having* (already) *forgiven you all trespasses."*

Before I go back and look at another word, let's look at Colossians chapter 3, since we're already in that. And let's look at verse 13. And again, Paul repeats this twice in two chapters to drive it home. And oh, most of Christendom has a hard time swallowing this, I know they do. But here it is again.

Colossians 3:13
"Forbearing one another, (remember, he's writing to believers congregated in an assembly) *and forgiving one another, if any may have a quarrel against any: even as Christ forgave you, so also do ye."*

Now look at that verse very carefully. Is there any demand in that verse that you forgive your enemy before you can be saved? NO! That's already done by the Grace of God. You're forgiven. But now since you and I are forgiven, what should we be ready to do? Forgive whoever we have ought against, whether it's in the Church or neighborhood or whatever. **There is nothing stipulated in Paul's Gospel, nor his writings that first we have to forgive everybody before we can be forgiven like the Lord Jesus said during His earthly ministry under Law.** I had a question come the other day. Someone had heard it and they had missed it. The Lord's Prayer. The Lord's Prayer isn't appropriate for us today. The Lord's Prayer was under Law. It was to Israel. And it says *"forgive us our trespasses* (when?) *as we forgive those who trespass against us."* Now that's Law. And absolutely a Jew could not be forgiven until he went and forgave his neighbor. But that doesn't hold true today. We're forgiven by the Grace of God. And if we're forgiven, then why in the world can't we forgive our neighbor? That's the teaching.

Book 23 LESSON TWO * PART IV

Romans 8:26
"Likewise the Spirit (the Holy Spirit who is now indwelling us, according to Paul's teaching) *also helpeth our infirmities* (our weaknesses. There's not much we can do about it because we're dealing with the invisible, in the realm of the Spirit. But let God do it. God can strengthen us in our places of infirmity)*: for we know not what we should pray for as we ought: but the Spirit itself maketh intercession for us with groanings which cannot be uttered."*

That verse is kind of hard to comprehend, except to say I think that there will come places in our lives when we just don't know how to pray. We have an idea of what we want, but we can't put it into words. I've told my classes over the years, when you get to that situation, just be quiet, shut up and let the Holy Spirit commune for you. This is not necessarily a tongues experience. That's not what Paul is talking about. But we get to this place where the Holy Spirit actually intercedes on our behalf.

(23a) How can I know that I'm really saved ?

Book 34 LESSON ONE * PART III

Romans 8:14
"For as many (or all of you) *as are led by the Spirit of God, they are the sons of God."*
Listen, that's very exclusive to us. I get a kick out of the Biblical Archeological Review letters of the editor. Because some of these people write in and condemn people for being exclusionists. Of course we are, because the Bible is! And what's it excluding here? Lost people are not led by the Holy Spirit. They're out there on their own under the power of the god of this world. But believers are led by the Spirit of God. That's one of the indications that we have true salvation.

I had a letter the other day and it was a good question. "How can I know that I'm truly saved?" It's a good question. I wrote back and said, "There are several ways: 1. Do you have a hunger for the Word of God? If not I doubt if there's any true salvation because it just follows like daylight following dark, that when we become a child of God we hunger after His word. 2. Do you enjoy being with God's people? If you don't, then there's something wrong and I would re-examine my so-called salvation experience. 3. Do you enjoy prayer time, and taking your needs to the Lord? If not, I doubt if there's any relationship there."

But whatever, it's a thing of the heart and I can't look on the heart nor can anyone else, but you can self-examine. And I think it's Peter who wrote, *"make your call and election sure."* Well, what did he mean by that? Don't work a little harder, but just simply on the light of Scripture, examine yourself. Are you just depending on something that you have done, or are you depending on a solid faith in the Gospel wherein the power of God has been exercised? And when that happens, here it comes, as we saw in Galatians and now here in Romans, the Holy Spirit comes into our life and He begins to lead and guide and direct to the place where we don't have to have rules and regulations. The Spirit does that. Now here again, if we're led by the Spirit of God then we are the sons, or the born ones of God. That's one of the proofs of footing. Now let's go to verse 15 and again he's talking to believers here.

Romans 8:15
"For ye have not received the spirit of bondage again to (what?) *fear; but ye have received the Spirit of adoption, whereby we cry, Abba Father."*

Believers don't have to walk around in constant fear. We have respect for God and we revere Him, but we don't have to fear Him. Because we know He loves us. In fact, I'll never forget, and I think I mentioned this on a program a long time ago, somebody sent me a tape of their pastor's Sunday morning sermon. I learned a bunch from it. And that was that in John Chapter 13, where Jesus was dealing with Martha and Mary and Lazarus, all through that chapter, it wasn't how much Lazarus and Mary loved Jesus, but what was it? How much He loved them! And it was an eye-opener! And this is what people have to realize. It isn't dependent upon how much I love Him, although we're certainly going to love Him. But you see, the thing that's important is that we realize how much He loves us! Enough to die and suffer for us. Now then, when we have that kind of a salvation, the Holy Spirit bears witness with our spirit that we are the children of God.

Now do you see how that flies in the face of these people who say you can never really know? They say you can hope so or you can try and do the best you can, but you'll never really know? That's not what my Bible says. My Bible makes it so plain and mine is no different than anybody else's. But it makes it so plain that we can know that we have passed from death unto life. And here is another one. It's the witness of the Holy Spirit that we have that salvation, we have that we are children of God.

Book 26 LESSON ONE * PART II

Colossians1:4
"But since we've heard of your faith in Christ Jesus and of the love which you have to all the saints,"

Have you ever had someone ask you, "How can I know that I'm really saved?" It's a good question. I don't mind a bit if someone calls me and says, "Now Les, you're always talking about someone being a true believer. How can I know that I am a true believer? And not like multitude of others who are simply church members and sitting in their pew for an hour on Sunday morning and hope that they're okay. How can I know that I'm a true believer?" You know what my first answer is? "Do you love the Word of God?" And then I follow that right up with the second one. "Do you love being with God's people?"

In fact I just had a gentleman call last night and ask the same question and I said, "Okay. Do you have a love for the Word of God?" He said, "Yeah, I do for the last couple of years. I just can't get enough of it." I said, "Okay, then my next question is, do you enjoy being with God's people or would you rather be in some night club instead of a Bible study?" He said, "I hear you. I hear you." Well, that's just exactly what Paul is saying here. What was the proof of their faith? Their love for fellow believers! See, the world doesn't love us. The world would much rather have us be out there in some night club or some other place of amusement than to be in a Bible study. You know that. But we're to be the other way around. We'd much rather be with fellow believers studying the Word than being out there being entertained in some ungodly way. That's always the mark. And so here again he says that the proof of their faith was the love that they had for the saints or their fellow believers.

Now that doesn't mean that every believer is perfect. I don't think we even have to like every believer. There's a difference between love and like. Isn't that right? I hope I don't get my foot in my mouth. But I maintain there is a difference between liking someone and loving them and you don't necessarily have to do both. You've got to love them, but you don't necessarily have to like someone who rubs you wrong and doesn't have the same interests that you do. And you just certainly wouldn't say, "Well I just wish I could spend every day of the week with that individual." No, you don't have to like people all that much but we have to love them. And there's a big difference. Love is that which seeks the other person's highest good. These people had a love for the fellow saints.

Book 26 LESSON ONE * PART II

I Corinthians 15:1-4
"Moreover, brethren, I declare unto you the gospel which I preached unto you, which also ye have received, and wherein ye stand; By which also ye are saved, if ye keep in memory what I preached unto you, unless ye have believed in vain. For I delivered unto you first of all that which I also received, how that Christ died for our sins according to the scriptures; And that he was buried, and that he rose again the third day according to the scriptures:"

Now that's Paul's Gospel, and our Gospel and we must believe that for our salvation. So this is the primary thing, it supersedes anything else in all of Christendom. Then of course other things follow in their rightful place. Naturally we are to grow in grace. We are to grow in knowledge of the Word. We are to grow in our works and our activities for the Lord's business. Absolutely we're to be givers, and to be witnesses, and this is why we're left here. Because otherwise, would to God, that the moment that we're saved, He'd take us out of here. It would be far better. When Paul said that after seeing the things in glory that eyes have not seen, nor ears heard, the things that were prepared for those that love Him, I have to think we've got some glorious things awaiting us. It's going to be so glorious. Joy unspeakable, righteousness, music (I think), like mortal ear has never heard and it's all awaiting us once we enter into His presence.

(24a) What is the key to understanding the Bible ?

Book 27 LESSON ONE * PART III

I CORINTHIANS 4:3 - 6:11
Now let's come right back to our study, and begin I Corinthians Chapter 5. We love to hear when you write and say that you study right along with us. That just thrills our hearts. As you know we never try to promote any particular group or ourselves, but we just want to help people to understand The Bible, because it's the greatest Book on earth. But you know there are so many

that won't even attempt to read it because they say, **"Well I can't understand it."** But, oh yes you can, and the whole secret to understanding The Bible and having it come to life for you is this; pay attention to whom a particular Scripture is written to, and don't confuse Israel with the Church. God was careful in separating the two, and we should be also. And for the most part when God is speaking to the Church Age believer (that's you and I) He does this through the Apostle Paul's writings. A lot of the things that were applicable to Israel are not to the Church today.

But I always have to remind you that the things that God hated in the land of Israel He still hates today. God does not change. The God of Israel in Genesis is the still the same God that we deal with today, but He deals with us, the Church, under far different circumstances. We are now on resurrection ground, we are now being dealt with as people who are to believe for their Salvation that Christ died for our sins, was buried, and rose again, as recorded in I Corinthians 15:1-4, and not merely a Shekinah glory back there in the Temple in Jerusalem. We're not under a mandate to keep the Law and so forth. But nevertheless always remember that God has not changed in His attitude toward sin, and righteousness.

Book 13 LESSON THREE * PART III

You have to realize if you've been with me these past three and a half years (and many of you have been with me the better part of twenty years), that as we've come up through human history, God has changed His dealing with the human race. Now God didn't change. But He changed in His dealings.

In other words, when Adam and Eve were in the garden, God dealt with them under those circumstances. The garden was theirs to enjoy. God communed with them everyday. And everything was pretty simple. Then all of a sudden sin entered. And then what happened? A whole new ball game. Adam and Eve are expelled from the garden. All of a sudden they have to work with the sweat of their brow. Sin, and the curse is now on the scene. And that's certainly far different than it was in the garden. And that went on until it got so bad that God destroyed the whole human race with the exception of Noah and his family. Then they come out of the ark and what happened? Another whole different set of circumstances. Totally different than it was before the flood. And so that goes on. And then the next great event in history is the Tower of Babel. All those new generations of people coming out of the sons of Noah have gathered in rebellion. **That's what the tower of Babel really is. It's a place of rebellion.** And again, God intervenes and confuses all their languages and what happens? God scatters them.

Then He calls Abraham, and again it's something totally different. He now is going to deal with one special little race of people. That's why they are called **"The chosen race."** They're Covenant people. Again, that's totally different than what He's ever done before. Then along comes Moses about 1500 BC. At God's direction, Moses gives Israel the Law. You and I have no idea what it was to live under the Mosaic Law. That put such pressure on the Jew, and you need to remember it was far different than the law practiced by Judaism today. To live under the pure Law of Moses, was to live under the constant threat of what? Death! If they picked up sticks to build a fire on the Sabbath Day they knew that death was waiting for them. One act of adultery would result in the same thing. **There was no mercy. That was Law.** Then along comes the Apostle Paul and to the amazement of the Jew in his day, as well as the Jew to this day, Paul proclaims that you are not under Law, but under Grace. That's a whole different set of circumstances.

Book 29 LESSON THREE * PART I

You know I would like to get every person from whatever station in society or whatever age group interested in the Word of God. The Bible is still the greatest Book on earth, and it's not as difficult as most people have been led to believe. The secret to understanding the Bible is to separate some of these things that you cannot mix. And so this where we come in, especially with the apostle Paul and his writings. All of his writings are of Grace and Grace alone. So if there seems to be a contradiction in Scripture, see if it's under Grace or Law as the two won't mix.

Editor's Note: Paul's writings to the Gentiles (the Church) are the thirteen books of Romans through Philemon. This is the part of the Bible that a new believer should read first. Although Paul also wrote the book of Hebrews, he wrote it to the Jewish believers who had been saved under the gospel of the kingdom, the teaching of the twelve apostles of the circumcision (Jews). Hebrews was not written to the Gentiles.

Part B - Building Faith

(1b) What is the difference between Law and Grace ?

Book 37 Lesson One • Part I

Ephesians 3:2
"If ye have heard of the dispensation of the grace of God which is given me to you-ward."

Dispensation is word that I have refrained from using on the program purposely, simply because too many people have heard nothing but bad things about the word, even though they don't have any idea why. So I've known from day one that I had to be careful how I use this word, because I would turn people off before they would give me a minute to listen. But I think by now I have built enough credibility across the country that people won't get turned off when I use the word dispensation. **Remember Paul uses that word even in chapter 1 verse 10, so it's very Scriptural.**

Ephesians 1:10
"That in the dispensation of the fulness of time..."

We dealt with that several lessons back, but now in chapter 3 he deals with the dispensation of the Grace of God. **Well to qualify a dispensation, it's just a simple word from which we get the word** *stewardship* or *dispensing.* If we go to a pharmacy and give him our prescription, he then dispenses what the doctor has ordered, but along with dispensing the product he also gives you explicit instructions. You don't just take that medicine haphazardly, but rather you follow the instructions that came with the dispensing. Now bringing it back into the Scriptures, a dispensation was a period of time during which God laid particular dispensational instructions to the human race.

The best way I can illustrate dispensation from the secular world is our own presidential administration. And the one I like to use on this is the administration of Jimmy Carter and the one followed by Ronald Reagan. These were men with two totally different ideologies, but yet they both led the country under the same constitution. For a moment let's go back to the Carter years, as he builds his own administration. He appoints his own cabinet, he appoints men who have the same ideology that he does concerning how the country should be administered to. It wasn't so much the 4 years he was in the White House that made his administration, but rather what made the Carter administration was the ideology that he promoted by whatever he suggested to congress or how he handled foreign affairs, that's what marked the Carter administration, but it ended.

Then there was transition period, and from that dispensation of the Carter years we went to someone with a totally different view and that was Ronald Reagan. He too was under the same constitution, and his term of office also came to the place where it ended. Whether he served

4 or 8 years is moot. What counted was the kind of ideology that his administration promoted for the country. So in short what makes an administration was, **"What were they dispensing?"** Now you can bring that into Scripture and I think you have a beautiful analogy.

When God called Moses and the Nation of Israel out of Egypt, he brought them around Mt. Sinai. He called Moses up into the mountain. What did He give to Moses? Law. And Law was a dispensation. It was a dispensing to the Nation of Israel, God's demands upon the Nation as to how they were to worship, how they were to live; and all these things were part of that dispensation of Law. Whether it went 500 years or 1500 years is moot. What's important is**, what did God give Moses to tell the children of Israel? The Law.**

And of course the Law was in 3 parts. It was first and foremost the moral Law, the Ten Commandments. It was the ritual law - how to worship, and how to approach God with the sacrifices, and priesthood and so forth. Then it also had the civil law - how to deal with your neighbor and how to settle disputes and so forth. That was all dispensed at Mt. Sinai. But the Cross ended all of that. The Cross ended the Law, because that was when everything was fulfilled dispensationally of Law. But you see God in His wisdom could keep things secret as we see in Deuteronomy 29:29.

Deuteronomy 29:29a
"The secret things belong unto the LORD our God:..."

That means God can keep things totally secret as long as He wants to. And then He will reveal certain things when He is good and ready, and we've seen that all the way up through human history. So even though all the ramification of the Law was fulfilled at the Cross, yet we find that when we come into the early chapter of Acts, not a word has been said, **"That you're no longer under the Law."** There's not a word that's been said, **"That you no longer have to go to the temple, or keep the commandments as a system."**

That doesn't come until this man Paul comes and says, *"That if you have heard the dispensation of the Grace of God."* This is in total opposition to Law, and is now dispensed by Paul. Now if you will come back with me to I Corinthians chapter 4, and while you're looking for it let me remind you how dispensation was used in the Old Testament. When God was approaching Abraham, about beginning a nation through him and he didn't yet have a son, and so what did Abraham say to God?

Genesis 15:2
"And Abram said, Lord GOD, what wilt thou give me, seeing I go childless, and the steward of my house is this Eliezer of Damascus?"

What was Abraham saying? Eliezer was the man who managed all of Abraham's wealth. Not only did Eliezer dispense orders to the servants, but he also dispensed when to sell and when to buy. Now you want to remember Abraham was wealthy. Now why am I saying all of this? Because this is what Paul claims to be concerning the Grace of God. Have you got I Corinthians chapter 4? Let's start with verse 1.

I Corinthians 4:1
"Let a man so account of us, as of the ministers of Christ, and (what's your next word?) *stewards of the mysteries of God."*

Now if you're a Bible student you will catch on real quick that Paul is always referring to the mysteries that were revealed to him. And what are mysteries? Secrets. And Who kept them secret until revealed to this man? God did. And when God called Paul out of the religion of Judaism, and saved him on the road to Damascus, **He sent him down to Mt. Sinai and poured out on him for 3 years all the revelations of the mysteries. There are all kinds of mysteries that Paul speaks of in his writings, and since they were revealed to him he then became the steward of those mysteries.** And if he was the steward of them then he was the administrator of them. When we understand that, then this Book becomes as plain as a 300 watt light bulb. It just lays right out in front of you. **Of course this is a whole new administration or dispensation.**

You're going to find doctrinal things in Paul's writings that you won't find anywhere else in Scripture. But he doesn't cancel what went before, it's just an advance on it. Because now we're coming from the very small knowledge that they had way in the beginning, and it's just building, and building, and finally the promised Messiah came, and the Nation of Israel was in the promised land, they had the temple, but yet what did they do with the Messiah. **They crucified Him, and the Jews continued to reject Him in those early chapters of Acts, and in so many words God says, "That's the end of that dispensation of Law, we're now going to dispense something totally new."** It was just like moving from Jimmy Carter to Ronald Reagan. If you know anything about politics, it was as different as night and day between those two administrations. Well so is Grace and Law! You cannot mix them because they are so diverse, but it's the same God. God never changes, but He changes His programs. Now God says, **"Instead of all of the things that the Law demanded, I've already settled it on the Cross, now if you will just believe it I'll do everything that needs to be done."** People write constantly and proclaim, **"Oh what freedom they have found!"**

We've come now all these 2000 years and we're still reveling in this same Gospel that was begun by this apostle, and that is it's by faith and God's Grace alone. Now I'm talking about salvation. I'm not saying that you're saved by **Faith + Nothing**, and then you just go on and drift. No, No. But for salvation it's Faith and Faith alone, and then when that happens, God begins to work in and through us, and He doesn't expect us to become tremendous saints over night.

Editor's Note for clarification: It is the "drifting" (maintaining a lifestyle that is contrary to God's will) that is objectionable here. Salvation is by Faith + Nothing.

Lesson One • Part II

Paul Dispenses Grace - Ephesians 3:1-7
Now we'll be going right back to where we left off in the last lesson and that will be in verse 2. This Bible is for everybody not just for a certain group of people, and we want to be able to teach it in such a way that you can study it on your own, and search the Scriptures and see if these things are really so. The Book of Acts calls people who do that *Bereans*.

Acts 17:10-11
"And the brethren immediately sent away Paul and Silas by night unto Berea: who coming thither went into the synagogue of the Jews. 11. These were more noble than those in Thessalonica, in that they received the word with all readiness of mind, and searched the scriptures daily, whether those things were so."

So after these believers hear Paul they searched the Scriptures (of course that was the Old Testament in those days) to see if what Paul was teaching was in accord with the Scriptures. So now let's just pick the Scriptures apart word by word,

Ephesians 3:2a
"If ye have heard of the dispensation of the grace of God..."

Now that's where we stopped in the last lesson, and we're going to stay stopped for a bit, because I'm still not quite through with what I wanted to get across so far as, **"why does Paul define this dispensation of the Grace of God?"** Now always remember every word that Paul writes, as well as every word that the Old Testament writers write, was inspired by the Holy Spirit. None of these writings was just the will of a person. Even when Paul in so many words says, **"this is my idea"** it's still inspired, and never lose sight of that. Every word is here because the Holy Spirit wants it here. So when Paul says in Romans.

Romans 11:13a
"For I speak to you Gentiles, inasmuch as I am the apostle of the Gentiles,..."

Now that's not an egotistical man talking, but rather that's the Holy Spirit speaking exactly what He wants Paul to write. So in verse 2 let's see what he says.

Ephesians 3:2a
"If ye have heard of the dispensation of the grace of God..."

We spent nearly the whole last lesson defining a dispensation, and I hope it was clear enough. Now what is so different about Grace? **In Exodus chapter 3, up on Mount Sinai, God, spoke to Moses, and gave to him the Law, and then Moses takes the Law down the mountain and**

dispenses it to the Nation of Israel. So this was the dispensation of Law, and that's the way we look at it in Scriptures. Now some 1500 years later after the Damascus Road experience for Paul, the same God does something different, which is His prerogative, because He's Sovereign. **Now He calls out to Mount Sinai, a different man whom we know as the apostle Paul. And to Paul God reveals these doctrines of Grace, and Paul in turn dispenses these doctrines of Grace, not so much to the Nation of Israel, but to the Gentile world.**

(Mt. Sinai - Moses - Law - Nation of Israel)
The Cross
(Mt. Sinai - Paul - Grace - Gentile world)

Now of course in both cases the Law is going to have an influence on Gentiles, and Grace is going to have an influence on the Jew. But as a group the dispensation of Law was given through Moses to Israel, and the dispensation of Grace was given through the apostle Paul to the Gentiles. Now there's only one other place in the New Testament where that term is used explicitly, and that will be in Acts chapter 20, and let's look at verse 24. Now in all the other places in Paul's writings he may refer to this Gospel as the Gospel of Christ, the Gospel of God, My Gospel, and various others, but here in Acts chapter 24 and in Ephesians he refers to it as the Grace of God.

Acts 20:24
"But none of these things move me, neither count I my life dear unto myself, so that I might finish my course with joy, and the ministry, which I have received of the Lord Jesus, to testify the gospel of the grace of God."

Do you see how plain that is? Paul's whole ministry was to proclaim the Gospel of the Grace of God. Now I think it may be appropriate if we come back to Ephesians chapter 3, that now for a moment we can look at the word *"Grace."*

Ephesians 3:2a
"If ye have heard of the dispensation of the grace..."

Now like I said in the last lesson, **"very few people have any idea of the Grace of God."** I don't claim to know all that much, because it's beyond human understanding. How a Sovereign, Eternal, Creator God would do what He did simply because He loved the human race. He took on human flesh, walked among men for three years on the dusty roads of Israel, and then ended up going to the Cross to suffer the most horrible death ever invented, all because of His love for mankind. And through that death on the Cross He was able to pay the price of redemption for the whole human race, not just for a few chosen ones, but for the whole race. **Now listen, that's GRACE!**

And that's beyond our comprehension. He didn't have to do that. He could have just zapped the human race and started over. But from day one, from the time that Adam and Eve first sinned in the Garden of Eden, on up to the rebellious multitudes just before the flood, on up to the tower of Babel when again that group of humanity met in pagan consort, God could have zapped them, but He didn't. He let them go on until He was able to find one man 200 years later in the Ur of the Chaldees we know as Abraham, and begin again something totally different, all because He refused to give up on the human race. And why didn't He? **GRACE!**

So everything that God does, and the patience of God toward the human race is all because of His Grace. Now I call that one of God's attributes. It is something that is in the very make-up of the eternal God that prompted Him to pour out all this unmerited favor and love on a rebellious human race. All we have to do is just look around us today, and just stop and think for a moment, why does God put up with it when every thing is flying in His face in total rebellion? All God would have to do is speak the Word and we'd all be gone. But God doesn't do that, and why doesn't He? **GRACE!**

Now you see under the Law that wasn't the case. Law was demanding, Law as I've said so often is what? Severe! It was severe, and there was no bending it. If you broke the Law back in it's pure early stages, invariably the penalty was death. So that was the Law, and there wasn't Grace in that except it was the Grace of God getting a way for man to come back, but in reality Law was legalism, it was severe, it was the very opposite of Grace. But now on this side of the Cross we have the same God who gave the Law and all of it's severity to Moses for Israel, God now opens the window of heaven and through this apostle's writings we have the opening of the door of **GRACE!**

Now some people say, "Well don't you make too much of Paul?" No. Paul knew only one thing, and that was **"Christ crucified for our sins, and risen from the dead," and you can't find that anywhere else in Scripture that you are to believe that for salvation except in Paul's writings.** So we don't elevate Paul above that. But you see God, as He kept things secret as we saw in our last lesson, **has decided that it's through this man that He would reveal the things that had been kept secret.** That's why Paul, over and over, uses the term **"revelation,"** how God revealed to me such and such, and he writes over and over again.

Now the other argument that we sometimes get, and praise the Lord we don't get many. We get very few arguments from all the mail we get, **and when we do get an argument its usually over water baptism. And in every instance the party will try to make it sound that if you're not baptized in water, then you can't be saved.** And when I write back and answer that this is what Paul has said, then they'll come right back and say, "But we go by what the Bible says, not what Paul says, or we use the whole Bible, we don't just use Paul."

Well if that be the case, and you're going to argue that you do what the whole Bible says then I take you right back to Leviticus chapter 5. This is a fun exercise, it really is, because it says it so plainly. Now I could use any other portion of the Old Testament, but this one says it so clearly, and it's not real deep theologically. It's just an everyday possibility for anyone of us.

Leviticus 5:1-2
"And if a soul (or person) *sin, and hear the voice of swaring, and is a witness, whether he hath seen or known of it: if he do not utter it, then he shall bear his iniquity.* (he has to tell the priest what someone has said or he's guilty.) *2. Or if a soul* (or person) *touch any unclean thing, whether it be a carcass of an unclean beast, or a carcass of unclean cattle, or the carcass of unclean creeping things, and if it be hidden from him; he also shall be unclean, and guilty.* Now for sake of time come on down to verse 5.

Leviticus 5:5
"And it shall be, when he shall be guilty in one of these things, that he shall confess that he hath sinned in that thing: 6. And he shall (that's a command) *bring his trespass offering unto the LORD for his sin which he that sinned, a female from the flock, a lamb, or a kid of the goats for a sin offering: and the priest shall make an atonement for him concerning his sin."*

Now do you know what I say? That's what the Bible says. Isn't it? Just as plain as day. Do you bring a sacrificial offering when you touch anything dead? No. Does God expect you to do it? No. **Why? Because this was Law.** This is all part of what Moses instructed Israel, and we're not under that economy. But we're under the economy of Grace with the apostle Paul. So when people say I go by what all the Bible says, they get their foot in their mouth before they can turn around, because there are so many things back here that cannot be done today. So what's the difference? You've got to separate Law from Grace.

Paul will never tell you that if you touch something dead, you go and offer a sacrifice some place does he? No. **So always keep these things straight that when I say we have to listen to the apostle Paul the apostle to the Gentiles (Romans 11:13), that doesn't mean we don't read the rest of Scripture**. That doesn't mean it isn't profitable - of course it is, because it shows us the very mind of a Holy God. It shows us what it was like to live under the yoke of bondage which was what the Law really was. It's what Peter called it in Acts chapter 15, and it's what Paul called it in Galatians. It was a yoke of bondage, but now under Paul's teaching of Grace, we've been set free from all that. Now coming back to Ephesians chapter 3 for a split second, and I know I used some of this in the last lesson, but let it sink in. It's so important!

Ephesians 3:2
"If ye have heard of the dispensation (or the economy, or the administration) *of the grace of God* (and like I've shown that Law came to Israel through Moses. How in the world did the doctrines of Grace get to the Gentiles? Well the next part of the verse tells us) *which is given me to you-ward:"*

Do you see what that says? You have no idea how many times I've had someone at my now famous kitchen table, and **I will tell them this very concept, that all of our doctrines of Grace come from Paul. They'll always say, "Well where do you get that?"** Well here's one good example, and this is just one. They'll read that verse, and say, "I don't see what you're getting at." Then I always come back and say, "Well then you didn't read it." And they always come back with, "Yeah I did." So I have them read it as many times as it takes, usually about 3 or 4 times, and then they normally say, "Oh I never saw that before." I dare say there are multitudes just exactly like that. And here it is, **"The dispensation of the Grace of God which was given to Paul, and Paul through inspiration and by the Grace of God have brought it to us Gentiles.**

Now isn't that easy? Now let me show you from Scripture what we're talking about. My there's so much of it I hardly know where to start. Come back with me to II Corinthians. I was debating whether to use Galatians first or Corinthians, but just for sake of chronological order of the Bible we'll start here in II Corinthians. Remember just like Paul had to deal in I Corinthians with the Corinthian believers who wanted to follow Peter's teachings rather than Paul. Others wanted to follow Jesus' earthly ministry teachings rather than Paul, and their whole concept was that Paul was something less than those fellows at Jerusalem. And this is what Paul had to overcome and we covered this in detail when we taught the Corinthian letters. But this is just review.

II Corinthians 11:5
"For I suppose I was not a whit behind the very chiefest apostles."

Wow! What does that say? I was not a half of step behind Peter. See, they were trying to put Peter up above him. And that the chiefest apostle would have to be Peter most people would say. Now if Paul's not behind him, where is he? Well he's either beside him or ahead of him. Now for the next one, stay in the same chapter and come down to verse 22. Now this verse puts Paul out a step ahead. This is speaking of the Jerusalem leadership which would include the twelve, as well as some of the other head people of the Jerusalem assembly.

II Corinthians 11:22-23a
"Are they Hebrews? so am I. Are they Israelites? so am I. Are they the seed of Abraham? so am I. 23. Are they ministers of Christ? (I speak as a fool) I am more:..."

See how plain that is? **That's the Holy Spirit writing through the pen of the apostle Paul, that Paul is more the minister of Christ than anybody back there at Jerusalem. And this is what we have to understand.** Now let's go on to one more in the next chapter.

II Corinthians 12:11
"I am become a fool in glorying; (and Paul didn't like to boast, but he had to in order to convince especially the Corinthians that he was a special instrument in God's hand) *ye have compelled*

me: (you've forced me) *for I ought to have been commended of you:* (it was this man who had brought these people out of their abject paganism. It was his message that set them free, and brought them into a relationship with Christ. It was this man's Gospel that brought these pagans into a life of morality and hope for eternity) *for in nothing am I behind the very chiefest apostles, though I be nothing."*

Evidently there were some Jewish believers in the congregation who knew all about Peter and the eleven, and were stirring up these Gentile believers saying that Paul didn't have the authority to lead the Corinthians. So Paul tells them he's not behind Peter one bit, in fact he's in front of him. So that should tell you that Paul is the man that is given, and ordained of God to go to the non-Jew, the Gentiles, and he claims it over and over, the same as God did back when He was talking to Ananias back in Acts chapter 9.

Acts 9:15a
"But the Lord said, unto him, (Ananias) *Go thy way:* (to Paul) *for he is a chosen vessel unto me, to bear my name before the Gentiles,..."*

Now turn on over to the Book of Galatians chapter 1, and this is all to back up his claim in Ephesians chapter 3:2:

Ephesians 3:2b
"...the dispensation of the grace of God which is given me to you-ward:" And the *you-ward* is speaking of Gentiles. So now let's look in Galatians 1.

Galatians 1:11
"But I certify you, brethren, that the gospel which was preached of me is not after man. (Paul is saying he's not following in some other man's footsteps) *12. For I neither received it of man, neither was I taught it. But by the revelation of Jesus Christ."*

Paul got all of his doctrines of Grace, to include this Gospel we must believe for salvation, from Jesus Christ Himself. It was a revealing, a secret that had been kept secret in the mind of God according to the verses we looked at in the last lesson. So here in verse 12 that's what Paul is claiming. **That what had been kept secret and is now revealed to this apostle, came by revelation of Jesus Christ. Now when I teach Paul's epistles I always emphasize that this revelation was after our Lord's death, burial, and resurrection, and that makes all the difference in the world.**

See Jesus couldn't even preach His death, burial, and resurrection for salvation, because it hadn't even happened yet. He tried to tell the twelve about it, but they never got it, according to Luke 18:31-34, but it just wasn't in the economy of that system of Law for Israel and the Jews to understand the Gospel of Grace. It just wasn't meant to be! So now let's look at what Paul says in verse 15.

Galatians 1:15
"But when it pleased God, who separated me from my mother's womb, and called me by his grace,"

The other night I took the Strong's concordance, and I counted all the times that *Grace* was used between Matthew 1:1 and Acts chapter 9. How many times do you suppose it was? Sixteen times, and then it wasn't even used as a doctrinal term, but rather as the word Grace. From Acts chapter 9 until the end of Paul's letters I counted eighty-four times Paul had used that word. Six times more is the word Grace referred to in Paul's epistles than everything that went before his writing. Now that's shocking isn't it? And yet it shouldn't be, because this is the apostle of Grace. I have a book at home, I think the title is **The Apostle of the Soul Set Free.** It was a biography of the apostle Paul. I didn't like the book all that much, but I sure did like the title. Now that says it all doesn't it? Now in the short time we have left let's look at verse 16.

Galatians 1:16a
"To reveal his Son in me, that I might preach him among the heathen;..." (Gentiles)

That's Paul specific calling, to take this Gospel of Grace to the Gentile world. And that's why I put it this way over the years, that as the Law was given to Moses on Mt. Sinai for Israel, Paul goes out to Mt. Sinai, and God gave him the doctrines of Grace for us. Now that's beyond human comprehension. Now finishing the verse.

Galatians 1:16b-17a
"...immediately I conferred not with flesh and blood: 17. Neither went I up to Jerusalem to them which were apostles before me; but I went into Arabia..." (that would be Mt. Sinai)

Then Paul goes on to say that this whole mystery of the Gospel was revealed to him, and that why I'm always stressing Paul's apostleship, and spending most of our time in his letters.

(2b) What is the difference between the Peter's gospel and Paul's gospel ?

Book 17 LESSON TWO * PART III

We are getting close to a portion of Scripture that I think has been totally confused by almost all groups, and we're just going to take it for what it says. We're not going to spiritualize it, or allegorize, it we are going leave it right where it is. Verse 36:

Acts 2:36a
   "Therefore (because of all that has just taken place. Israel has had The Messiah for three years,

performing signs and miracles, they crucified Him, God raised Him from the dead, and sent the Holy Spirit, and everything is falling into place) *let all the house of Israel..."*

Now you can't put us Gentiles in this verse, unless you force it. Peter is speaking to Jews on Covenant grounds. It's the fulfilling of the Covenant which God made with Abraham. Let's pause for a moment and go to Chapter 3, so you'll know what I'm talking about. And again Peter is preaching to a Jew-only crowd.

Acts 3:24,25

"Yea, and all the prophets from Samuel and those that follow after, as many as have spoken, have likewise foretold of these days." What days? Everything that has just taken place. According to Peter, the Crucifixion, Resurrection, ascension and coming of the Holy Spirit was prophesied. Look at verse 25:

"Ye are the children of the prophets, and of the covenant (only the Nation of Israel. All prophecy is directed to the Nation of Israel, they are the ones that will be at the core of these prophetic events. Even the horrible events in Revelation will be directed primarily at the Jew. But the whole world will also reap the fallout from these events. Jeremiah 30 tells us it's the time of Jacob's trouble) *which God made with our fathers, saying unto Abraham, 'And in thy seed* (through the Nation of Israel) *shall all the kindreds of the earth be blessed.'"*

So Peter is on Covenant ground. He's still on the basis that everything that has been since Abraham, that is: the Nation of Israel was to receive the Redeemer, The Messiah, The King and the Kingdom, and it would be through Israel that God would gather the Gentiles. I never like to leave people with the idea that God had cast off the Gentiles. Oh, not at all. But He was going to use the Nation of Israel on Covenant grounds to bring them to Salvation. Even right here God has never said a word to anybody that He's setting the Covenant promises aside for awhile. He hasn't told anybody yet that they don't have to keep Temple worship, or keep the Law. He hasn't told people they must believe in His death, burial and Resurrection for their Salvation. Not a word about that as of yet. You can't find it here. And that is what I try to tell people to understand. Don't take my word for it. **Search the Scriptures, but be sure you understand that the Scripture is putting Salvation on His death, burial, and Resurrection. Remember, there is never any reason to force anything into Scripture. Just leave them where they are. You can't put a square peg in a round hole without doing a lot of damage.** So here Peter is still on Covenant ground. Back to Acts 2:36:

Acts 2:36

"Therefore let all the house of Israel (He's talking to Jew only) *know assuredly, that God hath made that same Jesus, whom ye have crucified, both Lord and Christ."*

Now we have to compare Scripture with Scripture. Come to the Book of Galatians, and just look at the difference in the language. We just saw Peter accusing the Nation of Israel of killing their Messiah, and now look what Paul tells us here in the Church Age.

Galatians 1:3,4a

"Grace be to you and peace from God the Father, and from our Lord Jesus Christ, Who gave himself for our sins,...."

And that's Paul's theme all through his writings. It's as different as day from night with Peter's message. Peter's sermon just doesn't fit Paul's doctrine at all. And it wasn't supposed to. God hadn't revealed Paul's message yet. It's still a secret kept in the mind of God. Now back to Acts verse 37:

Acts 2:37

"Now when they heard this (heard what? That they were guilty of crucifying their Messiah. And remember, Peter isn't just talking to 40 or 50 people. He's got thousands out in front of him listening out there in that Temple complex. This is the feast of Pentecost and they have come from everywhere as we seen in verses 9-11) *they were pricked in their heart, and said unto Peter and to the rest of the apostles, 'Men and brethren what shall* (what's the pronoun?) *we do?'"*

Remember Peter is addressing this great crowd of Jews on Covenant ground. He has accused them of killing their Messiah, and now they are so convicted that I suppose in one way or another word gets up to Peter as he is speaking. And they say, **"Well, Peter, what in the world are we** (and remember that pronoun) **supposed to do?"** Now that is the question coming from the Nation of Israel.

Book 17 LESSON TWO * PART IV

Let's pick up again in the Book of Acts and for a short review we will start at Chapter 2 verse 36. Remember this is a Jewish feast day that is being celebrated. Jews from the then-known world have come to celebrate the feast of Pentecost. This is one of the seven feasts listed in Leviticus 23. Now it's on this day of Pentecost that this huge crowd of Jews are out there in the Temple area and Peter, through the power of the Holy Spirit, is addressing this great gathering. And regardless what nations these Jews have come from, they are hearing it in their own language. And this is the miracle of it all. Peter is speaking to Jew only (with an occasional proselyte). There is no Gentile ground here. God doesn't put Gentiles in this group and neither should we. It's a Jewish feast day, a Jewish crowd, a Jewish speaker, and a Jewish message. And now verse 36:

Acts 2:36,37

"Therefore let all the house of Israel know assuredly (this is all twelve tribes that are repre-sented here, and God knows who they are)*, that God hath made that same Jesus, whom ye have crucified, both Lord and Christ."* Peter is accusing these Jews of killing Christ their Messiah. *"Now when they heard this they were pricked in their heart, and said unto Peter and to the rest of the apostles, Men and brethren what shall we do?"* And before we look

at Peter's answer, I want to take you back to Acts Chapter 16.

In Chapter 16, Paul has begun his missionary journey throughout western Turkey. Earlier in this chapter the Holy Spirit directed him over into Greece. One of the first cities he approached there was Philippi. And that is where he met Lydia, who was the first European convert. After the conversion of Lydia, he is arrested and beaten along with Silas, and cast into the lower dungeon of the jail, as in verse 25. The setting is completely different than in Acts 2. This is all Gentile ground, a Gentile prison, a Gentile jailer, This Gentile jailer may have witnessed Paul and Silas preaching, and saw their arrest and beating. Now he was given charge over these two men along with the rest of the prisoners.

Acts 16:25-29

"And at midnight Paul and Silas prayed, and sang praises unto God; and the prisoners heard them."

"And suddenly there was a great earthquake (we still haven't left the economy of signs and miracles, and wonders. These will pass off the scene in Paul's ministry at a little later time. But at this time we have a miraculous earthquake with a distinct purpose), *so that the foundations of the prison were shaken: and immediately all the doors were opened, and every one's bands were loosed."*

"And the keeper of the prison awaking out of his sleep, and seeing the prison doors open, he drew out his sword, and would have killed himself, supposing that the prisoners had been fled." The Roman authority would have killed him if prisoners had escaped.

"But Paul cried with a loud voice, saying, 'Do thyself no harm: for we are all here.'" Although they could have fled they didn't, because this is a Sovereign God at work.

"Then he called for a light, and sprang in, and came trembling, and fell down before Paul and Silas,"

Why did this pagan Gentile jailer pick Paul and Silas out of all his prisoners? Somehow, God let him know that here was the answer to his dilemma. He's got all these prisoners loose, ready to flee, but they are staying there. God lets that jailer know the answer to his problem, but it's going to be a lot more than a bunch of prisoners, it's going to be the man's own soul.

Acts 16:30

"And brought them (Paul and Silas) *out, and said, Sirs, what must I do to be saved?"* Now look at the comparison.

Peter, preaching in Acts Chapter 2, is dealing with the Covenant Nation of Israel. And they say in verse 37, *"What must we do?"* But God doesn't deal with Gentiles on Covenant ground. He deals with us as individuals. Every individual has to ask that same question. *"What must I do...?"* Let's compare the answers each were given. In Acts Chapter 2, it is very clear, anyone can understand it. I'm leaving every word the way it's in your Bible and mine. I'm not changing a thing. Israel says, "What must we do?" Look at Peter's answer.

Acts 2:38

"Then Peter said unto them, 'Repent, and be baptized (the next two words are crucial) *every one of you in the name of Jesus Christ for the remission of sins, and ye shall receive the gift of the Holy Ghost,'"*

Everyone of them would have to be converted and accept Christ as their Messiah for God to pick up where He had left off. He would have sent back The King and set up the Kingdom. Peter also tells them this in Acts 3:26. Look at the message. Peter says, ***"Repent and be baptized."*** Who began that message? John the Baptist. John was the herald of The King, and his message was, ***"Repent and be baptized."*** That was for the Nation of Israel. Now compare this with Paul's answer to the Gentile in Acts Chapter 16. Paul is not talking to the Nation of Israel, he's talking to a Gentile. And when this Gentile asks what he must do to be saved, what does Paul tell him?

Acts 16:31

"And they (Paul and Silas) *said, 'Believe on The Lord Jesus Christ, and thou shalt be saved, and thy house.'"*

Does it say Repent and be baptized? No, and if that was the criteria it would have been in here. That was the Jewish program, and by this time it has fallen through the cracks because Israel is rejecting it again. God has now turned to the Gentiles through the Apostle Paul, without Israel. So the jailer said, ***"What must I do?"*** The answer is simple: ***"Only Believe on The Lord Jesus Christ."*** Now when you know the rest of Paul's message, he only had one Gospel to believe: ***"That Christ died for your sins, was buried and rose from the dead." You can find that message in many places in Paul's letters, for example I Corinthians 15:1-4.*** Believe the Gospel. And it's no different for Gentiles today, and the Jew as well. That is the criteria tonight. **We have to believe the Gospel and nothing else**. You search Paul's letters from Romans through Hebrews (and Hebrews is more Jewish than the rest and there is a reason for that), and show me one place where Paul teaches repentance and baptism for Salvation. You won't find it. Paul doesn't teach it. Paul's message is a different economy and you can't mix them. A lot of people try to. Our Lord didn't mix them and neither should we. The verses in Galatians 2:7-9 exist because they were two different messages. That's why Peter says Paul's message of Salvation is hard for him to understand in II Peter 3:15-16. To the Jew it was repent and be baptized. To the Gentile it is believe the Gospel. See how simple that is. Now let's come back to Acts 2 and make another tremendous comparison. Read verse 38 again:

Acts 2:38

"Then Peter said unto them, 'Repent, and be baptized every one of you in the name of Jesus Christ for the remission of sins,....'" The whole Nation of Israel had to repent and be baptized.

Winning the whole world has never been implied with Paul. In Acts 15, when even James had to agree that God is using Paul to go to the Gentiles, what was the expression that James used? Calling out a people for His name. That doesn't imply 99 or 100%. Christianity has always been just a small percentage. But we should always be ready to share the Gospel that Paul presents to everyone we come in contact with when the opportunity presents itself. I get a kick out of the Gallop polls, the last one I saw was 60% of Americans were professing Christians. That's a joke because 60% of the Bible belt aren't Bible believing Christians, let alone other vast areas of our country. But it's always been that very small percentage, and it hasn't changed that much. Another comparison here in verse 38:

Acts 2:38
"...and ye shall receive the gift of the Holy Ghost,"

I've had questions asked of me about this for many years, and let me ask you a question. What was the prerequisite in this verse for receiving the Holy Spirit? Repentance and baptism. That is the first part of the verse. Look at it again:

Acts 2:38
"...Repent, and be baptized every one of you in the name of Jesus Christ for the remission of sins, and ye shall receive the gift of the Holy Spirit."

Is there any mention of the death, burial, and Resurrection? Any mention of the shed blood for atonement? Not a word. But only the name. When you talk about the name of someone, what does that imply? Who he is. If I say the name of one of our Presidents, what do you associate that with? The White House. You speak the name and immediately it's the position that you're tied to. So, Peter doesn't mention death, burial, and Resurrection. But what were they to put their faith in? Who Jesus was. He was The Christ their Messiah, and they had killed Him. But God had raised Him from the dead. They were to repent and be baptized for the remission of sins and then they would receive the gift of the Holy Ghost. In Acts Chapter 10, we have Peter at the house of Cornelius, a Gentile. This is seven years after the Cross. Not a Gentile has been saved. Back in Acts 2, the Jews had to repent and be baptized, then they could receive the Holy Spirit. Now look at what it says here:

Acts 10:44
"While Peter yet spake (he hadn't come to the end of his message) *these words, the Holy Ghost fell on all them which heard the word. "*

And we know they all believed. Have they been baptized yet? No, these are Gentiles who haven't heard anything of the Law. But the moment they believed Peter's message the Holy Spirit came down, and the amazing thing is God had to prove to Peter and these six other Jews that God was doing something totally new, and that was saving Gentiles! Not on the basis of repentance and baptism, **but the moment they heard the word and believed**. Peter is still tied to that Jewish economy, so when he sees what is happening he commands these Gentile believers to be baptized **after** the fact instead of before as we saw in Acts 2:38:

Acts 10:47
"Can any man forbid water, that these should not be baptized, which have (past tense)

This isn't a contradiction, this is not Chapter 10 contradicting Chapter 2, but rather a change of events. Ten is Gentile and Two is still Jew. Acts is a transitional book, so always be aware that what was good for the Jew under that Jewish economy seems like a contradiction, but it's not, it's only God changing the program. The moment we believe for our Salvation the Gospel of Grace, that Jesus died for our sins, was buried, and rose from the dead, the Holy Spirit baptizes us and we are saved. Don't put the message that Peter preached and the message that Paul preached in a blender and mix it all up and expect to understand it. That will give you heartburn, and you will never be able to see what you should clearly believe for your Salvation. But if you will realize that God is changing the program when He goes to the Gentiles, and leave the Scriptures right where they are, I believe the Scriptures will be opened to you. So many people come into my classes and almost immediately have their eyes opened. I don't do that, the Holy Spirit does that when you search the Scriptures.

Editor's Note: Peter's gospel, called the gospel of the kingdom or the gospel of the circumcision, was preached to the nation of Israel under the law of Moses. Paul's gospel, called the gospel of grace or the gospel of the uncircumcision, was preached to the Gentiles under grace. Whether we are Jew or Gentile, Paul's gospel is the way of salvation for us in this present age of grace.

(3b) What part of the Bible should new believers be reading ?

Book 29 LESSON TWO * PART II

Now we'll pick up again where we left off, and what we're trying to show is how this next order of the resurrection comes about and of course that would be the main harvest: the Body of Christ. Before we begin though I would like to share that last evening we got a phone call from a gentlemen who had a friend who was an alcoholic and in a treatment center. He had been to visit her, and told her that this was probably her last chance and it was time that she got interested in the things of the spiritual. So he left this lady a couple of my tapes, and the reason he called was to tell me that from those tapes she had gotten saved, she was right with The Lord, and he was just so thrilled he couldn't get over it. So this is our whole purpose, whether you're watching by way of television or by a tape or through the printed page. The reason we teach is to help folk understand what the Bible is really all about. Remember, this is God's Word and He has left it with us to prepare us for eternity. That's the only reason we're here. This life of 70, 80, or 90 years is not even a split second compared with eternity.

We're in I Corinthians Chapter 15, and we've been talking about the doctrine of the resurrection, which is basic to our Christian faith, and at verse 20 we saw Paul sort of shift gears and now he breaks down how the resurrections are going to take place. They are not going to be all at one event, but rather first we had the first-fruits when Christ rose from the dead and those

Jewish believers who came out of the graves after He did in Matthew Chapter 27.

Matthew 27:52,53a
"And the graves were opened; and many bodies of the saints which slept arose. And came out of the graves after his resurrection,...." Then Paul said in I Corinthians Chapter 15:23:

I Corinthians 15:23
"But every man in his own order: Christ the first fruits; (and) *afterward they that are Christ's at his coming."*

Which of course would have to be the believers of the Church Age. That's us believers. So in our last lesson that was the purpose of taking you all the way back to the Book of Acts and bringing us through those early chapters when Peter was still dealing with the Nation of Israel and how then God raised up Saul of Tarsus. He made it plain as day that now this man was going to be sent to the Gentiles. And of course we saw all that in Acts Chapter 9, and we left him as they had lowered him in a basket over the wall because of the threats on his life. Now I want you to turn to Galatians Chapter 1, and in this little chapter Paul again brings us up to date as to what took place after he fled from Damascus. Now remember God is going to use this one man to take the message of salvation primarily to, but not exclusively, the Gentile world, although Jews are certainly going to be available for this same salvation. Let's start with verse 11.

Galatians 1:11
"But I certify you, brethren, that the gospel which was preached of me is not after man."

Now you know I'm a stickler for words, and the Holy Spirit never puts in excess words or never cuts it short, but rather He puts in everything that we need. Now look at that verse. If Paul is going to be preaching the same Gospel that Jesus and the Twelve preached then why in the world does He identify that the Gospel he preached as not being after man? Why those extra little words in there? Why didn't he just say, "I certify you, brethren, that when I preach the Gospel?." But he doesn't put it that way. He says rather, "the Gospel which was preached of me." Now that identifies him, and if you'll come across into Chapter 2 he does it even more clearly. Now years later in Chapter 2 when he meets with Peter, James, and John, and the other leaders at the Church there in Jerusalem he's going to have to give an account of what he's been preaching to these Gentiles. Now look at verse 2 of Chapter 2.

Galatians 2:2
"And I went up (to Jerusalem) *by revelation, and communicated* (he made it crystal clear) *unto them that gospel which I preach among the Gentiles,...."*

And again why didn't he just say, "the Gospel?" Well, that would have left a gap, so he clarifies it by saying, "I communicated unto them that Gospel which I preached among the Gentiles." Do you see how that clarifies everything? All right, now let's come back to Chapter 1 and see how all this came about because Paul is reviewing this. Remember when he writes Galatians this is about twenty years after his conversion in Acts Chapter 9. I think a lot of people lose sight of the chronology of some of these events in the New Testament. Saul of Tarsus was probably saved on the road to Damascus around 37 AD and then after his three years of desert training in Arabia it's 40 AD before he goes out into the Gentile world. Then he has that counsel at Jerusalem, which is in Acts 15 and Galatians 2 in AD 52 and so that's about 12 years after he began his ministry. Then the first letter that he writes, according to my time-table, is the Thessalonian letters and they're written some 12 or 14 years after he began his ministry. So you see, time keeps rolling on. This isn't all just mashed together. It's all spread out over a period of 20 or 30 years. In Galatians Chapter 1 he is writing about 58 or 59 AD Remember, if he began his ministry in 40 AD then this is 18 years later when he starts writing these Epistles.

Galatians 1:11,12
"But I certify you, brethren, that the gospel which was preached of me is not after man. For I neither received it of man, neither was I taught it, (by men) *but by the revelation of Jesus Christ."*

Now that tells you something. If Paul received everything that he is preaching and writing from The Lord Jesus Christ, where is Christ at the time of all this revelation? Well, He's in Heaven! He's in glory! After His resurrection! I'm always pointing this out. We hear so much of our preaching and our Sunday School material from the four Gospels. And there is nothing wrong with it to a degree. But that all took place before the work of the Cross. But this man is going to have the Lord Jesus telling him these things after the work of the Cross is accomplished, after He is ascended back to glory and now He's going to tell this man, Paul, what to tell the whole world. Not just the Jew. Not just the Gentile, but all the world. Now let's read on.

Galatians 1:13
"For ye have heard of my conversation in time past in the Jews' religion, (remember that's what he was when he was a persecutor. He was a religious Jew) *how that beyond measure I persecuted the church* (or assembly) *of God and wasted it:"* He absolutely persecuted them. He tore them up. He killed and imprisoned them. Anything he could do to stop anything concerning Jesus of Nazareth.

Galatians 1:14a
"And profited..."

He was a religious big-wig, and he probably gained a tremendous amount of wealth. And from that period of time I think Saul of Tarsus was married and had children. I think as a result of being sold out now to Christ, he had to put all that behind him. He lost it all. And I think that was all included when he said that everything he ever owned he counted but dung. Why? Because now he had a far higher commission in life than gaining wealth or taking care of a family.

Galatians 1:14

"And profited in the Jews' religion above many my equals in mine own nation, being more exceed-ing zealous of the tradition of my fathers." That would be Judaism and religion Now verse 15 and what's the first word? "But." Here he came out of all this religion and all of the benefits of it, but the flip side of it is that God had something else for the man.

Galatians 1:15

"But when it pleased God, who separated me from my mother's womb, and called me by his grace," He didn't deserve God's grace. If anybody didn't deserve it, Saul of Tarsus didn't. But God called him by his grace for what purpose?

Galatians 1:16

"To reveal his Son in me, (for what purpose?) *that I might preach him among the heathen,* (Gen-tiles) *immediately I conferred not with flesh and blood:"*

Here is his whole purpose, that God has brought this man on the scene for the distinct purpose of taking the Gospel of Grace to the Gentiles. **(Faith in His death, burial, and resurrection for salvation, and nothing else.)** Now, granted, it's going also to spill over to some Jews, but not many. You know, it's almost a total reverse of the Old Testament. There, God was dealing only with the Jew but a few Gentiles picked up some of the gleanings. And the same thing here. Saul of Tarsus, now Paul, is going to go primarily to the Gentiles. But there are a few Jews that come into the Body of Christ. Now in the last part of verse 16, just put yourself in Saul's shoes, running outside the walls of Damascus, not really knowing where he was going, pitch dark, no explicit instructions yet of where to go. All God had said was that he was going to suffer for His Name. Now if you had been in Saul's shoes, just outside the wall of Damascus and you put your old mind in gear, where would you have headed?

I know where I would have gone. Where would you have gone? Back to Jerusalem and look up Peter, James and John! He knew that those were the fellows who had been with Jesus for three years. He knew that they headed up the group that he had been trying to destroy. And now when he suddenly realized that the One that he thought he was trying to obliterate, was the very God that he thought he was serving, common sense tells me that the man should have headed right straight back to Jerusalem and poured out his heart to those Twelve men and shared with them everything that had happened, and confessed the fact that he had been dead wrong about Jesus, and now he was ready to serve Him. But he doesn't do that. Why? There's a purpose in all of this. A divine purpose. A sovereign purpose. And look what he says in the last part of verse 16:

Galatians 1:16b

"...immediately I conferred not with flesh and blood:" Now who do you suppose he was referring

to? The Twelve! He didn't go back to Jerusalem. He didn't confer with them. Now let's read on.

Galatians 1:17
"Neither went I up to Jerusalem to them which were apostles before me; (now that sets it clear doesn't it?) *but I went into Arabia, and returned again unto Damascus."*

We know from another chapter in Galatians, what was in Arabia? Mount Sinai! And so that's where The Lord took him. Now we have to feel that from the account in the book of Acts, he must have been down there three years. And then from that, three years of experience at Mount Sinai in the desert, and now he's ready to take the message of grace to the Gentile world. Let's read on.

Galatians 1:18
"Then after three years I went up to Jerusalem to see Peter, (not until. And by this time he has all these revelations. The mysteries are beginning to unfold and now he can go see Peter. Not to learn everything thing Peter knew but to share with Peter some of these new revelations. I've said it so often, Peter never did get them all. He never could comprehend all these revelations that the apostle Paul had received.) *and abode with him fifteen days."*

Now let's come back to Romans Chapter 16 and verse 25. And now at the end of this tremendous book of doctrine, the Book of Romans, (and it's doctrinal from verse 1 to at least Chapter 16) here in Chapter 16 and verse 25 comes a subtle statement, and it should blow our minds, but too many people don't even know it's in here. Look what he says:

Romans 16:25
"Now to him that is of power to stablish you (believers) *according to* (the Gospel? No. What?) *my gospel* (see how he identifies it) *and the preaching of Jesus Christ, according to the revelation* (or revealing) *of the mystery,* (the secret that's been kept in the mind of God) *which was kept secret since the world began,"*

Now isn't that plain? Why can't people see that? That here this mystery which is the whole circle of Paul's doctrines were kept secret until God revealed them to this man. Most of which came out in that three years at Sinai and the deeper revelations that come out in Ephesians. In his prison epistles, The Lord may have poured out of these deeper doctrines while he was sitting in prison in Caesarea waiting to go to Rome. Because, you see, after he'd spent that year and a half in Caesarea, he gets to Rome under house arrest and that's when he writes what we call his prison epistles: Ephesians, Philippians, Colossians, and Philemon. So those 18 months in prison probably were not wasted at all, because that's when The Lord revealed these tremendous, deeper things to him. Now let's go to Ephesians Chapter 3 and we'll start at verse 1. And remember this is just sort of an overview of Paul getting to the place where the Lord can use him to start calling out that next great body of resurrection: the Body of Christ, the Church.

Ephesians 3:1,2

"For this cause I Paul, the prisoner of Jesus Christ for (whom?) *you Gentiles. If you have heard of the dispensation of the grace of God* (now watch how it came. He doesn't say "which came to you by Jesus Christ". It doesn't say, "which came to you by Peter, James and John." It doesn't say, "by way of Abraham". What does it say?) *which is given me* (and then where did it go?) *to you-ward:"*

Do you see how plain that is? I had a gentleman sitting at my kitchen table one night and I had him read that verse and he said, "I know what you're driving at." So I said, "Read it again." I think he read it three or four times before he finally just almost batted his eyes and he said, "I never saw that before." I said, "Well, you're typical. That's the way people read their Bibles." **They read it but they don't read it**. But when he saw that the Holy Spirit inspired the apostle Paul to say that this Grace of God was given to him **to give to us,** there was the process. But how many people understand that? That's why I'm always telling people when they call or write and tell me that they are relatively new believers, and they want to know what part of the Bible should they be reading. Paul!!! Because this is where it's at for the Church Age. Now you don't throw the rest of the Bible away, you know that. But it's Paul that reveals all these various doctrines. So now verse 3 of Ephesians 3.

Ephesians 3:3

"How that by revelation (the same word he used in Galatians) *he* (The Lord Jesus Himself) *made known unto me the* (what?) *mystery; ..."*

Now we covered all the mysteries in earlier lessons. And they are that whole composite of truth that makes for the Church Age. And they all come from the pen of the apostle Paul. I was talking to someone they other day, and they said, " Why do you make this much of Paul?" And I said, "Let me ask you something. I don't care what denomination handle you have. Do you have a pastor and deacons and Church elders?" He said, "Well, yes." I said, "Where did you get the instructions for them?" Well, he didn't know. I said, "Well, I'll tell you. You got it from Timothy. And who wrote Timothy? Paul! Does your Church practice The Lord's table?" He said, "Oh, yeah." I said, "Where did you get it?" He thought maybe when Jesus said it. I said, "No, Jesus didn't put anything on it. All He said was, "This is My body and this is My blood, but He didn't give any instructions for the communion service. So where did we get it? From I Corinthians 11." And down the line you can go with every facet of what 99% of Christendom practices doctrinally. They get it from Paul. And yet they'll never give him the time of day. It's amazing isn't it?

Editor's Note: Paul's writings to the Gentiles (the Church) are the thirteen books of Romans through Philemon. Although Paul also wrote the book of Hebrews, he wrote it to the Jewish believers who had been saved under the gospel of the kingdom, the teaching of the twelve apostles of the circumcision (Jews). Hebrews was not written to the Gentiles.

(4b) What is the one true church ?

Book 29 LESSON TWO * PART III

Ephesians 4:4-6
"There is one body, and one Spirit, even as ye are called in one hope of your calling; One Lord, one faith, one baptism," (not three, as a lot of people are depending on, and that's not what the Book says now as you can see. We've moved on into another administration or dispensation) *One God and Father of all, who is above all, and through all, and in you all.*

Ephesians 3:5,6
"Which in other ages (generations) *was not made known unto the sons of men, as it is now revealed unto his holy apostles and prophets by the Spirit; That the Gentiles should be fellow-heirs, and of the same body and partakers of his promise in Christ* (how?) *by the gospel".*

Not by works, or baptism, or some other phenomena. Just by the Gospel. That's the only way. The Gospel, how that Christ died, was buried and rose again as we find in I Corinthians 15:1-4 and Romans 10:9-10. Now let's come across to Chapter 4, still in Ephesians. Now this is an interesting series of verses.

Ephesians 4:4a
"There is one body, ..." There it is again. You don't see that in Peter's preaching. You don't see that in Christ's earthly ministry. But all through Paul's writing you find this term, "the Body". Let's read on.

Ephesians 4:4b,5
"... and one Spirit, even as ye are called in one hope of your calling; One Lord, (absolutely, there's only one Name given among men whereby we must be saved) *one faith, one baptism,"*

I always smile when people say, "Well, I'm of the Catholic faith," "I'm of the Methodist faith," "I'm of the Baptist faith," "I'm of this faith." What do they do with a verse like this? There aren't all that many faiths. There's one faith and only one. That's what The Book says.

Book 36 LESSON ONE * PART IV

Ephesians 1:22-23a
"And hath put all things under his feet, and gave him to be the head over all things to the church, 23. Which is the body..."

Most people think that last verse should read, **"And hath put all things under his feet, and gave him to be the King over all things to the church."** But you see that's not what it says. But rather **"God hath set Him to be head of all things to the Church, which is His Body."** Now if we are the Body, are we decapitated without a head? No! Now let's come back to I Corinthians chapter 12, and look at that. In these verses we're going to look at, he gets down to such simplicity that it's almost ridiculous, but Paul is trying to drive the point home. What is the Body of Christ? Well it's just like this human body, it's composed of billions of cells. And every cell whether it be a fingernail, or an eyeball, or an ear drum has a different make up and each is important. So you see Paul is using the analogy of a human body as an example of the Body which is His Church. Now let's look at it.

I Corinthians 12:12
"For as the body (the human body) *is one, and hath many members,* (hands, feet, eyes, etc.) *and all the members of that one body, being many, are one body:* (before we go any further, what controls the body? The head!) *so also is Christ"*.

Paul is making that same analogy. You and I as believers are members of a Body of which Christ is the head. And we're just as connected in this Body of Christ, as our head is to our own human body. Looking at some more of the analogy in verse 15.

I Corinthians 12:15
"If the foot shall say, Because I am not the hand, I am not of the body; is it therefore not of the body? 16. And if the ear shall say, Because I am not the eye, I am not of the body: is it therefore not of the body?" Then let's see what Paul says in verse 18.

I Corinthians 12:18
"But now hath God set the members (that is you and I as believers) *every one of them in the body, as it hath pleased him."*
Now in our mother's womb, and I've used this analogy often. One of the miracles of reproduction is that as the mother prepares that little baby in the womb you don't have fingernail cells going any place but to the fingers. And all these separate cells go exactly to the right place. And at the end of that 9 months whenever the baby is complete, then you have birth. That's miracles of miracles. Well God is doing the same thing in a Spiritual realm. He is building the Body of Christ of believers from every walk of life from around the planet. The Chinese, or Jew, or any other nationality when they become believers are just as much a part of the Body of Christ as we are. And we're all connected to that one source, which is Christ the head. Now come on down to verse 27.

I Corinthians 12:27
"Now ye are the body of Christ, and members in particular."

God never loses sight of our individualism. God hasn't lost us in the crowd, we're not just a number in God's mind, He knows us as an individual. Now that's the Body of Christ.

Now come back again to the Book of Ephesians chapter 1.

Ephesians 1:22-23a
"And hath put all things under his feet, and gave him to be the head over all things to the church, 23. Which is the body, the fulness..."

Now if you have a marginal Bible, the other word for *fullness* is *complement*. As members of the Body of Christ we have become a complement. Now the best way to explain that is to go all the way back to Genesis where everything begins. We'll start in chapter 2.

Genesis 2:18
"And the LORD God said, It is not good that the man should be alone; I will make him an help meet for him."

Now you take the Hebrew root, and what do you suppose that word help meet is in our English? **Complement**. Or a better definition for it would be, "Someone called along side to help." Do you see that? That's the whole idea of a husband and wife relationship even to this day. The wife is that complement to the man that really completes him and brings the help that he needs, and that's what Eve was to Adam. This was all set in type of course looking forward to the greatest union that could ever take place which was the marriage between Christ and the Church. Now for a moment let's go back to the Book of Romans chapter 7. My how these verses just drop into place. Remember Paul is writing to believers.

Romans 7:4
"Wherefore, my brethren, ye also are become dead to the law by the body of Christ; (His physical body that was crucified) *that ye should be married to another, even to him who is raised from the dead,* (not just to escape hell fire, but also) *that we should bring forth fruit unto God."*

We're to be worth something to God, we're not to be deadwood. We're to be working, and bring forth fruit for His honor and His glory. Now coming back to Ephesians chapter 1.

Ephesians 1:22b-23a
"...and gave him to be the head over all things to the church, 23. Which is his body,..."

And that's a concept that few believers, I think, have any idea that we're members of a living organism. Now you know as well as I do that as long as we're living our body is a composite of living things. Our cells are alive, our enzymes are alive, and as soon as they die, we dead. All right it's the same way with the Body of Christ. The Body of Christ is not an organization like the country club. I know that's what most Churches are getting to be like I'm afraid, but that is not the true scriptural definition of a local Church. We are to be a living organism, with life.

Not physical life, but rather spiritual life. And that life is enhanced by fellowship, by the Word, by prayer, and all because we're connected to the head who is in heaven. God knows we're waiting for the day when there won't be that huge space between the head and the Body. Why? Because one day we're going to be brought into union with Him, and we're going to revel throughout all eternity in His presence, and that's something to glory in.

Book 38 Lesson Three • Part IV

Ephesians 5:23
"For the husband is the head of the wife, even as Christ is the head of the church: and he is the saviour of the body."

Now always remember that the word "Church" does not mean that building on the corner. As I was thinking about these things last evening, I remember when Iris and I were first married. She was from Oklahoma and I was from up in Iowa, and her expression always was, "The Church house." "We're going to go to the Church house." Yeah, I see you nodding your head. Well up North in Iowa, and for most people today, that's almost an unknown term. Oh I used to ride herd on her for saying that, and would ask, where do you get that? Well she would say, **"that's what it is!"** But I had never heard of such a thing, we just called it the Church. But you know what? She was right, it is the Church house, that building is not the Church.

That building is just brick and stone. The Church is made up of the true believers who meet **in** that Church house. So I was completely wrong on that one, but according to our culture this is the way we've come to look at it. **The Church is made up of the believing element, "the Body of Christ." and that's the way Paul always uses the word *Church*.** The word in the Greek is "Ecclesia" and you can spell it with k's or c's, it doesn't make any difference, and is always translated with one or two exceptions, as Church, but it should be defined as "A called out assembly."

So the called out assembly is the Body of Christ when Paul uses it, but it's not that way in other passages. For example in Acts chapter 7 we find Stephen speaks of the Church which was in the wilderness. Well now it wasn't a building with a steeple, you all know that. Neither was it a Church that practiced the Lord's Supper, and had pastors, bishops, and deacons. But rather it was the children of Israel, recently come out of Egypt. So why in the world does the New Testament call them a Church? Well they were a called out assembly of people recently in Egypt and now around Mount Sinai, but for goodness sake they weren't a Church as we think of the word Church. So when you see the word Church, this is why Paul almost always identifies it as *"The Church which is His Body,"* which makes a big difference from the word Church that's maybe used elsewhere in Scripture.

Ephesians 5:23b-24a

"...even as Christ is the head of the church: and he is the saviour of the body. 24. Therefore as the church..."

This composite of believers around the whole world that makes up the ***True Body of Christ,*** whether we're Methodists, Baptists, Lutherans, Catholics - that's moot. If we're born again and children of God, we are automatically in that ***Body of Christ,*** and that ***Body of Christ*** will be meeting in Church buildings. But always remember that not all people meeting in those Church buildings are in the Body of Christ. That depends of course how much of the "Truth" is promoted. **If the people in that particular building believe for their salvation that Jesus Christ died for their sins, was buried and rose again, + Nothing, then these people are what are called "true believers, and are part of *the Body of Christ!"***

Book 18 LESSON THREE * PART IV

John 4:15-20

"The woman saith unto him, `Sir, give me this water, that I thirst not, neither come hither to draw.' Jesus saith unto her, `Go, call thy husband, and come hither.' The woman answered and said, `I have no husband.' Jesus said unto her, `Thou hast well said, I have no husband: For thou hast had five husbands; and he whom thou now hast is not thy husband: (Sounds familiar doesn't it?) in that saidst thou truly.' The woman saith unto him, `Sir, I perceive that thou art a prophet. Our fathers worshipped in this mountain; and ye say, that in Jerusalem is the place where men ought to worship.'"

We've got to go back into Israel's history, when the Kingdom was divided under Rehoboam and Jeroboam. The Temple was in the Southern Kingdom of Judah, and it carried on as usual. So what did the Israelites of the Northern Kingdom set up? A secondary temple worship. They had their own counterfeit as it were. The presence of God wasn't in it. It was another man-made religion. They didn't realize that God was dealing with Israel at the Temple in Jerusalem. Now I need to make another point as we go along. All through Israel's religious history, Jerusalem is the headquarters of God's operation. For the New Testament Church there is no earthly headquarters. That's the vast difference. The Church today is headquartered not on earth, but in Heaven! And even though Antioch was more or less the fountainhead of where the Gospel went out to Gentiles, yet the Scriptures never place Antioch as the headquarters of the New Testament Church. Nor is Jerusalem. There is no headquarters of the New Testament Church.

(5b) What is the primary function of the local church ?

Book 28 LESSON TWO * PART III

Ephesians 4:4-10

"There is one body, and one Spirit, even as ye are called in one hope of your calling; One Lord, one faith, one baptism," (not three, as a lot of people are depending on, and that's not what the Book says now as you can see. We've moved on into another administration or dispensation) *One God and Father of all, who is above all, and through all, and in you all. But unto every one of us* (from the greatest to the least He has given these gifts of the Spirit that He lists here.) *is given grace according to the measure of the gift of Christ. Wherefore he saith, 'When he ascended up on high, he led captivity captive, and gave gifts unto men.* (Absolutely He did.) *[Now that he ascended, what is it but that he also descended first into the lower parts of the earth? He that descended* (that of course was in His three days and nights that He was in the tomb) *is the same also that ascended up far above all heavens, that he might fill all things.]'"* Look at the gifted men he gives to the Church in verse 11.

Ephesians 4:11

"And he gave some, apostles; (and they even faded off the scene after the apostolic age ended. We don't have apostles in the Church today, but they were part of it even when he was writing Ephesians.) and some, prophets; (they also faded away because we now have the printed Word. Once the Word came into print there was no longer a need for gifted men to speak forth the Word, but even so, Paul still lists them here in Ephesians. Now here's where we are today.) and some, evangelists; and some, pastors and teachers;"

Those are the three basic gifts that the Church needs today. Men who are evangelists and can preach salvation, and probably going from place to place, we all understand the role of an evangelist. And then there's the man who is the gifted person to be a pastor. We know that not all of God's men can be pastors, and not all can be teachers. But these are the three basic gifts that are explained here in the Book of Ephesians, and now look also at verse 12. Why did God give the Church these three categories of people?

Ephesians 4:12

"For the perfecting (the maturing of believers, getting away from the milk bottle, and learning to eat the meat of the Word) *of the saints, for the work of the ministry, for the edifying of* (not for the evangelist, pastors, and teachers, but for whom?) *the body of Christ:"*

Now I've maintained for years that the primary purpose of the Church (and I don't care what denomination that is), is to so feed its members that those members can go out and become soul winners among the world in which they live. That's the way they did it in the early Church. They didn't have great evangelistic campaigns, they didn't have great coliseums full of people, but oh listen, they turned the Roman Empire upside down. And how did they do it? By just simply every believer being taught from the Word that he could be a living testimony to the world around him, and this is the criteria for us today. Oh, to be so taught in the Word that you can be a testimony wherever you go, whoever you are. I don't care how little education that you have, you can be a gifted person in God's program for today.

Romans 7:4
"Wherefore, my brethren, ye also are become dead to the law by the body of Christ; (that is His crucified physical body) *that ye should be married to another, even to him who is raised from the dead, that we should bring forth fruit unto God."*

Now I think when we taught Romans we brought this out. What is the primary purpose of God bringing man and woman together in a marital relationship? Fruit. And what's the fruit? Children. That not the sole purpose, but the primary purpose. Well it's the same way here. What is the primary purpose of God uniting Himself to us as members of the Body of Christ, and claiming us as His own. We are to be fruitful and bring forth spiritual children. Now we're all getting anxious I trust for the Lord's soon return. We are seeing the world just plunging into the end-time phenomena, and the things that are getting bad are going to only get worse. While you're in Romans stop with me at Romans 11:25 because here's the whole concept that as in a physical marriage God expects the fruit of that marriage to be children so also the fruit of the believer should be other believers, and we call that soul winning. And soul winning has to be done scripturally.

Romans 11:25
"For I would not, brethren, that ye should be ignorant of this mystery, (secret) *lest ye should be wise in your own conceits; that blindness* (a spiritual blindness) *in part* (one day this blindness will end) *is happened to Israel, until the fulness of the Gentiles be come in."*
Now what's the fulness of the Gentiles? When the Body of Christ is complete. When God has finished drawing that last person into the Body of Christ then we're out of here. After that happens God will pick up where He left off with the Nation of Israel. Now coming back to II Corinthians Chapter 11 and reading verse 3 again.

II Corinthians 11:3
"But I fear, lest by any means, as the serpent beguiled Eve (in that first marital union) *through his subtilty, so your minds should be corrupted from the simplicity that is in Christ."*

If Eve is a symbol of the Church, the Body of Christ, then it stands to reason that it's the Church that Satan is constantly attacking. Satan knows that it's in the realm of the Church that he has his greatest opposition. Now we hear over and over, "When good men do nothing, then bad things happen." And Satan knows that, so if he can neutralize the Body of Christ to where it says nothing then he can have full say.

Book 29 LESSON TWO * PART III

Ephesians 3:5,6
"Which in other ages (generations) *was not made known unto the sons of men, as it is now*

revealed unto his holy apostles and prophets by the Spirit; That the Gentiles should be fellow-heirs, and of the same body and partakers of his promise in Christ (how?) *by the gospel".*

Not by works, or baptism, or some other phenomena. Just by the Gospel. That's the only way. The Gospel, how that Christ died, was buried and rose again as we find in I Corinthians 15:1-4 and Romans 10:9-10. Now let's come across to Chapter 4, still in Ephesians. Now this is an interesting series of verses.

Ephesians 4:4a
"There is one body, ..." There it is again. You don't see that in Peter's preaching. You don't see that in Christ's earthly ministry. But all through Paul's writing you find this term, "the Body". Let's read on.

Ephesians 4:4b,5
"... and one Spirit, even as ye are called in one hope of your calling; One Lord, (absolutely, there's only one Name given among men whereby we must be saved) *one faith, one baptism,"*
I always smile when people say, "Well, I'm of the Catholic faith," "I'm of the Methodist faith," "I'm of the Baptist faith," "I'm of this faith." What do they do with a verse like this? There aren't all that many faiths. There's one faith and only one. That's what The Book says.

Ephesians 4:6
"One God and Father of all, who is above all, and through all, and in you all."

Let's look on down into verse 12 of Ephesians 4. Why do you suppose we're seeing all these references to the Body all of a sudden, in the book of Ephesians? More than we did in Romans or Corinthians. Paul's writings are a progressive revelation just like the Bible as a whole. Now when Paul first begins his letters he does not make that big a deal over the Body of Christ. In Romans just that one mention. In I Corinthians, one or two mentions. But now as you come into the book of Ephesians and Paul has had further revelations, this is one of the prison epistles. And he has now been sitting in prison in Caesarea for a year and a half and all of these deeper things come and now that's why you see more about the Body in Ephesians than you did in Romans and Corinthians. It's part of this greater revelation of our position in the Body, which is in Christ.

Ephesians 4:12
"For the perfecting (maturing) *of the saints, for the work of the ministry, for the edifying of the* (what?) *body of Christ."*

Do you see that? Now, let me make a point. Not every church member across the world is a member of the Body of Christ. In fact, I'm going to stick my neck out and say a small percentage of them. I don't care what church you belong to. Mine included. Yes, I'm a member of a local church. Some people call and ask. I love my pastor and I think it's mutual. But there are members of my church that are as lost as lost can be and they are not in the Body of Christ. I don't know who they are because I'm not judging. I'm not looking at somebody and saying, "Well, you're not in the Body." In fact I told somebody the other day, and I'll tell my whole television audience, don't ever look at anybody, I don't care how far down the tube they are, don't look at them and say, "Well, you're going to Hell", because you don't know that.

Salvation may come to that person at some future date and you don't know that. And so, please, don't ever tell someone that. That's God's prerogative, not ours. And the same with judging whether someone is a believer. I can't and neither can you. **Only God can see the heart**. But I do know from the Scripture and from everything else that bombards us, there are a lot of bonafide church members who are not members of the Body of Christ. Only The Lord himself places a person into the Body of Christ. Denominations can't, your preacher can't do it, a priest can't do it. This is something that only the Spirit of God can do. So, what is the purpose of all the things that God has been doing on behalf of the Church? To edify the Body of Christ, the true believer!

(6b) How can we help others to be saved ?

Book 38 Lesson One • Part I

Maturing in God's Word
Ephesians 4:12-24

As we begin this new book, let me remind each true believer that we're all laborers together for our Lord. We are part of what Paul calls in *I Corinthians 3:9 "...God's building..."* As we study I know there are countless millions who are so hung up on tradition, and they based their very eternal destination on some of these traditions Tradition is something that has been passed down from generation to generation, and many never bother to check the Scripture to see if these traditions are really true for the Body of Christ believer. **I just thank the Lord that over half of the New Testament was written by Paul for the Body of Christ, who gives us** *can't miss instruction* **for eternal life.**

Last lesson we left off in Ephesians chapter 4. Today we'll pick up with verse 12. Remember that in verse 11, Paul leaves the Church with evangelists, pastors and teachers as we discussed in the last lesson. These are specially gifted men that God is going to provide for the Christian community. I think it also ties in with I Corinthians chapter 13, the love chapter. It's almost the same kind of scenario, only we shake out off the superfluous things and we end up with the three things that in the end will abide. And what are they?

I Corinthians 13:13
"And now abideth faith, hope, charity, (or love) *these three; but the greatest of these is charity."*

Those are the things that remain with us even today. These three words in Paul's epistles just keep popping up. Now all three may not be together all the time, but watch for those words. Now coming back to where we were in Ephesians chapter 4, and we have much the same thing. So forth of the various gifts and so forth, that people make so much ado over even today, they've more or less just fallen by the way side, but three of them remain. These three are as absolute as anything can be even today, and what are they? **Evangelists, pastors, and teachers**. Those are the three main criteria for any local group of believers. Now verse 12, and what's the purpose of these three?

Ephesians 4:12
"For the perfecting of the saints, (notice Paul said to *perfect the saints*, not the lost. and what's the purpose again?) *for the work of the ministry, for the edifying of the body of Christ:"*

You know I'm always stressing that I think too much of Church activity is geared in the wrong direction, not that it's all that bad, but so much Church activity is supposedly directed to lost people. Oh we've got to save the lost, most Churches will say, and I'm also concerned about the lost, but the best way to reach lost people is not wait for that poor preacher, or Sunday school teacher to do it all, **but every ordinary believer should be in the position to open the Scriptures to lost people**, and that's what I think Paul is referring to here. Now look at it again in that light. All evangelists, pastors, and teachers are given for what purpose?

Ephesians 4:12
"For the perfecting (or maturing) *of the saints, for the work of the ministry, for the edifying of the body of Christ:"* This is where all Paul's effort is being directed to the to edifying the believer. Now verse 13.

Ephesians 4:13a
"Till we all come in the unity of the faith, and of the knowledge of the Son of God,..."

Now those of you who hear me teach over a period of time, know that I'm always stressing that there's no use trying to go out and witness to people if you don't know what you're witnessing about. **You have to know the subject, and you need to be able to show the lost the correct Scripture so they can see with their own eyes**. If you ask an auto mechanic, or some other person in a specialized field about their profession, they show how professional they are real quick with their knowledge of the subject. But if you asked them something that's out of their field, they would clam up, because they don't know. Well it's almost that ridiculous when we try to send people out to witness to the lost, when they know nothing about the Word of God. So the whole purpose in Paul's writings is to edify the believer, and now let's look and see what the believer is supposed to do.

II Corinthians 5:18

"And all things are of God, who hath (past tense) *reconciled us to himself by Jesus Christ, and hath given to us* (the believer) *the ministry of reconciliation; 19. To wit,* (that is to say) *that God was in Christ, reconciling the world unto himself, not imputing their trespasses* (sins) *unto them;* (they're forgiven) *and hath committed unto us the word of reconciliation.:"*

In other words, we're to tell a lost world that because of Christ's death, burial, and resurrection, He has already reconciled them, but they have to believe that beautiful Gospel. And how are they to believe it?

Romans 10:14

"How then shall they call on him in whom they have not believed? and how shall they believe in him of whom they have not heard? and how shall they hear without a preacher (or proclaimer?) Paul tells us someone must present this Gospel to them. Now finishing our thought with verse 20 of II Corinthians chapter 5.

II Corinthians 5:20a

"Now then we (as ordinary everyday believers) *are ambassadors for Christ,..."*

Now what's an ambassador? He's a representative of his home country, but he's living in foreign territory, and everything that he does is being viewed by the foreigners. Everything that he says is being analyzed by the people in the country which he is serving. Now folks that's exactly where you and I are. We are in foreign territory whether we know it or not. Everyday that we live we see it more and more, I mean the opposition is rising against Christianity. We're in foreign territory! **Paul tells us as believers our homeland, and citizenship is in heaven, and we're to be ambassadors**.

Now let me ask you something, would any president in his right mind send somebody to Japan to be an ambassador from my background, for example. Would he just send an ordinary dirt farmer over there to represent this country? Why I wouldn't know how to even begin a conversation. So before we send an ambassador to a foreign nation by an appointment, usually of the president, and the congress has to OK it, what do you expect that person to have in his background? Everything that prepared him to be an ambassador. **You wouldn't send anyone over there with no education or background, but isn't that exactly what we do with most Christians? We send them out into that world of wolves with no background, they have no knowledge of the Scripture, and as soon as the scoffer hits them with something, they absolutely melt, they don't know what to say or where to find it.**

This is why we have to teach the Word, this is why God has left evangelists, pastors, and teachers. The believing community has to be prepared to go out into the world and win the lost. We're to have a heart for lost people, of course we are. God has a heart for lost people, but you see too often we put the cart up in front of the horse, and we wonder why it doesn't work

Book 37 Lesson Two • Part IV

I Corinthians 2:14
"But the natural man (the unbeliever. I don't care if he's in church every Sunday. If he's still unsaved and in the natural he) *receiveth not the things of the Spirit of God;* (it's impossible for him. Why?) *for they are foolishness unto him: neither can he know them, because they are spiritually discerned."*

So when you're talking with unbelievers, and you try to express some of the deeper things in Scripture, then expect them to look at you with a blank look because they can't help it. The Bible says, *"They can not know about these things. The spiritual things must be spiritually discerned."* So the unbelieving world will argue and fuss with you and give you all their ideas, but listen, it's nothing but secular gibberish. But when they finally get the Spirit of God, then they can certainly comprehend. That's why Paul makes it so common for the believer to understand these deep things of God, and he expects us to. Now let's go back to the Book of Ephesians.

Ephesians 3:17-18
"That Christ may dwell in your hearts by faith; that ye, being rooted and grounded in love, (that is the love of God that brought us unto Himself. That we) *18. May be able to comprehend with all saints what is the breadth, and length, and depth, and height;"*
We can step into the whole spectrum of spiritual understanding, and the unbelieving world can't get that. But oh listen, for us, it's all here if we'll just search it out. Now then verse 19.

Ephesians 3:19
"And to know the love of Christ, which passeth knowledge that ye might be filled with all the fulness of God." (Read that verse again)

Ephesians 3:19a
"And to know the love of Christ,..."

Remember a program or two back when we were following *the "unsearchable riches of Christ?"* And I mentioned, "How can you and I, mere mortals, comprehend the fact that the *Eternal Sovereign Creator God* condescended to be born of an ordinary little lady in Israel, to be born under the humble circumstances of Bethlehem, and then go through 30 years on this old planet for the sole purpose of going to that Cross." Now listen that's beyond human comprehension. But what did it? *"The Love of God!"* How God loves the human race! And how He paid the very extent of the very riches of heaven to accomplish a plan of redemption!
Now remember lost humanity is under the clutches, chains and control of a powerful, powerful being. Oh, never lose sight of that. And in order for God to bring salvation to the human

race, first after taking upon Himself all the sins of this human race, He also had to break the powers of Satan. He literally had to break the bands of Satan that held everything in it's power, which He accomplished at the Cross. And then again you repeat that for every believer that is saved, then God has to do it all over again, breaking the power of the Satanic forces that hold us. Keep your hands in Ephesians, but for a moment let's come back to II Corinthians chapter 4, and look at this for a moment so you can see what I'm talking about.

II Corinthians 4:3-4
"But if our gospel be hid, it is hid to them that are lost: (now remember every human being on the face is lost until they're saved) *4. In whom* (in lost people) *the god of this world hath blinded the minds of them which believe not, lest the light of the glorious gospel of Christ, who is the image of God, should shine unto them."*

So who's the culprit? Who is keeping lost people lost? Well Satan is! We're in a society that you almost cringe to use the term, "Satan." People think you're a fundamentalist kook if you use that term. **But listen, the Bible explicitly tells us that his power is tremendous, and only the power of God can break his blinding the unbeliever**. And that's where I think prayer comes in. Oh let me give you another one that I use. Come back to Acts chapter 16, and Paul has been up in northern Greece, and comes to Philippi.

Acts 16:13-14
"And on the sabbath (remember that early on in Paul's ministry, he's still coming out of the law background, and this of course was the Saturday Sabbath, and so these were Jewish women no doubt) *we went out of the city by a river side, where prayer was wont to be made; and we sat down, and spake unto the women which resorted thither. 14. And a certain woman named Lydia a seller of purple, of the city of Thyatira, which worshipped God*, (she was Jewish and worshipping the God of Abraham, and this Lydia) *heard us; whose heart the Lord opened,* (now before the Lord could open her heart to believe Paul's Gospel, what other power did God have to exercise? He had to break the blinding power of Satan. This Lydia was no different than anybody else. Just because she believed in God, doesn't mean she wasn't blind to the truth of the Gospel, for she was blinded. But here we have the perfect account of how the Lord opened her eyes, and heart, the Lord broke the bands of Satan) *that she attended unto the things which were spoken of Paul."* (Lydia believed Paul's Gospel and became a believer.)

Now this is all part and parcel of what we're up against even in our own day. Satan has blinded the eyes of those that believe not and only the power of God can open their understanding. Now let's come back to Ephesians chapter 3, and let's read verse 19 again.

Ephesians 3:19
"And to know the love of Christ, which passeth knowledge, that ye might be filled with all the fulness of God."

We can't comprehend what love it took to drive Him to the Cross. And all the fulness of God is what we're to be filled with. Now I don't think any of us understand what that is do we? I don't think there's ever been a human alive, at least not on this side of the apostle Paul that has really understood the fulness of God. We can't even come close, but potentially it's there for us. Now verse 20. Here Paul ends this prayer.

Ephesians 3:20
"Now unto him that is able to do exceeding abundantly above all that we ask or think, according to the power that worketh in us,"

What a prayer request on behalf of you and I. Just for a moment let's come over to the Book of Colossians and look at another prayer for believers.

Colossians 1:9
"For this cause we also, since the day we heard it, (that is their salvation, we) *do not cease to pray for you, and to desire that ye might be filled with the knowledge of his will in all wisdom and spiritual understanding;"* Does that ring a bell? It's almost the same thing we were looking at in the Book of Ephesians. Now verse 10.

Colossians 1:10-14
"That ye might walk worthy of the Lord unto all pleasing, (remember God never tells us to be a thorn in people. We are not to be obnoxious, or to make a fools of ourselves, but rather we are to be a living example of the love of the One who died for us.) *being fruitful in every good work, and increasing in the knowledge of God;* (now that's a constant thing isn't it? We don't get all this knowledge of God all at once, and say, 'well I've arrived.') *11. Strengthened with all might, according to his glorious power unto all patience and longsuffering with joyfulness; 12. Giving thanks unto the Father, which hath made us meet to be partakers of the inheritance of the saints in light: 13. Who hath delivered us from the power of darkness, and hath translated us into the kingdom of his dear Son: 14. In whom we have redemption through his blood, even the forgiveness of sins:"*

My goodness, what a prayer request for us. And that's for every believer, not just for the preachers and teachers, but rather it's for everyone of us. Now back to Ephesians and we'll wind up the chapter.

Ephesians 3:21
"Unto him be glory in the church (the Body of Christ) *by Christ Jesus throughout all ages, world without end. Amen."*

In other words this isn't the end. Eternity is out there in front of us, but our Lord Jesus Christ will never change. He is the same, yesterday, today, and forever!

Book 7 LESSON THREE * PART I

I Corinthians 1:18
"For the preaching of the cross is to them that perish foolishness;"

At some point in the next few lessons we are going to come back to the New Testament and show that so much of what we are hearing today is leaving out the Cross. And we can't do that. No one can be saved by simply believing in Jesus. It has to be the work of the Cross. And so Paul states that here. The world may think the preaching of the Cross is foolishness, but to us that are saved, it is the power of God. It takes the power of God to save us, to set us free from the shackles of sin And that power can never be released from God until we **BELIEVE THE GOSPEL. That Christ died, was buried and rose again.**

I may say it again before these next four lessons are over. I always tell people that it's not because I'm getting senile, but I repeat a lot of these things purposely for emphasis, because the Scripture does. What we have to understand is that today, even among evangelical Christians, there is too much use of what I call "clichés." Now, you know what a cliché is? It's just a little coined statement, that we've learned to use in the proper places.

I think too much of Christianity is using clichés which, if the person fully understands the whole Gospel picture, that cliché may say it all. But too many don't. You say, "what are you talking about?" You have all heard the expression (I've used it and imagine you have used it) "Well, I've accepted the Lord Jesus as my personal Savior." Now, there is nothing wrong with that, but what is it? It's a coined phrase. It's not in the Bible! You show me one verse where it says that if you will take Jesus as your Lord and personal Savior, that you will be saved. It doesn't say that.

Now, if you take the Lord Jesus Christ as your personal Savior, based on the fact that He, the very Son of God, became flesh, went to the Cross, shed His blood, was buried, and rose from the dead, and you put that whole truth into your cliché, then I have no problem with that. But how many people can do that? Another one we like to use is, "Well if you just believe in Jesus." Which Jesus are you believing in? Are you believing in the Jesus of the three years that He ministered to Israel, **or are you putting your faith in that Jesus that went to the Cross, and rose from the dead?**

Do you see what I'm saying? How many times have you heard the expression "Well if you'll just take Jesus into your heart," and again, there is nothing basically wrong with that, except, unless the person who is taking Him into his heart, understands that the only reason you can have Christ in your heart, is because He died on that Cross. This is what worries me, that people are being led into a false security by simply taking a shortcut, or clichés without knowing the full truth of the matter. **So we are saved by the power of God, from the preaching of the Cross.**

Editor's Note: In summary we see that:
1. Every believer should be in the position to open the Scriptures to a lost person through their knowledge of the scripture.
2. Only the Lord can open someone's heart.
3. When we have the opportunity to share the scripture with someone we should clearly share the Gospel with them, first and foremost. Corinthians 15:1-4

(7b) Will God talk to us ?

Book 4 LESSON ONE * PART IV

Genesis 12:14-17
"And it came to pass, that, when Abram was come into Egypt, the Egyptians beheld the woman that she was very fair. The princes also of Pharaoh saw her, and commended her before Pharaoh: and the woman was taken into Pharaohs house (becoming part of his harem). *And he entreated Abram well for her sake: and he had sheep, and oxen, and he asses, and menservants, and maidservants, and she asses, and camels. And the Lord plagued Pharaoh and his house with great plagues because of Sarai Abram's wife."*

In the Old Testament days God dealt more directly than He does today. In fact, I was thinking the other day as I was getting ready for this lesson, there is a good book by Sir Robert Anderson entitled: The Silence of God. It is rather hard to comprehend. It is written in Old English, more or less. It seems like an odd title, but Sir Robert Anderson was a Bible scholar as well as the head of Scotland Yard. He must have been a layman. But, he was a tremendous Bible scholar. In his book, he draws this analogy of God constantly dealing in an intrinsic way with the Old Testament characters. But when we get to our Age of Grace, God is comparatively silent because we have The Book. God doesn't have to talk to us audibly. God doesn't have to appear to us in the miraculous. I always have to qualify that. That doesn't mean that I don't believe God cannot miraculously answer our prayers. Sir Robert Anderson makes a point of the fact that in this Age of Grace it is as if God is silent, compared to His dealing in the Old Testament,.

Think about that. We just don't expect angels to appear. I told someone at a class one night, "If all of a sudden on my way home at 11:00 at night I'd see a bunch of angels on the highway, do you think I could take it? I know I couldn't. I don't think you could either!" What if all of a sudden God would just appear as He did back in the Old Testament? It would crack us up. We're not prepared for that. And God doesn't expect us to be. Indeed, God is silent today compared to the days we are reading about. Here, God even appeared to pagan Pharaoh and revealed to him that, "This lady out there is not what you think she is. She is a man's wife."

Genesis 12:18,19
"And Pharaoh called Abram and said, `What is this that thou hast done unto me? why didst thou

not tell me that she was thy wife (God told him, but Abram had not)*? Why saidst thou, She is my sister? so I might have taken her to me to wife: now therefore behold thy wife, take her, and go thy way.'"*

Book 28 LESSON TWO * PART III

I Corinthians 12:11
"But all these (the things that he has listed up there in verses 8, 9 and 10) *worketh that one and the selfsame Spirit, dividing to every man severally* (differently) *as he* (the Holy Spirit) *will."*

Do you see that? So it's not for you and me to go and say, "Oh I want this gift, or that gift," No, you just take the gift that God has given you. Now I think the greatest thing we can do is just simply say, "Lord here I am, I'm available, use me." And let Him direct you where He want to use you. I've told people this for years that I don't wait for God to say something out loud, He's never spoken to me out loud, but I'll tell you how He talks to me, and that's with open and closed doors. He gets us just exactly where He want us. If something doesn't fly and the door closes, don't push against it, you just take it that God doesn't want you in that direction. You will find another open door someplace else so just take that one. And then from the Word, His Word can just impress you so much. Another one is by prayer, and that's some of the ways that we can find what God wants. But just to simply go to God and say, "I want the gift of such and such, no I don't think this is what the Bible permits. We are to leave that up to the Holy Spirit.

Book 37 Lesson Two • Part III

I Corinthians 3:16
"Know ye not that ye are the temple of God, and that the Spirit of God dwelleth in you?

Now again to just point out Paul's revelations and I think this is all part of the mysteries, did you ever read that the believers were indwelt by the Holy Spirit of this in the Old Testament? No way. Now they knew of the Holy Spirit, but you want to remember like David and Samson, the Holy Spirit would come upon them, but He wasn't there permanently, He could leave at the drop of a hat. And of course that's what happened to Samson. When the Holy left off with Samson he was as weak as a dish rag. But when the Spirit was upon him, he had all kinds of power.

Now here Paul is making it so plain then that the Spirit of God dwelleth in you. How do I know the Holy Spirit lives within me? I don't feel Him in there. I don't hear Him talking to me. I'm not one of those who hears God talk out loud. I've never yet heard Him talk audibly to me. Now I think He affects our thoughts, and as we study the Scriptures God speaks to us through His Word. But to hear Him say, "Now Les I want you to do this." I've never had that happen, and I'm a little bit dubious when people talk like that, because the Bible doesn't teach that. But we do have the indwelling Person of the Holy Spirit living within us. Now back to Ephesians chapter

3. So Christ in the Person of the Holy Spirit is dwelling in our hearts as believers. By faith is the only way of knowing.

(8b) What is the meaning of baptism ?

Book 14 LESSON THREE * PART III

Matthew 3:3
"For this is he that was spoken of by the prophet Esaias (see it's also in Isaiah. I took you back to Malachi but Isaiah also speaks of John the Baptist) *saying, `The voice of one crying in the wilderness, `Prepare ye the way of the Lord, make his paths straight.'"* You know all about John, so now I would like for you to come quickly down to verse 6:

Matthew 3:6
"And were baptized of him in Jordan, confessing their sins."

Think for a moment. Can you think of any other subject in Christianity that will cause more controversy, more anger, more disruption of fellowship and more everything else that you can think of, than baptism? Oh, I've experienced it over and over. I see people who seemingly have real sweet fellowship until all of a sudden they realize they didn't agree on baptism and then, oops, there goes their friendship. **Now there's something wrong when something can cause such division amongst believers.** And I guess I'd have to say it's because we have so many different views of this baptism. Some feel that it's mandatory for salvation. Some, that it has nothing to do with salvation. Some in sprinkling, some in immersion. So you have all of these conflicting ideas, and I think it's a pity.

Now we are going to see what the Scripture says. **But here, John no doubt about it, maintains that if these Jews of Israel are going to show saving faith in the fact that their King and Kingdom is here, then they would have to show it with the baptism of repentance.** And that is why it is always called the **"Baptism of Repentance."** The two could not be separated. These Jews were repenting then of their failure of the system of law, and everything else. They were now preparing their hearts and minds for the King and His Kingdom. I have a question for you. Why baptism? That throws a curve at almost everyone. Now remember that we are dealing with the Jew, and if you go back to the Old Testament economy, in order for the priest to be prepared for service the first thing they had to do was wash, wash, and wash some more. They had lots of practice at washing. **Throughout the whole system of the Law of Moses there was that constant washing to show to the very mind of Israel that sin was a filthy thing. This is what we are dealing with here. Sin!**

That is why leprosy is used as a picture of sin. Now most of us don't know how horrible a man with leprosy can look, especially in the final stages. It is beyond comprehension. And that's what sin does. Naaman, the Syrian General, had leprosy and the servant just begged him to go to the prophet of Israel and be healed. So he ends up with Elisha, and the old prophet doesn't even come but rather sends his own servant out, and tells this big Syrian General to do what? Go dip in the Jordan River seven times. Well he finally did, and what happened? He was healed of his leprosy. Now the water didn't do it. God did it because Naaman, as reluctant as he was, was still exercising faith. But that dipping in the Jordan River indicated a cleansing. In the same way, the priesthood with their wash, wash, wash, were merely emphasizing their need for a spiritual cleansing. The water in no way could do that. **Remember, we looked at Scripture a couple of lessons back where Israel was told that every Jew was to be a priest of God. What little rite had to happen before they would be ready for a priesthood? They had to be washed. And they experienced that symbolic washing with their baptism. Now that is all you can put on it. Nothing more!**

I guess one of the biggest questions has been, **"Why was Jesus baptized? He didn't have any sin to repent of."** But again, He came to be a prophet, priest, and King, and in order to fulfill all of the requirements of the priesthood again, symbolically what did He have to experience? The washing. So as He went down into that baptism in the Jordan, he symbolically fulfilled the washing of the priesthood, and at the same time He identifies Himself with His Covenant people the Nation of Israel. Do you see how everything just fits so beautifully together? There is a reason for it, but we have to understand it.

Book 3 LESSON ONE * PART I

I Corinthians 12:12,13
For as the body is one, and hath many members, and all the members of that one body, being many, are one body: so also is Christ. For by one Spirit are we all baptized into one body, whether we be Jews or Gentiles, whether we be bond or free; and have been all made to drink into one Spirit."

Now, does the Holy Spirit baptize with water? No! So, this is not talking about water baptism, yet nearly every Christian group will not accept a person for membership without water baptism. Do you really believe that every member in your congregation is a born again child of God? Of course not! We are all members of congregations where there are unbelievers who have been baptized under whatever form of baptism their particular group uses. There are still people coming into every group who are totally unsaved; they're baptized and they are members there, but they are **not** members of the Body of Christ. There will be no unbelievers in the Body of Christ because that's the work of the Holy Spirit - to immediately place or baptize them into the Body of Christ. The reason Paul uses this analogy of the human body is that some believers' roles are no more that that of a little pinkie finger. Some may even have the role of a little toe, which most people never see. Others may be in more visible roles, but every one of us, regardless of where God has placed us in the Body, has a function in that Body, be it small or great.

We'll get back to Romans 8 in moment, but here in I Corinthians 12, it shows very clearly what God expects of His children. Here, Paul mentions the gifts that really amount to something; the very gifts Christ uses, by an act of the Holy Spirit, to search the heart. The Holy Spirit will never place an unbeliever into the Body of Christ. None of us can examine someone else close enough to screen him from the membership in our local church. We can't do it, and we're not supposed to. That's why Jesus gave the illustration during His earthly ministry of the "tares and the wheat." Years ago, when I was teaching in that concept of the tares and the wheat, an agronomist at the college brought in some tares and wheat. You couldn't tell the difference, but one would never give a grain and the other would. It's the same way in the church. We can't judge and say, "That church member is not a child of God." That's not our job. But, we have to be aware that in the Body of Christ there are no false professors - only the genuine believer is in the Body of Christ, and that's the only Christ there is.

So that's the membership you'd better be sure of. Don't worry about whether you are member of the biggest church in town or the smallest; just be sure you are a member of the Body of Christ, and remember the qualification: **It's for all! "For by one spirit we were baptized into one body!"**

Book 8 LESSON ONE * PART IV

Romans 6:4
"Therefore we are buried with him by baptism into death: (many people will disagree, but I'm convinced this is not a water baptism. Water baptism cannot do what Paul is talking about here.) *that like as Christ was raised up from the dead by the glory of the Father, even so we also should walk in newness of life."*

No baptism can give new life. Only the power of God can do that. So I am convinced, maybe contrary to the way I was taught in my earlier years, that **this is Baptism of the Holy Spirit.** Paul speaks of this in I Corinthians Chapter 12. I hadn't intended to do this but I feel the Spirit is leading this way for a reason, so let's look at this verse. **In Chapter 12 is what I consider the only valid baptism for us in this Age of Grace.** And it's a baptism that human hands cannot touch; it's a baptism that a lost person can have no part in. In water baptism, we can never be sure of a person's salvation.

I was brought up in a congregation where candidates for baptism were examined very thoroughly, yet I've come to the conclusion in my later years that there is no way a group of men, or pastors, can truly determine a person's salvation. We can hear their testimony and come to some human conclusions, **but we can never look on the heart. That is something that only God Himself can do**.

I've told my class that I don't think it will actually happen this way, but if it were, and we get to glory, we are suddenly going to realize that a lot of people are there we didn't think would be. And there are going to be a lot of people not there that we thought should be. We probably won't have that kind of knowledge, but just hypothetically if that were the case, we would be surprised and disappointed. But we can't look on the heart, only the outward veneer to reach a conclusion. But that's not the heart. This is where the Scripture says also "Judge not!" Consequently this is the baptism that Paul refers to here in verse 12:

I Corinthians 12:12,13
"For as the body (that is this human body. In other words from head to toe, we are controlled by one central nervous system, one mind, one brain) *is one, and hath many members, and all the members of that one body, being many, are one body* (ten fingers and toes if we are normal)*: so also is Christ."*

And here Paul is referring to the Body of Christ. Now, verse 13, and this may shock some people, but again I'm not changing or twisting the wording, we are going to leave it exactly where it sits.

I Corinthians 12:13
"For by one Spirit (notice that Spirit is capitalized, so it is in reference to the Holy Spirit.) *are we* (and remember Paul always writes to believers. What's the next word?) *all* (not just a favorite few, or a special elite, but how many? **All** But of course that's according to God's determination of who is a believer, whether weak or strong, spiritual or carnal) *baptized into one body,"* So reading the verse again: *"For by one Spirit are we all baptized into one body, whether we be Jews or Gentiles, whether we be bond or free; and have been all made to drink into one Spirit."*

Let me qualify the Body of Christ, which of course came on the scene in the New Testament, I think after Pentecost. Some people disagree with me, and that's fine. But you search the Scriptures until you are sure you can prove me wrong. But I'm convinced that the Body of Christ didn't necessarily begin at Pentecost, because Pentecost was strictly a Jewish holiday, with a Jewish message. **When the Gospel of Grace begins to go out to both Jew and Gentile, especially at the church in Antioch, in Acts Chapter 11, where it says that the believers at Antioch were the first to be called Christians; this was about 10 years after Pentecost.**

That's where they were first called Christians. Not the Jewish believers in Jerusalem in those previous years. But when Gentiles started coming in **by faith** in the Gospel of the grace of God, they were now called Christians as the Scriptures says, so that's where I feel the Body of Christ began when Paul begins to preach this message of Christ's death, burial, and resurrection. And by faith and faith alone without the Law. And as men and women began to believe that, then the Holy Spirit baptized, or placed them, into the Body of Christ, the Church. Now, I asked my class the other night, as I have over the years, as I don't care what denomination you are a part of it doesn't make any difference, the question is still valid: is every member on your church roll a genuine born again Christian? No. Remember we are not to judge, but we know for a fact that they are not all true believers. What about the unbeliever? Are they members of the Body of Christ? No, they can't be. They are unsaved. Only the saved go into the Body of Christ. **So this is where I get the premise, that the only baptism that really counts for eternity is this one.** The one that places the true believer into the Body of Christ. Let's also look quickly at Ephesians 4. Again, Paul writing to believers says:

Ephesians 4:4,5
"There is one body, (The Body of Christ) *and one Spirit,* (The Holy Spirit) *even as ye are called in one hope of your calling. One Lord, one faith, one baptism,"* How many? ONE. Do you see that?

So you can have your name on as many church rolls as you wish. **But unless you are in the Body of Christ you are doomed.** The Scripture makes it so plain. But if you are a child of God, you are in the Body of Christ by virtue of the placing it there by the Holy Spirit, as Paul makes it so plain. And then as members of the Body of Christ, we all maintain our individuality, we all have unique place in that Body, and yet we are all what? ONE. That's also why, when you walk into a room full of fellow believers, are you a stranger very long? No. I've experienced it and I know you have. I've had people from far off states come into my class, and on the way out they will say, **"The minute I stepped into this room I felt at home"** And that is as it should be, because when you are with fellow believers there is that **oneness** that any other group can never experience.

Book 33 LESSON THREE * PART IV

THE TRUE INTENT OF THE LAW IS CONDEMNATION

GALATIANS 3:15-29
Now this lesson will finish book 33, and I find that unreal. That means we've come to Tulsa 99 times to do these tapings of *"Through The Bible."* Before we begin, let's review where we ended our last lesson. Paul is writing to Gentile believers for the most part and says -

Galatians 3:26
"For ye are all the children of God by faith in Christ Jesus."
And as I mentioned in the last lesson when Paul speaks of faith in Christ he's speaking of that whole finished work of redemption, which is faith in His death, His shed blood, His burial, and His resurrection. Paul stresses constantly the power of His resurrection.

Galatians 3:27
"For as many of you as have been baptized into (your denomination?) *Christ have put on Christ."*

Well that's the way most people read it, isn't it? Sure. You ask the average individual, how did you become a member of your Church? Well I was baptized into it! But you see that's not what the Scriptures says. Here it says, **"that you have been baptized into Christ."** Now there's not a drop of water in this verse. It's as dry as a bone, and to follow up with another verse come back to Romans chapter 6, and you have the same thing. I'll never forget the first time I heard a guest preacher in one of our previous churches where we were members, and this preacher preached from Romans 6 and when he said there wasn't a drop of water in this third verse we thought he was way out in left field. And at that time I was probably one of the strongest, but oh I can see now that he was 100 % right because there is no water in Romans chapter 6. Here it's basically the same thing as what Paul is saying in Galatians chapter 3.

Romans 6:3
"Know ye not, that so many of us as were baptized into (not into a denomination or church, but rather into) *Jesus Christ were baptized into his death?"*

If you've been placed in Christ then before you can get there you had to be identified with His death. And how have I always put it? When Christ died, God saw every one of us on the Cross in the Person of Christ, because He died in our place, and this is what God saw. He saw you and I crucified and that's what He means in Galatians 2 when Paul says -

Galatians 2:20
"I am crucified with Christ: nevertheless I live; yet not I, but Christ liveth in me;..."
Now just as surely as God saw us on the Cross in the person of Christ, He also saw us in the tomb. So here we are in the tomb, we're buried with Him. Not by water but by virtue of God determining that now since He's paid the sin debt for all that believe, and appropriate it then yes God said, "You're dead, you're crucified, I saw you in Christ, I saw you buried with Him in his death, in His tomb, and so also we've been resurrected with Him to a new life. We are totally different people as a result of this power of His resurrection, and so it's a God thing. God in His Omnipotence, in His power, in His Omniscience, in His ability to work in the area of the invisible, He has placed us in all of these places.

In the area of the invisible He has seen everyone of us crucified with Christ. In the area of the invisible He saw everyone of us in the tomb with Christ, and in the area of the invisible He has resurrected everyone of us to a new life. How often haven't I made this illustration? If you were to go down to the morgue and accompany a pathologist in a autopsy, would you ever see the soul of a person? Would you ever see their spirit? Of course not, it's invisible. Does that mean that it's not for real? You better believe it's for real or you wouldn't be here. But the soul and spirit are invisible, and that's where God works, in the area of the invisible. He works in the area of our soul and spirit, and human hands can't touch that. **You can baptize this old body a hundred times and it's not going to change the soul and spirit**. Remember this is only an outer tabernacle, but only God can work in the area of the soul and spirit. I wish people could understand that. Looking at the verse again.

Romans 6:3
"Know ye not, that so many of us is were baptized into Jesus Christ were baptized (or identified) *into his death?"* And then to verse 8:

Romans 6:8
"Now if we be dead with Christ, (in other words if we've been crucified with Him, if we've been buried with Him then) *we believe that we shall also live with him:"*

How are we going to live with Him? By His resurrection power. Do you see that? We've been raised in resurrection power. We're a new person, we're a whole new being, and now we are placed into Christ. How? Now on your way back to Galatians stop at I Corinthians chapter 12. These are verses that we use over and over because they are so foundational and so simplistic. You don't have to have a seminary degree to understand some of these verses. They're so simple but most people don't understand them. Also keep in mind that Paul tells us in Ephesians now in this age of Grace that there is only **one baptism** and then I Corinthians tells us what baptism that is.

Ephesians 4:4-5
"There is one body, and one Spirit, even as ye are called in one hope of your calling; 5. One Lord, one faith, one baptism,"

I Corinthians 12:13
"For by one Spirit (the Holy Spirit, it's capitalized) *are we all* (believers of Paul's Gospel for salvation) *baptized into one body,* (the Body of Christ. Now here's another verse that is as dry as a bone. There is not a drop of water in this verse. It's the work of the Holy Spirit working in the area of the invisible placing you and I now in that new resurrected personage into that relationship with Christ.) *whether we be Jews or Gentiles, whether we be bond or free; and we have been all made to drink into one Spirit."*

There is no color line in the Body of Christ, we believers are **all** baptized into that Body of Christ, and we are **all** one in Christ. We just came back from a cruise on the Mediterranean, and we had 62 of us from various parts of the country. But you know what? In just a matter of 24 hours we had all come together as though we had known each other all our lives. Why? We were all believers. We were all members of the Body of Christ, and you're not strangers long when you're believers, and it's so beautiful. Now next week we'll be going back to Israel, and we'll have a different group and I know the same thing is going to happen again. That whole group of people is going to come together and by the time we come back it's going to be as close knit as family. It just shows the fact that when you become members of the Body of Christ there is that unity that nothing can take apart.

Now this is what comes **alone** from the writings of the apostle Paul. This isn't taught in the Four Gospels, this isn't taught in the Old Testament, but Paul is constantly at it. That when we have faith in the Gospel then we become a member of the Body of Christ. Now back to Galatians chapter 3. Now verse 27 is too good a verse to just casually go over, I'm going to spend some time in it. So if you have been baptized by that Holy Spirit's work into the Body of Christ, then something else has happened. What? You have put on Christ.

Galatians 3:27
"For as many of you as have been baptized into Christ have put on Christ."

Book 3 LESSON THREE * PART I

Romans 1:16
"For I am not ashamed of the gospel of Christ: for it is the power of God unto salvation to every one that believeth; to the Jew first, and also to the Greek."
He didn't say, "To everyone who repents and is baptized" or "to everyone who does according to man's traditions," but he said "to everyone that believeth"! He stated very plainly that if we believe this Gospel with all our hearts - that Christ died, was buried, and rose from the dead - then that Gospel becomes the very power of God Himself. The very power that created the universe is released on us, to us and in us so that we, by that power of God, become children of God. It is beyond human understanding, so we must take it by faith. The Bible says that is what the Gospel is, and when we believe it, God counts it as righteousness for us. But it is imperative that we be very careful what we believe!

(9b) What is the role of the Holy Spirit ?

Book 26 LESSON THREE * PART III

Now then Paul comes right into verse 16, which is tied to our lifestyle that's going to merit rewards or lack of it, by bringing up a completely new doctrine in Scripture. You don't find this in the Old Testament, you don't find Jesus teaching it, Peter and the eleven don't teach it, only Paul teaches it, and what is it? **"That God Himself is dwelling in this body."** Now that's a concept that you have to take by faith, because you didn't feel Him move in, you don't feel Him moving around in you, but He's there because the Book says He is. Now let's look at it.

I Corinthians 3:16
"Know ye not that ye are the temple of God, and that the Spirit of God dwelleth in you?"
Even these poor old carnal Corinthians were temples of the living God. To every believer, the moment he believes, the Spirit comes and indwells. Now usually when I teach young people (and that doesn't mean it doesn't apply to older folks), but I usually tell young people, "Now

look, when you go to some ungodly place, you're not going to check God at the door. You take Him wherever you go. You cannot check Him wherever you think it's not fit for Him to be, so you'd better be careful where you go. Because this body is the temple of the indwelling Holy Spirit and He comes the moment we believe!"

I Corinthians 3:16
"Know ye not that ye are the temple of God and that the Spirit of God dwelleth in you?"
Now that's plain language. You don't have to be a theologian to understand that. The third Person of the Trinity, as we refer to Him - God the Father, God the Son and God the Holy Spirit - the third Person of the Trinity comes and indwells the believer. That's why God can know every thought. Now that's scary, isn't it? God knows our thoughts. God knows every place we go. He knows everything we do. Because He's here in our heart. Now in your mind's eye, if you will, go all the way back to when Solomon built the Temple in Jerusalem, which was going to be the dwelling place of God. When the Temple was complete, and they dedicated it, what happened? Well, the presence of God in the Shekinah Glory came right down into that Temple there at Jerusalem. The presence of God dwelt in that dwelling place, which was the Temple Now that was just a foreview of this Age of Grace where, when God saves an individual, he immediately becomes a Temple, a dwelling place. And just like the Shekinah Glory came into Solomon's Temple in Jerusalem, the Holy Spirit comes into us. Not as visibly. It isn't manifested in much the same way, but according to the Book, this is what happens. And if the Book says it, we have to believe it. He is dwelling within us.

Book 23 LESSON TWO * PART IV

Romans 8:26
"Likewise the Spirit (the Holy Spirit who is now indwelling us, according to Paul's teaching) *also helpeth our infirmities* (our weaknesses. There's not much we can do about it because we're dealing with the invisible, in the realm of the Spirit. But let God do it. God can strengthen us in our places of infirmity): *for we know not what we should pray for as we ought: but the Spirit itself maketh intercession for us with groanings which cannot be uttered."*

That verse is kind of hard to comprehend, except to say I think that there will come places in our lives when we just don't know how to pray. We have an idea of what we want, but we can't put it into words. I've told my classes over the years, when you get to that situation, just be quiet, shut up and let the Holy Spirit commune for you. This is not necessarily a tongues experience. That's not what Paul is talking about. But we get to this place where the Holy Spirit actually intercedes on our behalf. Now, come back to I John. This is a different intercessory power that John talks about in his epistle.

I John 2:1
"My little children (who is he talking to? Believers! He doesn't call the unbelieving world his

children. It's the believing element that is being addressed), *these things I write unto you, that ye sin not* (now what have I stressed over the years - that we are under Grace and not under law. Grace is not license. Just because we're under Grace, just because the sin is always less than God's Grace, that doesn't give us license. And so John says the same thing. He begs the believer - sin not! Don't sin!). *And, if any man sin* (that's conditional. What are we going to do? We're going to sin! You might as well admit it), *we have an advocate with the Father* (now what is an advocate? It's an intercessor. We have Someone Who is interceding for us to the Father. And Who is it?), *Jesus Christ the righteous:"*

Absolutely He is! He is there 24 hours a day, every day of the year. I've told my classes over the years, and I think I've even said on the program, this is one of the miracles of our God. I'm sure that at any one moment of time, there are probably a million believers in all areas of the world that are approaching the throne room. But He hears every one as an individual. He doesn't hear just a mumble-jumble of voices coming up before Him. And so when we pray we have that assurance that He hears us and He knows all about us as a person. Now, back in Romans 8, the Holy Spirit is interceding on behalf of us. And again, I think we have all three Persons of the Trinity involved, even in our prayer life. All three Persons are working for us constantly. A little later in this chapter, no wonder Paul will write, **"If God be for us, who can be against us?"** We've got all three Persons constantly working on our behalf. Let's read on.

Romans 8:27

"And he that searcheth the hearts (this is the area in which God works. You and I can't look on each others hearts. I can't judge anyone, nor would I ever try. But God does) *knoweth what is the mind of the Spirit* (now hold it. Where, so far as you and I are concerned, is the Spirit? He's in us. Now, that's a concept that we cannot understand. A person of the Godhead dwelling in me? Absolutely! It's what The Book says. And again, we take it by faith that the third Person of the Trinity, the Holy Spirit is indwelling the believer. And it's through that Holy Spirit that God searches the heart of the believer), *because He* (the Holy Spirit) *maketh intercession for the saints according to the will of God."*

Does that leave out the Son? No! It just involves all three. The Holy Spirit intercedes on our behalf and the Son intercedes on our behalf to the Father. It's just fantastic.

Book 26 LESSON THREE * PART III

Now the question has come up and I think I answered it in my last newsletter, if I'm not mistaken. At the Rapture of the Church, and all the believers are taken out, does that mean the Holy Spirit is gone too? And you know, shortly after I'd sent my newsletter out with my answer, I was reading a well-known theologian and bless his heart (or mine), if he didn't answer it just exactly the same way. And that is; that just because the Holy Spirit goes out and finishes His role as indwelling the individual believer, doesn't remove Him from the earth. Because the Holy Spirit has always been the Omnipresence of God on the planet. You go all the way back to Genesis Chapter 1 and after the deluge of verse 2, when everything is under water, what moved upon the face of the deep? The Spirit! And so all throughout the Old Testament the Holy Spirit was evident, otherwise nobody could ever have knowledge of God. But He did not indwell the Old Testament believers like He does today. And the same way in the Tribulation - yes, as the indwelling Person of the Godhead, in the believer, that is going to end. But He's going to remain on the earth as the Omnipresence of God or else no one would be able to be saved during the Tribulation and we know they will be. So every believer then, in this Age of Grace in which Paul is dealing, is the temple of the Holy Spirit.

Book 43 LESSON TWO * PART II

All right, verse 6 (of II Thessalonians chapter 2) is where we quit in our last study, how that there has to be a restraining force now, beginning at some point in human history to hold everything in check lest things start rolling too fast and the anti-Christ would make his appearance before the right time. I think that is all that is implied here, is that God has instituted a restrainer so that the anti-Christ could not be brought on the scene ahead of time. Hopefully, we made plain that the restrainer is the work of the Holy Spirit, as he indwells you and I as believers.

In closing of the last lesson, I mentioned that even in Israel tonight, with the tremendous chasm between the secular (how shall I call it), the unbelieving Jews. They take no respect for the Scriptures, the Old Testament, as they are secular. They don't take God in their lives at all. In fact I was reminded, as I read that little article, when Iris and I were in Israel the very first time. That goes back too many years! We came out of the hotel dining room after dinner and a well dressed, Jewish business man said "You are from America, aren't you?" We said, "Yes." He said, "What do you think of our little country?" Well we were impressed with how far they had come in just those few years after the Six Day War. So, I just earnestly said, "It's amazing what God has done here!" Do you know what his answer was? **"God didn't have a thing to do with it. We did it."**

Well, see that's the secular attitude. They think God has nothing to do with it. But you see, on the other hand, you have that percentage in Israel who are still, what we would call *religious*. They are Orthodox and they are still spending their time in the Old Testament scriptures. But, it's gotten to the place that the secular part of Israel will be for anything that the religious segment is against. And visa versa. Whether it's political, economical, moral, whatever. As soon as those Rabbi's express themselves, the secular world comes up against it.

Well you see, we are in the same situation in America. Not quite to that extreme, but we are up against the same thing. Just as soon as we try to oppose something, then we are just called mean spirited. We are just simply against everything. Well, of course we are. **It is our responsibility as believers to stand against these things that we know are Biblically wrong.** Yet our nation has become so secular now, that regardless of what the outcome may be, they are going to be counter against us, simply because we are standing on the Scriptures. But, this is our role. This is why God has left us here. We can be used of the Holy Spirit to be a restraining force to hold back these forces of evil. Because we know, that the minute we are out of here (and we are going to see that in the next verse) that the wickedness is going to run rampant across the planet. And, that is what justifies the wrath and vexation of God. Now verse 6.

II Thessalonians 2:6-7a

"And now ye know what withholdeth (or the one who restrains) *that he* (the anti-Christ) *might be revealed in his time.* (or not before the time.) *7. For the mystery* (or the secret) *of iniquity doth already work:…"*

Now there is probably a debate, "When does Paul feel this mystery of iniquity began?" Did it begin as soon as he went out among the Gentile world with the Gospel? Possibly, but I prefer to think that this mystery of iniquity actually began at the tower of Babel. And, my reason for thinking that is **every false religion, even our modern day cults (and throw them in with the Oriental religions) - they all have their roots going right back to the tower of Babel.** Everything false goes back to the tower of Babel. Then if you have done any study at all of these false religions, you will notice that almost all of them, at the core of their belief system, are what they call, the mysteries. Now, you just think for a minute. The Oriental religions are mystery religions. And it is simply because only the inner sanctum of their priesthood have access to these mysteries. You will find this, all the way up through every false religion. And so this is what makes me think that this term *mystery* refers to all these false pagan religions that even Paul was confronting now, face to face, by bringing these people out of it. Indeed, the mysteries of paganism, of false worship, have been already revealed and were on the scene as Paul wrote this letter.

II Thessalonians 2:7a

"For the mystery (secret) *of iniquity doth already work:…"* It was permeating the whole human race. Now the next part is also interesting. There is a lot of debate over it, but I believe if you just look at it in the big picture, that Paul is dealing with the Body of Christ being taken out before this final seven years of wrath comes in. So he says in verse 7.

II Thessalonians 2 : 7b

"…only he who now letteth **(hindereth)** *will let* **(hinder)** *until he be taken out of the way."*

Now those are personal pronouns. So again, I am thinking you have to give the credit to the Holy Spirit. The personal pronoun that **"he who now hindereth,"** the indwelling Holy Spirit, is the same Spirit that we saw in verse 6 **"will hinder."** He's never going to stop. He's never going to give up. I have always felt that this hindering work of the Holy Spirit is such that until the Body of Christ is gone, it's going to be like a dam in the river. And the iniquity is just piling up and piling up, just like a large reservoir. All right, so look at the verse again.

II Thessalonians 2 : 7b

"...only he who now letteth (hindereth. Now I know that the King James says letteth, but again if you have a Bible with a marginal, they have all realized that the word meaning has changed 180 degrees. So the person of the Holy Spirit who) *will let,* (hinder) *until he be taken out of the way."*

Now, if the Holy Spirit is working in the believer today to withstand the forces of wickedness, then it stands to reason that as soon as he is taken out, it will be like the floodgates of wickedness that will come over the world.

Book 11 LESSON TWO * PART IV

The Holy Spirit today in the Age of Grace points people to God, the Son. This is the work of the Holy Spirit, to point lost people to the Son. For we believers, it's the Holy Spirit's work to teach and encourage and reprove us, so that we might in turn bring honor and glory to the Son.

(10b) How can we understand the Trinity ?

Book 1 LESSON Two * PART I

Genesis 1:26

God says, *"Let us make man in our image."* Scripture is always so accurate! Isn't it unique that the plural pronouns are used throughout this verse? Why do you think they were used?

Remember that in Lesson 1, we spent time discussing the Trinity. In verse 26, this triune God is speaking unanimously and simultaneously, saying "Let us make man in our image."

In Lesson 1, I pointed out that the word translated "God" in verse 1 is "Elohim," and it too, refers to the Trinity and is in the plural form. However, we went on to see in the New Testament that even though the entire Trinity was involved and at work in the creative acts recorded in the first few chapters of Genesis, that it was God, the Son, who actually spoke the word which caused creation to become a viable act. Whenever we get to any of the acts of creation, we are dealing directly with God the Son, Jesus the Christ (the anointed one). He is the one who actually spoke the Word, and things happened. That's why John's gospel begins, *"In the beginning was the Word."* I want to emphasize that "Word" indicates or denotes communication. You can't communicate, describe, or accomplish anything without putting it into words.

So God the Son was the One Who, by the spoken word, created everything that's ever been created, including man himself. But we cannot leave out the other two, God the Father, and God the Holy Spirit, because they're all three involved! So in the words of Verse 26, the pronouns are referring directly to the Triune God, but it's actually God the Son Who is speaking all this, including the first man, into reality.

Book 15 LESSON THREE * PART I

Acts 2:22,23

"Ye men of Israel, hear these words: Jesus of Nazareth, a man approved of God among you by miracles and wonders and signs, which God did by him in the midst of you, as ye yourselves also know, "Him (This Jesus), *being delivered by the determinate counsel and foreknowledge of God, ye have taken, and by wicked hands have crucified and slain:"*

Now what does the determinate counsel of God mean? The only way I can look at it is that the Trinity, the Triune God, Three Persons yet One, consulted within this Godhead before anything was ever created. They agreed within the Trinity, knowing everything that would take place: that fallen man would need a Redeemer, and salvation would be that Second Person of the Trinity Who would step down from the invisible Godhead, take on flesh, and go the way of the finished work of the Cross for man's redemption. Now all of that was foreknown and consummated in the thought-process of the Trinity. When I teach this, I don't imply that the Three sat down around a table and talked about which One would do what, as men would do. But within the Trinity of the Godhead, whether it was a split second or whatever, all three Persons of the Godhead had agreed that this is the way it would be done. And that's exactly what this verse means, *"...by the determinate counsel."*

Book 1 LESSON ONE * PART III

Hebrews 1:2

Verse 2 says; *"by whom* (Jesus) *also He made the worlds."*

These verses indicate that God (The Triune God), ordained all this to take place, but it was through Jesus (God The Son) that the words of creation were spoken. It's very difficult for us to understand the Trinity. Look at John 14:8. Philip says to Jesus, *"Lord, show us the Father."*

Jesus' answer to him in verse 9, was: *"'He that hath seen me hath seen the Father.'"* Now turn to Isaiah 9:6-7:

"For unto us (Israel) *a child is born, unto us a son is given; and the government shall be upon his shoulder, and his name shall be called Wonderful, Counsellor, The mighty God, The ever lasting Father, The Prince of Peace."*

This passage refers to Jesus, yet it calls Him, *"The Everlasting Father."* There is such intricacy in the Trinity. Father, Son and Holy Spirit are each separate and unique, yet they are One together. And we must be careful not to think of them as in order from top to bottom -

they are all co-equal. One is not more important, or more powerful, or more in control than any of the other two.

Book 25 LESSON TWO * PART I

Colossians 2:2,3

"That their hearts (and Paul is speaking of the believers up there in Laodicea in Asia Minor) *might be comforted, being knit together in love, and unto all riches of the full assurance of understanding, to the acknowledgment* (or the acceptance) *of the mystery of God, and of the Father, and of Christ. In whom are hid all the treasures of wisdom and knowledge."*

So we see that all treasures of wisdom and knowledge are hidden in the mysteries of God. What is the revelation here that the Old Testament is vague about? The Trinity! Now we know that the Old Testament has evidences of the Triune God, but you see this is why the Hebrews, and the Rabbi's even of our own present day, call Christians almost pagan because we worship three Gods. They don't recognize the Trinity back there in the Old Testament, and they still don't. But here is a revelation that God is a Triune God, and it's a revelation that Paul brings out that God is the Father, Son, and Holy Spirit.

Book 29 LESSON THREE * PART II

Colossians 1:13-15

"Who hath delivered us from the power of darkness, and hath translated us into the kingdom of his dear Son: In whom we have redemption through his blood, even the forgiveness of sins: Who (speaking of the Son up in verse 13.) *is the image of the invisible God, the firstborn of every creature: "*

Now Who is the invisible God? The Triune! The Trinity: God the Father, God the Son, and God the Holy Spirit. They're Spirit, and they were invisible, but out of that invisible Triune God stepped the Son, and He became visible. In the Old Testament economy it was a temporary thing, and then He would disappear, but in our New Testament account He became visible, tangible, touchable, He lived in the flesh by virtue of His Bethlehem birth. All right, it's the same God now manifested in the flesh by the Son.

Book 10 LESSON THREE * PART III

Psalms 2:2,3

"The kings of the earth set themselves (the rulers of the Gentile nations), *and the rulers* (of Israel), *take counsel together, against the Lord, and against his anointed, saying, Let us break their bands asunder, and cast away their cords from us."*

What's this about? Rome, Pilate and others in authority, consorting with the high priests and rulers of Israel to crucify the Messiah. In those final days of Christ's earthly life before He was crucified, what's the Jews position? When Pilate said, "I see nothing wrong with this man," they said, "We have no king, but Caesar. Away with this Man. We'll not have Him to rule over us. Crucify him."

That's the prophecy. They're rejecting His offer of ruling them as a benevolent King. They don't want any part of it. So they say, *"Break his bands asunder."* I'd like to stop a second. Do you see the pronouns here are plural? Where the people say, *"Let us break their bands asunder, and cast away their cords from us."* Why plural? Remember what I taught you way back in Genesis Chapter 1, Elohim is a plurality. It's a Godhead of three, not one. Here's the reason for the pronoun. Same way back in Genesis 1:26, when God said, *"Let us make man in our image,"* what are the pronouns? They're plural. Because Elohim is a Trinity. He's a plurality in the Godhead.

Book 32 LESSON ONE * PART IV

PAUL'S GLIMPSE OF GLORY
II CORINTHIANS 11:22 - GALATIANS 1:7
Let's pick up here in Chapter 13, and I'm not going to take this last chapter verse by verse, as you can read it at your leisure. However, I do want to close the Book with the final verse which is verse 14. This verse is probably the clearest statement concerning the Trinity that you can find anywhere in Scripture, next to Christ's baptism. I know when someone writes wanting to know where we get the idea of the Trinity (and if we can give them Scriptures for it), that the two we use the most are this one and where Christ was baptized:

Matthew 3:16,17
"And Jesus, when he was baptized, went up straightway out of the water: and, lo, the heavens were opened unto him, and he saw the Spirit of God descending like a dove, and lighting upon him: 17. And lo a voice from heaven, saying, `This is my beloved Son, in whom I am well pleased.'"

At His baptism you have all three persons of the Trinity there at one time. Now here in this verse we have the apostle Paul making reference also to the three Persons of the Godhead in a pure unadulterated statement. Now verse 14:
II Corinthians 13:14
"The grace of the Lord Jesus Christ, and the love of God, (The Father is implied) *and the communion of the Holy Ghost, be with you all. Amen."*

Now it's interesting that, normally when we speak of the Trinity, out of habit we put them in the order of God the Father, God the Son, and God the Holy Spirit. But when you look at this verse, there is something different. Paul changes the order of the three. Paul puts Christ first rather than the Father. Not that there is any change in the way the Trinity operates. Never. You've all heard me teach that there is no such thing as God the Father having power over God the Son, and over the Spirit or vice versa. They are all three co-equal. They are all three members of the Godhead. Let me take you, for a moment, to the Book of Colossians where Paul makes that same statement.

Here is where the Jewish people in their Old Testament background refer to Christianity as a polytheism. They call us a religion of three Gods. But we're not three Gods, it's three Persons in one God. And of course the Old Testament does not clarify that like it does in the New Testament.

Colossians 2:8,9
"Beware lest any man spoil you through philosophy and vain deceit, after the tradition of men, after the rudiments of the world, and not after Christ. 9. For in him (that is in Christ) *dwelleth all the fulness of the Godhead bodily."*

Now backing up a little bit to Colossians Chapter 1. And I think all of this gives us a clear picture that the Godhead is that invisible Spirit out of which God the Son stepped and became visible.

Colossians 1:15-19
Who (speaking of God the Son and the redeeming Blood in verses 13 and 14) *is the image of the invisible God,* (the Godhead) *the first born of every creature:* (in other words Christ was pre-eternal in His existence just like God the Father, and God the Spirit.) *16. For by him* (God the Son) *were all things created, that are in heaven, and that are in earth, visible and invisible, whether they be thrones, or dominions, or principalities, or powers; all things were created by him, and for him; 17. And he is before all things, and by him all things consist.* (or held together. Remember now this is speaking of God the Son) *18. And he is the head of the body, the church: who is the beginning, the firstborn from the dead;* (referring to His resurrection) *that in all things he might have the preeminence. 19. For it pleased the Father that in him* (Christ) *should all fulness dwell;"*

So the members of the Godhead are not One above the other, but rather they are all co-equal. Now returning to our text in II Corinthians. This is why, now, that Paul in complete liberty, and again, under the inspiration of the Holy Spirit, can sort of reverse the order that we normally use. Looking at verse 14 again:

II Corinthians 13:14
"The grace of the Lord Jesus Christ, and the love of God, and the communion of the Holy Ghost, be with you all. Amen."

Book 23 LESSON TWO * PART I

Romans 8:10,11

"And if Christ be in you, the body (the old Adam again) *is dead because of sin* (in other words Adam and the flesh was all under the curse, and this body is going to die if The Lord doesn't come to translate it. That's all part of the fall of man that death came in, and so all men has to die)*; but the* (Holy) *Spirit is life because of righteousness."* I think Paul is referring to eternal life, that life which will never end because of righteousness.

"But if the Spirit of him that raised up Jesus from the dead (here we have the implication again of the Trinity. God the Father used the power of the Holy Spirit to raise the Son. See how clear that is? So if He) *dwell in you, he that raised up Christ from the dead shall also quicken your mortal bodies by his Spirit that dwelleth in you."*

(11b) In the Age of Grace, what does the bread and wine (communion) speak of ?

Book 4 LESSON TWO * PART II

In the Age of Grace, what does the bread and wine speak of? The Lord's Supper; the Communion Table. The only way we can really identify that is to go back to Matthew's Gospel where we have The Lord's Supper. Jesus instituted The Lord's Supper at the Last Supper, at the Passover.

Matthew 26:20
"Now when the even was come, he sat down with the twelve."

Matthew 26:26,27
"And as they were eating, Jesus took bread, and blessed it, and brake it, and gave it to the disciples, and said, `Take, eat; this is my body.' And he took the cup, and gave thanks, and gave it to them, saying, `Drink ye all of it;'"

I'd like to ask a question. Did the disciples understand what all of this stood for? They didn't have the foggiest notion. They followed His directions, but there is no explanation by The Lord Jesus, or even by the writer of this Gospel account, that they had any idea what He was doing. So, we have to wait until we come to the writings of the Apostle Paul. Now we understand what it was all for. Turn with me to I Corinthians, Chapter 11. Here, again, is progressive revelation. The eleven there at the night of the Passover didn't understand it. Jesus didn't explain it; it wasn't time yet. The Lord's Table of the bread and the cup is a memorial of His death, and on the night of the Last Supper His death hadn't taken place yet.

I Corinthians 11:23-26
"For I have received of the Lord that which also I delivered unto you, That the Lord Jesus, the

141

same night in which he was betrayed, took bread: And when he had given thanks, he brake it, and said, `Take, eat; this is my body, which is broken for you: this do in remembrance of me.' After the same manner also he took the cup, when he had supped, saying, `This cup is the new testament in my blood: this do ye, as oft as ye drink it, in remembrance of me.'" Verse 26 gives us the explanation. *"For as often as ye eat this bread, and drink this cup, ye do shew the Lords death till he come.'"*

This is the purpose of The Lord's Supper. It is remembering what Christ accomplished on the Cross; that just as in ignominy and shame His Body was broken, the bread is broken. The pouring out of His Blood is, of course, in the cup. Back in Genesis we have the picture of His death, burial and Resurrection, but that's all.

Book 28 LESSON ONE * PART IV

Genesis 14:18
"And Melchizedek king of Salem brought forth bread and wine: and he was the priest of the most high God."

Now that wasn't what they normally used in the sacrifices of Abraham's day. So why in the world did Melchizedek offer bread and wine? Well, it was a subtle prophecy. Oh, it was so subtle because what was the bread and the wine, as Jesus administered it in Matthew 26, going to represent? The resurrection. **And that's what the whole idea of the Lord's supper is. It is to be a constant reminder that every time we partake of that bread and that cup it is a reminder of that finished work of the Cross. And this is the first time that's it's explained. In fact one commentator that I've read puts it this way**: "This is probably the first time that Jesus is quoted chronologically in the Scriptures, because the Four Gospels hadn't been written yet. Have you ever thought of that? The Four Gospels hadn't been written so Paul couldn't go to the Gospel of Matthew. But rather Paul's interpretation of the Lord's supper came by revelation. And isn't it amazing how God does everything in His own order, as before the Four Gospels were ever written Paul writes to the Corinthians the very same words. Now read on in I Corinthians, verse 26, and here is the doctrinal reason for the Lord's supper.

I Corinthians 11:26
"For as often as ye eat this bread, and drink this cup, ye do shew (or remind yourself of) *the Lord's death till he come."*

Now I'm going to point out two things. There is no stipulation from the apostle as to how often a Church practices the Lord's supper. I don't care if your denomination practices it every Sunday, that's your prerogative. If you want to practice it once a year that's also your prerogative. Because the word is whenever you have the Lord's Supper you had better have the right mindset when you do partake of it. And that is that you are reminding yourself that Christ died, His blood was shed, and He arose from the dead. And that's the only purpose of the Lord and it is to be a solemn experience. And again, the Corinthians were so abusing this b beautiful picture in type, by their indulgence with food, getting half drunk on too much w how in the world could they receive the impact of such a solemn service. So Paul had to upbraid them and tell them to stop it, because it was a solemn occasion. And as the last part of verse 26 says the Lord's table will not stop until the Lord returns. Now verse 27, and here comes the apostles description of what our attitude should be as we partake.

I Corinthians 11:27,28

"Wherefore whosoever shall eat this bread, and drink this cup of the Lord, unworthily, shall be guilty of the body and blood of the Lord. But let a man examine himself, and so let him eat of that bread, and drink of that cup."

When it says, "But let a man examine himself,..." I think that's the secret to behavior at the Lord's table. You don't examine the next person to you or judge someone else, but just look at your own heart, and attitude. Am I right with the Lord? Am I right with my fellow believers? And if you can say 'yes' and 'amen' to that, then you feel free to partake. If you can't, you'd better refrain, because then you are drinking and eating condemnation. Now verse 29.

I Corinthians 11:29

"For he that eateth and drinketh unworthily, eateth and drinketh damnation to himself, not discerning the Lord's body."

That is speaking of someone who partakes of the Lord's table with the wrong attitude. The Corinthians were going into that supper with almost an attitude of revelry, totally wrong. Many others of the Corinthians had a real thing against someone across the room, and their enmity was just like sparks, and Paul tells them that won't work. You can't take the Lord's table with that kind of attitude. Now verse 30. Since the Corinthians were guilty of many things that should have kept them from partaking:

I Corinthians 11:30

"For this cause many are weak and sickly among you, (in other words God was already chastising them by taking away their health) *and many sleep."*

What does he mean? They had died. Now there is a sin unto death recorded in one of John's little epistles, and we won't have time to look at it today, but John also tells us that we don't pray for it. Even though you think that someone is awfully out of step, you never pray, "Lord take them out." That's not our prerogative, but the Lord does have that prerogative. That if a believer will not shape up, and if a believer continues to walk in known sin, then yes, God will take them, because He's not going let anybody drag His name through the mud. Now we know there are people who have made profession of salvation, they've probably been members of the church,

...nd they're doing the same thing. And if the Lord doesn't deal with them, if the Lord doesn't chastise them, then Paul teaches in the Book of Hebrews that they are not His children.

Hebrews 12:5-8
"...My son, despise not thou the chastening of the Lord, nor faint when thou art rebuked of him: For whom the Lord loveth he chasteneth, and scourgeth every son whom he receiveth. If ye endure chastening, God dealeth with you as with sons; for what son is he whom the father chasteneth not? But if ye be without chastisement, whereof all are partakers, then are ye bastards, and not sons."

So the Lord had been chastening the Corinthians because Paul says:

I Corinthians 11:30
"For this cause many are weak and sickly among you, and many sleep."

Book 29 LESSON TWO * PART II

Ephesians 3:3
"How that by revelation (the same word he used in Galatians) *he* (The Lord Jesus Himself) *made known unto me the* (what?) *mystery; ..."*

Now we covered all the mysteries in earlier lessons. And they are that whole composite of truth that makes for the Church Age. And they all come from the pen of the apostle Paul. I was talking to someone they other day, and they said, " Why do you make this much of Paul?" And I said, "Let me ask you something. I don't care what denomination handle you have. Do you have a pastor and deacons and Church elders?" He said, "Well, yes." I said, "Where did you get the instructions for them?" Well, he didn't know. I said, "Well, I'll tell you. You got it from Timothy. And who wrote Timothy? Paul! Does your Church practice The Lord's table?" He said, "Oh, yeah." I said, "Where did you get it?" He thought maybe when Jesus said it. I said, "No, Jesus didn't put anything on it. All He said was, "This is My body and this is My blood, but He didn't give any instructions for the communion service. So where did we get it? From I Corinthians 11." And down the line you can go with every facet of what 99% of Christendom practices doctrinally. They get it from Paul. And yet they'll never give him the time of day. It's amazing isn't it.

(12b) Will God perform miracle healings?

Book 28 LESSON TWO * PART III

I Corinthians 12:9
"To another faith by the same Spirit; (now whether you know it or not, if you're a believer where did you get the wherewithal to believe the Gospel? From the Holy Spirit, because it's a gift,

and as we exercise that gift of faith we respond by believing. Also some have greater faith than others and there's nothing wrong with that.) *to another the gifts of healing by the same Spirit;"*

There's no doubt they exercised this gift in the early Church. We know that even Paul himself exercised this gift in the Book of Acts as he performed miracles. But by the time you get to his later letters there's not a word about these kind of miracles, and he doesn't perform them himself. One of his best friends, and fellow laborers in the work was sick on the island of Miletus, and was nigh on to death, but could Paul heal him? No. So what did he admonish the believers to do? The same as we do today; pray for him. And we know that Timothy evidently had a stomach ailment, and we know Paul didn't heal him, he gave him a remedy for it, but he didn't heal him. And it was the same way with many of his own catastrophes in his life experience. Did he get healed? No. The Lord brought him through them, but no sign of any miraculous healing. In this area of Scripture, remember, that it's only in the letter to this carnal Corinthian Church that he deals with these particular gifts. Now let's finish verse 10:

I Corinthians 14:22a
"Wherefore tongues are for a sign, not to them that believe, but to them that believe not: but (the flip side) *prophesying* (being able to speak forth the Word before they had the New Testament)..."*

So signs and all this is not going to accomplish all that much, but what will? Preaching the Word! This is what people need to hear today, people have to hear the Gospel (Ref. I Corinthians 15:1-4). They have to hear the plan of salvation, they don't have to see some kind of miracle, and I'm not condemning these people that can prove some miraculous manifestation. But they've got to prove it before I believe it. If they can prove it, then I'll say, "Yes, I know we have a God Who can perform miracles." I know God can heal miraculously, and I do not deny that.

Book 38 Lesson One • Part I

Ephesians 4:15
"But speaking the truth in love,..."
Not with the idea of causing a controversy, or argument, but rather in the spirit of love we are supposed to be sharing the Gospel with a lost world. We are to get so skilled with the Gospel and supporting Scriptures that when we get out into the work day world we'll be able to share in a moment if the occasion arises.

I got a call from a gentlemen from Mississippi just before we left to come up here this morning. And he had been to the pharmacy to pick up a prescription, and had seen a young mother with a super hyperactive child who was taking a prescription for being hyperactive. The mother had told him the medication works, but leaves the child in depression. This gentlemen said he felt so bad because he didn't have any advice for her. He said I couldn't tell her to just turn it over to

God, because here he is a believer and had his prescription in hand.

I said, "Did you share with her your knowledge of the Word and the power of prayer, and tell her that you would be passing out the prayer needs of that little fellow? Because I know that prayer works?" Jerry you know it works don't you? My we've made many, many prayer requests across our classes in Oklahoma. Now I don't believe in "healers" you know that, but I believe in the power of prayer. So we just need to learn to share with people how that God can meet our needs by simply making it an item of prayer, and we know that God can do it. Now He may not always answer the way we think He should, but He's still a prayer-answering God. Now these are all the things that Paul is referring to here.

Ephesians 4:15a
"But speaking the truth in love,..."

Letting people know that Christ loves them, and that He died for them, and that He defeated all the powers of Satan and death when He arose from the dead.

Book 41 LESSON ONE * PART II

Romans 5:1-2a
"Therefore being justified by faith, we have peace with God through our Lord Jesus Christ: (and now since we're justified and have peace with God) *2. By whom also we have access by faith into this grace wherein we stand,…"*

See you can't separate salvation from Grace. None of us deserved salvation, none of us deserved what Christ did for us, but it's all of Grace! And it's amazing how few believers understand that. Another place where Paul use this "peace with God" is in the Book of Philippians, and we looked at that not too many weeks ago. And in this portion of Scripture it's in relationship to our prayer life as we make request. We'll begin with verse 6. These are my two favorite verses when it comes to prayer.

Philippians 4:6
"Be careful (or worry*) for nothing; but in every thing by prayer and supplication with thanks-giving let your request be made know with God."*

There's no strings attached to that verse. That is a free access into the Throne Room of God to let all of our supplication and request be known, but with thanksgiving, but now verse 7. Regardless how God answers our request, and He may not spare our loved one who may be terminal, He may not grant healing to them. He may not saved a financial empire, or a marriage that we think needs to be saved. He may not answer the way we think that He should, but this verse 7 is the answer to every prayer.

Philippians 4:7
"And the peace of God, (that which was imparted to us the moment we believed. That we are no longer in a warfare against Him, we're no longer His enemy, but we are at peace with Him, and the peace of God) *which passeth all understanding, shall keep your hearts and minds through Christ Jesus."*

In other words you can't explain this peace you have with God, it's beyond us, but we know it's there, and it will keep our heart and mind.

(13b) How should someone that is saved deal with sin ?

Book 37 Lesson Two • Part I

Romans 3:23-24
"For all have sinned, and come short of the glory of God; (that's everyone of us. But look at the next verse.) *24. Being justified freely by his grace through the redemption that is in Christ Jesus:"*

Now you all know what redemption means? That's the process of God buying us back out of the slavery of sin. When I teach Romans chapter 3 I always use the analogy of the Roman slave market, and I think it's a very appropriate one, because it was very real. As the Romans would go out with their legions and they would conquer other people they would bring back, especially the younger people who were capable of slave duty, to Rome and they would end up in the slave market. And I drew the analogy, here we have a young blond, blue eyed fellow from northern Europe who finds himself in this market. Now that slave market was awful, because if you were bought out as a common slave you could end up doing any kind of horrible slave labor to include being sold to shipmasters to row their ships. It was awful, it was hot, and when they died, they just pitched them overboard. And if these slaves were not bought they could end up in the coliseums as meat for the wild animals. So that was the prospect of a Roman slave market.

But there was also the good side They could have a benefactor come and buy them out of the slave market. Say a benevolent slave owner would buy a slave and clean him up, give him a whole new set of clothes, give him light duty around his estate of trimming the lawns and so forth, and remember the Romans lived sumptuously. So here's this young slave who's been bought out of that horrible situation, and given this beautiful place to work, and have all the best food. Then one day this benevolent Roman owner comes and says, *"Young man I'm going to go one step further, I'm going to give you your freedom. I have bought your citizenship. You are free to go and do whatever you want to do."* Now the analogy I've always used before is, "What's this young man going to say? 'Listen you've done so much for me, and I have learned to love you so much, I don't want my freedom, but rather I want to stay here and serve you the rest of my life.'"

Now that's where I've always left that analogy. But you know what a lot of Christians are doing now? **What if this same young man would say, "I want to stay right here and serve you, but once a week can I go back into the slave market?"** Now isn't that ridiculous? Isn't that as ridiculous as you can get? Here he's been spared the horrors of the slave market, and that's where every lost person is, they're in Satan's slave market. Christ paid the price of redemption, He bought us out of it, and then we have the audacity to say, **"But can't I just go back and get a taste of that sinful world once in a while?"** Listen that's what Christians are doing when they go back into the world! And to me it just does not fit. I'm not saying we're going to be perfect, of course we're not. We all fail, we all sin, but to go back into gross sin, and just glibly say, **"Oh well, I'm saved and don't have anything to worry about."** I don't think a true believer can look at it that way.

When a true believer sins, they're going to be convicted as David was. And when David saw his sin, what does the Book of Psalms say he does? He wept tears of repentance, and oh how he bemoaned the fact that not only had he sinned against the humans that were involved, but against God. And when we sin, this is what we have to come back and realize. Well all of this I just sort of lob into the *"Unsearchable Riches of Christ."* It's beyond human comprehension. I can't understand it, and I don't think anyone else can. But does that mean, we just close our eyes, and say, "Forget it, I can't understand it anyway?" No. **You just keep digging, and learning, and keep getting more and more excited about what Christ has done for us. And not only just for the here and now, but for all of eternity to come.** Just like Paul says in I Corinthians chapter 2.

I Corinthians 2:9
"But as it is written, Eye hath not seen, nor ear heard, neither have entered into the heart of man, the things which God hath prepared for them that love him."

And that's about as much as it tells us about what we're going to enjoy in eternity. We don't know because the Bible doesn't tell us, but we know it's going to be fabulous. **What God has in store for us is going to be a million times better than the things you and I like to do down here, and it's all because of the** *"unsearchable riches of Christ."* Oh to have the knowledge that we can come into the very throne room of heaven in prayer and petitions is simply incomprehensible. Isn't it? Just think we can immediately come into the very throne room, without having to go through any rituals. We don't have to go into some prescribed place, at a prescribed time or God won't hear us. As you sit there and as I speak you can be in an attitude of prayer, and you're right in the throne room. Now that's all part of the *"unsearchable riches of Christ."*

Book 31 LESSON TWO * PART III

II Corinthians 7:12
"Wherefore, though I wrote unto you, (I Corinthians) *I did it not for his cause that had done the wrong,* (although certainly that man was involved) *nor for his cause that suffered wrong, but that our care for you in the sight of God might appear unto you."*

Now think about these things. What's Paul saying? If Paul would have treated this as the congregation was and just glossed over it, what would that have said to the congregation about him? Well he's no better than the rest of us. He looks at like we do so it must not be all that bad. But when Paul dealt with it, and he dealt with it severely, when he told them. "You deal with this man, and turn him over to the power of Satan that Satan can touch the flesh unless he turns around in repentance and gets right with God." I mean it's just a perfect picture of how you and I, even today, deal with sin because God hates it. God will never wink at sin even though He has paid for it and forgiven it through His death on the Cross, yet God is never going to wink at sin. He can't. So Paul tells us that all of us profited from this situation. Paul did, the congregation did, and certainly the guilty party did.

Book 41 LESSON THREE * PART IV

Colossians 3:12-13b
"Put on therefore, (as a result of all that Christ has done) *as the elect of God,* (the ones that God has saved by His Grace) *holy* (set apart) *and beloved, bowels of mercies, kindness, humbleness of mind, meekness, longsuffering;* (now verse 13. This is part of the Christian Grace.) *13. Forbearing one another, …"*

You know what I've always said? You don't have to like everybody, but you've got to love them. I mean there are some people that you like to be with a lot more than others, and that's perfectly normal. But whether we like them or not, we're to forbear them, and not be all angered and upset and have nothing to do with them, because everyone of us that have things that irritate others. I know I probably irritate people, but I thank God that they forbear with me, and that's what we have to do with others. But the one thing we can never compromise is our love. We love them regardless, see? Now reading on in verse 13, I'm going to go rather quickly now, because I think we can finish Colossians this lesson. These are all just plain logical, common sense admonitions from the pen of the apostle as to how to walk and live with a child of God.

Colossians 3:13
"Forbearing one another, and forgiving one another, if any man have a quarrel against any: (and we're going to, because we're human. We're going to have differences of opinion. We're going to have some unhappy situations, but don't let it destroy your relations. And if you have a quarrel,) *even as Christ forgave you, so also do ye."*

Now what does that tell you? **We're forgiven, we're totally forgiven, and I don't have to go back everyday and say, "Oh God forgive me." That's all done, it was done at the cross. A lot of people can't quite agree with me on that, and that's all right, but forgiveness is a done deal.** Now I know we have to still recognize our sins, and see them as God does. And I think we have to ask God for cleansing, and my whole approach to that is, the night that the Lord was washing Peter's feet. He came to Peter and what did Peter say?

John 11:8-10
"Peter saith unto him, Thou shalt never wash my feet. Jesus answered him, If I wash thee not, thou hast no part with me. 9. Simon Peter saith unto him, Lord not my feet only, but also my hands and my head. 10. Jesus saith to him, he that is washed needeth not save to wash his feet, but is clean every whit and ye are clean, but not all.

Peter had already been saved. He'd had his bath already, but by virtue of walking from that bath house to his home in the ancients, the streets were filthy, and before he could go into his own home, he would have to wash his feet. Well the picture of course is where we are. **We've been saved, we're forgiven, we're cleansed, but we're still in this old world, and as we go though this world our feet are getting dirty, and so what do we need? Cleaning!**

We don't need forgiveness, that's all done, but we need cleansing, and how do we cleanse? I just told somebody on the phone yesterday. How do you wash a strainer? A gravy strainer or a tea strainer, how do you wash it? You certainly can't run a piece of cloth through every little opening, so how do you wash a strainer? Oh you just swish it through the water, isn't that right? You just simply cleanse it with the washing of water. **Now that's what Paul uses in Ephesians, and this is what we have to do. We get daily cleansing, by the washing of the water, but what does Paul say the water is? The Word of God! Do you see that? Boy isn't that beautiful,? We don't have to come crawling to God every time we do something that is wrong, and plead that He forgive us.** He must get tired of that, and tells us, "I've forgiven you!" But we do need cleansing. We have to see our sin as He sees it and then be cleansed from it by the Word of God.

Book 9 LESSON ONE * PART IV

Hebrews 3:13
"But exhort one another daily, while it is called To day (while we still have this kind of an opportunity); *lest any of you be hardened through the deceitfulness of sin."*

Always stop and think. How do we recognize sin, and how do we deal with sin? I want it in only one word. **Faith.** Because, unless we can believe what God says about certain activities or certain acts, we don't know that it's sin. **But when God says it and we believe it, then we know what it is.** Our whole daily walk is prompted by faith in God's Word. Think about it. When

Romans 3:23 says that ***"For all have sinned and come short of the glory of God,"*** I always said that's the first step to salvation, to believe that I am what The Book says that I am. And that is, short of the glory of God. **It's taking God at His Word** concerning myself, concerning you. So faith is that which guides us not only into salvation, but all through our Christian experience. It's all based on what The Book says. Not what someone else says. People have told me and I appreciate it, **"You know, you don't condemn this and you don't condemn that. Do you notice that?"** I don't have to. I don't have to tell people, "Stop doing this and stop doing that" because as soon as they get into The Book and see what The Book says, by faith, then they're going to take appropriate action. I still maintain that if you get people into The Book, you get them to believe in what God says, and all those things that a lot of people scream about; they'll take care of themselves.

(14b) Are we supposed to give 10% of our income for a tithe ?

Book 30 LESSON ONE * PART IV

I Corinthians 15:58
"Therefore, my beloved brethren, be ye stedfast, unmoveable, always abounding in the work of the Lord, forasmuch as ye know that your labour is not in vain in the Lord."

We may not reap the rewards of our labor in this life. We may go to the grave as poor as church mice, but don't let that discourage you. God hasn't promised that, "Just because we're believers we're going to drive cadillacs, and live in mansions." No way, but God has promised that He is keeping a record of our earthly activities. Then one day we're going to cash in on the rewards in glory, and remember that Paul is always teaching that. We are to run the race for rewards. Now go to Chapter 16 to wind up I Corinthians. Here Paul is going to deal with something totally different from resurrection. Here he is going to come down to the nitty-gritty of, **"How we're to give."** Many people are hung up on the legal system of tithing. I've got nothing against giving. **But you are not under the tithe**. Now I know this is going to ruffle a few feathers, but remember the tithe was part of the Law. Tithing was given only to the tribe of Levi. I dare say if we could ask some of our Jewish friends whether they teach tithing today, I'd be very surprised if they would say yes. Because they, too, do not know who the Levites are so I just have to doubt that good Jewish people still tithe. Always remember that Paul never says tithe, because that was part of the Law, **but that doesn't say that God doesn't expect you to give**. Let's look how Paul puts it.

I Corinthians 16:1a
"Now concerning the collection (of money) *for the saints,..."*

Paul was always instructed to remember the poor saints at Jerusalem. Why? They had cashed in land and everything they had and brought the money to the feet of the Twelve disciples. It all went into a common kitty back there in Acts Chapters 2 and 3 in light of the Kingdom. But the Kingdom didn't come because the Jews had rejected it. So what happened to these poor Jewish saints? They had to live off the kitty and I imagine it was a pretty good existence for a while. But God took care of them through Paul's Gentile converts, and the money was taken back to Jerusalem for them. Now continuing on:

I Corinthians 16:1,2

"Now concerning the collection for the saints, (Jewish saints at Jerusalem) *as I have given order to the churches of Galatia, even so do ye* (at Corinth). *Upon the first day of the week* (not on the seventh day Sabbath. Why first day of the week? Resurrection day!) *let every on of you lay by him in store,* (as a tithe? No, but rather) *as God hath prospered him, that there be no gatherings when I come."*

Now that's one of the beauties of the Christian life, that's the beauty of God's Grace. He has left us with that free will. We can give as much as we want to, but God is not putting the thumb on our head, and saying, "You will give 10%! Now that's a guideline, and I'll always say that. God more or less lets it be known that 10% is a guideline for giving. But God's not going to zap you if you don't give 10%. Now you may lose some reward in glory, but you are under no mandate under Paul's teaching to give a set amount. That's up to you as a believer as God has prospered you. And God has enough respect for your free will as a believer that you're going to give as much as you can.

Paul told these believers at Corinth to take this offering before he came so that they wouldn't be under his influence. He wanted that all taken care of before he arrived. Paul doesn't want them to dig down in their other pocket and say, "Paul is here, and he'd better see how much I've given." But Paul wanted that all taken care of before he got there.

Book 31 LESSON THREE * PART I

Philippians 2:6,7a

"Who, (speaking of Christ Jesus in verse 5) **being in the form of God, thought it not robbery to be equal with God:** (because He was God, the God of creation, the God who owns everything in the universe) **7. But made himself of no reputation, and took upon him the form of a servant..."**

Now too often we read that word servant and we kind of glide over it without realizing what is the better term for servant? Slave. How much material goods did a slave have? None. He may be here today and gone tomorrow. The rowers in the ships of those days were down there in the stench-ridden hot areas of the ship. They rowed until they died and then they were just pitched overboard. How much of this worlds good did those fellows have? None. Well this is where the Lord Jesus took Himself. He took Himself to the depths of being a slave with absolutely nothing of this world's goods to call His own. Unbelievable? It is from the human side. I can't comprehend it, but it's what the Word declares. The Almighty God Himself in the Person of Christ became a slave in so many words. Now reading on:

Philippians 2:7b
"...was made in the likeness of men:"
Now imagine from the exalted area of the Godhead to come down to this earth, and become nothing more than a human being like the rest of us, how far can you go? And yet that's what He did.

Philippians 2:8
"And being found in fashion as a man, he humbled himself, (He didn't have to) **and became obedient unto death, even the death of the cross."**
Now why is Paul using that in relation to Christian giving? Well we have to take that same kind of attitude. If God, in the Person of Christ, was willing to leave that area of absolute control of the universe and took on the role of a slave for our salvation, then who are we to say, "Yeah, but I can't give anything." Now back to II Corinthians Chapter 8:

II Corinthians 8:10,11
"And herein I give my advice: for this is expedient for you, who have begun before, not only to do, but also to be forward, (zealous) **a year ago. 11. Now therefore perform** (or complete) **the doing of it; that as there was a readiness to will, so there may be a performance also out of that which ye have."**

What's Paul driving at? Well for the last year he has been encouraging these churches in Greece to get their offerings ready for the day when someone would come along and pick them up and transport them to Jerusalem. Now as I was studying this, I couldn't help but remember something that Gary, the station manager, had told me a long time ago. For those who are in this business of television that statistically - and I know that there are lies, and then there are statistics, but nevertheless statistics do have a certain amount of relevance here. But statistically, out of 300 people who may be listening to me over the next several weeks, most will say, "Now I'm going to send that man an offering." How many will actually get around to doing it? One. Isn't that amazing? But you see that's human nature, and Paul was dealing with the same thing. For a whole year they had been talking about getting these collections ready for the poor saints in Jerusalem. But they still hadn't done it. So Paul says, **"Let's get busy and complete it."** Paul wanted it all done before he got there so they wouldn't give because of his presence. And I understand exactly how he felt because you never like to make someone feel obligated to give just because you happen to be there personally on the scene. So this is exactly what he's talking about. Now verse 12. Remember this is all in regard to Christian giving, and notice there's not a word in here of him naming ten percent. He never says a tithe. All he's talking about is the general concept of giving.

II Corinthians 8:12
"For if there be first a willing mind, (remember everything we say or do has to begin with the thought process.) *it is accepted according to that a man hath, and not according to that he hath not."*

Now does God expect someone who is on a very meager income, maybe nothing more than just a little social security check, to give all that to ministry or some church? No way. More than once I've had to write to someone and tell them, "Now listen, if you're on a meager income I don't expect a dime." Now that's between them and God, and if they feel that God is still instructing them to give some then that's fine. But I never want someone on a meager income to feel obligated to support this ministry. Other ministries may not care, but I don't want it on this one. **But here God is making it so clear that giving is based on that ability to give**. And now in verse 13.

II Corinthians 8:13
"For I mean not that other men be eased, and ye burdened:"

In other words, Paul says, "He is not going to make anybody, whether they are wealthy or poor, to feel obligated to give because of his presence. Do you see that? Now he comes all the way down through verse 16 - 24 speaking of the men who would be coming along to pick up these offerings. And again he's showing the need for integrity in handling the affairs of God. Paul is telling the Corinthians that the men who are probably headed up by Titus, are men of integrity, they don't have to worry about turning over their offerings to them because they will get every penny of it to Jerusalem where it's supposed to go. Now I want to come quickly over to Chapter 9 and begin with verse 1.

II Corinthians 9:1,2a
"For as touching the ministering to the saints, (the poor saints in Jerusalem who had been left destitute because of their offerings into the common kitty back there beginning with Acts Chapter 2) *it is superfluous* (or it goes beyond saying) *for me to write to you: 2. For I know the forwardness* (the zealousness) *of your mind, for which I boast of you to them of Macedonia,..."*
In other words what was Paul actually doing on behalf of the Corinthian believers? He was boasting to other congregations on what a good job they were doing in making these collections. Now verse 3.

II Corinthians 9:3
"Yet have I sent the brethren, (these that will be picking up the offering) *lest our boasting of you should be in vain in this behalf, that, as I said, ye may be ready:"*

Now I think Paul is using a little psychology isn't he? He is building them up as he says, "Now look Corinthians, Titus, and the gentlemen that are already making collections up here in the poorest part of mountainous Greece, when they come into a culture and commercial center like Corinth, then it stands to reason there's going to be more wealth available than there would be up there in the mountains." So I think Paul is sort of setting them up and preparing them that these men are going to be expecting something of you, because you have so much more to offer than these poor churches up in northern Greece. Now reading on:

II Corinthians 9:5
"Therefore I thought it necessary to exhort the brethren, that they would go before unto you, and make up beforehand your bounty, (their offerings) *where of ye had noticed before, that the same might be ready, as a matter of bounty, and not as of covetousness."*

Do you see this constant drumming of the fact, "Now have this done when these fellows get there, don't put it off, don't procrastinate, have these offerings collected and ready so that they can pick it up and take it on to where it has to go there in Jerusalem. Now verse 6. **Here we come to the whole concept of Christian giving.**

II Corinthians 9:6
"But this I say, He which soweth sparingly shall reap also sparingly; and he which soweth bountifully shall reap also bountifully."

Now you want to remember that the vast majority of people in this day and time were agriculturally connected. So Paul is talking about sowing a crop of grain. And any farmer knows that if you sow half a crop of the required seed, you're not even going to get half a crop. Now you don't sow more grain than is necessary, but you put on the stipulated amount to get a full crop of grain. However, it's brought into the Christian experience on the same level. If you're going to be tight with your giving, if you're going to hold back when you have the ability to give, then God will kind of hold back on His blessing.

And that's exactly what Paul is teaching here. **Now I'm not a name it and claim it type.** I do not claim that if you give a $1000. dollars a year, then God's going to pour you out $3000. No way does this Bible teach that. But I think that we all realize that our God is so great that if we do it with the right attitude, we do it by faith, we can't out-give God. One of my favorite clichés is "**There is a line between faith and fantasy.**" By faith I can do certain things and realize that God is going to respond, but I can't be foolish. Fantasy would say, "Well I'm just going to give that ministry $500. because I just feel that God's going to turn back and give me $50,000." Now that's what a lot of people think, but it's not going to work that way. That's fantasy.

But we know that God is able, and here I must qualify. A lot of time we think that our giving should immediately have something returned in kind. But it's doesn't necessarily have to work that way. **Have you ever stopped to think of all of the potential expenses that God can spare you because you were liberal in your giving?** In other words, that old car may go another

155

50,000 miles where otherwise it may break down. You may end up as fortunate as Iris and I have over the years with practically no money spent for medical expenses. Do you know what I call that? That's the pay back. So you have to look at this whole thing on the big picture, not just in, "If I give a $100, will I get $500 back?" That's not the way to look at it, but rather look at the whole concept of how God is going to respond. Now verse 7. Here is the very foundation for our giving.

II Corinthians 9:7
"Every man (person) *according as he purposeth in his heart,* (and the Holy Spirit will motivate the heart) *so let him give; not grudgingly, or of necessity:..."* (legalism)

I can remember years ago a gentlemen up in Iowa was so upset that his particular pastor had came out to his farm, and looked at the size of his home, and furnishings, his car and pickup, and he turned around and said, "Well it looks to me like you should be able to give $600 a month." Well, how do you think the guy felt? He was totally turned off. He said, "Nobody is going to tell me how much I'm supposed to give." And I agreed with him. No one has a right to do that. That's strictly between the individual Christian and his Lord. Now reading the verse again.

II Corinthians 9:7
"Every man according as he purposeth in his heart, so let him give; not grudgingly, or of necessity: (legalism, or because somebody has laid it on you) *for God loveth a cheerful giver."*

Now if you have a marginal Bible the word *cheerful* in the Greek meant "Hilarious." How many people go to church on Sunday morning, and lay that offering on the plate with a hilarious attitude? Not many. They do it out of a sense of duty, they do it because they think somebody is laying a burden on their shoulder that they have to give. No you don't. If you don't want to give, and if you can't give hilariously, God in so many words says, **"I DON'T NEED IT, AND I DON'T WANT IT."**

But for a believer to give as God has prospered and do it joyfully, and give it to a place where the Word is honored, where the Gospel is proclaimed for salvation. (I Corinthians 15:1-4 or Romans 10:9-10) then God will give you the direction, and God will show you how much to give and where to give it. I wanted to take you back to the Book of Malachi, Exodus, and Leviticus, and the giving stipulations were all given to the Nation of Israel. All I ask people to do is go back and read Malachi 1:1

Malachi 1:1
"The burden of the word of the LORD to Israel (not the Church in the Age of Grace) *by Malachi."*

156

Book 31 LESSON THREE * PART I

Now remember believing what God says is the whole basis of studying and understanding the Word of God. Now granted we have to be careful. We're not going to bring into operation things that God told Israel to do back in the Old Testament. In fact we had a call from a person who said, **"Doesn't the Book of Malachi say to bring your tithe and offerings into the store house?" And I said "Yes, but doesn't the same Old Testament say bring me your sacrifices?"** The caller said "Yeah." Well then what are you going to do? Just because the Bible says to bring an animal sacrifice, are you going to go out and buy a lamb? Well of course not, we're not under that today, we know better than that. And yet it carries all the way through on everything. Just because the Old Testament told Israel to do something, that doesn't mean that's still valid for us today, and so we have to shake these things out. You can't just pick and choose what you want, like a lot of people are doing. Remember what was for Israel is completely different from what Paul tells us in the Church Age.

(15b) What does the Bible say concerning marriage ?

Book 27 LESSON TWO * PART II

I Corinthians 7:1
"Now concerning the things whereof ye wrote unto me: It is good for a man not to touch a woman."

So the question must have been, **"Is it right for men and women to marry?"** And you might ask the question, "How in the world could they come up with a question like that?" Well you must again realize the situation. You know I've always taught from day one that when you read a portion of scripture the first thing you determine is who wrote it, and to whom was it written, and the third part is, what are the circumstances. Well here we have Paul, the apostle to the Gentiles, writing to the congregation in the wicked city of Corinth who have come out of abject immoral, idolatrous background, and they are all hung up on this marriage relationship that now is Biblical compared to what it is in paganism. Now you want to remember that in paganism under idolatry, the marriage relationship didn't amount to that much. It was really just a place to propagate the family, but so far as any moral integrity, or fidelity of the marriage relationship, the pagans knew nothing of that.

And so now they are going off the deep end. **"Is it right for us to marry?"** Now don't misinterpret the last half of verse 1 when Paul says that it is good for a man not to touch a woman. He's not saying that they shouldn't get involved and get married. But he is saying in the light of these verses in Chapter 6 that as believers now men as well as women, have to be careful in their contact with people of the opposite sex in their everyday experience. And when Paul says, **"That it's good for a man not to touch a woman,"** and if I under stand the Greek at all, what he's talking about is that a man should not get physically involved with a woman to excite the sexual sense. He is certainly not bringing in the shaking of the hands with women. Even in the early Church they granted the "Holy Kiss" where they would embrace much like our middle easterners still do, and that also caused problems in the early Church, and so that was finally pushed out the back door.

So Paul is answering their questions, "It is not good for a man to touch a woman, not to embrace her, or get involved with her enough to excite the basic instinct of her or him." But he is not saying that they can't get married. And I know that a lot of people take this verse to mean that Paul is anti-marriage. No, he is not anti-marriage. In fact before we go any further let me show you some verses to back that up. Let's go to the Book of Hebrews for a moment. We've already seen what God said back there in Genesis concerning the marriage relationship, and that they were to replenish the earth, they were to have children, and they were to enjoy the marriage relationship. Now look what Paul writes in the Book of Hebrews, Chapter 13, and verse 4. And he's not going to utterly contradict this with his statement in I Corinthians Chapter 7, so you have to put the two of them together.

Hebrews 13:4a
"Marriage (As we understand it) is honourable in all, and the bed undefiled:..."
Now you know we've come mercifully away from Victorianism, which was the extreme in the other direction. Sex in Victorianism, was such a dirty word that it couldn't be mentioned in public, and it was almost taboo except for the purpose of child bearing. Well that certainly wasn't right, but now on the other hand we've gone too far the other way. Now completing verse 4 we find the other side of the coin opposite marriage being honourable, and the bed undefiled.

Hebrews 13:4b
"... but whoremongers and adulterers God will judge."
God is not going to wink at that. They're not going to get away with it, and they're going to face up with it some day. The Great White Throne Judgment is waiting for the lost, and they're going to come up before God with all this on their record. Now if you will come back again to I Corinthians Chapter 7 again.

I Corinthians 7:2
"Nevertheless, to avoid fornication, (or falling into the trap of immoral activity) *let every man have his own wife, and let every woman have her own husband."*

Now we have to be careful. Is the sole reason for getting married, not to be tempted to go out and be promiscuous? Well of course not, but it does have that redeeming effect, that if I have my wife, and she has me, then we're not tempted then to go out into the world, and be promiscuous with those we have no business being with. And so this is what Paul is saying. Also I've got to bring you back to that situation at Corinth with all their rampant prostitution, and for a young man it was a constant temptation. So Paul says, "rather than being tempted with that, have your own wife." Now verse 3:

I Corinthians 7:3

"Let the husband render unto the wife due benevolence: (we're living in a day where you see so much wife beating, and wife abuse. Well why is that? Well again it's because these people have not been taught plain, simple Biblical principals. And that is that a husband is to treat his wife as something that he would die for, and not as something that he can beat around the house. That was not God's intention of the marriage relationship.) *and likewise also the wife unto the husband."*

I had a letter recently asking why God condoned slavery? Why did He ever permit it to happen? Well, when you analyze the greatest period of time of human history, what percentage of the people were actually educated enough to carry on and be an entrepreneur, or be a good enough business person to make a good living. Not very many. The vast majority was totally illiterate, were totally incapable of decision making, and we saw that in Russia, after 70 years of communism. So under those kinds of circumstances a benevolent master was the best thing those people could have.

I think that most of you are aware that when slavery was holding forth in the South, there were masters like that. And those slaves loved them, didn't they? They had it better than they could have ever hoped to have it out there on their own. But you see man has totally again adulterated God's purposes, and instead of masters being benevolent they became bestial, and less than merciful, and then slavery became awful, and God never intended it to be that way. Well it's the same way here. The husband and wife relationship, if it's as God intended to be, should be a happy situation 365 days a year. There is absolutely no reason for husband and wives to be on a constant battle ground. I can say from experience, Iris and I have been married for 43 years and I think our kids will tell you that they have never heard us raise our voice at one another. It's not because we're so perfect, but rather because we know that The Lord is in control of our home. And this is way He wants it.

Book 1 LESSON Two * PART II

God has created man, as we saw last week, as the crowning act of His creation. Man is the epitome of His perfection. We are created in His image and given a will in order to be able to make choices of obedience or disobedience to God.

The whole concept of this thing compares to the very attitude of marriage in the human relationship. God has always had myriads of angels, but they were never created to have this special kind of love and fellowship relationship with God as mankind was. But in Adam, God deliberately created a will, and had Adam chosen to be obedient to God, He would have had someone with whom He could share this special love and fellowship throughout eternity. As I see Scriptures, this is the primary reason for man's creation in the first place - that God wants a creature that He can love and who will return that love to Him.

In a moment we're going to turn to Ephesians 5:22. I want to use this verse for a two-fold purpose:

1. To help our attitude concerning marriage and the home and the husband-wife relationship, and
2. To establish that this is the reason man was put here in the first place; because the relationship is so much the same.

I am of the conviction that if a home survives or doesn't survive, I blame the man. I know that there may be alternatives to that, but for the most part, I believe that the success or failure of a home and marriage is primarily the man's responsibility.

Ephesians 5:22-25: *"Wives, submit yourselves unto your own husbands, as unto the Lord. For the husband is the head of the wife, even as Christ is the head of the church: and He is the Saviour of the body. Therefore, as the Church is subject unto Christ, so let the wives be to their own husbands in everything. Husbands, love your wives, even as Christ also loved the church, and gave Himself for it;"*

The passage starts *"Wives, submit ... unto your own husbands,"* and it means not that the wife is meant to be a slave or a "go-fer," but rather that God has ordained the man to be the head of the home. The husband is not to be a taskmaster nor slave master, but rather he has been given the place of authority in the home. The very key to this verse is "as unto the Lord."
Verse 23 says: *"For the husband is the head of the wife, even as Christ is the head of the church: and He is the Savior of the body."*

Notice He is the Savior not only of the soul (as so many churches teach), but also of the body. Don't miss that God is just as concerned with the body as with the soul; He is vitally concerned with our entire being - spirit, soul and body.

Verse 24: *"Therefore, as the Church is subject unto Christ, so let the wives be to their own husbands in everything."*

So when we tie the husband-wife relationship to that of Christ and the Church, as this verse says we should, we find that there's no room for abuse in either the authority of the husband or in the submission of the wife. Everything is just so perfectly ordained if we will do it God's way! Verse 25 is the one I use for putting the responsibility for a successful marriage on the husbands.

"Husbands, love your wives, even as Christ also loved the church, and gave Himself for it;"
This is a COMMANDMENT! And interestingly, nowhere in the Scripture is the wife commended to love her husband. I know that Peter says mothers are to instruct their daughters in how to love their husbands, but that's a far cry from commanding it (in the husband-wife relationship). The reason that I tie this Scripture in with Genesis 1 is that God put man on the scene with a will so that when God would extend His love and grace and blessings on this creature, God expected love returned.

It's the same way in the marriage relationship, and I still maintain that (with rare exceptions) if the husband will truly love his wife Scripturally as Christ loves us, the Church, then it automatically follows that the wife is going to respond to that love. If a woman doesn't, then there's something wrong with her because God has created within her that responsiveness, so that when the man extends his love, she's going to respond, and you have a happy relationship.

(16b) How can you help an unbelieving spouse find the Lord ?

Book 27 LESSON TWO * PART III

I Corinthians 7:10-16
"And unto the married I command, yet not I, but the Lord, (so this is The Word of God) *Let not the wife depart from her husband: But and if she depart, let her remain unmarried, or be reconciled to her husband; and let not the husband put away his wife. But to the rest speak I, not the Lord: If any brother hath a wife that believeth not, and she be pleased to dwell with him, let him not put her away. And the woman which hath an husband that believeth not,* (still in paganism) *and if he be pleased to dwell with her,* (who is now a believer) *let her not leave him. For the unbelieving husband is sanctified by the wife,* (who is a believer) *and the unbelieving wife is sanctified by the husband:* (who is a believer) *else were your children unclean; but now are they holy. But if the unbelieving depart, let him depart.* (Paul says 'let the unbelieving spouse go if that's the way they want it.') *A brother or a sister is not under bondage in such cases: but God hath called us to peace. For what knowest thou, O wife,* (Who is a believer) *whether thou shalt save thy husband?* (who is lost) *or how knowest thou, O man, whether thou shall save thy wife?"*

Now we know that we can't save our spouse and the spouse can't save us, so what's Paul talking about? Well let me bring you back again to Peter's little epistle in I Peter Chapter 3. Here, especially in the city of Corinth, and this is the only letter where Paul deals with these things, and so consequently I have to feel that the Ephesians weren't under this kind of situation, nor the Philippians, or the Colossians. Maybe to a degree they were, but not like they were here in Corinth. It was just beyond comprehension, and everyone of these converts of Paul had been in idolatry. So if they were married then naturally they both were, so if one of them is saved and comes out of idolatry, and becomes a believing Christian then here we have in the home this division, as one is still in idolatry, and the other a believer. How were they going to handle it?

The same would be for missionaries who minister to people who have more than one wife in the family. We're so immune to all these things, we've been so protected in our American society, but these things were real to these people. Now look what Peter says here.

I Peter 3:1
"Likewise, ye wives, be in subjection to your own husbands; (sounds like Paul doesn't it?) *that, if any obey not the word,* (they're not a believer) *they* (the husbands) *also may without the word* (without preaching at them, without dragging them to church, without bringing them under the television ministry, without saying a word, that lost husband may) *be won by the conversation* (or manner of living) *of the wives,"* Now verse 2:

I Peter 3:2-4
"While they behold your chaste conversation (manner of living) *coupled with fear.* (a reverence fear, rather than being scared to death) *Whose adorning* (speaking of the Godly, believing wife) *let it not be that outward adorning of plaiting the hair, and of wearing of gold, or of putting on of apparel;* (but rather let her win the husband by) *but let it be the hidden man of the heart, in that which is not corruptible,* (that born again spirit within that believing woman) *even the ornament of a meek and quite spirit, which is in the sight of God of great price."*

Now what is Peter admonishing the believing wife to do? Listen, don't nag that unbelieving husband, don't preach at him, don't try to drag him to church because that's not going to work. So what does the wife do first and foremost? She lives an exemplary Christian life in front of him.

I remember when I was teaching up in Iowa, and I had a Saturday night teenager class, and we would have 45 or 50 kids that would come in every Saturday night for Bible teaching. One of the neighbors of the host home wanted to know, **"what in the world is going on in your house on Saturday night?"** So Gladys the host, said, **"well we have a Bible study for young people."** The neighbor lady wanted to know if there was a chance that she could come and sit off in the corner someplace, and listen and watch, and naturally there wasn't a problem with that. So this lady, who was a doctor's wife, had a lovely home, but her husband was something else. And they don't mind me telling this story on them, as they share it with everyone now. But anyway, she came to that class on Saturday nights over a few weeks time, and Mary Beth was gloriously saved.

Well it wasn't but a few weeks after that, and Iris and I were attending a wedding where she was also, and she met us out in the lobby of the church, and she started to weep - I mean weep. I said what in the world is the problem. And she said, "My husband John." I said, "Yeah, I've heard about John." You see John had more than one mistress, and his wife knew it, and as a result of her Salvation he became her number one burden. And so I took out my Bible and showed her these verses here in I Peter, and I told her that this wasn't going to be easy, but my Bible tells me that if you can do it, then God will do it. Well she said, "I'm willing to try." So I told her just to do what she knew John likes. If he loves a good T-bone steak have one ready when he comes in. If he likes hot apple pie, have one ready for him. Well to make a long story short, do you know how long it took to win John? 4 months. And old John told the story himself.

John said, " I was in my office one Sunday morning, and had just seen my last patient, and I was in a hurry to get out to the country club. I was just gong to spend the day boozing it up with my buddies. Before I could get out of my clinic, The Lord just came on me with such conviction that my wife was such a far better person than I could ever hope to be, that right there in my office I dropped to my knees and said 'Lord, I'm a sinner, save me, and The Lord did.'" And this man has now been a Church leader almost ever since. He is a living example of what a believing wife can do without saying a word.

Most women get the idea that they're going to drag their husband to church, and get everybody trying to collar him, and that's not the way to do it according to my Bible. I've also seen it the other way around. In one instance the husband came to the class first and was saved, and got a burden for his wife to be saved, but she wanted nothing to do with The Word of God when he tried to read it to her. But he just kept living the example, and finally one day The Lord in His Sovereign Grace caused a friend of hers, who was a believer, to just stop in for coffee one morning, and in the process of having a cup of coffee, led this lady to The Lord. And they are still living the exemplary Christian life together today. So I know this works. So back to I Corinthians, and this is all Paul is saying, that if a wife or husband finds themselves still in a marriage relationship with a rank pagan unbeliever, to just hang in there. Don't break up the marriage if at all possible, but live the example so that the day will come when they will open their heart to The Gospel (Ref. I Corinthians 15:1-4) and then you can have a happy marriage relationship, a happy home, and of course the children will more than likely follow suit.

Part C - Complex Questions and Others

(1c) Why did God require a blood sacrifice ?

Book 40 Lesson Three • Part III

Philippians 3:20a
"For our conversation (citizenship) *is* (where?) *in heaven…"*
How did our citizenship get transplanted from the earthly domain to heaven? Colossians 1. God the Father has transplanted us from darkness into the Kingdom of His dear Son.

Now that isn't so deep and yet very few people have this concept. **Very few people understand that when they were saved, they were literally made a citizen of a heavenly kingdom, which will tie us then to when Christ returns and sets up His kingdom on earth**. And we'll be part of that. So our citizenship is in Heaven. And lest you think it's a play on words, Paul, by inspiration, tells us exactly what heaven he's talking about. The abode of God. From whence we look for the Savior, the Lord Jesus Christ. And so that is what God has done by virtue of our faith in the Gospel. He has opened our eyes, broken those chains of darkness and He has transplanted us into the Kingdom of His dear Son. Now let's look at verse 14 of Colossians 1 and the first thing you're going to notice in these new translations is that the word "blood" isn't in there. And for whatever reason, I'm not going to make comment on it, but my good old King James still has it. And here it is.

Colossians 1:14
*"In whom (*that is in the Son up there in verse 13) *we have redemption through His blood, even the forgiveness of sins:"*

Now let's go all the way back to Hebrews and let's look at a verse that we haven't used for a long time. We certainly have in the past but it's been awhile. Hebrews chapter 9 and verse 22.

Hebrews 9:22
"And almost all things are by the law (back in the sacrificial economy) *purged with blood; and without shedding of blood is no remission."*

Now I call that an absolute. You know, they're trying to tell us today that there are no absolutes. I beg to differ. There are absolutes and this is one of them. **Without the shedding of blood there has never been any forgiveness of sin.** You go right back to the Garden of Eden and Adam and Eve had sinned and were expelled and what's the first thing that God does to restore them? He kills the animals. It was a blood sacrifice.

Now it's amazing how that Satan counterfeits everything that is perfect in God's economy and adulterates it in the process. Now if you know anything about paganism, if you've ever had missionaries come home, especially years back, from some of these almost uncivilized areas, what were they constantly doing in their tribal rituals? Killing animals, or roosters or birds and sprinkling or spattering the blood all over. Why? That was Satan's counterfeit. And so almost every culture up through human history has had a constant bath of sacrificial blood. But that was the counterfeit. That was the adulteration.

The true system of blood sacrifice was what God instituted with Adam and Eve and then bought it up and perfected it with the Law and the Temple worship. And it all was centered on the animal sacrifices. You know all of that. The Passover Lamb and I've shown you from Scripture that when Israel would sin a particular sin, there was a particular sacrifice that they would have to bring. It could be a turtledove, a goat or whatever, but it was always a blood sacrifice. **Because without the shedding of blood there has never been forgiveness. Now I know that today we don't hear anything anymore about the blood concept. But listen, it's the way the Sovereign God ordained it. That without the shedding of blood there can be no remission of sin.** And of course, I feel that the reason for that is that back in Genesis chapter 9 it tells us that life is in the blood. And you cannot get new life without death happening first and death is signified by shed blood. And so you follow this all the way through God's dealing with the whole human race leading up to His own supreme sacrifice, which had to be a shedding of blood. That's why He could have never been hung. He could have never died a death by hanging which was a typical capital punishment way of putting people to death. But it wouldn't have worked because then there wouldn't have been the shed blood. And it had to be a death where there would be that shedding of blood. It had to be! Because this is the way the Sovereign God ordained it and who are we to say that the shed blood is no longer of consequence. Well, anyone who does is in danger of Hellfire because without the shedding of blood there is no remission. Now let's see how Paul enlarges on it. Come back to Romans chapter 3 starting at verse 23.

Romans 3:23-24
*"**For all have sinned** (every last single human being) **and come short of the glory of God. 24. Being justified freely by his grace** (that unmerited favor) **through the redemption that is in Christ Jesus:**"*

Now you all know what redemption means. It's the process of paying the price and gaining something back. Now verse 25

Romans 3:25a
*"**Whom** (Christ) **God hath set forth to be a propitiation through faith in his (what?) blood,…**"*

You can't take that out. We have to maintain that it was His shed blood which was in accordance with His whole divine plan for the ages beginning with Adam and Eve's sin just outside the garden all the way up through the Old Testament economy of Law and temple worship, all bringing us up to the supreme sacrifice of all time, the death of Christ Himself. And that's when sacrificing stopped biblically. There was no more need for sacrifice once Christ died. Now the pagans kept it on. But biblically there was no more need for sacrifice.

But never forget that without the shedding of blood there is no remission.

Book 33 LESSON ONE * PART II

Leviticus 17:10-11
"And whatsoever man there be of the house of Israel, or of the strangers that sojourn among you, that eateth any manner of blood; I will even set my face against that soul that eateth blood, and will cut him off from among his people. (now this is God speaking) *11. For the life of the flesh is in the blood:* (this is why the Blood had to be sacrificed for the remission of sin. It was death for life.) *and I have given it to you upon the altar to make an atonement for your souls: for it is the blood that maketh an atonement for the soul."*

Now I'm going to make a point. What had to happen to the blood in the Old Testament sacrifices, as well as Christ's Blood for the atonement of sin? It had to be applied. It had to be sprinkled on the altar, it had to be sprinkled on the Ark of the Covenant's mercy seat, and Christ also had to present His Blood remember where? The Holy of Holies in heaven.

Book 4 LESSON TWO * PART II

Hebrews 7:14-17
"For it is evident that our Lord (The Lord Jesus) *sprang out of Juda* (not out of the tribe of Levi. He was not eligible to be a priest out the order of Aaron, having come out of the tribe of Judah)*; of which tribe Moses spake nothing concerning priesthood. And it is yet far more evident: for that after the similitude of Melchisedec there ariseth another priest, Who is made, not after the law of a carnal commandment, but after the power of an endless life. For he testifieth, Thou art a priest for ever after the order of Melchisedec."*

All the way from start to finish we have the connection of the High Priest of the Gentile and The Most High God. The Lord Jesus is not only The Most High, the possessor of Heaven and earth, but He is also the High Priest of the Gentile God so that you and I can rest assured that we have a High Priest interceding for us at the very Throne Room of Heaven itself. Not a high priest after the order of Aaron, but a High Priest after the order of Melchizedek.

On the day of atonement in Leviticus 21, the high priest once a year would take the blood of a sacrificed animal, make his way through the front part of the tabernacle, go in behind the veil, and sprinkle the blood on the Mercy Seat, which was the very presence of God under the Shekinah Glory. Israel's sins were then covered for that next year. Now that was the role of the high priest on behalf of Israel. Our High Priest had to do the same thing. Go to John's Gospel, Chapter 20. We cannot get a comprehension of Christ's role as our High Priest unless we can understand what He has done to fulfill that role. It is Resurrection Sunday morning. Mary Magdalene came to the tomb, saw it was empty, and ran back and told the disciples, who couldn't believe. Then Peter and John came running. I believe that although verse 9 tells us so much, most people are not enlightened on this. As Peter and John saw all the evidence there at the empty tomb, verses 8 and 9 tell us:

John 20:8,9
"Then went in also that other disciple, which came first to the sepulchre, and he saw, and believed. For as yet they (the Twelve, and Peter and John in particular) *knew not the scripture, that he must rise again from the dead."*

They had no idea He was going to rise from the dead until they saw proof of it; however, that isn't the point I want to make. Come down to the account of where Mary saw the tomb was empty. And she said, "Oh, where have they put my Lord?" As she turned, there stood The Lord Jesus, only she didn't know Him.

John 20:13
"And they (the two angels) *say unto her, `Woman, why weepest thou?' She saith unto them, `Because they have taken away my Lord, and I know not where they have laid him.'"*

John 20:15,16
"Jesus saith unto her, `Woman, why weepest thou? whom seekest thou?' She, supposing him to be the gardener, saith unto him, `Sir, if thou have borne him hence, tell me where thou hast laid him, and I will take him away.' Jesus saith unto her, `Mary.' She turned herself, and saith unto him, `Rabboni;' which is to say, Master."

What do you think Mary wanted to do? Embrace Him! He was alive! But what does He do? He holds her at bay and says:

John 20:17
"Jesus saith unto her, `Touch me not; for I am not yet ascended to my Father: but go to my brethren, and say unto them, I ascend unto my Father, and your Father; and to my God, and your God.'" Now back to Hebrews, if you will. Then I think we can put all this together.

Hebrews 9:11
"But Christ being come an high priest of good things to come (not after the order of Aaron, remember, but after the order of Melchizedek, the priest of the Gentile name of God), *by a greater and more perfect tabernacle, not made with hands, that is to say, not of this building* (where is it? - in Heaven);*"*

Remember what you just read in John; that Jesus, on that Resurrection morning, said to Mary

Magdalene, "Don't touch me until I have ascended to the Father." This is on Resurrection morning. We're not talking about the ascension of Acts. This is in John's Gospel on the Resurrection morning. Why did He have to ascend?

Hebrews 9:12
"Neither by the blood of goats and calves, but by his own blood he entered in (to the very throne room of Heaven) *once into the holy place* (the very presence of God, and as He presented His Blood...), *having obtained eternal redemption for us*

What role was He fulfilling? - High Priest! Not the high priest of Israel, but the High Priest of all. We don't have to leave the Jew out insofar as His High Priesthood is concerned because now, as a result of the Cross and the power of His Resurrection, He is the High Priest of all. That, of course, is what Melchizedek represented. Please go back with me to Romans, Chapter 3. I am always stressing that Paul is the one who has received the final part of our progressive revelation, except the Book of Revelation. But Paul brings everything to a head by asking the question:

Romans 3:29
"Is he the God of the Jews only? is he not also of the Gentiles? Yes, of the Gentiles also:"
See, nobody is left out. As a result of the work of the Cross, as a result of the work of His presenting His own blood in the very Throne Room of Heaven as our High Priest, everything has been satisfied. Everything is done that had to be done.

(2c) How was Lord Jesus Christ born without sin ?

Book 2 LESSON TWO PART I

Genesis 3:15
`And I will put enmity between thee and the woman, and between thy seed and her seed; it shall bruise thy head, and thou shalt bruise his heel.'"

In a previous lesson we pointed out that this verse is foretelling that long-running enmity between the powers of Satan and the powers of God, especially the Son of God Who would be coming on the scene as the Redeemer.

Turn now to Galatians 3:16. As we've said before, we must always qualify everything with Scripture, studying and comparing Scripture with Scripture to get the whole, correct picture. The "Seed of the Woman" is unique in Genesis 3:15, but we have to follow this thread all the way through Scripture, because the prophecy given in Genesis was looking forward to the coming of THE REDEEMER. Galatians 3:16, then helps us to qualify just Who this "Seed of the Woman" is.

Galatians 3:16

"Now to Abraham and his seed were the promises made. He saith not, 'And to seeds,' as of many; but as of one, 'And to thy seed,' which is Christ."

So we can always scripturally refer to the Lord Jesus as the "Seed of the Woman." Remember, as we've gone through our study from Genesis 1:26, when Adam and Eve were created through the time when they ate of the forbidden fruit, we have tried to emphasize the fact that first we must understand that Adam, as he was first created, actually contained the woman we now know as Eve. When Eve was later created (Genesis 2:21-22), the Bible makes it clear that she came out of Adam, because Adam had to be the "Federal Head" of the human race, and everybody, including Eve, would now come from that line of Adam. That's why Scripture tells us so plainly that the human race didn't come under sin by virtue of Eve, even though she had eaten first, but sin came upon the whole human race by way of Adam.

We have to understand that Eve was in Adam because even though God did not put the curse on Eve for having eaten herself of the Tree of the Knowledge of Good and Evil, yet she inherited that sin nature through Adam just like every other human being who's ever lived. All this should begin to tell us something!

For some reason or other, God had to keep the fault (or whatever you want to call it), that fell upon mankind through the curse from Eve. He had to somehow insulate her from it so that she would simply inherit her sin nature through Adam. She became a fallen creature, not from her own eating of the forbidden fruit which she did in ignorance, but rather because she was "in Adam." And even though she became a fallen creature and was under the anathema of sin just as much as Adam or anyone else, yet God did something with the long range view in mind, in order to provide "The Redeemer," because this Redeemer had to come through the woman and at the same time be free of the sin nature!

If you really stop and consider, most Christian people believe and ascribe to the virgin birth of Christ, and isn't it amazing that the Christ could be born of a woman who, out of the line of Adam, was a sinner like everyone else (Mary was not sinless!); that God could bring to pass the birth of the Christ Child from a normal female human being, yet her Offspring could be sinless and not pick up anything of the human element of the sin nature?

Why? This may get a little deep now, and unfortunately the average Christian never even considers this. However, we are teaching the very basics here and, consequently, some of the things just aren't too easy to understand. God expects us to study and grow and go into the deep things, as Paul calls them - "the meat of the Word."

Because Eve was somehow so insulated from propagating the sin nature, all of the females of the species have somehow still maintained that insulation from the curse that came by way of Adam.

To explain, the "seed of the woman" is called in medical terms "the ovum." When the female gets ready for reproduction, there is building within her all these potential "ovum" or "seeds." But those "ovum" will never become anything more than individual cells unless or until they are impregnated from an outside source - the father.

Physiologists say that in order for the young mother to become pregnant, one of the ovum becomes separated from the others and becomes impregnated; the first change is that the cells within the fertilized ovum begin to divide and multiply rapidly until they reach a count of 32 or sometimes 64; then suddenly, in the development of that little embryo that process of cell division and multiplication stops and the body cells begin to develop - the extremities: fingers, toes, feet, hands, etc. - to form the human body. Sometime further down the line, the original reproductive cells find their way into the fetus as a whole.

Remember back in studying Eve's creation, we pointed out that she was taken not just from Adam's rib, but from the "side chamber" of Adam, and it was probably the reproductive portion of Adam that is referred to as the "germ plasm" from which Eve was formed? She had to be insulated from any part of the curse of the sin nature so that these reproductive cells, beginning with and coming all the way down to Mary, and probably on down to us today, do not carry the curse from one generation to the next except through the father. It's only the father that precipitates what we call the circulatory system or the blood system.

This doesn't come easily to our understanding and you really must give this considerably thought. If the female of the species has been insulated from the effects of the curse in the area of reproduction, she cannot pass down from her generation to the next the curse of sin. That has to come through the father!

Physiologically speaking again, there is none of the mother's blood that ever becomes part and parcel of that little baby. The blood comes from the father. Always remember that!
Now, the line of the curse comes through the blood - through the father. So every human being, as we have been stressing through these early lessons in Genesis, is a born sinner by virtue of the fact that he has inherited it through his father, not through his mother, although she is just as much a sinner as the father is.

Why has all this happened? Why did God see fit to insulate the "seed of the woman" from the curse? He was looking down through the eons of time to the coming of "The Redeemer," because Christ had to be born of a woman, but yet He had to be sinless. Now, since the "ovum" or reproductive cells of the woman do not carry the curse, and God was the one who impregnated Mary so that she could become the mother of the Lord Jesus without benefit of a human father, Jesus could be born without that sin nature and that's why we call His, the "virgin birth."

The Lord Jesus could thus be born of a woman without the effects of the curse that came from the human father. He could be sinless, divine; His blood system did not originate with the human element, it originated with God. And yet since He was born of the woman, He was human; He had the same appetites that we have; He ate; He slept like we do, and yet was without sin!

(3c) Can a TRUE Christian fall from grace ?

Book 23 LESSON THREE * PART IV

We just want to teach The Word, and help people see what The Book says, and, just as important, what it doesn't say. Understanding The Book is really not that hard, and the best way to study is to compare Scripture with Scripture. Peter says:

II Peter 1:20
"Knowing this first, that no prophecy of the scripture is of any private interpretation."
That means that you cannot build a doctrine on one verse of Scripture here and there, because then you can build anything. But it's our prerogative to use all the Scriptures from Genesis through Revelation, and see that they fit. Seeming contradictions may arise, but when you study you find they're not contradictory at all. Usually it's because in one instance God is dealing with the Nation of Israel, and in another what may seem contradictory is His dealing with the Church Age. And there is a vast difference.

Book 23 LESSON THREE * PART II

Alright, now let's come on down to verse 33. Since Christ died, and God let Him, God permitted it to happen. He directed that it had to happen in order to purchase our Salvation. There would have never been a person saved, not even in the Old Testament economy, without the work of the Cross. It had to be to satisfy a Holy and Righteous God. Now, let's read:

Romans 8:33
"Who shall lay any thing to the charge of God's elect? It is God that justifieth."
Now, what does that word `elect' mean? Chosen. When you elect someone you designate them to be whatever you intend them to be, and the word `election' in the Greek is exactly that. It is an act of choosing, and that is what God has done with everyone of His believers. Now, I think I'll finish the chapter, and then I want to take you back to some of the statements that Jesus made Himself during His earthly ministry: that He has chosen us, and that no man comes to God on his own prerogative. Sometimes we like to think, "Well, I can just decide to go with God anytime I feel like it." Oh no you can't because you have to be back again in that chosen aspect, but on the other hand we have the Scriptures, "Whosoever will." So reading that verse again:

Romans 8:33
"Who shall lay any thing to the charge of God's elect? It is God that justifieth."

Not our neighbor, boss, husband or wife. We don't have to give an account to any of them. It's God, the Triune God, the Creator God, the sustaining God, He's the One Who determines who we are and what we are in the realm of the Spirit. Now, verse 34, so if He is the One Who has chosen us, if He is the One Who has forgiven us, if He is the One Who has taken us unto Himself, then:

Romans 8:34a
"Who is he that condemneth? It is Christ that died, yea rather that is risen again,...."
Now, do you see how Paul is constantly hammering that everything revolves around that finished work of the Cross? The fact that Christ died, His divine Blood had to be shed, because always remember:

Hebrews 9:22b
"...and without shedding of blood is no remission."
So without the shedding of Blood there is no remission. You can't bypass the Blood, it had to happen. So He's the One Who died, and rose from the dead, and He's the One Who is at the right hand of God interceding for us. He's the One Who is watching over us, and He is the one who promised, *"If God is for you, who can be against you?"* And never lose sight of that, but don't ever interpret that to mean that nothing bad can ever happen to a believer. Don't ever get the idea that the things of this world can't attack the believer. Satan can transform himself into an angel of light, and he does that often, and he can confuse the issue, but we have these promises, if we'll rest on them, that God is still in total control. God's Sovereign!

Now we're coming into a series of verses that will probably disturb one group of people of various denominations, and that is that group of people who feel that you can not be assured of your Salvation. They think that you have to hope you make it, you have to work like the dickens to hang on, and you have to be sure that you don't ever sin in such a way that you will lose your Salvation, and end up in Hell instead of God's Heaven. These verses are just going to fly in the face of that kind of thinking. I can't help it, because all I'm going to show you is what The Book says. Now, verse 35:

Romans 8:35
"Who shall separate us (and that means just exactly what it say) *from the love of Christ? shall tribulation,...."*

That word tribulation is used something like 29 times in the New Testament, and maybe with one exception that word is associated with the activity surrounding the believer. You go back into the Book of Revelation, in fact, let's turn to that book right now. Someday we're going to teach this part of Revelation - the letters to the seven churches in the opening chapters. Revelation Chapter2 verse 9. This is a letter to the church in Smyrna (verse 8) and Smyrna actually means to smell "just like myrrh," and myrrh does not exude its fragrance until it's crushed. This is exactly what the church at Smyrna was indicating, that the more persecution crushed those believers, the more they exuded their testimony. And you see that's why Satan had to give up persecuting the early Church because he couldn't get ahead of it. The more he persecuted the more it thrived, so he took the opposite attack, and that was to join them, and then Christianity began to slide. Let's read:

Revelation 2:9a
"I know thy works, and tribulation (God knew about their tribulation, and the Church at Smyrna was going through horrible pressure)*, and poverty, (but thou art rich)..."*

They were poor in material things because the persecution was taking them away from their income. It probably took them away from their job situation. It took all their wealth away if they had any. That was part of the persecution, but spiritually they were what? Rich! The Church today is just the opposite of that day, and that's what the letter to the Church at Laodicea was all about. Now, reading on:

Revelation 2:9,10
"I know thy works, and tribulation, and poverty, (but thou art rich) and I know the blasphemy of them which say they are Jews (believers)*, and are not, but are the synagogue of Satan* (they were impostors). *Fear none of those things which thou shalt suffer* (did believer's suffer? You bet they did)*: behold, the devil shall cast some of you into prison* (for their faith)*, that ye may be tried; and ye shall have tribulation ten days* (I think that ten days refers to ten distinct periods of time during the Roman Empire when the Church came under horrible pressure, but these believers didn't give up)*; be thou faithful unto death, and I will give thee a crown of life."*

Now, back to Romans again. So we're going to suffer tribulations, and as I mentioned before, it's only been in the last couple hundred years that western civilization, at least, has been able to guarantee the rights of the individual, and the freedom of worship, and so forth. But for the most part this has been unheard of. We're living in an extremely different time than most Christians had to live in, because we do have a government, that so far at least, guarantees our rights to assembly, and to religion. Verse 35 continuing:

Romans 8:35
"Who shall separate us from the love of Christ? shall tribulation, or distress, or persecution, or famine, or nakedness (Paul went through times of nakedness, and cold, he was thirsty, and hungry, and how did Paul die? Beheaded by the sword)*, or peril, or sword?"*

And there is nothing said that we will be spared the sword, but none of this will separate us from our Lord. Can the Devil bring in enough persecution to force a believer out of his place in the Body of Christ? Never! God has guaranteed that because of the work of the Cross we are secure. Not because of what we have done, not because of what we merit, but only because of what He has done, and let's never lose sight of that. We never maintain our assurance of Salvation and security because of who we are or what we are, or what we have done. That is never part of the picture. Everything that keeps us secure is that finished work of the Christ. Verse 36:

Romans 8:36
"As it is written, 'For thy sake (the sake of the Christ of the Cross) *we are killed all the day long, we are accounted as sheep for the slaughter.'"*

I read an account not too long ago about someone years back when Chicago was still the capital of the meat packing business. They would slaughter the cattle, sheep, and hogs all within one huge complex. A visitor was being taken on a tour and he just couldn't help but notice that as he went from the hog killing area, with all of the squealing and all the commotion that goes on with hogs, to the sheep killing area, what happened.

Utter silence, and I've witnessed that myself. I'll never forget that when they take sheep to the slaughter they have a goat. And that goat leads those sheep up to the place where they are to be killed, and then the goat slips out a side door. And then he goes back and gets another bunch. It's simply amazing, but those sheep go to their slaughter in utter silence.

And this is the analogy that Paul draws of the believer. We may someday just come to the place where we, too, will go like sheep to the slaughter. Are we going to scream and squeal like a bunch of pigs? No, because that's not the way God works. Do you remember what Isaiah said about the Lamb of God?

Isaiah 53:7
"He was oppressed, and he was afflicted, yet he opened not his mouth: he is brought as a lamb to the slaughter, and as a sheep before her shearers is dumb, so he openeth not his mouth."

Why? Because there was no need for Him to scream and argue, and so it has been with Christians down through the ages. Take a lot of the hunks and macho people of today, most of them think Christianity is for women and children. But they have it all wrong, because back in the days when persecution was running rampant it took ten times more man to stand up for the slaughter, to be burned at the stake, and to be put on the rack. You all know what the rack was, that was when their bones were all broken without killing them. That's when it takes a real man, and I bet most of those so called machos could never hold a candle to those saints. But Paul says this is all part and parcel of what God has imparted to us, the promise that even though we may have to go through these things, and many have, it will never separate us from the love of Christ.

And remember this life, even if somehow we could live to be 100, what is that compared to eternity? Eternity, never ending forever and ever and ever, and yet the human race will not consider that. All they look at is, what can I enjoy in the here and now? But you see this Book looks at everything in the light of eternity, and so this is why we have to take this blessed assurance that regardless of what may happen, nothing can separate us from our spending eternity with our Creator God. Well, let's move on to verse 37.

Romans 8:37
"Nay, in all these things we are more than conquerors through him that loved us."
Were those sheep, being led quietly to their death, conquerors? That's the analogy. We're led like sheep to the slaughter, but this verse says, "...yet we're conquerors." That's fantastic isn't it? So we don't have to mind being meek, and quiet, and coming under persecution, and doing without squealing like a hog. Because in the end we're still going to be more than conquerors, How? Through the One that loved us, that's where it is. You and I in the energy of the flesh can do nothing, we are nothing. Now verse 38 Paul says:

Romans 8:38
"For I am persuaded..."
What does it mean to be persuaded? Totally convinced. I think it was King Agrippa back in Acts Chapter 26 where Paul had been witnessing to him and what did old King Agrippa say to Paul?

Acts 26:28
"Then Agrippa said unto Paul, `Almost thou persuadest me to be a Christian.'"

But I don't believe that King Agrippa ever believed the Gospel and became a Christian, and do you know why? Because Agrippa could never be convinced that what Paul was telling him was true. And that's where a lot of people are today: they hear the Gospel (Ref. I Corinthians 15:1-4), they hear this Book taught, but they can't be convinced. They simply can't believe it. And I've had people approach me and say, "Well, what have you got?" And I'll tell them, but most will come back with, "But I can't believe that. I can't believe that's all it takes."

I'll never forget a young man in my class at Wilburton, OK. I think he's still receiving our tapes, and if so, I hope he hears this. He was one of these kids who from the time he was 5 or 6 years-old had no home life, no parents, he just literally made it on his own. He came up after class one night, and said, "Les, do you mean to tell me that I can have all of this free for nothing?" I told him, "Yes." He said, "I can't believe that." And then he told me of how he had to scratch and fight for every little bit of food that he had as a kid growing up. He said, "I just can't believe that." And I told him, "I'm sorry, but until you can believe it you can't have it." And so the young man left. But I'm hoping that sometime in the interim he will still come to his senses and see that, yes, all of this is ours for the taking, if we will only believe it. Now, continuing on with verse 38:

"For I am persuaded, that neither death, nor life, nor angels, nor principalities, nor powers, nor things present, nor things to come,"

Now, why do you suppose that the Holy Spirit inspired the Apostle Paul to start with death instead of life like we would normally put it? Stop and think for a moment, what's he driving at? Death is the easy way out. That's why we have so many suicides, they think that's their easiest way out. They can't cope with their problems, they can't cope with their circumstances, so they take their life, and that ends it as far as this life is concerned. But what about life? Oh, we're living in a world that's filled with heartaches and turmoils. A life that's lived with all kinds of oppositions to the home and family. Hey, life is difficult. Life is not easy. In fact, I was reading a book someone sent me a while back, and I almost had to quit reading it because all the writer was pointing out was all these things that make life difficult. True, but it wasn't necessarily what I wanted to be thinking about, so you see death is easy by comparison. But Paul tells us that even all the difficulties of life can't separate us from the love of God. Now, as we come to close of this lesson I wish I had more time for the next few words in verse 38: that is principalities and powers, nor things present, or things to come.

The word 'principalities' here in the Greek is 'Arche.' It deals with people who are in a high position. The word 'power' is from the Greek word 'Dunamis' from which we get 'Dynamo,' and it means energy. Paul is delineating here that principalities, the position, and the energy that comes from that position are going to do everything that they can to take us away from the love of Christ. But they can't do it. I wish I had time to take you to Ephesians in Chapter 6 to enlighten you even more. There the word 'powers' is used a little differently than in Romans. There it's not speaking of energy, but again, power as Jesus gave to the Twelve when they went out to perform the miracles. But, nevertheless, the powers that be in the realm of Satan are positioned and they are loaded with energy that seemingly never runs out.

LESSON THREE * PART III

IF GOD BE FOR US, WHO CAN BE AGAINST US?
ROMANS 8:31-39

Let's get back to Romans Chapter 8. I'd like to go back to those last 6 or 7 verses and pick out some things I neglected to bring out in the last lesson. But before I do I would like to say that I hope you're studying the Word with us, and learning what The Book says and what The Book doesn't say. The Scriptures are not just some gobbledy-gook, but rather written by the hand of God so that anybody can understand it. You don't have to be highly educated, or have a great theological education to comprehend the Scriptures. Now, of course, that's what precipitated the Dark Ages, when the church had gotten so powerful that they had pulled the Scriptures away from the common man and brought it into the monasteries because they felt only the monks and educated could discern the Word of God, but that's not what God intends. He wants all of us to become students, to learn how to study this Book. That's what Paul meant when he wrote to Timothy that we are to:

II Timothy 2:15
"Study to shew thyself approved unto God, a workman that needeth not to be ashamed, rightly dividing the word of truth."

I want to come back and cover some of these verses that we looked at in the last lesson. And someone had a question about verse 31 so let's turn to that verse now. Here is a verse that is so paramount to our Christian experience as a child of God, that we have to understand that those of us who have been called, we've been elected, we've been justified, we've been glorified, and that being the case:

Romans 8:31
"What shall we then say to these things (what's Paul talking about? That we've been justified, glorified, forgiven, and all these things that Paul alone teaches. How can we say that? Well, we can come to the conclusion if that's all true, then)*? If God be for us, who can be against us?"* And that's where God wants us to rest, there is no one that can condemn us because of verse 32.

Romans 8:32
"He that spared not his own Son, but delivered him up for us all,..."

And as we saw in the Book of Philippians The Lord Jesus Himself was obedient unto that kind of a death. Just like Isaac of old. A lot of those things back in the Old Testament were just a preview of what took place in the New. As Abraham laid Isaac upon the altar, is there anything in Scripture that indicates that Isaac struggled? Did Isaac fight back? But in complete obedience he let Abraham, his father, lay him upon that altar. Well, that was just a preview of how God the Son would react to the same situation, that He gave Himself up as we see in Philippians:

Philippians 2:8
"And being found in fashion as a man, he humbled himself, and became obedient unto death, even the death of the cross." Romans 8:33:

Romans 8:33a
"Who shall lay anything to the charge of God's elect?..."

I stressed a little bit in the last half hour that these verses just absolutely hammer home the idea that once God has put the finger on us, has elected us, and we have responded and we have entered into His tremendous Salvation, then who in the world can touch that? Nobody can touch it, because it's something that God has done, and don't let anyone ever tell you, "How can you be so conceited as to tell me that you know that you'll go to Heaven when you die, when no one can know." When someone talks like that, they themselves are totally unaware of true saving faith. Because if you have enough faith to believe the Gospel (Ref. I Corinthians 15:1-4), if your faith is sufficient to bring you into that Salvation, then you should have enough faith to take God at His Word, and the rest of it. And that is that you're His. No one can take us out of His hand, and we're going to see that in just a little bit. Verse 33 again.

Romans 8:33
"Who shall lay any thing to the charge of God's elect? It is God that justifieth."

Would God elect someone who somewhere down the road would chose to reject Him? I can't see it happening, and the reason I'm using that example is I had a fellow tell me that one time. I said, "Look, the Scripture says that God will never cast us out." He said, "Oh, I know that, but I could cast myself out." I said how? He replied, "By committing some horrible sin." I said, "Look, you can't touch yourself so far as being in that position in the Body of Christ any more than someone else can. We are totally, and I can't emphasize this enough; we are totally under the power of the Sovereign God, and nobody can supersede his power." These closing verses of Romans 8 are like the crescendo of a great orchestra. A crescendo is when that sound just builds and builds, and it's got your attention. It's been building throughout these first eight chapters of Romans, but now here comes this crescendo. I think Paul, if we could have heard him in person, would have just shouted it. "Look, nothing can separate us from the love of God in Christ!" We see this in verse 35:

Romans 8:35-37
"Who shall separate us from the love of Christ? shall tribulation, or distress, or persecution, or famine, or nakedness, or peril, or sword (we covered that in the last lesson. Verse 36)? ....*we are accounted as sheep for the slaughter. Nay, in all these things we are more than conquerors through him that loved us."*

Oh, not of what we have, not through any ability that I or you have, but what makes us conquerors? Christ Jesus. He became everything. What does the Book of Colossians say?

Colossians 3:17
"And whatsoever ye do in word or deed, do all in the name of the Lord Jesus, giving thanks to God and the Father by him."

And that is where we live and move, and there is nothing in us that can merit any favor with God, it is all of His Grace. And remember that Grace could never have happened if it had not been for mercy. We no longer have to cry for mercy because God poured out His mercy on Christ there on the Cross. His mercy has already been poured out. Since His mercy has been poured out, now He can give Grace. "Unmerited favor." We don't deserve any of this. Now, let's look again at verse 38:

Romans 8:38

"For I am persuaded, that neither death, nor life, nor angels, nor principalities, nor powers, nor things present, nor things to come,"

Go to Ephesians Chapter 6. I felt we had to do this part over since we didn't have time to cover it in the last lesson. Paul writes:

Ephesians 6:12

"For we wrestle not against flesh and blood, but against principalities, against powers, against the rulers of the darkness of this world, against spiritual wickedness in high places."

Not down in the gutter, not on skid row, but in high places. Now, that should wake us up. We're up against something that is beyond the normal. It's up here with tremendous power, and position. These powers are in high positions and let's compare the same Greek word 'powers' back in Matthew Chapter 10 so we get an idea of what Paul is really driving at when he says, *"For we wrestle not against flesh and blood, but against principalities, and against powers,"*

Matthew 10:1

"And when he (The Lord Jesus in His earthly ministry) *had called unto him his twelve disciples, he gave them power..."*

Now, that word 'power' is the same word in the Greek that we found back in Ephesians, and it was authority. So these principalities and powers have authority, and don't you ever doubt it. Don't you ever forget that Satan is powerful. My, he can transform himself into an angel of light. He is the one, according to II Corinthians 4:3-4, that prevents the lost from comprehending the Gospel. So this word is designated 'authority.' Another one is in Acts Chapter 26, and we see that same kind of a meaning. And this Scripture is going to be in regards to Paul, and it's the same Greek word again.

Acts 26:9,10

"I verily thought with myself (back in his pre-Salvation experience), *that I ought to do many things contrary to the name of Jesus of Nazareth. Which thing I also did in Jerusalem: and many of the saints did I shut up in prison, having received authority from the chief priests;"*

What does that mean? Paul was put in position to do what he was doing. Authority. Now, bring that back to what we saw in Ephesians:

Ephesians 6:12

"For we wrestle not against flesh and blood, but against principalities, against powers,..."

And they have authority. And that authority is Satan, and he is doing everything that he can, not only to frustrate the life of you and I as believers, but also to keep lost humanity in darkness.

And he will have that power until God breaks that power. Here again is why we have to come back to the very fact that God is the One Who opens our heart, God is the One through the working of the Holy Spirit Who gives us an understanding. Now, return to Romans 8 for a little bit, and then we may look at a couple of verses in John.

Romans 8:39
"Nor height, nor depth, nor any other creature (all of creation, there is nothing that has ever been created whether it's on the demonic side or on the righteous angelic side)*, shall be able to separate us* (or take us) *from the love of God, which is in Christ Jesus our Lord."*

Someone might say, "Well, that's Paul, and I don't have time for his teachings." Well, let's go back and see what Jesus Himself says. Let's turn to John's Gospel Chapter 6. And here Jesus is speaking:

John 6:37
"All that the Father giveth me shall come to me;..."

Who is making the first move? God is. Don't you ever believe anyone when they say, "Oh, seek this and that, and after God." because it's impossible. You and I can't seek God, because it not in us; no unbeliever is going to go running after God, it's not in him. If he suddenly has an appetite for the things of God, then God put it there first. And it's the same as Jesus is saying here:

John 6:37
"All that the Father giveth me shall come to me; and him that cometh to me (as a result of God moving him) *I will in no wise cast out."*

Now, Jesus said it in His earthly ministry that anybody that God has chosen, that God has elected, that God has sent to Him would in no wise ever be cast out. And that means what it says. Now, let's look at John Chapter 10. Ordinarily I don't like to raise my voice, but when I find out that there are people who totally don't understand this, and think I'm way out in left field, then that's why I have to show you what The Book says: It isn't what I think.

John 10:27,28
"My sheep hear my voice, and I know them, and they follow me: And I give unto them eternal life; and they shall never perish, neither shall any man (and man has been added by the translators so I prefer to leave it out. Neither shall any) *pluck them out of my hand."*

Now, compare that word *any* with what Paul has said in Romans Chapter 8, and what do you also include? The whole sphere of creation. Not just man, but neither the angelic powers, the Satanic powers, nothing can pluck them out of His hand. Now, can you believe that? Well, if you can believe that God in Christ died, and rose again for your Salvation, then you should be able to have enough faith to believe these things. You're His, and no one can take you away from Him. Now, you see the first thing I'll be accused of is, "Well, you're going to tell people that they can do what ever they want to do just because they will never be lost?" Never have I said that. Grace is not license! Don't ever get the idea that the Scripture teaches that since we're safe, that since we're secure we are free to do what we want.

So we believers live in constant awareness that we don't want to fall, or commit a sin. But we also have enough common sense to know that we could. I would hope that I would never fall into any great sin. We're all guilty of these mundane sins of everyday living, and thoughts.

But so far as falling into a great sin such as David did. Did David fall into sin? Was David a believer? Yes. Did David lose his Salvation? No. But oh, what did David know how to do? Beg for forgiveness, and of course he was back before the Age of Grace. But if you want to see a man, David to me was a "man's man." David was as manly as any person that ever lived. Yet as a man's man, we read in the psalms where he poured out his heart in sweat drops begging for forgiveness after he was convicted of his sin of adultery with Bathsheba, and of murdering her husband Uriah. He was a true child of God, otherwise it would have never bothered him. You can go all through Scripture and all the great people failed miserably.

Abraham for example, with his beautiful wife Sara, goes down into Egypt and what happens? "Sara, as beautiful as you are, they're going want you in their harem. There's nothing that I can do to stop it unless they kill me, so for goodness sake don't tell them that you're my wife, but rather my sister." That was sin. Did God kick Abraham out? No! Abraham had to come to the place of recognizing his sin as a believer. Look at Peter in the New Testament. In fact, I had a question from a listener the other day, "What did Jesus mean when He said to Peter there in the Book of Luke?"

Luke 22:31
"And the Lord said, `Simon, Simon, behold, Satan hath desired to have you, that he may sift you as wheat:'"

What did Jesus know that was just down the road in a matter of hours? Peters denial. And here, great big Peter, to probably a teenage girl, cursed and swore that he didn't know Jesus. He didn't have a thing to do with Him, and what happened? The cock crowed, and what happened to Peter? He wept bitterly. Why? He was convicted of his sin. Did that act throw Peter out? No! But he was reconciled immediately when he confessed his sin, and so it is with a believer in Paul's doctrines of Grace. Paul never gives us license to sin. John's little epistle at the back of your Bible tells:

I John 2:1
"My little children, these things write I unto you, that ye sin not. And if any man sin (we're going

to, and if we sin), *we have an advocate with the Father, Jesus Christ the righteous:"*

And then back in the Book of Revelation Chapter 12. My, don't ever think for a minute that believers aren't subjected to sin. I've never seen a true believer that just makes up his mind that he's going to go out and get drunk, or commit adultery, or cheat someone, but it can happen. But a believer has to be constantly on guard.

Revelation 12:10

"And I heard a loud voice saying in heaven, `Now is come salvation, and strength, and the king-dom of our God, and the power of his Christ: for the accuser of our brethren (believers) *is cast down* (Satan)*, which accused them* (believers) *before our God day and night.'"*

Now, if it's impossible for believers to sin, then Satan wouldn't have had anything to accuse them of, but he did, and he does, and he will until we're in The Lord's presence. Because as long as we're in this body of flesh we are going to be prone to fall. I like this simple analogy: most, if not all of you, have raised children, and when they were little and learning how to walk, did they just start walking? No, they fell, and what did a good mom or dad do? Kick them in the rear, and say, "What's the matter with you?" No. We picked them up, and lovingly set them on their feet, and got them started again.

Book 27 LESSON ONE * PART III

Galatians 6:1

"Brethren, if a man be overtaken in a fault, ye which are spiritual, restore such an one in the spirit of meekness; considering thyself, lest thou also be tempted."

You see we're all human. Every human being is just as prone to fall into sin as the next one, but hopefully if we're spiritually taught, and have kept these things, this won't happen. But it can happen to anybody. John is delineating that there were some sins that would not cause God to take them out of their physical life. But some sins He will, and I've seen it happen, and I'm sure you have where a believer will refuse to come away from his sinful lifestyle. You can deal with them, and deal with them, and all of a sudden, "Bingo." Just a sudden heart attack, or sudden car accident, and they're gone. Well God takes them home lest they keep on bringing reproach to His Name. And that's exactly what John is dealing with, and so he says:

I John 5:b

"...There is a sin unto death: (a believer can come to that place where God will take his life. Now then look at the very last part of that verse) *I do not say that he shall pray for it."*

In other words no believer or Church Body ever has the right to pray for the death of an erring believer, because that is never permissible, that's in God's hand. Now let's look at verse 17.

I John 5:17
"*All unrighteousness is sin:* (whether that sin be a little one or a great one) *and there is a sin not unto death.*"

Now what's implied here in verse 17? That some sins are gross enough that it will cause God to take that believer out ahead of time. Now let's come back to I Corinthians Chapter 5, and here's where we have it. This man is evidently committing a sin unto death if he does not repent of it, and turn around. If he's going to continue on living with his step-mother in a marital relationship, then God's going to take him out, and that's all there is to it. Now verse 5.

I Corinthians 5:5,6
"*To deliver such an one unto Satan for the destruction of the flesh, that the spirit* (soul) *may be saved in the day of the Lord Jesus.*"

Book 30 LESSON TWO * PART II

II Corinthians 1:21,22
"*Now he which stablisheth us with you in Christ, and hath anointed us, is God; Who hath also sealed us, and given the earnest* (or the down payment) *of the Spirit in our hearts.*"

Now there is another verse that is a perfect parallel with that and for that we have to go to the Book of Ephesians Chapter 1. Some of these days we'll be teaching this tremendous letter verse by verse. It's dealing with our position in the Body of Christ as believers.

Ephesians 1:13
"*In whom* (in Christ) *ye also trusted, after that ye heard the word of truth,* (and the word of truth is) *the gospel of your salvation:* (I Corinthians 15:11-4) *in whom also after that ye believed, ye were sealed with that holy Spirit of promise.*" Now that is part and parcel again of our salvation experience. We have been sealed, we have been marked by the Person of the Holy Spirit Himself. Now verse 14.

Ephesians 1:14
"*Which is the earnest* (and that means just exactly like we use the term today. He is the down payment. A sufficient down payment to make sure that the transaction is completed.) *of our inheritance* (which we will have by being joint-heirs with Christ, and that's going to hold it) *until the redemption of the purchased possession, unto the praise of his glory.*"

Book 41 LESSON TWO * PART IV

Colossians 2:13
"**And you, being dead in your sins** (absolutely, we were as under the control of the old nature,

our spirit was completely out of fellowship with God and so that's what Paul says we were in the world. We were dead in sin) *and the uncircumcision of your flesh* (by virtue of being Gentiles) *but hath he* (God) *quickened* (has regenerated our spirit. He has crucified old Adam and has given us a new nature. A divine nature) *together with him, having* (already) *forgiven you all trespasses."*

Now let's look at Colossians 3:13. And again, Paul repeats this twice in two chapters to drive it home. And oh, most of Christendom has a hard time swallowing this, I know they do. But here it is again.

Colossians 3:13
"Forbearing one another, (remember, he's writing to believers congregated in an assembly) *and forgiving one another, if any may have a quarrel against any: even as Christ forgave you, so also do ye."*

Now look at that verse very carefully. Is there any demand in that verse that you forgive your enemy before you can be saved? NO! That's already done by the Grace of God. You're forgiven. But now since you and I are forgiven, what should we be ready to do? Forgive whoever we have ought against, whether it's in the Church or neighborhood or whatever. **There is nothing stipulated in Paul's Gospel, nor his writings that first we have to forgive everybody before we can be forgiven like the Lord Jesus said during His earthly ministry under Law.** For example, The Lord's Prayer isn't appropriate for us today. The Lord's Prayer was under Law. It was to Israel. And it says *"forgive us our trespasses* (when?) *as we forgive those who trespass against us."* Now that's Law. And absolutely a Jew could not be forgiven until he went and forgave his neighbor. But that doesn't hold true today. We're forgiven by the Grace of God. And if we're forgiven, then why in the world can't we forgive our neighbor? That's the teaching. So twice in two chapters he says we have been forgiven of all our trespasses and all our sins. Now let's go back to Ephesians 2:1.

Ephesians 2:1-6
"And you (writing to these Ephesian believers) *hath he* (Christ) *quickened* (made alive. Same concept. As soon as we believe the Gospel, God imparted to us that new divine nature. He gave us the regeneration of the spirit. It's divine, eternal life that we are now partakers of) *who were dead in trespasses and sins: 2. Wherein in time past ye walked according to the course of this world* (everyone did) *according to the prince of the power of the air, the spirit that now worketh in the children of disobedience. 3. Among whom also we all* (he included himself) *had our conversation* (manner of living) *in times past in the lusts of our flesh, fulfilling the desires of the flesh and of the mind; and were by nature the children of wrath, even as others.* (doing what comes naturally like everybody else.) *4. But* (the flip side) *God* (not me, not I, but God) *who is rich in mercy, for his great love wherewith he loved us. 5. Even when we were dead in sins, hath quickened us together with Christ, (by grace ye are saved:) 6. Hath raised us up*

together, and made us sit together in heavenly places in Christ Jesus:" (see our position now as believers?) Now verse 8.

Ephesians 2:8
"For by grace are ye saved through faith; (plus how much? NOTHING! There's nothing else listed here. It's by grace through faith) *and that not of yourselves; it is the* (what?) *gift of God:"* How much work do you do for a gift? NONE! But, people are having all this stuff laid on them. There is nothing in here that says you've got to do such and such except believe that Christ has already done it. It's finished! And we can't add to it.

(4c) What really happened during Noah's flood ?

Book 3 LESSON ONE * PART III

NOAH, "SECURITY OF THE BELIEVER"
Turning to Genesis 7. We're ready to take a good look at Noah's flood, and I'm going to explode a lot of myths. There is a common picture that comes to mind when we talk about Noah's ark. We immediately get the picture of a little rowboat type thing with a little shed in the middle and a giraffe standing on deck looking over the edge. That goes back to our Sunday School materials when we were kids, and shows you how impressionable young minds are. The ark was not just a little row boat. Instead, as we pointed out a few weeks ago, the ark was an enclosed rectangular box. It was built, not to sail across the sea - it wasn't going anywhere in particular - but it was built to withstand the awful rigors of the flood.

The secret of this is in Gen. 7:11. The only thing that probably 99% of the people who have read of this flood have considered was the 40 days and nights of rain. Years ago, as I was teaching this, I had several pastors in my class. After class, one came up and said, "Les, you just shot out of the saddle one of my best sermons!" I replied, "I'll bet I know how you preached it. You said, 'it rained, and the water got ankle deep, and somebody said, 'Hey, old Noah was right,' and they came knocking on the door. When it got knee deep, a few more woke up; when it got up to their waists, a few more.'" He admitted he always taught it that way. It made a great sermon but it wasn't Biblical! They had no time to look for cover. It was instantaneous, absolute mayhem and cataclysmic destruction.

Genesis 7:10-12
"And it came to pass after seven days, that the waters of the flood were upon the earth. In the six hundredth year of Noah's life, in the second month, the seventeenth day of the month, the same day were all the fountains of the great deep broken up, and the windows of heaven were opened. And the rain was upon the earth forty days and forty nights."

The seven days referred to in verse 10 are those "seven days of grace" we mentioned in a previous lesson. After Noah, his family and the animals were all on the ark, the door was left open and the gangplank down and anyone who wished, still could have come in, but no one did. Then, God shut the door. "In the second month" - When months are mentioned in Scripture, April is considered the first month of the year, so this would have been the month of May. ... "On the same day all the fountains of the great deep burst open, and the floodgates of the sky were opened." Here is the secret. On one day everything hit and hit hard. It didn't just begin to rain with water rising slowly (previously, in Genesis 1:6,7, we noted that after the earth was flooded during a previous judgment, not on man, but probably on an angelic kingdom. God was preparing it for human habitation).

Genesis 1:6,7

"And God said, `Let there be a firmament in the midst of the waters, and let it divide the waters from the waters.' And God made the firmament, and divided the waters which were under the firmament from the waters which were above the firmament: and it was so."

I'm of the conviction that at that point in His restoration, God raised half of the water that had been flooding the planet and placed it in a huge vapor belt somewhere out in space; that laid the foundation for the amazing spring-like weather that enveloped the planet from one end to the other. The earth had a constant spring-like climate, and because it was constant, there was no "weather;" no storm clouds; and the Bible can accurately say it never rained, but that God watered the things that needed water from beneath.

In Genesis 7, as Noah was building the ark and started talking of a great rain to come, the people probably couldn't understand what he was talking about. Even though as we have discussed, the technology of that day was fantastic, probably something equivalent to what we have today or more, yet they couldn't comprehend water coming down from above because they'd never experienced rain. All of a sudden it began to rain all over the planet, and that was the first time the people probably began to give credence to what Noah had said. But before they had time to react to that thought all the fountains of the great deep were broken up. Analyze that for a moment. What do we usually think of when "the deep" explodes out above the surface? We call it a volcano. So if you can picture it in your mind, (and I'm going to get you to expand your imagination here as far as I can), all around this planet there were volcanic eruptions, and along with these eruptions there were gigantic earthquakes. This whole planet went into convulsions. There was no time to knock on Noah's door. There was no time to find a high place or climb a tree. It was instantaneous judgment.

And, it didn't just last an hour or two; it continued for months and the whole planet was turned completely inside out by these tremendous acts of God. The problem with people (even believers), is that we fail to understand that with God nothing is impossible. God handling this old planet is like you or me handling a marble or ball bearing. It's that simple in His power - He can do with it whatever He wants. He controls all the forces of nature and outer space, and this was all brought to bear in the early months of what we refer to as Noah's flood. Remember years back, the old front-loading washing machines had a window in the door - and when the machine was started, you could see the suds and the clothing start to roll violently. That's much the way the earth would have looked as Noah's flood started. It was complete turmoil.

We have plenty of archaeological proof for this. In fact, if you get into a study of the flood, all around the earth you'll find a soil product called "loess" which comes solely from volcanic action. In every place on this planet there has been laid down, (even on our ocean floors), a tremendous amount of "loess," and the only logical time that this could have been laid down is during the flood, with all its volcanic action. Along with the flood, we also have a disappearance of much of the land surface of the pre-Noah time. We believe that the land surface of the earth from the time of Adam until the flood of Noah's day, was much larger than it is today. Seventy-five percent of the earth's surface is water today. Only a small portion of it is land, and only a small percentage of that land surface is habitable. Most of it is uninhabitable.

Up until the time of Noah, the earth was beautiful, tremendously productive with vegetation beyond our imagination, and highly populated. I have a friend who was in the space program back in the 1960's. He and a friend of his calculated how many people could have been here from the time of Adam until Noah (about 1600 years). They had an easy mathematical time approaching four to five billion people. The reason for that (and we've witnessed this in recent years) is once you get to a certain level, population doubles. Once it doubles, it begins to grow exponentially - to just explode. So, we can be confident that at the time of Noah's flood, the earth was highly populated and had tremendous technology. But when the flood came, there was no time to escape. It was complete and instantaneous, and for that reason there is not much evidence of the things before Noah's flood except in fossil records. And the only logical way to view the fossil records, is that they are a direct result of the flood. Scientists are going to scoff at this.

Turn to I Timothy 6 in the New Testament. I am an avid supporter of good science. I love science, and I love people who have the intellectual and physical fortitude to go into it. It's an exciting discipline. But we have to be honest, and scientists aren't always honest. In I Timothy 6:20, the Apostle Paul is writing under the inspiration of the Holy Spirit and he says:

I Timothy 6:20
"O Timothy, keep that which is committed to thy trust, avoiding profane and vain babblings, and oppositions of science falsely so called:"

Paul is saying, "Timothy, watch out for the false sciences." True science never disagrees with Scripture. True science and Scripture always fit "hand in glove." But, it's these false sciences, the man-made sciences, that cast all the belligerent reflections on the Word of God. They are not true sciences. The reason some sciences are false and not true sciences is that, in them, every-thing is based on what man thinks. They can actually prove nothing in the laboratory. Compare that to mathematics, which is a true science, because you can never change the makeup of true mathematics. You cannot change the true workings of physics or chemistry, either. But a geologist can come along and say, "Well, we think `such-and-such'," and then the next generation comes along and they are taught that theory as a truth or absolute fact. I've got no argument with theory. If someone wants to come up with a bizarre theory, and he will tell his students in the classroom that it is "strictly theory - we can't prove it," then I don't object to that. I've even told kids in high school classes, "if your teacher makes it plain that what he's teaching is simply some man-made idea, and that it's only `theory', I'm not going to complain." But, educators usually come in and say, "That's the way it was," and I have a problem with that.

Public television programs such as "Nova" are very interesting, but gullible people believe everything that's said. You can only determine so much from fossil records. The rest is interpolation and assumption. Here's good example. Go into any basic college geology course and the first thing they throw at their students is a "geologic column," an "evolutionary geologic column" or time scale. They teamed up with evolutionary biologists and have divided the structure of the surface of the earth into various strata which they associate a particular time period with. That time period is dependent on the fossils found in that one strata. If near the bottom they have found a very simple life form, they maintain that that is the oldest rock on the earth, it's the farthest down from the top, and consequently, the very earliest of life forms are found in this layer.

Then, as they find in higher strata ... say, reptiles, they say, that naturally you'll find them throughout all the earth's structure in this level, and it's the next higher form of life, because its "evolved" from those simplest of life forms into the reptile. The next up from reptiles is, I believe, birds, and so on up that geologic column. All that sounds so believable, because as wind and erosion, etc. pile this material up, naturally the oldest would be at the bottom, and at the top would be the fossils of man. It all sounds so logical. But, what they don't tell people is that nowhere on earth have they ever found these fossils in this clear order. Never! They are all mixed up. Granted, there may be levels of sandstone or rock of some kind, with only primordial forms. But, it's not on the bottom! It may be way up on top! Study the Geological Time Scale Example A on the next page.

So, it's a lie, and our kids fall for it. Then they come home and tell their parents that they can no longer believe the Bible because their geology professor has "proved" that evolution is the only thing that makes sense. What the teacher doesn't tell them is that these are only theories - they can't prove it - but, they tout them as truths. Some other verses in the New Testament that we need to look at are in II Peter 3:1-6:

II Peter 3:1-6
"This second epistle, beloved, I now write unto you; in both which I stir up your pure minds by way of remembrance: That ye may be mindful of the words which were spoken before by the holy prophets, and of the commandment of us the apostles of the Lord and Saviour: Knowing this first,

that there shall come in the last days scoffers, walking after their own lusts, And saying, 'Where is the promise of his coming?' for since the fathers fell asleep, all things continue as they were from the beginning of the creation. For this they willingly are ignorant of, that by the word of God the heavens were of old, and the earth standing out of the water and in the water: Whereby the world that then was, being overflowed with water, perished:"

Verse 2 refers to "words spoken beforehand by the holy prophets" or the Old Testament. Verse 3 says we should "know" or expect that there will be those who will mock and scoff at Biblical truths. And, as we discussed a few chapters ago, these people are "willingly ignorant," as it says in verse 5, they do not want to know any different, they won't listen to anything different than what they are teaching. If you were to speak to a geology professor and point out that the theories he purports as truths have discrepancies because things just
aren't consistently as he says on the earth's surface, they are all mixed up in various levels; and that you believe it was Noah's Flood, he'll just laugh at you, because he doesn't want to believe that there was ever a flood. We know from the chronological record, that Noah's flood could not have taken place more than 5000 to 6000 years ago, and that blows their millions and millions of years theories 'out of the water'! So, they totally reject Noah's flood. You will never find a current college or university textbook on geology mention Noah's flood; they totally reject and ignore it.

This is where we come into the controversy of what is being taught our children. Some states have tried to pass laws that if schools are going to teach evolution, they also have to teach creationism; and the educators reject it, because it makes a fallacy of everything they are trying to teach our kids. What takes more faith? Believing something like evolution that is a figment of somebody's imagination, or believing the true record? I believe it would take a lot more faith to believe the false than it does the true.

An oilman, if he were a true geologist, would say … "Wait a minute! In the oil business, we rest on geology." My answer to him would be, "Tell me, would it put oil in any different strata if it were laid down by Noah's flood as opposed to evolution?" No, it wouldn't change anything, the oil would still be in the same places. I've had some geologists in my classes, and they have been able to reconcile this. They will say something like, "If I'm going to believe any of God's Word, then I have to believe all of it. I can reconcile the fact that there is oil and gas in certain places, there are coal deposits in certain places, because of the Scriptural records, and I don't have to go back and say that a geologist says 'such-and-such.'"

We have to be careful and make our young people aware that science is not always honest. I remember when the U.S. astronauts were making the "moon walk." The same friend I told you about earlier was involved in that project. If you'll remember, before they went to the moon, they had one big fear of landing there - that they would sink into the dust. When they got there and found that that dust was only about twelve inches deep, the whole scientific community was so shocked that they immediately went to work building an instrument that they could place on the moon's surface on the next trip, which would measure how much and how fast this lunar dust was collecting on the moon. They just couldn't believe that there were so few inches of

Example of A

GEOLOGICAL TIME SCALE

Read From Bottom to Top.

TIME PERIODS ROCK SYSTEMS	TIME EPOCHS ROCK SERIES	APPROX. DURATION MILLION YEARS	APPROX. PERCENT TOTAL AGE	LIFE FORMS
QUATERNARY	RECENT PLEISTOCENE	1		Rise and dominance of Man.
UPPER TERTIARY	PLIOCENE MIOCENE		2	Modern animals and plants.
LOWER TERTIARY	OLIGOCENE EOCENE PALEOCENE	65		Rapid development of modern mammals, insects, and plants.
UPPER CRETACEOUS LOWER CRETACEOUS		75		Primitive mammals; last dinosaurs; last ammonites. Rise of flowering plants.
JURASSIC		45	5	First birds, first mammals. Diversification of reptiles; climax of ammonites; coniferous trees.
TRIASSIC		45		Rise of dinosaurs; cycadlike plants; bony fishes.
PERMIAN		45		Rise of reptiles. Modern insects. Last of many plant and animal groups.
PENNSYLVANIAN } CARBONIFEROUS		75		First reptiles. Amphibians; primitive insects; seed ferns; primitive conifers.
MISSISSIPPIAN				Climax of shell-crushing sharks. Primitive ammonites.
DEVONIAN		50	9	First amphibians, first land snails. Primitive land plants. Climax of brachiopods.
SILURIAN		20		First traces of land life. Scorpions. First lungfishes. Widespread coral reefs.
ORDOVICIAN		70		First fish. Climax of trilobites. First appearance of many marine invertebrates.
CAMBRIAN		50		First marine invertebrates, including trilobites.
PROTEROZOIC } PRE-CAMBRIAN ARCHEOZOIC		About 3000	84	First signs of life. Algae.

Age of oldest dated rocks: about 3,500,000,000 years.

lunar dust on its surface, if the moon was billions of years old. They decided to make a special instrument to measure how much dust was filtering to the moon's surface in a given period of time, and set it up on their next trip. When they went back the next time, they measured it and were aghast that instead of some infinitesimal, immeasurable amount, there was a fraction of an inch of dust, which indicated that the moon couldn't be more than ten thousand years old, at the most!

My friend told me that when the scientists got that information, they buried it, so that the public wouldn't find out, and it remained hidden until just a few years ago, when in the Tulsa World, I saw a little article on the back page that gave that fact. The scientists didn't want the public to know that, because, it simply blew their theories of millions upon millions of years being involved in the evolution of our solar system. So, this brings us back to the false, so-called "sciences." We have to take them with a grain of salt.

I remember a few years ago, a fellow showed me an article in one of the prestigious archaeology magazines, in which they were refuting the existence of a little town mentioned in the Old Testament. He asked me about it. I told him to wait just a little while, because one thing about archaeologists, they are honest enough that when they find something in line with the Scriptures, they'll announce it. And sure enough, it wasn't even a year later that that very magazine had to admit that the little town that they had said `never existed,' had been found, according to the Biblical record. Every time they scoff at the Old Testament record, all you have to do is set back and say, "The Bible is the true record. This is the Word of God and God does not lie."

The entire scientific community tonight will not recognize Noah's flood, because it totally changed everything so that the history of this planet, instead of going back millions and millions of years, in actuality, goes back to Noah's flood. Even carbon 14 dating cannot be accurate beyond the flood, because it is based on a continuous degeneration under continuous circumstances. Those continuous circumstances were interrupted at Noah's flood. The whole planet was wrapped in volcanic ash and volcanic smoke from the center of the earth; along with that, there was a deluge of the water, that totally changed the face of the planet. If you've ever seen pictures of what a rampaging river flood can do, taking everything in its path, you've got a glimpse of what was taking place on the entire surface of the planet. There was total destruction from pole to pole; and from East to West. No one knew what hit him!
In our next chapter, we'll look at some things that archaeologists can't explain. If they'd just give the flood the credit for it, they'd have all their questions answered.

(5c) How was Noah's Ark a picture of the eternal security of a TRUE believer ?

Book 3 LESSON ONE * PART I

NOAH, "SECURITY OF THE BELIEVER"

The ark was tremendous in size and capable of holding all the Bible says it did. Most important, the ark was a picture of our Salvation. The Hebrew word "pitch," used in conjunction with the ark, is the same word that's translated "atonement" in other Scriptures. The pitch sealed the ark against the waters of judgment making it a place of safety for those within. The Blood (atonement) of Christ makes our salvation secure. If a person is not "under the Blood" he does not have Salvation! Also, God was in the ark when He made the invitation to Noah, his family, and all of creation to enter the ark. It was time for judgment to fall. But after the animals and Noah and his family were securely inside the ark, God left the door open another seven days so anyone else could come into that ark of safety; but none came.

Genesis 7:16
"And they that went in, went in male and female of all flesh, as God had commanded him: and the LORD shut him in."

Underline that last phrase in your Bible; it's tantamount to New Testament doctrine. It says, "The LORD closed it behind him." The word "LORD" in all capital letters in the Old Testament always refers to "Jehovah." With maybe a few exceptions, Jehovah is God the Son - Jesus' Old Testament revelation. When the LORD, Jehovah, God the Son, invited them into the ark, He became the gyroscope that maintained the safety of the ark throughout the flood, and when we look at the flood closely, we'll see it was more than just calmly rising water. **So, God shut the door!** There was only one door in the ark, and in the New Testament, we are told over and over there is only **"One Door!"** John 10:1-14 uses the analogy of the Sheepfold Door: the only door to the sheepfold is The Lord Jesus. Peter also makes this plain in Acts 4:

Acts 4:12
"Neither is there salvation in any other: for there is none other name under heaven given among men, whereby we must be saved." Later on Paul uses this analogy in I Corinthians 3:11:

I Corinthians 3:11
"For other foundation can no man lay than that is laid, which is Jesus Christ."

This is the reason there was only one door going into the ark, and when that door was shut, there was no possible way anyone else could enter. There was only one window in the top of the roof, but it could not have provided access to someone from the outside. There was probably a band just under the eve or roof-line of the ark for ventilation, but the water couldn't splash into it as the seas rose. All these things are pertinent to our own Salvation experience. There's only one door to Salvation, and when we enter that door, God seals it. There's not a human latch on that door - **God shuts us in!**

With that background (as there is so much controversy and confusion today about the whole concept of eternal security, I am teaching it as I believe The Lord has revealed it to me, for that is where my responsibility lies), coming from the perspective of the ark, we want to stop and analyze this particular doctrine. Are we secure once we've entered into the ark of safety? Is the Blood of Christ sufficient to take us through those times of testing and the final judgment? Go to Romans 8. We have established that God "shut the door," and it was the pitch - the Atonement as it were - that sealed out those waters of judgment for Noah. It's the Blood of Christ that secures us from any judgment from whatever source. This is a tremendous promise for us. Can God lie? **Absolutely not!** If we believe The Bible is the inspired Word of God, then if God said it, that settles it! There's no controversy. Verse 1:

Romans 8:1a
There is therefore now no condemnation to them which are in Christ Jesus,..."

That's conditional! That's qualified! That doesn't cover the whole human race. But for those members of the human race that are *"in Christ Jesus"* the promise of God is that we will never face condemnation. I don't use the rest of the verse given in the King James Version because almost every scholar that has looked into these things maintains that the last part of verse 1 was never in the original manuscripts. It has only shown up in a few, and they feel that somewhere along the line, someone who was not inspired added that portion that reads "...who walk not after the flesh, but after the Spirit." It comes up again later in the chapter where it is appropriate.

*"There is therefore now **no** condemnation..."* That means exactly what it says! There is nothing that God can bring against us in condemnation if we are in Christ Jesus! Why? For the same reason that once Noah and his family went into the ark, and the door was shut and the ark was sealed against the waters of judgment, no harm could come to them. In the first seven chapters of the Book of Romans, the Holy Spirit has been mentioned only once or twice. That's what leaves Paul in such a dilemma in Chapter 7 verse 15 when he says, *"For that which I do I allow not: for what I would, that I do not; but what I hate, that do I."* Then he breaks out in Chapter 8 with the remedy, The Holy Spirit. In this short chapter, the Holy Spirit is mentioned nineteen times! Verse 14:

Romans 8:14
"For as many as are led by the Spirit of God, they are the sons of God."

Not they "might be," or they can "hope to be," but they are! That's a present tense verb. Take a contemporary situation, a husband and wife with two or three children. One of the children becomes a belligerent renegade - he is an embarrassment to everything the family stands for. Finally, his parents say, "He is such an embarrassment that we don't even want him to partake in the inheritance. Let's go to the law and totally disinherit him. Let's not even recognize him as a son." And so they do. But know matter where that child goes, whose blood is flowing through his veins? His Parents'!

195

It's the same way here. Once we have entered into this kind of a relationship, and we have become bonafide children of God by virtue of all the acts of God that are attendant to our Salvation, who can change that? No one, it can't be done. We may think that God should kick someone out of His family, but the Scripture stands. If that person has **genuinely** entered in, he is in permanently. This is where I make the qualifications. I am a firm believer in eternal security only for those who have been genuinely saved. For a genuinely saved person, there is no condemnation. But I'm not talking about people who may have gone through some set of rules whereby they became church members and automatically by rote repetition are qualified as a Christian. I don't buy that! People who just simply walk the aisle, following whatever procedure may be given to them, and doing it by rote repetition, are not **genuinely** saved.

That's not Salvation. But for the person who has genuinely come under the power of The Holy Spirit, and has genuinely believed the Gospel with all his heart, then I have to maintain what the Scripture says, *"There is therefore now no condemnation..."* He is a child of God and always will be. Let's read on starting with verse 15:

Romans 8:15-17

"For ye have not received the spirit of bondage again to fear; but ye have received the Spirit of adoption, whereby we cry, Abba, Father." **"...ye have received..."** - this is past tense, it's been done! We come into that relationship with God as complete, mature sons. That is brought about to a fuller extent in verse 16:

"The Spirit itself beareth witness with our spirit, that we are the children of God:" There are no if's, and's, but's or maybe's! We are children of God! The Spirit makes us know we are sons of God.

"And if children, then heirs; heirs of God, and joint-heirs with Christ; if so be that we suffer with him, that we may be also glorified together."

Look at these promises! If we're children, then we are heirs of God; and if we're heirs of God, then we are joint heirs with Christ. Do you know what it means to be a joint heir? It means that everything that is His is ours. But on the other hand, everything that is ours is His also! Many believers don't like to accept that thought. Just as surely as everything that's God's is now ours, He expects that everything that's ours is His. If he expects it, He doesn't command it - He doesn't demand it. And this is the beauty of **Grace**.

Occasionally, people say things that just make my day. One night as I was leaving, I heard a dear lady that I know has been a believer for years saying to a friend, "It wasn't until the last two or three weeks that I've come to understand the Grace of God." We had been discussing Genesis where Ishmael came on the scene. Hagar had become pregnant by Abram and she was causing such trouble in the home that Sarai finally said, "Abram, get her out of here, I can't stand it." So Abram did. But God came on the scene and told Hagar to return to Sarai's tent. Why didn't He just leave her in the desert where she and her son finally ended up anyway? Because of God's eternal purpose in this situation. It would be a living example of a New Testament truth.

A few years later, Abraham's son of promise, Isaac was born. He was the one that God has said in the beginning would be born. As Isaac became a young boy, Ishmael made life miserable for him. Then God entered the situation directly and instructed Abraham to send Hagar and Ishmael out into the wilderness, for Ishmael will not live under the same roof with the son of promise, Isaac. That sounds almost cruel, but God did all this because Paul was going to use that as an allegory in Galatians 4:21-31:

Galatians 4:21-23
"Tell me, ye that desire to be under the law, do ye not hear the law? For it is written, that Abraham had two sons, the one by a bondmaid, the other by a freewoman. But he who was of the bondwoman (Ishmael) *was born after the flesh; but he of the freewoman* (Isaac) *was by promise."* Ishmael stood for Law and legalism; Isaac stood for Grace. To prove those two can't let live under the same roof, Paul says:

Galatians 4:29,30
"But as then he that was born after the flesh persecuted him that was born after the Spirit, even so it is now. Nevertheless what saith the scripture? Cast out the bondwoman and her son: for the son of the bondwoman shall not be heir with the son of the freewoman."

So even as Ishmael was sent out, so also must Law and legalism be sent out, because Law and legalism cannot live under the same roof with the son of promise, Isaac, who represented Grace. We have to come to the understanding that we live under Grace - the very grace of God which is beyond our human comprehension! That's the only reason I can stand here and teach that if you are once a genuine born again child of God, you can never be cast out. Arguments arise by those who say, "I know so and so who did such and such." My answer is, if God hasn't begun a disciplining process in their lives, I doubt if they have ever been genuinely saved.

The Bible makes it so clear that if you're a child of God and you begin to waver in your walk, He will begin to discipline you. Then we also can see that the Bible says that if discipline doesn't work, and we get rebellious, God will take us home. He's not going to let someone stay and continue to bring reproach to His Name. Remember I used the illustration of the Redeemer, and how one was bought out of the salve market and totally removed from anything that would tie him to the slave market. His Roman master gave him his freedom so that he could go anywhere in the empire with a purchased citizenship. What was the servant likely to say? "You, my master, have done so much for me, I want to stay here and be your servant." That's exactly how Salvation works. Once we have come into the grace of God and comprehend all that God has done for us, how can we help but want to serve Him? We're going back to Romans 8:22. This is a whole different thought in here and we'll come back to it another time. Paul continues:

Romans 8:22,23

"For we know that the whole creation groaneth and travaileth in pain together until now. And not only they, but ourselves also, which have the firstfruits of the Spirit, even we ourselves groan within ourselves, waiting for the adoption, to wit, the redemption of our body."

Paul says that we as believers have the "firstfruits of the Spirit." He goes on to say that we are waiting for the "redemption of our body." Most believers have sat under teaching about the Salvation of the soul, but I've found as I've gotten into The Word, that God is not just concerned for the soul, but He is concerned about the redemption of the whole person: Body, Soul and Spirit. In light of that, turn to I Corinthians 12. We're following this same concept, that once we enter into that ark of safety (which for us is the Gospel of Salvation - that Christ died, His Blood was shed, He was buried and He rose again) and when we believe that with all our hearts, then we enter into eternal redemption. In I Corinthians 12: 12,13, we see Paul expressing this concept of being in the "Body." Instead of the ark, he uses the illustration of the human body as a type of the "Body of Christ." The human body is made up of all its various parts; fingers, toes, eyes, etc. These are all different organs with different functions, but they all operate under one center of operation in the mind and make up **One Body**.

I Corinthians 12:12,13

For as the body is one, and hath many members, and all the members of that one body, being many, are one body: so also is Christ. For by one Spirit are we all baptized into one body, whether we be Jews or Gentiles, whether we be bond or free; and have been all made to drink into one Spirit."

Now, does the Holy Spirit baptize with water? No! So, this is not talking about water baptism, yet nearly every Christian group will not accept a person for membership without water baptism. Do you really believe that every member in your congregation is a born again child of God? Of course not! We are all members of congregations where there are unbelievers who have been baptized under whatever form of baptism their particular group uses. There are still people coming into every group who are totally unsaved; they're baptized and they are members there, but they are **not** members of the Body of Christ. There will be no unbelievers in the Body of Christ because that's the work of the Holy Spirit - to immediately place or baptize them into the Body of Christ. The reason Paul uses this analogy of the human body is that some believers' roles are no more that that of a little pinkie finger. Some may even have the role of a little toe, which most people never see. Others may be in more visible roles, but every one of us, regardless of where God has placed us in the Body, has a function in that Body, be it small or great. We'll get back to Romans 8 in moment, but here in I Corinthians 12, it shows very clearly what God expects of His children. Here, Paul mentions the gifts that really amount to something; the very gifts Christ uses, by an act of the Holy Spirit, to search the heart. The Holy Spirit will never place an unbeliever into the Body of Christ. None of us can examine someone else close enough to screen him from the membership in our local church. We can't do it, and we're not supposed to. That's why Jesus gave the illustration during His earthly ministry of the "tares and the wheat." Years ago, when I was teaching in that concept of the tares and the wheat, an agronomist at the college brought in some tares and wheat. You couldn't tell the difference, but one would never give a grain and the other would. It's the same way in the church. We can't judge and say, "That church member is not a child of God." That's not our job. But, we have to be aware that in the Body of Christ there are no false professors - only the genuine believer is in the Body of Christ, and that's the only Christ there is.

So that's the membership you'd better be sure of. Don't worry about whether you are member of the biggest church in town or the smallest; just be sure you are a member of the Body of Christ, and remember the qualification: **It's for all! "For by one spirit we were baptized into one body!"**

(6c) What is the unpardonable sin ?

Book 15 LESSON TWO * PART II

MATTHEW REVIEW: UNPARDONABLE SIN:PARABLES OF LUKE 15: THE SECRETS OF THE BODY NOT REVEALED

Take your Bible and join in with us for this study. Once you get into the Book of Books you just can't beat it. It is just so fabulous. So many people have the idea it's just a musty, dusty, old Book and just a bunch of Bible stories, and it's not. Everything fits from cover to cover, and it's all written so miraculously. That's why we know it's not an ordinary Book, but rather the Divine, inspired Word of God, and is everything that God said it is. As I've said before, I just want to look at the "overall plan of the ages," as someone has put it, and hit some of the high points, and some of the passages that questions arise from.

In Matthew Chapter 12, beginning with verse 31, we have a few little verses that have raised so many questions. This passage used to bother me also, but when you come to any portion of Scripture, be ready to constantly ask questions from your own point of view. Right here we have what people normally call the **"unpardonable sin."** When something is unpardonable, that means it's going to be your doom. In other words, if you are guilty of the unpardonable sin, then you have no hope of glory, and are headed for the lake of fire. I've looked at these verses in the knowledge that, the only sin that is going to condemn anyone, Jew or Gentile, black or white, rich or poor is not any particular thing we have said, or deed we have done. There is only one thing that will condemn a person to the lake of fire, and that is **"UNBELIEF."**
We are not talking about **unbelief** here, we are talking about something that is spoken. Let me prove my point. Before we look at Matthew 12, let's look at the Book of Hebrews Chapter 3 for a moment. Maybe I can make my point from the reverse end. I don't want someone to go through life scared to death that maybe they have committed the unpardonable sin, which most people feel, according to Matthew 12 is blasphemy against the Holy Spirit. Blaspheming the

Holy Spirit is a sin, and there is no doubt about it. But if I understand Scripture correctly, there is no sin that the Grace of God doesn't reach beyond. In other words, the most violent of sinners are still candidates of the Grace of God. But what do they have to do? **"BELIEVE."**

I think the Apostle Paul wrote the Book of Hebrews that we are now going to look at. He is taking the experience of Israel having just come out of Egypt, with God leading them to the Promised Land. When they got to Kadesh Barnea, who's idea was it to send in spies? It certainly wasn't God's. God had never intended for them go search out the land. God said, **"Go in and take the land, and I'll send in hornets ahead of you and drive the people out."** But Israel couldn't even take God at His word at that point in time. So they hedge and say, **"Well let us spy it out first."** God in His goodness then condescended to their request and said, **"Alright, choose out twelve men and let them go in."** And that was one of the biggest mistakes that Israel ever made. Ten of them said, **"Oh, we can't do it. There is no way we can drive out the Canaanites, we are as grasshoppers in their sights."** God had already said that He would drive them out. So what was their problem?

Hebrews 3:15-18
"While it is said, 'To day if ye will hear his voice, harden not your hearts, as in the provocation (in other words, as Israel was there in the wilderness). *For some, when they had heard, did provoke: howbeit not all that came out of Egypt by Moses. But with whom was he* (God) *grieved forty years? Was it not with them that had sinned, whose carcasses fell in the wilderness? And to whom sware he that they should not enter into his rest, but to them that* (what?) *believed not?'"*

They had committed many sins of immorality; the golden calf; all pagan practices of worship. But God is not holding that against them - He doesn't even mention that, as vile as it was. He could forgive that kind of sin. But what was Israel's problem? **"UNBELIEF."** They couldn't believe what God had said.

Hebrews 3:19
"So we see that they (the children of Israel) *could not enter in because of unbelief."*

Has anything changed? No! God can forgive to the uttermost, any sin except the sin of *UNBELIEF (*when people refuse to believe that Christ died for them, paid their sin debt, and rose from the dead in power. And that's all He's asking). So believe it for your salvation! If a person refuses to believe that Gospel, then that person's doom is sealed. Remember Hebrews 11:6 says to you and I in the Age of Grace:
Hebrews 11:6
"But without faith it is impossible to please him...."

Let's go back to Matthew 12 and look at the unpardonable sin. We need to leave this verse right where it sits. This is God dealing with the Nation of Israel. This doesn't mean that we can't take some warning from it. I certainly don't tell people to go out and blaspheme the Holy Spirit, because after all, God will forgive you. I would never do that. All I'm saying is that this is something that doesn't fit Church doctrine. If you can learn to leave these things where they belong, you don't have to pigeonhole them, and say you'll come back to this at a later time. It's so perfectly set. So to the Nation of Israel He says:

Matthew 12:31,32

"Wherefore I say unto you, All manner of sin and blasphemy shall be forgiven unto men: but the blasphemy against the Holy Ghost shall not be forgiven unto men. And whosoever speaketh a word against the Son of man (Christ)*, it shall be forgiven him: but whosoever speaketh against the Holy Ghost, it shall not be forgiven him, neither in this world* (age)*, neither in the world* (age) *to come."*

Now let's look at a parable that explains this so beautifully in Matthew 21. Jesus is speaking again to the Jews:

Matthew 21:33,34

"Hear another parable: `There was a certain householder, which planted a vineyard, and hedged it round about, and digged a winepress in it, and built a tower, and let it out to husbandmen, and went into a far country:'"
"And when the time of the fruit drew near, he sent his servants (to get some return on the investment that he had made) *to the husbandmen, that they might receive the fruits* (or profit) *of it."*

Matthew 21:35-42

"And the husbandmen took his servants, and beat one, and killed another, and stoned another. Again, he sent other servants more than the first: and they did unto them likewise. But last of all he sent unto them his son, saying, `They will reverence my son.' But when the husbandmen saw the son, they said among themselves, `This is the heir; come, let us kill him, and let us seize on his inheritance.' And they caught him, and cast him out of the vineyard, and slew him, When the lord therefore of the vineyard cometh, what will he do unto those husbandmen (and remember this is Jesus asking the Jew). *They say unto him, `He will miserably destroy those wicked men, and will let out his vineyard unto other husbandmen, which shall render him the fruits in their seasons.' Jesus saith unto them, `Did ye never read in the scriptures, The stone which the builders rejected, the same is become the head of the corner: this is the Lord's doing, and it is marvellous in our eyes?'"*

Matthew 21:43-45

"Therefore say I unto you, `The kingdom of God shall be taken from you, and given to a nation bringing forth the fruits thereof. And whosoever shall fall on this stone shall be broken: but on whomsoever it shall fall, it will grind him to powder.' And when the chief priests and Pharisees had heard his parables (plural, not just this one, but everyone that He had spoken)*, they*

perceived that he spake of them."

They suddenly understood that Jesus was pointing His finger at them. Now what was the parable all about? God called the Nation of Israel out, and gave them the Covenant promises. He called them His son, His favored nation. And He dealt with them through the Old Testament years by sending the prophets. What did they do to the prophets? They killed them. We always like to talk in terms of the Trinity. So let's look at it this way. Remember the Jew only knew about God the Father. So God the Father sent the prophets to His Covenant people and they killed them, or threw them in the dungeons. They refused to hear them. Did God cancel the Nation of Israel because of that? No. God sent His only Son next, The Christ. And Christ presented Himself to the Nation of Israel, on the basis of the covenants that we have been emphasizing for months. And what did they do with the Son? They killed Him. So these Pharisees are picking up on it. He's talking about them. And so it is in all of Jesus' parables.

But we have one Person of the Trinity left out. The Holy Spirit. Let's look at the Scripture that pertains to the Holy Spirit. And if you can't go along with this, don't worry about it. I've always said in my teaching there is room for you to disagree on some things, and this is one of them. But to me it makes sense in light of the fact that there is one sin that condemns us, and that is **unbelief** concerning the Gospel. In other words, I maintain, someone could blaspheme the Holy Spirit tomorrow or next week and God can still save him in this Age of Grace. But let's not lose sight of what the unpardonable sin is dealing with, and that is Israel the Nation! She is the one that is coming under this anathema of God.

Now go to Acts Chapter 6. Israel has rejected the overtures from the Father by killing the prophets. They rejected the overtures of the Son by killing The Christ. But how are they going to deal with the Holy Spirit, because here is the unpardonable part now - how they deal with third Person of the Godhead. He could forgive the first two, but not the third one. We have, in Acts Chapter 6, the appointment of seven men, normally referred to as deacons. They get the word "deacon" from the description of their duties. We find in verse 3 that the early Jewish church in Jerusalem was having some problems and so the following happened:

Acts 6:3
"Wherefore, brethren, look ye out among you seven men of honest report, full of the Holy Ghost and wisdom, whom we may appoint over this business."

Acts 6:5
"And the saying pleased the whole multitude: and they chose Stephen, a man full of faith and of the Holy Ghost,..." Now we have the Holy Spirit mentioned twice in two verses. So Stephen comes before this whole Jewish crowd.

Acts 6:15

"And all that sat in the council, looking steadfastly on him, saw his face as it had been the face of an angel."

What is permeating Stephen? The presence of the Holy Spirit. It was so radiant they could see the difference. Go to Chapter 7 verse 2. Now watch the language of whom Stephen is addressing:

Acts 7:2

"And he said, `Men, brethren, and fathers (all Jews), *hearken; The God of glory appeared unto our father Abraham,...'"* Can any Gentile claim that? Of course not.

If you ever want the history of the Nation of Israel in a nutshell, read this whole chapter. It even gives a lot of little details that the Old Testament leaves out.

Acts 7:54

"And when they (these Jews) *heard these things, they were cut to the heart, and they gnashed on him with their teeth."*

Acts 7:55

"But he, being full of the Holy Ghost (do you see the emphasis over and over that the Holy Spirit is on display here?), *looked up steadfastly into heaven, and saw the glory of God, and Jesus* (not sitting but rather) *standing on the right hand of God,"* In a future lesson, we'll pick up the reason these Jews got so mad when they heard Stephen say that Jesus was standing.

Acts 7:58-60

"And cast him out of the city, and stoned him: and the witnesses laid down their clothes at a young man's feet, whose name was Saul. And they stoned Stephen, calling upon God, and saying, `Lord Jesus, receive my spirit.' And he kneeled down, and cried with a loud voice, `Lord, lay not this sin to their charge. And when he had said this, he fell asleep (died).'"

From this point on, what is the future as we see here in the Book of Acts concerning the Nation of Israel? All down hill. And why? Because they had now committed that unpardonable sin of not only rejecting the Father and The Son, but now had also rejected the Holy Spirit. And for nearly 2000 years, what has the Jew been going through? Suffering, turmoil, in a state of spiritual blindness. Here in America they are pretty fortunate, but overall for all this time, basically they have been going through the mill. But when this age ends and we come into the next age, which is the millennium reign, Israel is going to come into God's goodness and Grace. If you don't like that approach about the unpardonable sin you don't have to agree. But for me it fits so beautifully, because we have left it in place. Notice we didn't take it out of the Nation of Israel and try to put it in the Church Age, but left it right where it was, with the Jewish economy.

Another point I would like to make is this. After the stoning of Stephen and the Holy Spirit aspect, the next event of importance in the chronological unfolding is the conversion of what great man? Saul of Tarsus (Paul). Even though Peter will go to the house of Cornelius in Acts Chapter 10 (after Saul is converted in Chapter 9), Chapters 11 and 15 mention Peter, and from there to the end of the Book of Acts Peter is never mentioned again. Why? Israel is now falling out of all the things that God had been promising, and now here comes Paul with the Body of Christ, the predominately Gentile Church. When we study the Book of Acts, I'll show you the transitional aspect of this Book, how God deals with His Covenant people Israel under the Law with all the Old Testament promises; and how when they rejected it, God now does something totally different - something the Old Testament knew nothing of. He turned to the Gentiles with the Apostle Paul.

(7c) When was the earth created according to the Bible ?

Book 1 LESSON ONE * PART IV

Turn to Genesis 1:1,2. Last time we talked about Christ's being the Person of the Godhead who called everything into being. We talked about how the Hebrew word "Barah" indicates not only creation, but perfect, beautiful creation. God can't create something that isn't perfect and good. Throughout Chapter 1 of Genesis, we see that as God made things, He inspected them and recorded that "it was good." Yet, when we come to verse 2 of this Chapter we read: "*And the earth was without form and void, and darkness was upon the face of the deep.*"

That hardly sounds perfect and beautiful. Rather it implies a "mess," chaos. If God, in verse 1, created the earth beautiful and perfect, (we have no indication of the time element between these two verses) and now, in verse 2 it's less than that, it's obvious that something drastic has happened. That beautiful creation of verse 1 has been changed into something ..... "without form, void, covered with water, and enveloped in darkness."

This is the first flood. A flood condition existed over the entire face of the planet. This may be an explanation of why God told Noah in Genesis 9:13,15: "*I do set my bow in the cloud, and it shall be for a token of a covenant between me and the earth...And I will remember my covenant, which is between me and you and every living creature of all flesh; and the waters shall no more become a flood to destroy all flesh .*"

Why would God make so big an issue of not ever destroying the world again in this manner? Because He made this covenant with Noah, following the second worldwide flood which destroyed all life. "*And darkness was upon the face of the deep.*" Here the earth was covered with water and that which God had originally created perfect and beautiful was undone. All we can do to understand this situation is to search the Scriptures for an explanation. Turn in your Bible to Ezekiel 28:13-15. Remember when you study Scriptures, ask yourself questions about what you're reading. What is being said; about whom is it being said; who's doing the talking; etc. Now verses 13-15:

"Thou hast been in Eden the garden of God; every precious stone was thy covering, the sardius, topaz, and the diamond, the beryl, the onyx, and the jasper, the sapphire, the emerald and the carbuncle, and gold: the workmanship of thy tabrets and of thy pipes was prepared in thee in the day that thou wast created."

"Thou art the anointed cherub that covereth; and I have set thee so: thou wast upon the holy mountain of God; thou hast walked up and down in the midst of the stones of fire."

"Thou wast perfect in thy ways from the day that thou wast created, till iniquity was found in thee."

Now, let's look at these verses phrase by phrase:

"You were in Eden, the garden of God;"

Who do we know, according to Scripture, was in the Garden of Eden?

God * Adam * Eve * Satan

"...every precious stone was thy covering, the sardius, topaz, and the diamond, the beryl, the onyx, and the jasper, the sapphire, the emerald and the carbuncle, and gold."

These beautiful gemstones mentioned here are mentioned again in the book of Revelation in the description of the New Jerusalem. (Again we see that what began in Genesis, we will see ending in Revelation).

"...the workmanship of thy tabrets and of thy pipes was prepared in thee in the day that thou wast created."

Now, because we know that God is not a created being, this indicates that the passage must refer to Adam or Eve or Satan.

"...Thou art the anointed cherub that covereth;"

In Scripture, people are never referred to as cherubs or angelic beings; so here we see that God is addressing an angelic being, and through the prophet Ezekiel, is revealing that angelic being to us. So we can deduce that this passage is referring to Satan. The term "covers" in Hebrew refers to "rule." So we see that this angelic being is a ruling being.

"...and I have set thee so:"

God says, "I placed you there." This angelic being was ruling because he was placed there by a sovereign act of God.

"Thou wast upon the holy mountain of God;"

Again, in Scripture, unless a specific mountain or land area is mentioned, mountain is normally used to indicate a "kingdom" rather than just a "hill" somewhere. So God says to this angelic being, Satan, "you ruled over a kingdom I gave you."

"Thou hast walked up and down in the midst of the stones of fire."
These stones of fire refer to the gemstones named in the verses above. So we see that this angelic creature was ruling, by God's sovereign command, over a kingdom that was literally impregnated with these precious jewels, these glorious gemstones along with all the other beauties of nature. We see all these gemstones referred to again in Revelation 21 as a part of the New Jerusalem coming down - restoring the world to its original beauty of Genesis 1:1:

"Thou wast perfect in thy ways from the day that thou wast created, till iniquity was found in thee."
In verse 15, God is continuing to speak to this angelic being, describing his perfection "until" - a time word. At some specific point in time, this angelic being lost, dropped, destroyed his perfection and iniquity or unrighteousness was found in him. What was his problem? Turn to

Isaiah 14:12-14. Here the prophet says,
"How art thou fallen from heaven, O Lucifer, son of the morning! How art thou cut down to the ground, Which didst weaken the nations! For thou hast said in thine heart, 'I will ascend into heaven, I will exalt my throne above the stars of God; I will sit also upon the mount of the congregation, in the sides of the north; I will ascend above the heights of the clouds; I will be like the Most High.'"

In verse 12 we discover the name of this angelic being - "Lucifer," along with his actions "which didst weaken the nations." These nations refer to angelic kingdoms over which he had dominion, because mankind was not yet made for him to have rule over.
Now, look what he says. ..... (Notice all the "*I will's*"). "*...I will ascend into heaven, I will exalt my throne above the stars of God;...*"

This angelic being, Lucifer, was not satisfied with all God had given him. Instead, he wanted even more - even to usurp the very power and position of God. Satan is still trying that. Remember his temptation of Jesus as recorded in Matthew 4:8,9?

"Again, the devil taketh him up into an exceeding high mountain, and sheweth him all the kingdoms of the world, and the glory of them; and saith unto him, 'All these things will I give thee, if thou wilt fall down and worship me.'"

He still attempts to bribe us into worshipping him today in much the same way.

"I will sit also upon the mount of the congregation, in the sides of the north;"
The "*sides of the north*" are where some theologians get the idea that heaven is located somewhere behind the northern sky. It may or may not be. We can only speculate on this and we have more important things to contemplate.

"I will ascend above the heights of the clouds; I will be like the Most High."

Here God is quoting the heart thoughts of this creature. Lucifer is saying (and still is saying) in his heart, *"I will be like the Most High."* This angelic being has everything he could possibly expect ever to have: he's beautiful, he's surrounded by beauty over which he has total dominion. But the one thing he lacks that is not within his grasp is to be God or higher than God.

Soon in our studies we'll be coming to Genesis 3:1-6. We'll see Eve in the garden. She has everything she could possibly want: a perfect home, a perfect husband, a perfect environment. And what does Satan tempt her with? "If you'll eat the forbidden fruit, you'll be `like God.'" And she falls for it!

This is what I refer to throughout the Scripture as "The Lie" - that human beings can be "like God." When you hear that touted, don't believe it! Certainly we are sons, children of God; and Paul tells us in Phil. 3:20-21 that our bodies shall be changed to be like Jesus' glorified body, but we're never going to become God. That would be impossible. And that's the LIE! As this world is so fast winding down, with all the false teachings and movements like the New Age or "Shirley McLainism," what is the pitch we hear being offered by the cults? "You're going to become God." When the Antichrist shows up, he's going to promise everything including this LIE in order to get control of the world.

Always be aware as you study the unfolding of the human experience that Satan's big lie, the one most people will fall for, and the basis for all the cults is this very one, "You will become God," or "You will become like God." Lucifer found out that he could not become God, and God brought him down. Consequently, as a result of that judgment the earth became changed from what it was in Genesis 1:1 to what it is recorded as being in Genesis 1:2.
Look near the back of your Bible to the little book of Jude, verse 6. This describes the angels being chained, awaiting judgment. This ties in with a passage in Revelation 12:3-4 which reads:

"And there appeared another wonder in heaven; and behold a great red dragon, having seven heads and ten horns, and seven crowns upon his heads. And his tail drew the third part of the stars of heaven, and did cast them to the earth ..."

We see that this angelic being, Lucifer, who ruled over an angelic kingdom, in his rebellion against God, actually convinced one-third of the angelic host of heaven to follow him in his rebellion, and they are referred to in Jude as "fallen angels," locked up and awaiting judgment. These are not the precursors of demons. The Bible doesn't tell us just where demons do come from, only that they exist as a part of Satan's forces of evil.

Looking back at Genesis 1:2, now we see that the earth is "without form." In judgment on Lucifer, God destroyed the earth and knocked him out of his place of authority and rule over that beautiful creation to become the great "adversary" or enemy of God. And God, in his sovereignty has permitted that.

Satan, Paul tells us, can transform himself into an angel of light (II Cor. 11:14). Don't believe the cartoon portrayals of Satan as dressed in red leotards, with horns and a tail and carrying a pitchfork; or as Milton described him as "the one who stokes the fires of hell." Satan is a powerful angelic being with great cunning and intellect. He is limited only by the sovereign power of God. Satan will do anything to promote his own ends. He'll even promote good and beautiful things if, by doing so, he can keep a human being from seeing the truth of God's Word. Don't sell him short! He's got tremendous power! In Genesis 1:2, we find that God's beautiful creation of verse 1 has been destroyed because of Satan's (Lucifer's) rebellion. It was destroyed by water.

In verses 3-19 in Chapter 1, the work described being done by God does not actually refer to works of creation, but rather to works of restoration. In verse 2 the earth and all that was on it did not cease to exist - it just became dysfunctional. Verses 3-19 record the steps God took to restore his creation of verse 1 to a functional condition - to restore it to what it had been before the rebellion. There's not a word in the Hebrew text that refers to creation in these verses, and we don't see that "creativity" of God until we get to verse 20 where animal life is introduced, and later of course, when Adam is created.

In verse 3, the Almighty, Triune God, through the Person of Jesus Christ, as we see in the New Testament, says, "Let there be light." It doesn't say He created it - just that He made it functional. He removed whatever had hidden the light from the scene.

Verses 4 & 5: "*And God saw the light, that it was good: and God divided the light from the darkness. And God called the light Day, and the darkness He called Night. And the evening and the morning were the first day.*"

Some like to say that this could be a day of any amount of time. However, the description of the separation of light from darkness really indicates a 24-hour day, in my opinion. It is the beginning of time as we know it. We are creatures of time. We are governed by it, slaves to it. It's an integral part of our human experience.

Science says all creation is composed of three things:
Space * Matter * Time
If you remove any one of these factors, you have nothing. All creation as we know it is matter traveling through a given amount of space in a given period of time. Everything concerning time is based on our 24-hour day. Everything in space is meticulously timed. The scientists can tell us when to expect a comet, even though it's been out of sight for years, based on a time table governed by the laws of nature God established at creation. Ships navigate by the stars because

their movement is regular, dependable. All of human experience is tied to God's creation of time in verses 3 through 5. This is the only way we can comprehend that in six 24-hour days God got everything ready for the human experience, and then on the 7th day He rested.

For the next session, read verses 6 through 19 of Genesis chapter 1. You'll see no reference to "creation," but rather a replenishment or restoration of what had been before. Remember, it is by faith we have understanding of God's Word. We believe it because God said it. We know God's Word is true because hundreds of sometimes even thousands of years before it was accomplished, God prophesied and recorded what would happen later. The virtue of God's Word is established by the prophesies already fulfilled. ..... They are the proof of the Scriptures.

Book 1 LESSON Two * PART I
FIVE DAYS OF RE-CREATION

We're going to pick up right where we left off in the last chapter. I hope you had opportunity to read Genesis 1:6-23 as I suggested in preparation for today's lesson. Please take note that the language used in these verses is not that of creation, but rather that of restoration. God has taken that which the previous verses (Genesis 1:2-5) indicate was under water and darkness as a result of a previous judgment, and restored it to a functional condition. When we get down to verse 20, we'll see that God again, through an act of creation, brings forth the animal kingdom, and from verse 26 through the end of the chapter, the human race.

Verse 6: *"And God said, Let there be a firmament in the midst of the waters, and let it divide the waters from the waters."*

All you have to do to understand this verse is to analyze the wording carefully. The word "Firmament" is what we would normally refer to as our atmosphere - our sky. It may involve or include a certain portion of what we would call space, the planets closest to earth, but generally speaking, we will consider the firmament as earth's atmosphere.

Looking closely at this, the Word says here that God is going to divide the water that is presently covering the planet (as a result of an earlier judgment). The earth is in a state of total flood - what we previously called the "First Flood." God, the Scripture says, is going to divide these flood waters and move part of them out above our atmosphere. We can picture that as a vapor belt out in space surrounding the earth. This same vapor belt will later be brought back on earth at the time of "Noah's Flood," but for now, let's just picture it out in space with the remainder of the water left covering the planet's surface.

Verse 7: *"And God made the firmament, and divided the waters which were under the firmament from the waters which were above the firmament; and it was so."*
God accomplished what He had spoken in verse 6.

Verse 8: *"And God called the firmament Heaven. And the evening and the morning were the second day.”*

God names the firmament (atmosphere) *“heaven.”* Previously we talked about the three heavens mentioned in Scripture:

1. The 1st Heaven which is the earth's atmosphere; the area in which the birds fly. The Scriptures even use that terminology; *“The fowls of the Heavens;”* (Jer. 9:10).

2. The 2nd Heaven which we now understand as “space;” ... that area where the stars and planets are.

3. The 3rd Heaven, mentioned in II Cor. 12:2 when Paul speaks of his own experience of being caught up into the very presence of God. The 3rd heaven then is the abode of God - what we normally think of as heaven.

What we have in verse 8 then is that the earth's floodwaters have been divided with half being above the atmosphere in the “vapor belt” in the first and maybe part of the second heaven, and the remaining half covering the earth.

I'd like to give a little consideration to this vapor belt because it gives rise theoretically to the idea, much to the consternation of science today, of the earth's having had a “greenhouse effect” from the beginning. As the illustration indicates, this vapor belt was such that it shielded the earth from the damaging and harmful rays of the sun. But even more, with this moisture in place, the rays of the sun were diffused or bent through the belt so that the sunbeams could not directly strike the planet's surface. Consequently the entire earth - from pole to pole - was tropical.

Archaeological evidence shows that at one time this had to be the case. Scientists have found tropical plants and animals buried deep in the frozen snows of the polar regions, particularly in northern Siberia. We know by this evidence that this old planet at one time had a constant tropical temperature and the best way to explain this is that this vapor belt provided a greenhouse effect and the world as we understand it was of one temperature.

This also explains as the Scriptures do, that it never rained, but rather was watered from beneath. This vapor belt provided no opportunity for rain or weather phenomena of any kind, because as the sun's light rays were diffused equally around the globe rather than striking the planet's surface directly as they now do, there was no shift in temperature, no increase or decrease of atmospheric pressures. Everything remained pretty much constant.

This condition gave rise on earth to that beautiful, constant, calm weather of the pre-Noah's Flood experience of man. It was perfect beyond our comprehension. Verses 9 and 10:
“And God said, Let the waters under the heaven be gathered together unto one place, and let the dry land appear; and it was so. And God called the dry land Earth; and the gathering together of the waters called he Seas; and God saw that it was good.”

In these verses, God separates the waters left on earth making dry land appear; and gives names to the land, "Earth," and the waters, "Seas." Verse 10 goes on to say that *"God saw that it was good."* It was perfect! When God calls something "Good," there's absolutely nothing amiss! Now, with the dry land having been established, and the sunlight's being able to come through, albeit diffused, the natural order once again comes on the scene as the earth "brings forth."

Verses 11 and 12: *"And God said, Let the earth bring forth grass, the herb yielding seed, and the fruit tree yielding fruit after his kind, whose seed is in itself, upon the earth; and it was so." "And the earth brought forth grass, and herb yielding seed after his kind, and the tree yielding fruit, whose seed was in itself, after his kind; and God saw that it was good."*

There's no word here of creation. All these things have been here before, and now with the earth's having been brought back to a place of production, these things just naturally come on the scene. The seeds were already there - they just needed the right conditions to "bring forth." We've had things happen in recent times that makes this so believable. Even though it is necessary to take the Word by faith, and some things talked about in Scriptures are beyond our comprehension, yet it's appropriate for us to see the logical aspect of God's dealing with mankind and His creation.

Just a few years ago, maybe 10, Mount St. Helens just blew it's top and totally devastated the area around it. Now, just a few years later (only moments or hours in God's scheme) people are already starting to write about how beautiful the new growth and new vegetation is and how the wildlife is coming back even better than it was before.

So, it's logical that when God restored the productivity to the earth, it just naturally came back into existence. There was no need for creation - it was already there - it just needed the right conditions to produce.

Verse 12 is actually a repetition of verse 11, but notice, if you will, the use of the phrase "after his kind," again and again. This flies in the face of evolution, doesn't it? That's why there is that constant and on-going argument between adherents to the Genesis account of creation and evolutionists.

God emphasizes over and over in these verses that everything was created in its "own kind." We know through our studies in biology and botany and other earth sciences that you cannot take something of one species and cross it with something of another species - something totally different. There are times when scientists can seemingly take cells from one species and they'll survive for awhile - but only for a short while, because God has said, "everything after its own kind," and there's just no room for such a thing as the evolutionary process which says that everything came from one cell.

Remember a few years ago when there was quite a furor that for burn patients, the best therapy they had was to cover the burns with pig's skin? They could actually take thin layers of pig's skin and place it over the human's burned areas, and because the pig's skin would "breathe" or let air pass freely, it worked well in enhancing the healing process in the human physiology. But it was only a temporary fix. After a few days, those cells in the pig's skin would die and just slough off.

Now, an evolutionist says, "See, that shows that everything came from the same place." But the creationists say, "It just shows that there was one Mastermind in creation." Everything that God has created has come from that one "Mastermind," so even though there may be similarities and there are things that seem analogous, that does not tell us that they came by way of evolution, but rather that the same Creator is the instigator of all of it.

Verse 13: *"And the evening and the morning were the third day."*

As we discussed in a previous lesson, I believe that this refers to a regular 24-hour day as we know it today. We're not talking about things suddenly just being created out of nothing as they were in Verse 1, but they're coming back on the scene quite naturally.

Verses 14 and 15: *"And God said, Let there be lights in the firmament of the heaven to divide the day from the night; and let them be for signs, and for seasons, and for days, and years; And let them be for lights in the firmament of the heaven to give light upon the earth; and it was so."*

Again, in verse 14 it doesn't indicate that God created the lights. They've already been there - we don't know for how long, and He merely makes them functional again. Whatever He had placed over the earth in that 1st catastrophe between verses 1 and 2 that made darkness and water cover the earth and blotted out the sun, moon, and stars, God here just simply removes and they come into view and are able to do what they were originally created to do.

Verse 15 is a simple statement of fact and we believe it. When God says, *"It was so,"* we can trust He knew what He was talking about!

Verses 16, 17 and 18: *"And God made two great lights; the greater light to rule the day, and the lesser light to rule the night; He made the stars also. And God set them in the firmament of the heaven to give light upon the earth. And to rule over the day and over the night, and to divide the light from the darkness; and God saw that it was good."*

If you'll look in a good Hebrew-English dictionary, the word translated *"made"* in verse 16 doesn't even come close in meaning to the word *"create"* that we discussed in Lesson 2. Again, this word is more in line with the idea that He simply made them operational. It doesn't say that He brought them out of nothing like the Hebrew word "Barah" does in verse 1. Verse 17 says God placed them in the "firmament of heaven," and this refers to the 2nd heaven that we discussed above - the depths of space in which revolve the galaxies.

"And God saw that it was good." Remember that God was getting everything ready for the appearance of the human race. The earth, as we saw in Lesson 1 was created to be inhabited (Is. 45:18), and verses 2 through 19 describe the process of getting it ready for mankind.

(8c) How can God send people to hell that have never heard the Gospel ?

Book 24 LESSON TWO * PART II

John 1:7-9

"The same came for a witness, to bear witness of the Light, (Speaking of Christ) *that all men through him might believe."* How many? All! Not just a few, but He came that all might believe. In verse 8, John the Baptist wasn't that Light.

"He was not that Light, but was sent to bear witness of that Light. That was the true Light, (Jesus the Christ, and here's something that I had never seen before) *which lighteth every man that cometh into the world."*

It says, "He lighteth every man," and The Book doesn't lie. Now I know a lot of us get all hung up when we realize that people down in the jungles of the Amazon valley, and in certain other spiritual dark places of the world have never heard the Gospel (Ref. I Corinthians 15:1-4). And we can't comprehend a Righteous God sending them to an eternal lake of fire. But listen, The Book says over and over that for some reason or other they have received the Light. They have a certain amount of knowledge. I can't explain it but that's what The Book says, and that's what it says right here, that when Christ came into the world, ***"His light lighteth every man that cometh into the world."*** Now that's a future tense verb, so it wasn't just speaking of those living at Christ's time, but rather it was also speaking of those coming on the scene even today. They have received somehow or other the Light. Let's go to Titus Chapter 2, and another verse that I've even struggled with myself, but I take it by faith. I believe it with all my heart, and mind because The Book says it. Here the Apostle Paul is at the end of his earthly ministry, he's going to be martyred before much longer. But look at this amazing statement, and remember it's Holy Spirit inspired. It's The Word of God.

Titus 2:11

"For the grace of God (That unmerited favor that God has poured out on the whole human race) *that bringeth salvation hath* (past tense) *appeared to all men."* Not just a favored few, but all men. Now let's back up to Romans that has thrown a curve at a lot of people, and it's hard for me to teach it because it just seems so impossible, but it isn't because The Book says it.

Romans 1:18,19a

"For the wrath of God..." And remember we're not under the wrath of God today, but rather the Grace of God. But His wrath is coming, it's getting closer every day, and one of these days God's going to have His stomach full, and He's going to start pouring out His wrath. Now reading on:

"For the wrath of God is revealed from heaven against all ungodliness and unrighteousness

of men, who hold the truth in unrighteousness; Because that which may (Now watch this) *be known of God is manifest in them..."*

'Manifest' is a multi-type term. There isn't just one little segment of knowledge, they have a whole bunch, just like a manifold on a V-8 engine has 8 port holes. That's one for every cylinder, that's a manifold, and the same word is associated with this word manifest. A complete unveiling of knowledge.

Romans 1:19b,20
"for God hath shewed it unto them. For the invisible things of him from the creation of the world are clearly seen, being understood (See?) *by the things that are made, even his eternal power and Godhead; so that they* (the whole human race) *are without excuse:"* That doesn't mean we can just sit in our living room and let the world go to Hell. But the constant admonition is that we are to promote the Gospel to the ends of the earth. Absolutely we are.

Book 21 LESSON TWO * PART II

Romans 3:26b
"... that he (The Lord Jesus) *might be just* (or fair),..."*
I remember sometime ago that someone presented the same question in a book or some material I was reading, and I've always had that question in my mind for as long as I can remember, just like everyone else. How will God justify sending someone to the eternal Lake of Fire when so far as we know they have never had an opportunity to hear the Gospel (Ref I Corinthians 15:1-4). The human response is this, "But God, that's not fair, because they never had a chance." Whoever presented that question said this, "You know the only way we can answer that dilemma is that God is never unjust, or unfair. So in His own higher way of thinking, God knows how He will take care of it. We can't comprehend it. But remember that God can never be unfair. He is totally just in all of his dealings.

(9c) Will there be degrees of punishment for those sentenced to hell ?

Book 14 LESSON ONE * PART IV

Now here we are at the end of the thousand years reign and rule of Christ and we are at the Great White Throne. It's up in space somewhere. It's not on the earth, because the earth has fled away. So now in the resurrection of the unjust, they are brought back bodily because that's what resurrection denotes. Now, back to Revelation 20. Here the lost stand before the Lord, Who in their case is the Judge, and not the Savior. As Judge, He shows them their record, and there will be degrees of punishment. Jesus made that so plain, when He said to the people of Capernaum in Matthew 11, the following:

Matthew 11:23,24
"And thou, Capernaum, which art exalted unto heaven, shalt be brought down to hell: for if the mighty works, which have been done in thee, had been done in Sodom, it would have remained until this day. But I say unto you, `That it shall be more tolerable for the land of Sodom in the day of judgment, than for thee.'" So He makes it very plain that the people of Capernaum would suffer more in their eternal doom, than the horrible people of Sodom.

Book 36   LESSON TWO * PART II

Revelation 20:5a
"But the rest of the dead lived not again until the thousand years were finished..." So there's coming a day when they're brought back on the scene to have their day before our Lord to see what degrees of punishment they will receive in the **Lake of Fire**.

Revelation 20:5b
"This is the first resurrection."
Now this is always confusing, because it's not talking about the rest of dead in the first part of verse 5, but the ones up in verse 4. They were in the first resurrection which was the resurrection unto life.

Revelation 20:6
"Blessed and holy is he that hath part in the first resurrection: (the believers) **on such the second death hath no power, but they shall be priest of God and of Christ, and shall reign with him a thousand years."** Now come on down to verse 11.

Revelation 20:11-15
"And I saw a great white throne, and him that sat on it, (which will be Christ) **from whose face the earth and the heaven fled away; and there was found no place for them. 12. And I saw the dead,** (the lost who have been down in Hell in torment ever since they died) **small and great, stand before God; and the books were opened: and another book was opened, which is the book of life: and the dead** (those spiritually dead who never entered into salvation) **were judged out of those things which were written in the books, according to their works. 13. And the sea gave up the dead which were in it; and death and hell delivered up the dead which were in them: and they were judged every man according to their works. 14. And death and hell were cast into the lake of fire. This is the second death.** (remember a believer will never face second death, because we experience our second death when we identified with Christ when He died on the cross. Remember Paul says, `we are crucified with Christ!') **15. And whosoever was not found written in the book of life was cast into the lake of fire."**

So these unbelievers will be resurrected out of Hell and given a body that is fit for the Lake of Fire. That sounds horrible doesn't it? But that's what the Book says.

Book 34 LESSON TWO * PART IV

Galatians 5:10
"I have confidence in you through the Lord, that ye will be none otherwise minded: but he that troubleth you shall bear his judgment, whosoever he be."

Now those are strong words aren't they? In other words Paul is saying, "Whoever it is that is bringing in this false teaching, and is leading you away from the Gospel of Grace, his judgment is sure." He's going to one day stand before the Great White Throne where only lost people will stand, and he's going to be judged, absolutely they are. I've said for years that preachers and theologians who mislead people are going to have the hottest corner in the lake of fire, because they are misleading multitudes.

(10c) What is the origin and role of the various races of people ?

Book 3 LESSON TWO * PART II
The map below covers the area of the Mediterranean Sea and shows Jerusalem, the Sea of Galilee, the Jordan River and the Dead Sea near the lower end of which lie the ancient cities of

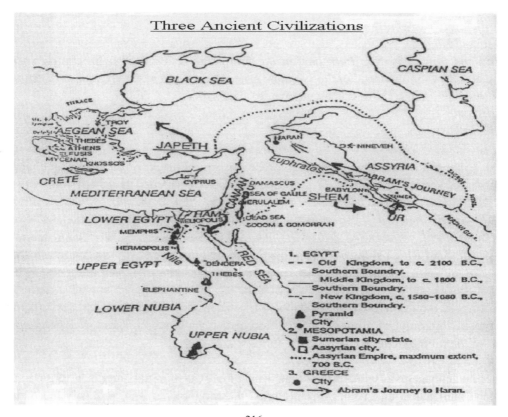

Sodom and Gomorrah. This whole area is called the land of Canaan throughout Scripture and today is the land of Israel. We will continue to refer to it as the land of Canaan, because the Canaanites, the offspring of this grandson of Noah were occupying the land of Canaan. This carries all the way into the coming of the Nation of Israel. We'll soon get to that in Genesis 12, which I consider to be the benchmark of Genesis. From that chapter we get the setting of everything that leads into our own doctrine in the Church Age. When it comes to the choosing of a bride for Isaac, Abraham had been told by God that Isaac was not to marry a Canaanite woman. It goes back to what happened in Genesis 9. We have to go slowly; there's a reason for everything. This is not a bunch of Jewish myths cooked up around a campfire. This is the literal unfolding of God's detailed program - it all fits. Nothing is in the picture that doesn't belong there. After Canaan is cursed, Noah says in verses 26 & 27:

Genesis 9:26,27
"And he said, `Blessed be the LORD God of Shem; and Canaan shall be his servant. God shall enlarge Japheth, and he shall dwell in the tents of Shem; and Canaan shall be his servant.'"

I've always been careful not to imply that through these three sons of Noah and because of the curse placed on the son of Ham that God has made some races inferior or others superior. We are going to see the whole human race coming from these three men and they are going to be different in their roles. I like to use the word "role" in more places than one. For example, in the game of football, the team's lineman has a different role than a running back, and a wide receiver has a totally different role from the quarterback. Some are on camera much more than others. But if you remove one of those team members, what happens? The people who are most visible can do nothing because each member of that team has to play out his role for the whole thing to work. It's the same way now with these three basic races of humanity - none is superior over the other, but each has its own particular role to fill.

What are the roles that God has stipulated? The offspring of Ham who, in the next chapter are predominately responsible for the building of the Tower of Babel, make their way to the land of Canaan. From Canaan we know there took place a migration south into southern Africa and southern Arabia, and they were probably the forebears of the Queen of Sheba. Then, from the Euphrates River we have the establishment of the offspring of another son of Noah, Shem. From the line of Shem we will follow predominately the man Abraham, who becomes the father of the Nation of Israel as well as the Arabs. So the Middle Eastern people are primarily the descendants of Shem. And then from the Tower of Babel, as they migrated up toward western Russia and Europe, we find the offspring of Japheth (the white race or Caucasians). The offspring of Japheth will migrate to Europe, Scandinavia, Great Britain, western Russia and the northern coasts of the Mediterranean.

Reflect on human history. We know that from the Tower of Babel, some of the population moved toward the orient, China. From China, the Mongolians were probably the ones who migrated across the Pacific, becoming the forerunners of the American Indians. Never forget, those people had a tremendously advanced civilization. The Chinese were way ahead of the Caucasians when it came to materials such as silk and spices, to mathematics, and many other areas. So there is no superiority in the Caucasians over some of the other races, but the role they were assigned to play is different. When God said in verse 27 that He would enlarge Japheth, I believe we can see where it came about. Go to Acts 16. Until this time, the Caucasians or Japhethites were barbarians. Historically, when Rome was at the pinnacle of its power, it was overrun by the Gauls from the North who sacked Rome and burned it. They were the people of Europe. So these Japhethites had little impact on the human race until Acts 16. Paul had been spending time in Asia Minor - today's Turkey. Go to verse 6:

Acts 16:6
"Now when they had gone throughout Phrygia and the region of Galatia, and were forbidden of the Holy Ghost to preach the word in Asia,"

After being in Asia Minor, Paul had planned to go to the east, but the Holy Spirit stopped him and sent him west to Greece instead, and from thence the Gospel went to Europe and simply overwhelmed it. As the Gospel went over Europe, the people there were prompted by their convictions to go to America. We see now, in the last several hundred years how the Caucasian race has taken things that were lying dormant for so long and exploded them with their intellectualism and technology; yet I think the engine behind it was Christianity itself. Again, all of this ties together. Paul would have gone back to Asia but the Holy Spirit said, "No, I want you to go to Europe," and from Europe the Gospel came to us.

LESSON TWO * PART III
BABEL, "FALSE GODS"
Remember, we saw that after the flood, Noah and his family were given instructions to repopulate the earth and begin to cultivate it. Following our last session, one of my students mentioned to me that he had heard somewhere that prior to the flood there had been no fermentation. Nevertheless the Scriptures make it clear that the alcohol got the best of him and he became drunk. A sad commentary on all this is in verse 28 where it says:

Genesis 9:28
"And Noah lived after the flood three hundred and fifty years."

Isn't it amazing that there is never another mention of Noah's activities after this drunken episode? The only reason I can give for this is that the catastrophe that occurred to him in verses 20-22 destroyed his testimony. We as believers have to be so careful. The devil is constantly out to trip us up and if we fall far enough, we can certainly lose our testimony. It doesn't take long, either! I think everyone, even in the secular world knows that it takes a lifetime to build a reputation, but it only takes a moment to destroy it. It can happen politically, in the business world, and even in Christian circles. I think perhaps this is the reason that Noah lost his influence. We're going to see in the moments that follow how the entire human race began to decline spiritually almost immediately after the flood, in spite of all the knowledge that Noah and his sons had concerning the will of God.

These were adult people who went into the ark; they had complete memory of everything that was before the flood. It would be just as if you and I found ourselves in the ark and when we came out following the flood, we'd remember all the technology that we had enjoyed, all the things that were on the earth before the catastrophe. So it was with Noah and his family. These eight people had complete recollection, and it was only the grace of God that kept things from moving along too fast and kept technology from erupting again until God was ready for it to do so, as we've seen in the last eighty or ninety years. So these three sons of Noah, who with their wives came out of the ark, became the parents of the three great classifications of people that then overspread the earth. You might break it down this way:

1. Out of the line of Shem came all the great "religions" (although I don't like that word), Islam, Judaism, and Christianity. When I refer to the line of Shem, the primary man is Abraham.
2. Out of the line of Ham we have a lot of the original discoveries and inventions as we'll see in Chapter 12.
3. Out of the line of Japheth, even though they were primarily uncivilized barbarians, came a people that became expert in the arts, sciences, music (the Beethoven's and Tchaikovsky's), and the inventors of the industrial revolution (not taking credit away from contributions made by Oriental immigrants who came to America).

Come back to the migrations of the peoples as the Bible lays them out, and as we illustrated last time. The Japhethites migrated into what is present day Europe and western Russia; the Hamites ended up primarily in the land of Canaan and points south; and the sons of Shem populated the lands of the Middle East. I also prefer to put the oriental peoples in the line of Shem (although I may be wrong in that). Those three basic groups of people come from these three sons of Noah. Let's go to Chapter 10. We won't examine this chapter verse by verse, but I want you to see that the sons of Japheth are mentioned in verses 2 through 5. In verse 6 we have the genealogy of the Hamitic people:

Genesis 10:6,8,9
"And the sons of Ham; Cush, and Mizraim, and Phut, and Canaan."
Then, it's important that you look at verses 8 and 9:
"And Cush begat Nimrod: he began to be a mighty one in the earth. He was a mighty hunter before the LORD: wherefore it is said, `Even as Nimrod the mighty hunter before the LORD."
Keep this fact in mind because we're going to be talking about Nimrod for the next few moments. He was the son of Cush who was the son of Ham. However, to keep moving genealogically through the chapter, go down to verse 21. There we pick up Shem's offspring. Out of the

line of Shem we'll come to the family of Abraham in the last part of Chapter 11. Terah, the father of Abraham came out of the line of Shem. Also in those verses is something I think is very interesting (though there is no way for me to prove it) in Chapter 10, verse 25:

Genesis 10:25
"And unto Eber were born two sons: the name of one was Peleg, for in his days was the earth divided, and his brother's name was Joktan."

What I'm referring to is the so-called "theory of the continental drift." It states that the continents of the world were at one time together in one land mass. If you look at a map today, you'll see that with some effort and imagination the earth's continents could be fitted together like a jigsaw puzzle. For instance, the eastern coast of South America could easily be matched to the western coast of Africa. I'm not saying this is true, but I am saying it is possible that the continents drifted apart and wound up as we now know them, and if they did, it was during the lifetime of Peleg, for it was during his lifetime that the earth was divided.

(11c) What does the Bible say about false religions and horoscopes ?

Book 3 LESSON TWO * PART III

Genesis 11:2-4
"And it came to pass, as they journeyed from the east, that they found a plain in the land of Shinar; and they dwelt there. And they said one to another, "Go to, let us make brick, and burn them throughly.' And they had brick for stone, and slime had they for morter. And they said, `Go to, let us build a city and a tower, whose top may reach unto heaven; and let us make us a name, lest we be scattered abroad upon the face of the whole earth."

Again, I have to feel that this was all done at the instigation of Semiramis and under satanic influence. Logically, these people knew that they didn't have Jack's beanstalk. They knew they couldn't build a literal tower into the very throne room of Heaven, but what they were instituting here was a false, anti-god, ungodly system of worship whereby Satan inspired them to think they could usurp the very heavens of God Himself. This is nothing new to Satan. He has thought it before and still thinks today that he is going to defeat God in His purposes. They built this tower, not as something high through which they can walk to enter Heaven, but rather as a system of approach to Heaven, and hence it was the introduction to false worship. As we go through the Scriptures, we will continually refer to the fact that every false religion on this planet today no matter what it is or where, has its roots at the Tower of Babel. This is the beginning of false pagan worship.

Archaeologists have found that at the top of the Tower of Babel were all twelve signs of the zodiac. I maintain that today the horoscopes and the signs of the zodiac are of the underworld, the occult and should be left alone. Again, this is another way that Satan has adulterated something that was originally in God's program. I believe that before the flood, Adam and the early believers understood the Word of God, not from the written page, but from the stars. They had an intrinsic knowledge of the constellations and all these things - but as the Word of God written in the stars. However, as the human race degenerated, Satan took that which was spiritually perfect, adulterated it, and turned it to his own purposes, so that when we get to the Tower of Babel, this knowledge of the stars is turned into something that we call now, the occult. The horoscope and everything associated with it is not of God, but is of the counterfeiter, the Adversary. Remember, every false religion that ever has been, that is now, or that will come in the future, has its roots in the Tower of Babel.

Consequently, we haven't left Babel behind. Go to Revelation 17, where John deals with the false worldwide religion that is going to come on the scene during the final seven years of tribulation. This is written in symbolic imagery, but it certainly portrays a literal truth. John sees this woman, symbolic of the world-wide religious system, arrayed in purple and scarlet colors and decked with gold, precious stones and pearls which speak of tremendous wealth. If you look at the religions in the world today, the cults and false teachers draw in tremendous wealth daily, and ultimately they're going to come together to amalgamate all this wealth. This is what John sees symbolically.

Revelation 17:4,5
"And the woman was arrayed in purple and scarlet colour, and decked with gold and precious stones and pearls, having a golden cup in her hand full of abominations and filthiness of her fornication:" I maintain that this was not a physical fornication, but a spiritual one, an adulterating of spiritual things which God hates. Verse 5:
"And upon her forehead was a name written, MYSTERY, BABYLON THE GREAT, THE MOTHER OF HARLOTS AND ABOMINATIONS OF THE EARTH."

Clear back here in Revelation we find it - we haven't left Babylon behind, not by any means. Here it is, a great religious system coming on the scene, and all this is already here. We're seeing it grow by leaps and bounds in the New Age Movement. I warn people constantly that it's creeping into the churches and it sounds so good, but it's Babylon - it's Babel.

(12c) What is the origin of the customs and traditions associated with Christmas, Easter, and April Fool's Day ?

Book 3 LESSON TWO * PART IV

BABEL, "FALSE GODS"

Turn to Genesis 11 and we'll touch on some things from our last lesson - things related to the

Tower of Babel. Some of the customs and traditions that are still with us today have been with us so long we don't even know where they originated. For example, everyone is familiar with the Easter egg hunts that we have on Easter, and the Easter bunny; Santa Claus at Christmas and the Christmas tree; and every one of these things got its start at the Tower of Babel! As pagan worship was instituted in conjunction with the Tower of Babel, the first thing Semiramis started was the idea that her son, Tamar, was a son of god. We are coming full circle today! The more you understand Genesis the more you can understand what is taking place today. They weren't satisfied with just the male god figure, so they introduced female "goddesses," which became the very core of the mythologies of ancient Rome, Egypt, Greece and Babylon. And it didn't stop there!

Along with the worship of the female goddesses such as Venus and Diana, came the fertility rites - sexuality. As a part of the pagan worship, the ancient temples such as the one of Ephesus dedicated to Diana and those of other goddesses, were nothing but glorified houses of prostitution done in the name of religion. This all went hand-in-hand with pagan worship. And in the fertility rites, they went back to nature. As one approaches the spring equinox, March 21 and 22, there is new life coming up all around, and that new life speaks of fertility. So when they put all this together, they formed their fertility rites around the worship-center of the spring equinox. Again, Satan was becoming the great counterfeiter because whether he had foreknowledge of what he was doing or not, also associated with the spring equinox would be our celebration of the Resurrection of Christ.

Of course our Easter is timed according to the Passover of Israel as given in the Old Testament, and all of the Israeli feasts and time keeping was based on the moon's phases - either the new moon or the full moon. So way back at the Tower of Babel, they instituted the fertility rites in association with the spring equinox, and thereby we have the rabbit and eggs associated with our Easter, supposedly indicative of new life. But remember, it's pagan in its origin.

It's the same way with our customs at Christmas which is close to the first day of winter - the winter solstice of December 21 and 22. Again the ancient pagans instituted the worship of the evergreen tree because it, alone was still showing signs of life when everything else looked dead. The ancient Europeans actually began worshipping the evergreen tree and had the custom of the burning of the "Yule log" - all coming out of this pagan system associated with the Tower of Babel. Back in the early days, during the first, second and third centuries a lot of these pagan people were coming into the "church." However they came into the church without having a genuine Salvation experience, and merely came to enjoy the worship service. So it wasn't long before they began introducing some of their pagan practices into the church and the church accommodated them, so here we are some 1900 years later and we take these things for granted. I want you to know where they come from, for they have no place in our present day church.

I'm not telling people to throw away the Christmas tree (we have one), or to spoil Christmas and tell your kids that there's no such thing as Santa Claus, (maybe I should!), but I'll tell you this, anytime I see a Santa Claus going down the aisle of a church I won't go back there, because Santa Claus does not belong in a local church. He is a symbol of paganism, a symbol of the commercial world, and we should never mix it in with Christianity. Now, as I said before, I'm not telling people to take away the fun of Santa Claus as long as they don't associate it with the birth of Christ. Also, I don't think that Christ was born on or around December 25. We know that He wasn't born in the winter time because the shepherds don't stay out in the fields in Judea in December - it's too cold! (Again, I just pass this out in speculation, because I can't prove it from Scripture), but I personally think that April 1 would really more likely be the time of His birth.

I read one theory - and that's all it is, because nobody really knows when He was born - and that person speculated that Jesus was born in September, and the December 25th date was more likely the time of His conception. This would bring His birthday into September ... And he may be right. The reason that I think April 1 would be the more likely date is that I believe Adam was created and brought on the scene on April 1st. God stipulated to Israel that April was to be the first month of the year, so everything in Israel's calendar back in biblical times began with April 1st. I think that Christ was probably resurrected on an April 1st, also. Like I said, I can't prove any of this, but I think there are a lot of things associated in God's time table with the first day of the month of the biblical year - the month of April.

In addition, to kind of put the frosting on the cake, I think that Satan adulterated that day, April 1, with what we now call "April Fool's Day," or "All Fool's Day," which again came out of the occult practices and not from Scripture.

(13c) What does the Bible say about capital punishment ?

Book 3 LESSON TWO * PART I

Genesis 9:5,6
"And surely your blood of your lives will I require; at the hand of every beast will I require it, and at the hand of man; at the hand of every man's brother will I require the life of man. Whoso sheddeth man's blood, by man shall his blood be shed: for in the image of God made he man."
That puts man head and shoulders over anything else in creation, because we were created in God's image and God so ordained that the life of His created man is in the blood. This carries through in all the animals and birds, also; but God puts the stipulation on the life of a human being as not being cheap, but rather, of intrinsic value to God. There are many areas of the world where life is cheap; where they think nothing of killing people by the hundreds and thousands. We've witnessed it profusely in the last several years - First, in Far East in the killing fields of Cambodia and Vietnam, and more recently in the Middle East. It is nothing new to the human race, but it is not the way that God ordained it. He declared that man was to be of intrinsic value,

his life was not to be taken lightly, and if someone did take the life of a fellow human being, the stipulation was that the murderer was to be put to death by his fellow man. We call this, in the vernacular of Bible study, the instigation or the beginning of human government. In other words, before the flood, man didn't have the authority from God to control behavior by capital punishment or by incarceration in jail, or anything else. But, at this point, God designed that man would have authority over his fellow man (under God) and if a man were guilty of murder or some other crime, then the authority of human government was to take that person and deal with him accordingly.

"Capital punishment" has never been rescinded throughout Scripture. There are some things that have changed, but this still stands as God's law for the human race. Mankind, particularly sociologists, who hear me state this will probably "go into orbit;" they try to tell us that capital punishment is barbarian and is not fit for a civilized society. But, what is causing many of our problems? Why is crime increasing every day? I recently read in the Tulsa World that crime last year increased by 27%. It is doing so because we are not deterring it by a severe enough punishment. Let's look back at the New Testament, to Romans 13, again to compare Scripture with Scripture. Paul, writing to the Church in Rome, in particular; and the Church through the ages, in general, is laying out so clearly the role of government. We are blessed in America, and think that we have the best government in the world, but it has its weaknesses and problems. Even though it may be the best the world has ever seen, we're not to take advantage of it, but to recognize what a blessing good government is. Verse 1:

Romans 13:1
"Let every soul be subject unto the higher powers. For there is no power but of God: the powers that be are ordained of God."

"The Higher Powers" refer to government - the authority over us. God gives that power to rule us to the government. Even to a Saddam Hussein?!! Yes, ordained to them, too. Personally, I believe that this "Operation Desert Storm" war that has just ended might very well have been a fulfillment of Jeremiah 50 and 51, where the prophet describes the total annihilation of the nation of Babylon (which Saddam Hussein claims Iraq is).

Even Hitler was ordained of God! I've always said that the German people got just exactly what they deserved. Now, horror of horrors, I heard on the news recently, that there are now video games circulating among the young people of Europe, in which the role of the game player is the head of a concentration camp and the `point' of the game, is for him to put his subjects to death and cause them to suffer - the worse the prisoners suffer, the higher the player scores. This is simply preparing the world for the awful things that are to come upon human society. Nevertheless, the governments have been ordained of God for the good of Christian people. Many times they do not fulfill that calling, but as I said earlier, nations get what they deserve! If someday we loose our beautiful, democratic way of living, it will probably be because we've brought it upon ourselves. Paul continues:

Romans 13:2-4
"Whosoever therefore resisteth the power, resisteth the ordinance of God: and they that resist shall receive to themselves damnation. For rulers are not a terror to good works, but to the evil. Wilt thou then not be afraid of the power? Do that which is good, and thou shalt have praise of the same: For he is the minister of God to thee for good. But if thou do that which is evil, be afraid; for he beareth not the sword in vain: for he is the minister of God, a revenger to execute wrath upon him that doeth evil."

Whoever resists his local government, resists the plan of God! Whenever you meet a policeman, you shouldn't fear him (if you are a law-abiding citizen), but rather enjoy the sense of security that he is there to protect you. But, if you are a lawbreaker, you should feel terror, because God has ordained that he bring you to justice. We've lost that! Our young people have lost all respect for authority. Criminals know that statistics show that 70% of them can get out of jail within eight months of their conviction, so they have no fear of the authorities. The only thing that holds the fabric of society together, is a healthy fear and respect for the law - human government. Go back now to Genesis 9. As we see in verses 5 and 6, human government was established to maintain law and order, to protect the lives of the citizens; and in order to deter crime - murder in particular - God instituted capital punishment.

Any nation that practiced capital punishment in the past had a relatively low crime rate until they abolished it. One of the most visible examples of this is the nation of France. Until sometime in the 1970's, France still used the guillotine to execute murderers. They had so few murders in France each year that you could practically number them on one hand, But, … "society" said, "that's barbaric, it's a holdover from the dark ages," and so capital punishment there was abolished. Immediately, their murder rate skyrocketed like that of other nations without capital punishment. I am convinced that capital punishment is a legitimate deterrent to murder and major crime. We see so clearly in Genesis 9, what the Word of God says in this regard. The Word is true! I make no apology for it. The stipulation is made in verses 5 and 6:

Genesis 9:5,6
"And surely your blood of your lives will I require; at the hand of every beast will I require it, and at the hand of man; at the hand of every man's brother will I require the life of man. Whoso sheddeth man's blood, by man shall his blood be shed: for in the image of God made he man."

This is why life is precious, and we're not to take it lightly or to make of it something cheap!

(14c) What was the purpose of circumcision ?

Book 4 LESSON THREE * PART I

Genesis 17:6,7

"And I will make thee exceeding fruitful, and I will make nations of thee, and kings shall come out of thee. And I will establish my covenant between me and thee and thy seed after thee in their generations for an everlasting covenant, to be a God unto thee and to thy seed after thee."

Here is an interesting tidbit. It used to bother me how you could determine when the word seed was referring to the children in generations, or when it was referring to the seed of the woman in Genesis 3:15, which we know is Christ. It has been hard to determine. The word seed in the Hebrew is the word "zera." It is like our word sheep. Now our word sheep, whether it is singular or plural, is still sheep. It is the same with this Hebrew word "zera." The only way you can determine if it is singular or plural is by how it sets in the text. It is the same with our word sheep. If you were reading a sentence which talked about a flock of sheep covering the mountainside, you would immediately know the word is not singular, but plural. On the other hand, if you were shown a picture of someone shearing a sheep, by context what do you know? - that we are talking about `one.' Whenever the context refers to a vast number of people who are Abraham's seed, we are not talking about Christ, but about the generations of Israel. Turn with me to Chapter 21 where we will see the singular use of the word.

Genesis 21:12

"And God said unto Abraham, `Let it not be grievous in thy sight because of the lad, and because of thy bondwoman; in all that Sarah hath said unto thee, hearken unto her voice; for in Isaac (one person) *shall thy seed* (singular) *be called.'"*

Turn to Galatians, Chapter 3. I want you to be mindful of Genesis 3:15 (without having you turn there), where as soon as Adam and Eve had fallen, God made the prophetic promise that the seed of the woman would be the Redeemer and the One who would make the way back to God possible. Now in Galatians, Paul writes:

Galatians 3:16

"Now to Abraham and his seed were the promises made. He saith not, And to seeds (plural)*, as of many; but as of one, And to thy seed* (singular)*, which is Christ."*
Is it falling into place? In the Old Testament whenever we have the singular approach to the seed of the woman, it speaks of Christ; but when the plural is used with the generations following Abraham, then that is what it's referring to. Back to Genesis 17:

Genesis 17:8

"And I will give unto thee, and to thy seed (plural) *after thee, the land wherein thou art a stranger, all the land of Canaan, for an everlasting possession; and I will be their God."*

They can say what they want about God being through with the Nation of Israel, and about God transferring the promises made to Israel to the Church. But that flies in the face of what the

Scripture says. The Bible plainly teaches that no matter what the Israelite or Jew may do, God is still going to maintain the Covenant He made with Abraham clear back in 2000 BC If you are watching the Middle Eastern situation with an open mind, you realize the present day Jew is still the offspring of Abraham. Although we are not yet into the Jewish aspect of the Tribulation, etc., it is all coming. Everything in the Middle East is setting the stage for when the curtain will rise, and God will again pick up where He left off with His Nation of Israel back in the Book of Acts.

Genesis 17:9,10

"And God said unto Abraham, `Thou shalt keep my covenant therefore, thou, and thy seed after thee in their generations (again we are talking about the line of people). *This is my covenant, which ye shall keep, between me and you and thy seed after thee; Every man child among you shall be circumcised.'"*

Remember this is years after that original Covenant. This is even some time after that Deed we saw in Chapter 15. But now God is going to, you might say, cement this whole thing with a blood Covenant. I think that is the best way we can look at it. Have you ever watched movies of the ancients where they made a covenant with one another? They would take a knife blade and put a little slit in each hand. They would then shake hands and literally mix their blood; it was a blood covenant. I think this is the whole aspect of the institution of circumcision. God now has a blood Covenant with the Nation of Israel, or the children of Abraham. So Abraham was given all the instructions of how circumcision was to be instituted even though he, himself, was ninety-nine. From then on, every child of Abraham was to be circumcised at the age of eight days.

I believe medical science will back me up that an infant's blood coagulation reaches its peak at the age of eight days. In this present day we get our young mothers in and out of the hospital so quickly, that circumcision is accomplished before the child reaches eight days. When my mother gave birth to my little sister, the hospital stay for delivery was fourteen days. That gave the doctors ample time to circumcise the boy babies at eight days of age. This is all Scriptural.

Book 41 LESSON Two * Part III

The Uncircumcision. That was the Jewish term for a non-Jew. He was the Uncircumcised. And a lot of times they would add the word, "dogs." "Uncircumcised Dogs" is what they thought of Gentiles. Now, I'm going to give you one more. Come back a few more pages to Galatians chapter 2 and verse 7.

Galatians 2:7

"But contrariwise, when they (the leadership of the Jerusalem Jewish assembly) **saw that the gospel of the uncircumcision was committed unto me, as the gospel of the circumcision was unto Peter;"**

Now how many classes of people do you have? Two! Paul and Barnabas were the apostles of the uncircumcision or the Gentiles. Peter, on the other hand, and James and John and the other of the disciples, were the apostles of the circumcision, or Israel. I could stand here for another hour on that alone. **Why do you suppose Jesus chose the twelve inside of Israel? Because they were to be the apostles of Israel. That's why He told them not to go to the Gentiles in Matthew 10:5**. Why do you supposed He chose the apostle Paul outside of Israel? Because he was to be the apostle to the Gentiles. And so all of this just fits together. But what I'm trying to show you here is the terminology, the uncircumcision, is the non-Jewish world of which you and I are a part. The circumcision was the Jewish world. Now, let's go back to Ephesians chapter 2 and verse 11. I'm almost sure I'm not going to finish these two verses in this half hour.

Ephesians 2:11b
"….who are called Uncircumcision by that which is called the Circumcision in the flesh made hands." In other words, the Jew would refer to the Gentiles as uncircumcised. Now let's go to verse 12.

Ephesians 2:12
"That at that time (while God was dealing with the circumcision, Israel) *ye* (uncircumcision, Gentiles) *were without Christ, being aliens from the commonwealth of Israel and strangers from the covenants of promise, having no hope, and without God in the world:"*

That was the lot of the Gentile world. Because God was dealing with Israel. But the day came when Israel rejected everything and God turned to the Gentile world through this apostle. Now, come back to Colossians chapter 2 and I'm going to try and take this slow enough that I don't leave everybody totally confused. But now let's look at Colossians chapter 2 and verse 13.

Colossians 2:13a
"And you, being dead in your sins and the uncircumcision of your flesh,…."

Now you tie the two together. Why were they dead in their sins? Because they were outside the covenants of Israel, outside the citizenship, they were Gentiles. And so this is what Paul is saying – This was our past. We were dead spiritually, mostly because we were Gentiles and were outside the covenant promises. And so as the uncircumcised physically, we were dead spiritually but what has God done? He's quickened us. He's made us alive. What has happened? Come up to verse 11 and I'll leave this half hour in total confusion, I'm afraid.

Colossians 2:11a
"In whom (Christ) *also ye are circumcised with the circumcision made without hands,…."*

What is he talking about? A spiritual circumcision with which the flesh had nothing to do with. Now, I guess the Lord must have instituted circumcision in the flesh knowing that the day would come when it would be the perfect example of spiritual circumcision. And this is what we're going to see in these two verses. I'm not going to finish it in this half hour, I know I can't. So now then, we who in the flesh, uncircumcised, in the spirit we are circumcised, not the fleshly circumcision, but a spiritual one. I hope I can put it on the board in the next half hour and clarify it. And that simply means that God has done something spiritually that was a good example of that which practiced in Israel physically. And that was cutting off that which is superfluous or no longer needful. That's the whole concept.

Now for you and I as believers, what did God cut off that was now superfluous? The old Adam! The old Adam has been cut off. It's been crucified with Christ and we'll pick it up in our next half hour so hang by a string if you can. But anyway this is the whole idea of these two verses – that yes, in the flesh we're uncircumcised, we're Gentiles. But spiritually we've been circumcised by virtue of the old Adam being crucified with Christ, cut off, and is no longer something that we have to deal with as far as eternity is concerned because it has been done by God Himself.

Book 41 LESSON Two * Part IV

Now back to where we left off in Colossians chapter 2. You know I didn't finish my thoughts in the two verses 11 and 13 dealing with circumcision and our being dead in sins, but now we are circumcised Spiritually and we've been made alive Spiritually. So come back with me to verse 11 and 13 and let's read verse 13 again first.

Colossians 2:13
"And you being dead in your sins (a Spiritual death) *and the uncircumcision of your flesh,* (that's where we were genetically. We're not in the family of Abraham, but rather we were Gentiles) *hath he* (God) *quickened* (or made us alive) *together with him,* (which of course ties us to His death, burial, and resurrection. And the moment we beloved that Gospel of Salvation, God forgave us.) *having forgiven you all trespasses:"* Now we'll come back to forgiveness a little later, but for now let's also look at verse 11.

Colossians 2:11
"In whom (Christ Who is the fullness of the Godhead of verse 9) *also ye are circumcised* (now we are circumcised, not in the flesh, but Spiritually) *with the circumcision made without hands, in putting off the body of the sins of the flesh* (remember circumcision depicts a cutting off of that which was superfluous. So for the believer now we have had something cut off which is no longer necessary and it is the old Adam.) *by the circumcision of* (or by) *Christ:"*

(15c) What is the Gospel that will be preached during the tribulation ?

Book 12 LESSON ONE * PART I

ANTI-CHRIST - "FALSE PROPHET"
Turn to Revelation 7. The Book of Revelation primarily deals with those final seven years before the return of Christ at His Second Coming; then the setting up of His Kingdom upon the earth.

This seven years is primarily God dealing with the Nation of Israel; however, all the world will become involved. Remember Jeremiah 30:7?

Jeremiah 30:7
"Alas! for that day is great, so that none is like it: it is even the time of Jacob's trouble; but he shall be saved out of it."

We'll look at this verse more in detail later. It's God dealing with His Covenant people and for this reason they are still coming back to their homeland, getting ready for these final seven years.

The best way to study Revelation is not to try to take it chronologically, but find the events at the beginning, at the middle, and at the end of the Tribulation, and then fill in the gaps. Chronologically it won't make all that much sense to you. The past several lessons we have been looking at things at the beginning. **1. The appearance of the Anti-christ** when he will sign that seven-year peace treaty with the Nation of Israel, which will again kick God's time clock back in gear, as it has been stopped now all during the Church Age. **2. The appearance of those two witnesses.** They will come to the Nation of Israel in Jerusalem. And they will begin proclaiming God's Word to the Nation of Israel, and out of the ministry of these two... **3. God is going to seal and commission the 144,000 young Jewish men** whom God will use to circumvent the globe. They won't be preaching the Gospel of Grace as we know it, but, rather, they will be reverting back again to the Gospel of the Kingdom as it was being proclaimed at the time of Christ and Peter and the eleven.

There is a vast difference between the Gospel of Grace and the Gospel of the Kingdom. When you understand that, the Bible is much less confusing. At that time, the Age of Grace has ended and the Church is gone. A person will no longer have the opportunity to join a local congregation. But rather these 144,000 will be telling the world that the King is coming. After all, that was the message in Christ's earthly ministry. He Himself referred to it more than once as the Gospel of the Kingdom. The King and His Kingdom were about to come on the scene. Of course Israel rejected that, and the King was crucified. God raised Him from the dead, called Him back to heaven to sit at the Father's right hand until His enemies should be made His footstool. That `until' signifies the time when He will once again deal with His Covenant people of Israel.

Book 10 LESSON THREE * PART IV

Matthew 24:14
"And this gospel of the kingdom..."

This Gospel of the Kingdom. **Not the Gospel of Grace. We preach today the Gospel of**

Grace that you must believe for your salvation, that Jesus died for your sins, was buried, and rose from the dead. Jesus Himself revealed that to the Apostle Paul, and Paul alone, in I Corinthians 15:1-4, Romans 10:9-10 and many other places in Paul's writing. **But Jesus and the twelve preached the Gospel of the Kingdom which is believing for salvation that Jesus was the Messiah, repentance, and baptism.** This is found in Matthew 3:2, Matthew 4:17, Mark 16:16, Acts 2:38 and many other Scriptures in the four Gospels and the Book of Acts through at least Chapter 15. So this gospel of the Kingdom:

Matthew 24:14b
"...shall be preached in all the world for a witness unto all nations; and then shall the end come."

Isn't that plain? **But you have to know which Gospel. Paul tells us in Galatians 2:7-9 that there were two Gospels, one that he (Paul) preached to the Gentiles (uncircumcision) by revelation from Jesus Christ. And the other that John the Baptist, Jesus, Peter and the 12 preached to the Jews or Nation of Israel (circumcision). So as you study, notice who is speaking and who is being spoken to.**

Book 11 LESSON THREE * PART III

Matthew 24:14
"And this gospel of the kingdom shall (at a future time.) *be preached in all the world for a witness unto* (how many?) *all nations; and then shall the end come."*

Now, you see how simple that is when you put it in the right prospective. I've had good friends of mine lift this verse out of context, and say we have to get the Gospel into every nation before the Lord can come. That's not what Jesus was talking about. The Gospel of Grace is a calling out a people for His Name, absolutely. But it's going to end, and the Tribulation is going to come in and then Jesus said, **"The same Gospel of the Kingdom that He preached in His three years of ministry will be proclaimed again during the Tribulation."** Now can you keep that? Put that up here. Just stop and think. If that Good News is proclaimed to every nation on earth, that the King is coming, it will last for the whole seven years. Notice Jesus did not mention the Church Age and the Gospel of Grace. He skips over it from His ministry to the Tribulation. And that will be the message that the 144,000 young Jewish men will preach to the world. The King is coming, and indeed He will be!

Editor's Note: After the rapture takes place, the Age of Grace will have ended. Then during the tribulation, the 144,000 young Jewish men will be teaching the Gospel of the Kingdom. The message will be that the Kingdom is at hand and the Messiah, the King, is coming, as it was prophesied. Therefore, repent of your sins and be baptized with water.

(16c) Is the gift of tongues for the Church today ?

Book 28 LESSON TWO * PART IV

ETERNAL EXCELLENCE OF LOVE
I CORINTHIANS 12:1 - 14:3

As we continue in I Corinthians Chapter 12, Paul has been explaining that the Body of Christ, that invisible make-up of all believers from wherever they are on the planet, and of whatever background, every true child of God becomes a member then of that Body of Christ. And that is a revelation that was given only to the Apostle Paul, because you do not see the Body of Christ taught until Paul comes and shares the revelations that he got from the ascended Lord. And that is what we'll be emphasizing in Chapter 15; a chapter about the resurrection. You see the resurrection of Christ was at the core of all of Paul's preaching.

But here Paul has been addressing problems because the Church was still so carnal, they had not grown spiritually. Now it's interesting that of all the things he has dealt with in Corinthians from Chapter 1, where they had divisions of whom they were following, and going to court against each other, and the problem of immorality in the Church, he also had to deal with the tongues phenomenon, which it had also become a problem. He does not address it as some aspect of their spirituality, because it had become a problem. It had upset the function of the local Church, and they were causing disorder, and he has to address it. So all these things had been in answer to questions that they had written to Paul requesting some answers. Tongues were unique in the Corinthian Church, and this is what I can't get over in my own study, as we never see again in any of his other churches tongues even mentioned. We only find tongues at this carnal Church at Corinth, and that should tell us something.

But for now let's get back to where we left off, and here Paul is dealing with the Body of Christ which is composed of people who have been baptized by the Holy Spirit. Now that Holy Spirit baptism is not an emotional phenomenon, or a physical thing, because you or I never felt a thing, or didn't know anything had happened when the Holy Spirit baptized us into the Body. We know it happened only because the Book says so, and that's the only way we know that we were placed into the Body of Christ, and we have to leave it at that. We don't try to look for some emotional thing or feeling. I've told people so often that word *feeling* is not used in the Scriptures. We take these things by faith, and not by feeling. Now let's look at verse 23:

I Corinthians 12:23
"And those members of the body, which we think to be less honourable, (remember in the last lesson I used the little toe as an example. It's very seldom seen, and we probably think it's totally useless until you lose it, because if you lose your little toe it inhibits walking, and balance. It may be the place of less honor, but it is still important, so also are the less noticed, and less

honored members of the Body of Christ.) *upon these we bestow more abundant honour; and our uncomely parts have more abundant comeliness."* In other words, that's just the way that God works. He takes the foolish things of this world and confounds the wise. He says in another place in I Corinthians that He took the things that are not, to confound the things that are, and it's basically on this same premise.

I Corinthians 1:27
"But God hath chosen the foolish things of the world to confound the wise; and God hath chosen the weak things of the world to confound the things which are mighty;" Now let's look at verse 24:

I Corinthians 12:24
"For our comely parts (the best part of our appearance) *have no need: but God hath tempered the body together, having given more abundant honour to that part which lacked:"*

Isn't that amazing? As I was studying this I couldn't help but think of parents who have had a retarded child, maybe even the Down Syndrome child. We've talked to several who have had this kind of child and even though they had several children, the Down Syndrome child was always the most responsive. That was the child that they poured their love to in such a very special way, and every parent that has one will tell you that same thing. They are the most lovable, and the most easy to love of all children. Well I think Paul is saying the same thing here, we take the weakest believer, the one that the world would think, "Well, the Church certainly can't use that person." But that's the very one that God wants us to enhance, and to bring them to the forefront. Now verse 25, all of these things are for one purpose.

I Corinthians 12:25,26
"That there should be no schism (or division) *in the body;* (That is the Body of Christ) *but that the members should have the same care one for another."* In other words, every believer in God's eyes deserves the same amount of love and compassion as the next one.

Verse 26:
"And whether one member suffer, all the members suffer with it;...
And again he's going to use the analogy of the human body and what is it? You hit your thumb with a hammer, and the whole body is shot with pain. It's the same way with the Body of Christ, if a believer is hurt, then the whole Body hurts with it. Now verse 27.

I Corinthians 12:27
"Now ye are the body of Christ, and members in particular."

As an individual, we don't just come into the Body of Christ as a number, but every one of us is an individual in God's sight, whom He knows. And He knows our every need, and He knows our every heartache and joy. So many times Christians pray, and we think, "Oh it's just another sound to God." No it's not! It's just as if you are the only one in the throne room with Him, and that's the kind of God we serve. Now verse 28, and again here's the list that he has in Corinthians compared with the one we saw in the Book of Ephesians.

I Corinthians 12:28-31
"And God hath set some in the church, (that is the local Church) *first apostles,* (we know they went off the scene) *secondarily prophets,* (we know that has left, because we now have the printed Word) *thirdly teachers, after that miracles, then gifts of healings, helps, governments,* (or administrations) *diversities* (the ability to speak more then one language, and that's what the word tongues in the plural always implies; it was known languages, and they were able to communicate the Gospel to those of a different language.) *of tongues."*

"Are all apostles? (of course not, the Church would get lopsided.) *Are all prophets?* (No) *are all teachers?* (No) *are all workers of miracles?* (Of course not) *Have all the gifts of healing?* (No) *do all speak with tongues?* (absolutely not) *do all interpret?* (No) *But covet* (or desire) *earnestly the best gifts: and yet shew I unto you a more excellent way."*

And that's why I taught Chapter 13 first, because all of this, even to be an apostle, even to be a gifted man, at especially in the Church at Corinth, if they didn't exhibit the love of God in what they were doing, then they were better off staying at home. Just don't even do it, if you can't do it in that attitude of love. Now since we've covered Chapter 13, let's go right on over to Chapter 14.

I Corinthians 14:1
"Follow after charity, (love) *and desire spiritual gifts,* (don't request them specifically; ask the Lord to use you) *but rather that ye may prophesy."*

Now remember the word `prophesy' is not being able to tell the future as we think of Daniel or Isaiah, but to simply speak the Word of God. Share the Word, that's what it is to prophesy, and that's what every believer should desire. "Lord give me that ability to just share your Word with people, whether it's believers who need to be taught, or the unbeliever who is still out there in darkness, Lord give us that opportunity to speak forth the Word. " Now verse 2 which reads:

I Corinthians 14:2
"For he that speaketh in an unknown tongue (Now watch the language here because the word "unknown" is italicized. So it's been added by the translators, because even way back at the time of the King James translators, they really didn't know how to handle this word tongue in the singular, because, like I explained in an earlier lesson, this denoted a sound that had no phonetics to it. It could not be reduced to writings, it was just a guttural sound , and had no pronunciation.) *speaketh not unto men, but unto God:* (because only God could understand it) *for no man*

understandeth him; howbeit in the spirit (Now it's a small s so it's not the Holy Spirit, but in his mind and his own thinking processes) *he speaketh mysteries."*

Those things are beyond the ordinary human comprehension. Now before we go any further, come back to what we just read: that the person speaking in this so-called *"unknown"* tongue, or in this unwritten tongue, was speaking to God. Let's go back to the three times in Scripture when the Holy Spirit delegated this miracle of speaking in tongues to men, and there are only three times. The first is in Acts Chapter 2, and here is our first example of the gift of speaking in tongues, but it's plural so it's languages, and of course it's back when God was still dealing with the Nation of Israel. And here it was on the day of Pentecost. I've always maintained that Pentecost was a Jewish feast day, and Gentiles had nothing to do with Pentecost.

Acts 2:1-4a
"And when the day of Pentecost was fully come, they were all with one accord in one place. And suddenly there came a sound from heaven as of a rushing mighty wind, and it filled all the house where they were sitting. And there appeared unto them cloven tongues like as of fire, and it sat upon each of them. And they were all filled with the Holy Ghost, and began to speak with other tongues,..."

Other languages, because there were Jews there from all over the then-known world all speaking different languages. Now the miracle of Pentecost was that God gave these apostles for sure this gift to speak all the languages of the people that were out there in that massive crowd in front of them. And then you come down to verse 6:

Acts 2:6
"Now when this was noised abroad, the multitude came together, and were confounded, because that every man heard them speak in his own language."

This is the first time in Scripture that we have a manifestation of the Holy Spirit given to men - this gift of speaking known languages, but which was not intrinsic to their own education. In other words, where did Peter and most of the disciples come from? Galilee. They were uneducated fishermen, and all of a sudden here they are speaking the various languages that were evident there on the day of Pentecost. It was miraculous, and it was the work of the Holy Spirit, but as Paul said in I Corinthians, who were these men talking to? Other men, and what was the purpose? To bring them salvation. That's the whole purpose of this Book from cover to cover. The purpose is that mankind might hear the plan of salvation, and it was the same way at Pentecost. Peter and these other disciples were promoting the Gospel of the Kingdom, that Jesus was the Christ, but they were doing it in languages that everyone could understand, so it had a divine purpose.

Now the next time this happens is in Acts Chapter 10. And Peter is now up in the house of a

Gentile, the Roman, Cornelius. You all know the account, how that Peter, contrary to his own desires, is forced by God to go up to the house of Cornelius. And you remember the last thing Peter said as he goes through the door: "Cornelius, you know it is an unlawful thing for me, a Jew, to come into the house of another nation. But God has shown me." In other words, there was a distinct divine purpose in Peter coming up to the house of Cornelius. Now, as he is preaching and is probably expounding about Jesus of Nazareth, and how He had come to be Israel's Messiah and Redeemer and King, I imagine as Peter was laying all of this out, in the back of his mind he was thinking, "Why am I giving this to Gentiles?" He had no idea that there was something moving in God's purposes that He, God, was now going to go out to the Gentile world. He certainly was not aware that in the previous chapter (I don't know how many months previous to this, but not many), that God had saved Paul of Tarsus and had told him He was going to go to the Gentiles. I don't think Peter knew that yet. But here he is in this Gentile house of Cornelius and is proclaiming the Gospel of the Kingdom that Jesus and the Twelve preached: that Jesus was the Christ, the Messiah, Repentance, and water baptism, which was in a different administration, and is completely different from the Gospel of Grace that was given to the Apostle Paul, and the Gospel that we believe for salvation. (Ref. I Corinthians 15:1-4) Now let's look at verses 44 and 45:

Acts 10:44,45a
"While Peter yet spake these words, the Holy Ghost fell on all them which heard the word." Now you want to remember, this was in the confines of a gentlemen's house. This wasn't in a great coliseum. This was in the house of Cornelius, a Roman officer. But as Peter was preaching, the Holy Spirit fell on that house full of Gentiles. Verse 45.
"And they of the circumcision (these Jews) *which believed* (they were like Peter. They had recognized Jesus was the Christ) *were astonished,....."*

Now we pointed all this out when we taught the Book of Acts, that these Jews, six men who came with Peter for a total of seven, were just utterly astonished that these Gentiles were hearing a salvation message and believing it. Now in order for God to prove to these seven Jews that He was doing something totally different than had ever been done before, what does He do? He proves it with these Gentiles speaking other languages. Not just the Latin, in which they had grown and probably practiced. Maybe not even just Greek that they probably used in their military conversations, but now:

Acts 10:45b,46
"....as many as came with Peter (these six Jews) *because that on the Gentiles also was poured out the gift of the Holy Ghost.* (how did they know?) *For they heard them* (the Gentiles) *speak with tongues* (known languages) *and magnify God..."*

Were they talking to God? NO! They were talking to fellow men and they were magnifying God in the presence of these seven Jews, as well as the members of the house of Cornelius, and there is no manifestation of an unknown language here or a guttural sound. It was speaking languages. That's the second time that the Holy Spirit was manifested by giving the gift of speaking more language than they were normally living with. Now the third and last time that this happens in the whole of Acts is in Chapter 19. The first time it happened to Jews in Chapter 2 - strictly Jews. The second time it happens - to a whole house of Gentiles. Now the third time it happens it's another unique little group. Small in number, but they were representative of another larger group and we'll look at it here in Acts 19 and verse 1.

Acts 19:1-6

"And it came to pass, that, while Apollos was at Corinth, Paul having passed through the upper coasts came to Ephesus: (where a church had been founded) *and finding certain disciples,* (we know they were Jews because he says they are) *He said unto them, `Have ye received the Holy Ghost since ye believed?' And they said unto him, `We have not so much as heard whether there be any Holy Ghost.' And he said unto them, `Unto what then were ye baptized?' And they said, `Unto John's baptism.'* (John the Baptist) *Then said Paul, `John verily baptized with the baptism of repentance,* (that was to the Nation of Israel and John baptized in Jordan with the message of repentance) *saying unto the people, that they should believe on him which should come after him, that is, on Christ Jesus.' When they* (these Twelve men) *heard this, they were baptized in the name of the Lord Jesus. And when Paul had laid his hands upon them,* (these twelve Jews) *the Holy Ghost came on them; and they spake with tongues* (languages other than their own) *and prophesied."*

Now those are the only three times in the whole Book of Acts, in fact in all of Scripture, where the Holy Spirit manifested Himself by giving out the gift of speaking a multitude of languages. They were known languages. They were languages that could be understood if somebody happened to be in that same room with that same background. There was no need for interpreters. No emotional upheaval. This was just simply the working of the Holy Sprit to the third category of people that God would be dealing with in the Book of Acts. Remember what they were. Chapter 2 - with the Nation of Israel. Chapter 10 - with the Gentiles in the house of Cornelius. Chapter 19 - with those who were in the transition. They were Jews who had been saved under John's baptism, but they had known nothing of Paul's Gospel and now the Body of Christ and these further revelations. And those three categories are the only ones that came under the manifestation of the power of the Holy Spirit to speak in languages other than the ones they normally practiced.

Now let's go back to Chapter 14 and remember that whenever the Holy Spirit was manifested in the Book of Acts, it was for a divine purpose and that was to prove something. It was to show Israel that God was now moving in the work of the Holy Spirit. It was to prove to the Jews in the house of the Gentiles that God was now saving Gentiles. It was manifested in these twelve Jews to show that there was now a change in the overall program. It was not longer based on John's baptism and Christ's earthly ministry. It was now based on that which followed the work of the Cross, His death, burial and resurrection.

I Corinthians 14:3
"But he that prophesieth speaketh unto men to edification, and exhortation, and comfort." Paul said in verse 1 that the one that they should really long for is the gift of speaking the Word of God. That's the number one criteria and in verse 3 he re-emphasizes it again.

I Corinthians 14:3
"But he that prophesieth speaketh unto men to edification. (to lift him up, support him) *and exhortation* (to encourage him. Every one of us need to be encouraged throughout our daily walk) *and comfort."*

Now we know that we're in this old world which is under the curse, and a lot of people are hurting. How can we best comfort them? By proclaiming to them the Word of God.

LESSON THREE * PART I
RESURRECTION OF THE BODY
I CORINTHIANS 14:4 - 15:19

Now let's open our Bibles to I Corinthians Chapter 14. And again, before I start teaching I would like to get into the background, because I'm finding out there are very few people who know the circumstances that surround a particular Book or Letter, so we should always know the circumstances, and that makes all the difference in understanding. Remember that Paul is writing to these weak, carnal, fleshly, believers that have just come out of abject immorality in Corinth. He's writing to correct them because they had so many problems. So the whole theme of I Corinthians is to correct problems, and this whole letter has to be studied in that light.

Also remember the reason, I think, the Holy Spirit prompted Paul to write the love chapter, which is Chapter 13, and to sandwich it in between 12 and 14, which are filled with problems. Chapter 13 was to soften his approach in order to prepare the ground. Because Paul realizes, as well as anybody, that the only way that you can bring people around to the truth is in the spirit of love, you don't slap them in the face with anger, or ridicule, and put them down as some kind of dummy, but in the spirit of love bring them around to the truth. So as we pick up our study in Chapter 14 don't lose sight of what he wrote in the love chapter. Remember love is still the greatest of all the things so far as God's dealing with mankind is concerned. Verse 1:

I Corinthians 14:1
"Follow after charity, (love) *and desire spiritual gifts,* (gifts is italicized, and personally I like to use the word `things' instead of gifts) *but rather that ye may prophesy."*

Remember the greatest spiritual thing at this time was to prophesy or to speak forth the Word of God, because at the time that Paul is writing to these early Churches there is still no New Testament written. The Four Gospels haven't been written and won't be written until many years after Paul's letters. His own letters have not gone out as the Word of God as yet. He certainly hasn't written to the Corinthian Church before, so you have to realize that these early primitive, apostolic Churches were experiencing their growth and reaching out into the pagan world without benefit of the written Word. Where would we be today if we didn't have the Book. I mean this is all that we have to go on, but they didn't have that so what did they have to depend on? Gifted men. And they had to be gifted to the point that they could now teach people the Pauline doctrines, and not that which was still coming out of the Old Testament, or there would have been pandemonium. So Paul realizes through the Holy Spirit that this was the most important thing a local Church could have, and that was men who could proclaim the truth of God's Word without benefit of having it in print. Now does that help? Paul said in Chapter 13 and verse 10 that the time would come when that gift would fade away. And it is no longer a valid gift, because now we have the printed page. Now of course to be a pastor or teacher it's still a gift, and it's delineated as such. But once the printed Scriptures came into being, Paul's letters come into the right format. Then we got the Four Gospels, and Book of Acts, and so forth, and our New Testament is complete, and now there is no need for that kind of gifted men.

I had an interesting phone call the other day, and ordinarily I wouldn't share something like this with you, but I imagine that if the gentlemen hears it may get his attention. And that phone call reminded me of gifted men who didn't have the Word of God, and he was such a kind, benevolent type or I would have hung up on him sooner than I did. At first I didn't get what he was driving at, but finally he came out and in so many words said, "Les, you're just like everybody else, you are teaching men's words, and I wish I could sit down with you and teach you what God has said." Well, the bells began to ring, and the red flag started to fly, and I said, "Wait a minute, what are you trying to tell me? That you are the only one who has received the revelation of the true Word of God?" He replied, "Yeah." I said, "I'm sorry, but this conversation is ended," and I hung up on him.

I had a note in the mail from him yesterday, and he couldn't figure out why I hung up. I didn't fly off the handle I just said, "You're way out in left field, why do you think I have the camera constantly putting the Scriptures on the screen!" I said that's the Word of God, not what someone like you has supposedly received, and this is what I'm constantly trying to drive into peoples' thinking - that it doesn't matter what I say or think, but rather what does the Book say? This is why I prefer the Word of God on the screen rather than myself, and we have to understand that, yes, in the early Church it did take men with that kind of a gift, but today we have the Word of God. And the Word is in such a format that anyone can understand it, and it can feed a hungry heart. So when Paul speaks of this gift of prophecy it was under a whole different set of circumstances than what we've got today.

I Corinthians 14:2a
"For he that speaketh in an unknown tongue..."

And we defined all that in our last lesson, and when you see the word "tongue" in these two chapters, 12 and 14, in the singular, and with the added word *unknown* italicized by the translators, it's talking about a bunch of sounds that cannot be reduced to print. They are not phonetic, there is no way anyone can write them down, it's just a bunch of noise. And Paul is going to make this so evident later through this chapter. But when you see the word "tongues" plural, then he's talking about languages. And even in the city of Corinth there were probably five or six languages being used constantly. There was Latin, Greek, Spanish, Hebrew, and Aramaic, so those languages made up the city of Corinth, and it all enters into the picture of these Chapters 12 and 14. Now here he's speaking of the tongues movement, it's an unknown language that no one can print, so this is why the translators call it an unknown tongue. Continuing on in verse 2:

I Corinthians 14:2
"For he that speaketh in an unknown tongue speaketh not unto men, but unto God: (God is the only One who can make anything out of it if it were possible.) *for no man understandeth him; howbeit in the spirit* (small "s" so that's man's spirit) *he speaketh mysteries,"*

And I mentioned this in the last letters about some of the pagan religions and their mysteries. And so Paul is saying here what they're doing is using their own make-up or personality, and they are speaking things that to anybody else is nothing but a mystery. Now verse 3:

I Corinthians 14:3,4
"But (the flip side) *he that prophesieth* (or speaketh forth the Word as a gifted individual) *speaketh unto men to edification,* (lift them up) *and exhortation, and comfort."* Now verse 4, and I'm not going to make a lot of comment, because the Book speaks for itself.

"He that speaketh in an unknown tongue edifieth himself; but he that prophesieth (and speaks forth the Word of God) *edifieth the church."*
When someone claims to have had a tongues experience, according to the Book, who are they edifying? Themselves. It's an ego trip, and that's what it amounts to. Now reading on in verse 5.

I Corinthians 14:5
"I would that ye all spake with tongues, (That's plural, which means languages. Paul is saying it would be nice if you could just go up into northern Greece, or other countries and speak the dialects that those people do. Today I'd say the same thing, and those of you who have kids out on the mission field know what I'm talking about. My, wouldn't it have been great if your son or daughter could have gone to the mission field, and picked up the language the next day? But instead they had to go to language school to learn the language before they went to the field. So Paul knew what he was talking about. He said, "It would be great if you all spoke several lan-

guages.") *but rather that ye prophesied: for greater is he that prophesieth than he that speaketh with tongues, except he interpret, that the church may receive edifying."*

Let's take that little congregation in Corinth, and let's say that most of them were able to understand Greek. Now there were probably some even in Corinth that couldn't understand Greek, all they could understand maybe was Hebrew or Aramaic. Paul says, "Now it would be great if you could come into this congregation and be able to teach and preach in a language that they could all understand." My, what a great gift that would be, because that's what people needed, they had to hear the Word, because they couldn't go home and read it.

I Corinthians 14:6
"Now. brethren, if I come unto you speaking with tongues, (these different languages) *what shall I profit you, except I shall speak to you either by revelation, or by knowledge, or by prophesying, or by doctrine?"*

Those are the things that count. People even today need doctrine as very few professing believers today have a good solid understanding of doctrine. I've learned over the years that most Catholics, Baptists, Methodists, Presbyterians, or just about any other denomination don't really know what they believe. And if you doubt that, just ask people what they really believe, and most of them can't tell you much. I say that sincerely, and this is what Paul is saying. Even the Corinthians were so weak in the fundamentals, but oh, they were emotional, they had a lot of enthusiasm, but that in itself is not enough. So Paul says:

I Corinthians 14:6b,7
"...except I shall speak to you either by revelation, or by knowledge, or by prophesying, or by doctrine." What's the profit? Now verse 7.
"And even things without life giving sound, whether pipe or harp, except they give a distinction in the sounds, how shall it be known what is piped or harped?

What is the Apostle Paul is saying here? Unless somebody picks up an instrument that knows how to play, knows how to bring out the right tone at the right time within the score, what do you have? A bunch of noise. In fact I've been to a few concerts in my life, and especially if you go to a concert of a symphony orchestra, and before they lift the curtain what are those musicians doing back there? They're tuning their instruments at the same time and it's just a bunch of noise, there's no melody, or harmony, or anything worth listening to, you can't hardly wait till the curtain goes up and you can hear some real music. Well here, Paul is saying the same thing. Look at it again:

I Corinthians 14:7
And even things without life giving sound, (Musical instruments, when they're giving sound) *whether pipe or harp, except they give a distinction in the sounds,* (The right note at the right

place) *how shall it be known what is piped or harped?"*

How can you make a melody? How would you know what song they're playing? Well, you don't. Now verse 8, and Paul is using simple illustrations, and I really don't have to comment on them.

I Corinthians 14:8
"For if the trumpet give an uncertain sound, who shall prepare himself to the battle?"

Now you want to remember that the Romans used the trumpet for battle commands much like you have seen in the movies and like our American Calvary did with their riders and so forth. They had a particular trumpet sound for each command, and every soldier knew what it was. And it was the same way in the Roman army, when the trumpet was sounded they would know whether to retreat, attack, or whatever. And Paul is using that analogy here. Now what if the trumpeter didn't know his command? What if he was just blaring out a bunch of sounds, what would the poor troops do? They would just be looking at each other wondering what they were supposed to do. It would cause confusion. Now verse 9:

I Corinthians 14:9
"So likewise ye, (see how plain this is?) *except ye utter by the tongue* (this organ in your mouth) *words easy to be understood, how shall it be known what is spoken? for ye shall speak into the air."*

Common sense? Yeah. In fact I've even given this illustration before: I remember years ago I was reading a book by one of the deep, deep theologians of that time, and I would just have to go back and read it over and over. I mean, it was just so hard to dig any of the truth out of it, because it was written in such complicated language. So one morning while Iris was fixing breakfast, and I was sitting at the table, and I had just read a paragraph to her, I said, "Honey, do you know anything that the guy is saying?" And she said, "No, what's he saying?" Well, I just spit it back out into plain, ordinary laymen's language, and then she said, "Oh, is that what he said?"

And this is what has happened across the whole spectrum. We've got men that are such theologians that they talk above the heads of the average individuals. And you know what I'm talking about. You pray with me that every time I teach that I can take these same truths and keep it so simple that a six-year-old can understand it. And this is what Paul is saying, what good does it do to come in with high-sounding intellectual statements if people don't know what you're talking about. The Word of God is simple, I explained just yesterday the Gospel (Ref. I Corinthians 15:1-4) to a man I'm sure had never heard it before. I put it in such simple language that I know he went down my driveway with no doubt what it would take to gain heaven. I don't know whether he will or not, but I tell you what, he's going to stand responsible someday, because I laid it out as plain and simple as it can be laid out. And this gentleman just stood there and said, "I've never heard that before." Of course not, most people haven't. Now verse 10:

I Corinthians 14:10
There are, it may be, so many kinds of voices in the world, and none of them is without signification."

Do you know what Paul is talking about here? You go out even into the animal kingdom and what are sciences learning more and more everyday? That even the animals communicate one with another. Those of you who are quail hunters know if you flush out a covey, the first thing you hear is they start whistling. Iris and I were out fishing a while back, and our dog scared up a wild turkey, and she flew right over where we were fishing, and after a while we could hear her start to cluck, and her little ones who were back in the woods started to answer. What were they doing? Communicating. And those sounds weren't jibberish, those little turkeys knew exactly what momma was saying, and momma knew exactly what they were saying. And we've found that throughout the whole spectrum of the wild animal kingdom that they communicate. The same is true with sea creatures, they all communicate. Men, whatever the background, whether we're European, or Asiatic, we all communicate and this is what Paul is saying, and that's why God gave us that ability to communicate.

I Corinthians 14:11
"Therefore if I know not the meaning of the voice, (If I don't know what someone is saying) *I shall be unto him that speaketh* (like) *a barbarian, and he that speaketh shall be a barbarian unto me."*

What's he talking about? He can't understand, and if that be the case what purpose is there in making a sound if it isn't going to communicate. So how much understanding will come between a barbarian, an uncivilized person, and a cultured man like Paul? Nothing!

I Corinthians 14:12
"Even so ye, forasmuch as ye are zealous of spiritual gifts, seek that ye may excel to the edifying (or promoting, or the lifting up) *of the church."* Not just one person or two, but the whole congregation.

I Corinthians 14:13
"Wherefore let him that speaketh in an unknown tongue (here's that singular again) *pray that he may interpret."* I know that to most of our tongues people, (and I'm not condemning them, because the last verse of this chapter says that he doesn't forbid it), unless this sound can be reduced to something understandable, you're beating the air. That's what this chapter is pointing out. Verse 13 again:

I Corinthians 14:13

"Wherefore let him that speaketh in an unknown tongue pray that he may interpret."
And for what purpose? To communicate. Otherwise it's just so much lost energy, and time. And we're going to see in our next lesson that it had gotten to the place even in Corinth where it was just causing commotion in the local congregation, and no one was being edified by it. So the whole purpose of this chapter is in the spirit of love to bring these people to a solid understanding.

LESSON THREE * PART II
RESURRECTION OF THE BODY
I CORINTHIANS 14:4 - 15:19

Now let's just jump right into where we left off in the last lesson and that would be verse 14, and here Paul is admonishing the Corinthians to take stock of what they were doing, and realize that all that glitters isn't gold. And that's all I'm saying, because I'm not condemning the folk who claim to have spoken in tongues, or I won't look down my nose at them, but all that I do ask everyone in the spirit of Chapter 13, the love chapter, is to analyze this whole thing in the light of what God wants, not what men want. You know we're living in that era of instant gratification regardless of what area of our life we may be looking at. But listen, we have to line everything up with the Word of God or we're on thin ice. And that's all I try to do. I don't try to browbeat people into everything the way I see it. You can disagree with me on things and that's fine, but on the other hand I think it's my responsibility, since the Lord has given me this avenue of teaching, that we show what the Word says. Now verse 14, and to me this is so plain, where Paul, now speaking in the first person says:

I Corinthians 14:14

"For if I pray in an unknown tongue, (there's that singular again, that sound that can't be reduced to a phonetic sound or to writing) *my spirit* (small "s"- his own personality) *prayeth, but my understanding is unfruitful."*

How much plainer can you get? Even for the individual, what good does it do, Paul says, to speak in a language that you don't know what you're talking about, and I know their answer, "Well, God does." But the Book doesn't say that He does. We know that God being Omnipotent, He certainly can if He wants to, but there is nothing in here that indicates that this is what God expects people to do.

I Corinthians 14:15

"What is it then? I will pray with the spirit, (Paul is saying, `I will pray from my innermost being. His own spirit - small `s') *and I will pray with the understanding* (Now how many of you would talk to God in prayer, whether it be in thanksgiving or supplication, or whatever thing you might have on your mind - what good would it do to talk to God in some language that you don't know

what you're saying? Even if God is able to discern it, what if you can't? You don't know what you're asking for, and this is what Paul is pointing out. Whatever you do while communicating with God, do it in understanding.) *also: I will sing with the spirit,* (I know that sometimes we're too laid back. I know from Scripture that there were times when people sang and danced before the Lord, and there's nothing wrong with singing, or an exuberance in our Christian Spirit, absolutely nothing, but again, it has to be tempered with common sense.) *and I will sing with the understanding also."*

I Corinthians 14:16

"Else when thou shalt bless (That is the food) *with the spirit,* (small "s" - your being) *how shall he that occupieth the room of the unlearned say `A-men' at thy giving of thanks, seeing he understandeth not what thou sayest?*

In other words, you're asking the blessing over a table around where many people are sitting, and if you supposedly pray in an unknown tongue how will the people around the table know when you're finished? Verse 17:

I Corinthians 14:17,18

"For thou verily givest thanks well, but the other is not edified. (and then in verse 18 Paul makes a graphic statement) *I thank my God, I speak with tongues* (Plural - Languages) *more than ye all:"*

Now for years I've said this is what Paul is driving at, and now some of the great scholars are beginning to write it in their books. What's Paul saying? That when he went into some of these various areas and different tribes and dialects, and different languages, could he communicate? Yes. He had that special gift, Christianity was just getting off the ground, and he had this gift to speak whatever language was necessary. So here in verse 18 Paul is speaking of languages with which he could communicate the Gospel. Now verse 19:

I Corinthians 14:19,20

"Yet in the church I had rather speak five words with my understanding, that by my voice I might teach others also, than ten thousand words in an unknown tongue. brethren, be not children in understanding: howbeit in malice (And that's not a very nice word) *be ye children, but in understanding* (grow up and) *be men."* Do you see how plain all of this is? Now verse 21:

I Corinthians 14:21

"In the law it is written, `With men of other tongues (Languages) *and other lips will I speak unto this people; and yet for all that will they not hear me, saith the Lord.'"*

Here Paul is quoting from the Book of Deuteronomy, and we're going to go back and look at it in Chapter 28: And naturally this is directed to the Children of Israel.

Deuteronomy 28:49

"The LORD shall bring a nation (of foreign people) *against thee from far, from the end of the earth, as swift as the eagle flieth; a nation whose tongue thou shalt not understand:"*

Now here the tongue refers to their language. Whether it was the Babylonians that He was referring to or some other nation, there would come a time in Israel's history that a foreign nation would over-run them, invade them, and the Jews would have to listen to them talking in their language as they were being occupied. Do you see that? Now it wasn't an unknown tongue, but it was a language that the Jews wouldn't be able to understand. It was a warning, "Listen, you're going to have people in your midst that you're not going to like to have around, you're not going to be able to understand what they say, they're going to be foreigners." And so this is exactly what Paul is referring to now in I Corinthians when he says in verse 21 again:

I Corinthians 14:21,22

"In the law it is written, 'With men of other tongues (or other languages) *and other lips will I speak unto this people;* (by occupying them) *and yet for all that will they not hear me,' saith the Lord. Wherefore tongues* (This ability to speak in languages) *are for a sign,..."*
To the Jew, and we find that in I Corinthians Chapter 1, and verse 22, and again, all we're going by is what the Book says.

I Corinthians 1:22

"For the Jews require a sign,..."

Now stop and think, how long has Israel been demanding signs? Well, it goes all the way back to when Moses was first called out of the desert, and even Moses the Jew did not believe that he was supposed to do what God wanted him to do. And so how did God prove it to him? He said, "Throw your shepherd rod on the ground." And you all know the account, and what happened? It became a serpent. Then the Lord said, "Pick it up," and it became a shepherd's rod again. What was God trying to show Moses? That He is in it. He is going to take him back to Pharaoh. And then Moses said, "Yeah, but when I get to Pharaoh he's not going to believe that I'm supposed to lead the children of Israel out." And what does God tell Moses and Aaron? The same thing: "You throw your rod down and it will become a serpent," and all these signs were not so much for Pharaoh's benefit, but rather for Moses' and Aaron's. To prove to those two men that God was going to do the supernatural. He's going to bring Israel out of Egypt. So all the way up through Israel's history you have the supernatural, and you come into Christ's earthly ministry, and I've taught it and I've taught it until I'm blue in the face. Why did Jesus perform miracle, after miracle? To prove to the Jew that He was Who He said He was. It was signs. And remember when we taught the Book of John there were seven miraculous signs, and every one of them had a whole train-load of truths for the Nation of Israel. They didn't mean that much to the Gentiles, but they meant everything to the Jew. And now Paul comes in even as he writes to a Gentile congregation and says:

I Corinthians 1:22,23a

"For the Jews require a sign, and the Greeks seek after wisdom; (Now look at the flip side in verse 23) *But we preach Christ crucified,..."*

Do you see the difference? Now let's come back to Chapter 14, and again he comes back with that same concept that tongues, the ability to speak all the languages such as he had, were for a sign.

I Corinthians 14:22a

"Wherefore tongues are for a sign, not to them that believe, but to them that believe not: but (the flip side) *prophesying* (being able to speak forth the Word before they had the New Testament)..."*

So signs and all this is not going to accomplish all that much, but what will? Preaching the Word! This is what people need to hear today, people have to hear the Gospel (Ref. I Corinthians 15:1-4). They have to hear the plan of salvation, they don't have to see some kind of miracle, and I'm not condemning these people that can prove some miraculous manifestation. But they've got to prove it before I believe it. If they can prove it, then I'll say, "Yes, I know we have a God Who can perform miracles." I know God can heal miraculously, and I do not deny that. Now finishing verse 22:

I Corinthians 14:22b

"...prophesying serveth not for them that believe not, but for them which believe."

Now what's Paul talking about? To bring them growth in their Christian experience. To bring them so they wouldn't be blown about with every wind of doctrine. Well let's just sort of skim through these next few verses, and then I've got to deal with another hot potato in this day and time: "What about the women's activity in the local Church?" Well, we'll come to that in a few minutes, but before we get there let's skim verses 23 through 33.

I Corinthians 14:23

"If therefore the whole church be come together into one place, and all speak with tongues, (languages) *and there come in those that are unlearned, or unbelievers, will they not say that ye are mad?"*

Do you know what the Greek root word for *mad* in the King James is? Maniac. That's where the word maniac came from. He says, "They'll come in off the street, look at you, and will say you're a bunch of maniacs, you're mad." Now verse 24.

I Corinthians 14:24-26

"But if all prophesy, (or speak forth the Word) *and there come in one that believeth not, or one*

unlearned, he is convinced of all, he is judged of all: (Because he's hearing the Word of God, see the difference?) *And thus are the secrets of his heart made manifest; and so falling down on his face he will worship God, and report that God is in you of a truth.* (if he can hear the Word) *How is then, brethren? when ye come together, every one of you hath a psalm, hath a doctrine, hath a tongue, hath a revelation, hath an interpretation.* (now if you had all that at once you'd have confusion) *Let all things be done unto edifying."* If you're wondering what he's driving at, verse 40 puts the cap on it.

I Corinthians 14:40

"Let all things be done decently and in order." That's what the Book says, it's not what I'm saying. The Book says, *"Let all things be done decently and in order."*

Part D – The End Times

(1d) What is the sequence of events in the end times ?

Book 14 LESSON TWO * PART I

I Corinthians 15:51
"Behold, I shew you a mystery; We shall not all sleep, but we shall all be changed."
In other words, when the Body of Christ is finally finished and the last one has been brought in, there is going to be an out-calling of those who are alive and remain, by virtue of a change from this body to the new glorified body. All of those who have died in Christ during this Church Age will be resurrected with their new bodies. And we call that the Rapture of the Church.

After that happens, we find God picking up where He left off with the Nation of Israel. Remember, out of the 490 years that had been determined on the Nation of Israel, 483 of those years ended at the Crucifixion of Christ. Daniel 9:26. That left seven more years to make the prophecy complete. We call it the seven years of Tribulation. And that is what the whole Book of Revelation is all about. It is the unfolding of this final seven years of God dealing with the human race in general. But the Nation of Israel in particular. Then, as we found in the Book of Revelation, tying it all in with Daniel, we find that the very opening event of this final seven years, is the appearance of the Anti-christ. He will sign a seven-year peace treaty with the Nation of Israel. The treaties that have been signed by Israel with Palestine and Jordan, have caused a lot of confusion. Some people think that this is the peace treaty that Daniel speaks of in Daniel 9:27. But as far as I'm concerned, this treaty they have just signed is nothing but an agreement to agree or disagree. I don't think it will hold much water for long. But we know the Anti-christ is going to come on the scene, and he will be born of woman, flesh and blood. He will be much like Judas and will be used of Satan to fulfill Satan's aspirations. He will come on the scene as a tremendous political manipulator. He will be a charismatic type individual. He will be able to walk into any kind of summit meeting and command attention. They will listen to him, and, consequently, he will bring himself to a place of having the power of making that peace treaty with Israel as we referred to earlier.

The opening of the seven years will not only reveal the Anti-christ, but also his letting the Nation of Israel resume their Temple worship, with their animal sacrifices, and other Law-related rituals. We know that, even as we speak, the Nation of Israel has everything ready to resume Temple worship. However don't have the place where the Temple must be built. But they **will have** when the right time comes. It may take an act of war or nature for the Mosque of Omar to be destroyed. But we do know that Israel will have Temple worship for the first 3 1/2 years, all with the approval of this man Anti-christ. So today, this is Israel's anticipation, that they will have their Messiah and their Temple worship. But remember, Israel is looking for their Messiah to come the **first** time, because they don't recognize that Jesus Christ was the Messiah.
At the opening of the Tribulation, there will be the two witnesses (Revelation Chapter 10). We studied how these two will be on the streets of Jerusalem. They will begin a witness of Jehovah

God to Israel. Out of their preaching will come the sealing of the 144,000 young Jews who will come on the scene, but **not** to preach the Gospel of Grace, **Faith in the Death, Burial, and Resurrection of Jesus Christ for salvation,** we have had here in the Church Age. They will be preaching the Gospel of the Kingdom, that Jesus, John the Baptist, and the twelve preached **that the King is Coming. Repent and be baptized**. That certainly will be good news for that period of history. They will preach this message all over the world. I think that shortly after the Tribulation begins, the Russian confederation will invade Israel. God will destroy them on the hills of Israel, so that will be a quick removal of those nations as enemies of Israel. And as we studied about the seals being removed, we found that one-fourth of the human race will be destroyed. By the time we come to the mid-point of the Tribulation, we find that the two witnesses will be killed and their bodies will lie on a street in Jerusalem for 3 days. Then they will be resurrected and the whole world will see them ascend back to Heaven.

Then at the mid-point of the Tribulation, the Anti-christ will come into the Temple in Jerusalem, and make war on the Jews. He will defile the Temple and set himself up as God, and force the Jew to worship him. Consequently, they will come under the horrible persecution of this man. Also at the mid-point, we find that Satan is cast down from Heaven for the final time. He knows his time is short (3 1/2 years) so now not only must the earth endure the wrath of Satan, but also in the Scriptures, this last 3 1/2 years is known as the Wrath of God. That is going to be a double-barreled unloading upon this planet. On one hand, from the Satanic forces, and on the other from a righteous God. You and I as human beings can't comprehend what that last 3 1/2 years will be like. The scenes we see in Rwanda, and what we saw in the Holocaust, as awful as they were, will only be a drop in the bucket as compared to these final 3 1/2 years. Remember what Jesus said in Matthew 24.

Matthew 24:21
"For then shall be great tribulation, such as was not since the beginning of the world to this time, no, nor ever shall be."

As those various judgments come to pass, don't forget that the whole reason for all of this is to pay off the mortgage that Satan is holding on the earth. Remember, Satan picked up the mortgage on the earth when Adam lost it the moment he sinned. We saw in Revelation Chapter 5, a scroll that has the seven seals on it (the mortgage that Christ will pay off). Paying off the mortgage is really the whole scope of the Tribulation. As a result, the curse will be lifted from the whole planet. Having now consummated these seven years, Christ will return at His Second Coming, and destroy the remaining armies at Jerusalem in the battle of Armageddon. As a result of the curse being lifted, and the defeat of Satan, the earth will be made for a renovation project, which God will accomplish in short order, making it ready for the Kingdom.

Christ will then set up His Kingdom on earth and it will be glorious. The earth will be brought back like it was in the Garden of Eden. Now comes the thousand-year reign and rule with Him upon this earth. I remind my classes that the Kingdom has been spoken of and prophesied all the way through the Old Testament. The coming of the King and the Kingdom. But it isn't until we get to Revelation that we have a time frame attached to it of a thousand years. The Old Testament speaks of it as being forever and eternal. Well, we have to reconcile some things then: why does Revelations speak of a thousand years? The reason the first part of it must be limited for a thousand years is this: as a result of the events of the Tribulation, most of the world's population is going to lose their lives. Most of those who have become believers as a result of the preaching of the 144,000 will have been martyred, and they will be resurrected with the Old Testament saints at a later time.

By the time we come to the end of the seven years, Isaiah 24:6 says, **"There will be few men left."** However, there will be survivors. Some of whom have heard the message and believed will be mostly Gentiles. They will become the seed stock for the Gentile nations to repopulate during this thousand-year rule. And the rest who survive will be lost. We then find these two groups standing before God as the Kingdom is set up in Matthew 25:32-46. They are noted as sheep and goats. One group, the sheep, will inherit the Kingdom. The other group, the goats, will go into everlasting punishment. We will also have another flesh and blood group that will go into the Kingdom, and that is the remnant of Israel. We saw that they went down into the mountains Southeast of Jerusalem at the mid-point of the Tribulation, and we found that in Matthew 24:16. God will feed, clothe, and protect them there for the final 3 1/2 years. They go out in unbelief, but will believe when they see Christ at His Second Coming. They will then be the seed stock to go into this Kingdom to repopulate it for the Nation of Israel.

Coming into the Kingdom with Christ ruling and reigning as King, we have the Gentile believers, and the believers from the remnant of Israel. These two flesh and blood groups will be responsible to repopulate the whole world. There will be a tremendous population explosion. The curse is lifted, there will be no pain in childbirth, and these children that are born will live the entire thousand years. There will be no sin, and Satan will have been locked up these 1000 years. It will be like the Garden of Eden, but on a world-wide basis. The children coming from these believers, though they are born with the old sin nature, do not have a tempter to exploit it, since Satan is locked up during that time. However, keep in mind that they have been living under the rule of the King, Who is benevolent. Also, these children have not had to make a choice for, or against God, as you and I and the rest of the believers had to make. So we find at the end of the thousand years that Satan must be released just for a little season. This will be a time of testing for the children. They will have to exercise their free will even as we did. And to give a choice, there has to be more than one option.

So Satan is brought back for the sole purpose of giving these new generations of children that choice to choose between Christ or Satan. Satan is given the opportunity to present his options to these children. And just like he did to Eve in the Garden of Eden, it will be that same type of temptation. Because the Kingdom has been so glorious, who could want anything different?

Remember, Eve had it that good, but what was Satan's ploy with Eve? **"You can be like God."** And I think the same thing will happen here. I think he will say, **"You've got it perfect, but you're still not God. Wouldn't you like to be like God?"** And the vast majority will follow him hook, line, and sinker. After they have made their choice, and when they try to come against God, He will destroy them with fire. That then will be the end of time as we know it. After all that has happened, it's time for the Great White Throne judgment, where all the lost will be resurrected out of hell to be judged by Christ, and then sent to their final doom in the lake of fire. Jesus tells us there will be degrees of punishment for those going into the lake of fire, depending on their works here on earth. Now in our next lesson we will be going into Revelation Chapter 21 and verse 1:

Revelation 21:1
"AND I saw a new heaven and a new earth: for the first heaven and the first earth were passed away; and there was no more sea." That means the Kingdom will be lifted off the planet long enough for a whole new planet to come on the scene. I think I'll have the reason for that in our next lesson.

(2d) What is the rapture ?

Book 6 LESSON ONE * PART IV

Now, let's look at how the Church Age is going to end. Just turn on over in Corinthians to Chapter 15, and we'll quickly look at this. There's coming a day, and we think it's real soon, the way things are happening in the world, I don't see how it can be put off much longer. But, we are fast approaching the day when the last person will be brought into the body, and that vessel will be full, and God's going to have to take it out of the way.

I Corinthians 15:52
"Behold, I show you a mystery; We shall not all sleep, but we shall all be changed, in a moment, in the twinkling of an eye, the last trump: for the trumpet shall sound, and the dead shall be raised incorruptible, and we shall be changed."

Now, here again, these teachings you won't find anywhere but Paul. Nowhere has it ever hinted that there's ever going to be a day when living people are suddenly going to be translated. **"Behold I show you another mystery,..."** another secret. **"We** (that is believers) **shall not all sleep** (or die)**, but...",** we have to be what?...**"Changed" "In a moment, in the twinkling of an eye,"** in the split second of an eyelash, (at) **"...the last trump: for the trumpet shall sound, and the dead in Christ"** Those who have been part and parcel now of the Body of Christ. Not the Old Testament saints. Daniel says he has to wait. We'll look at that in another lesson. But now, it's the Church Age saints. These who are in the body. **"At the last trump: for the trumpet shall sound, and the dead shall be raised incorruptible, and we...** Paul says (and he expected to be alive) **...shall be changed."** In other words, when the trumpet sounds, and if we're living – and I think we will be, the dead in Christ will rise first and then we will suddenly take flight and we will go up with him. Now, in order to culminate all of this we have to go to 1 Thessalonians Chapter 4. Here, **some people just simply refuse the concept of the Rapture; and when they do that, they have to throw Paul away first.** This is because Paul makes so much of it, and here is probably the clearest language in I Thessalonians:

I Thessalonians 4:13
"But I would not have you to be ignorant, brethren, concerning them which are asleep, that ye sorrow not, even as others which have no hope."

"But I would not have you to be ignorant, brethren (same language), *concerning them which are asleep,"* (that is our loved ones who have died), *"that ye sorrow not, even as others which have no hope."* In other words, if we, as believers, have lost loved ones, we don't have to weep and wail and carry on like the heathen do. Because **we're going to see our loved ones again someday.**

I Thessalonians 4:14
"For if we believe that Jesus died and rose again, even so them also which sleep in Jesus will God bring with him."

"For if we..." what's the word? **Believe!** It doesn't say if we are repenting and are baptizing. It doesn't say if we join the church. **It says if we believe.** But we've got to be careful what we believe. Don't just believe in God. **We believe that Jesus died and rose again.** There's the Gospel. So, if we believe the Gospel, even so them also who sleep, or who have died, in Jesus; God will bring them with him. Now, watch the language. We know that the believer, as soon as he dies; his spirit and soul take flight to where? **The presence of Christ in Heaven.** And there they wait for this day of resurrection to be reunited with the believers resurrected body.

I Thessalonians 4:15,16
"For this we say unto you by the word of the Lord, that we which are alive and remain unto the coming of the Lord shall not prevent them which are asleep. For the Lord himself shall descend from heaven with a shout, with the voice of the archangel, and with the trump of God: and the dead in Christ shall rise first:..."

"For this we say unto you by the word of the Lord, that we which are alive and remain unto the coming of the Lord shall not prevent..." – or go ahead of, *"...them which are asleep. For the Lord himself shall descend from heaven,"* now you remember Isaac. He met Rebecca where? Part way, away from home. *"...The Lord himself shall descend from heaven with a shout, with the voice of the archangel, and with the trump of God: and the dead in Christ shall rise first:..."*

I Thessalonians 4:17
"Then we which are alive and remain shall be caught up together with them in the clouds, to meet the Lord in the air: and so shall we ever be with the Lord."

"Then we which are alive and remain shall be caught up together with them (everybody) *in the clouds* (that is in the atmosphere), *to meet the Lord* (Where?)... **in the air:...**" And then we go back into Heaven with Him to go before the Judgment Seat of Christ, and have the marriage of the Lamb; and then we'll be ready to come back with Him seven years later, as time reckons it, at His Second Coming; as He comes then to ...**stand on the Mount of Olives**... as it says in Zechariah 14. Read it when you have a minute at home. Those first six or seven verses. It says in part, *"...in that day his feet shall stand on the Mount of Olives."*

The other night I was teaching in Acts Chapter one, **"...and there he stood with the eleven, and he went up, and the angels said, 'why stand ye gazing up into Heaven, this same Jesus in like manner as you have seen him go, shall come again.'"** I don't say these things to be funny; I try to make it clear. He left how? **Head first!** He's coming, how? **Feet first.** And He's going to stand on the Mount of Olives just as sure as it's there tonight; and that will usher in the Kingdom. And when He comes, we're going to come with Him. In fact, I always like to use two prepositions – and that probably helps you remember as well as anything. **When He comes at the Rapture, He's going to come for us. When He comes at the Second Coming, He comes with us.**

Editor's Note: Les further explains in Book 25, Lesson Two, Part I that it is from the words "caught up" that we have coined the word "rapture" - caught up to meet the Lord in the air. We are not told when in the timeline the rapture will occur, only that it will take place before the seven-year tribulation period begins.

Book 41 LESSON TWO * PART II

Now let's come back and continue our study about this mystery given to Paul in Romans 11:25. Nothing in Scripture foretold that there would be a long 1900 + period of time that Israel would be spiritually blinded as we have seen them be. But now let's see when the Scripture says that will be. Looking at the last part of verse 25 again we find:

Romans 11:25b
"...that blindness in part (not forever) *is happened to Israel, until..."*

Now those of you who have heard me teach for a long time know that **"until"** is a time word. I shocked one of my classes a couple of weeks ago. They all know that I've always taught that there is no way we can know the day, month or year that The Lord is coming for the Church. It's an eminent return, but we never set dates. Then I just shocked that class when I said, you're all wondering when the Church is going to be raptured. Well I'm going to tell you exactly when it will be raptured, and some thought that I had gone out into left field. When is the Church going to be raptured? When the last person has been saved and completes the "Body." Now I don't know what day, month, and year that will be, but that is the **"until."** Israel is going to remain blinded **"until."** The rest of the verse reads:

Romans 11:25b

"*...that blindness in part is happened to Israel, until the fulness of the Gentiles be come in.*"

Now what's the fulness of the Gentiles? The Body of Christ.

(3d) When does the Bible indicate that the tribulation will begin ?

Book 1 LESSON ONE * PART I

Consider the timeline in relation to II Peter 3:8:

"*But, beloved, be not ignorant of this one thing, that one day is with the Lord as a thousand years, and a thousand years as one day.*"

Consider it is also in conjunction with Genesis Chapter 1 in which the creation of the world, the universe, and all that is in them, including mankind is described as being completed in six days.

Notice that the first six days of creation were for man's benefit (Isaiah 45:18 says that the earth was formed to be inhabited), but the seventh day was for God - a day of rest. So, consider the following hypothesis: If 1,000 years is to God as a day, according to the timeline, we can see that man has just about used up his "six days" or 6,000 years (if our calendars are at all accurate). Are we about to enter into God's day - the "seventh day" or the final 1,000 years?

We are seeing the signs of the times in the wars, earthquakes, famines, and pestilences we hear about on the news daily. Terms being used today such as "global economy," "global politics," and "new age" are all indicative of the fact that we are very close to the end of our age. The stage is being set for Daniel's 70th week (see Daniel 9).

Book 16 LESSON TWO * PART III

John 9:16
"*Therefore said some of the Pharisees, This man is not of God, because he keepeth not the sabbath day. Others said, `How can a man that is a sinner do such miracles? And there was a division among them.'*"

Move on to Chapter 11. We've come through the blind man which was healed of blindness which he had since birth; sin is mentioned as well as with the impotent man; they were next to the pool which indicated a need for cleansing. Now to Lazarus and he's dead.

John 11:17
"*Then when Jesus came, he found that he* (Lazarus) *had lain in the grave four days already.*"

What does I Peter say in regard to a day in God's mind? A thousand years is but a day, and a day is but a thousand years. So, picking up the analogy that we are dealing with the Nation of Israel just like the blind man who had been blind since birth, how long has the Nation of Israel literally been spiritually dead? 4000 years. That takes you back to Abraham at 2000 BC So, I think the four days of Lazarus' death is an indication that Israel, nationally, is spending 4000 years spiritually dead. But what will happen at the end of the 4000 years? She will be brought back to life. I realize this is a little bit backwards, but come back to verse 6; hopefully you are getting the picture. But here in verse 6, word came to Jesus that Lazarus was sick, and they knew that if Jesus would come that He could heal him.

John 11:6
"When he had heard therefore that he was sick, he (purposely) *abode two days still in the same place where he was."* And then what will He do? He will go to where Lazarus is and raise him from the dead. Look at the Book of Hosea for a moment:

Hosea 6:1,2
"COME, and let us return unto the LORD: for he hath torn, and he will heal us; he hath smitten, and he will bind us up." The pronouns here are the Nation of Israel.
"After two days will he revive us: in the third day he will raise us up, and we shall live in his sight."

What are the two days? Well the two days since the Cross is how long? 2000 years. What's going to be the third thousand years? The Kingdom. See how beautifully this all fits. Now, back to Lazarus for a moment. He calls Lazarus forth. Does Lazarus contribute anything? Nothing. Remember he came out of the tomb. And that is the picture of Israel. One day they are going to be called back to life, nationally, and we will get to it in our next lesson.

(4d) Will the rapture occur before the tribulation ?

Book 25 LESSON TWO * PART II

Acts 15:7
"And when there had been much disputing, Peter rose up, and said unto them, `Men and brethren, ye know how that a good while ago God made choice among us, (that is from among the Jewish believers) *that the Gentiles by my mouth should hear the word of the gospel, and believe.'"*

Now after Peter goes through all his explanation, you come down to verse 12:

Acts 15:12-14
"Then all the multitude (that is of these Jewish believers there at Jerusalem) *kept silence, and gave audience to Barnabas and Paul, declaring what miracles and wonders God had wrought*

among the Gentiles by them. And after they had held their peace, (they finally settled down and listened to some common sense approach to all of this) *James* (who was moderating the meeting) *answered, saying, Men and brethren, hearken unto me: Simeon* (or Peter) *hath declared how God at the first* (that would be at the house of Cornelius) *did visit the Gentiles, to take out of them* (the Gentiles) *a people for his name."*

Now what is that? The Church, which is his Body. So for the last 1900+ years now the Church is being formed mainly by Gentiles who are being called out from among what they are, pagans or whatever, and becoming members of the body of Christ. Now as we've already seen then, as soon as that began, the Jews got envious and began to oppose it everywhere that Paul went. And God put a blindness upon the Nation. Remember, I'm always teaching and always reminding people, God deals with the Jew on two levels: National and personal. Now when he blinds them nationally, that does not take away the personal opportunity for Salvation. So don't ever think that God's being unfair. A Jew still has every opportunity for Salvation that we do, but it's on a personal basis and not on a national. So God is now calling out Gentiles as a people for His name, which is what we refer to now from Paul's epistles, as the Church which is His Body, the Body of Christ.

Now I'd like to use this analogy. I had just read an article, written by a physiologist, or he might have been an embryologist. He dealt with the fetus in the womb. And of course I'm not going to tell you anything you don't know, but I think it's such a beautiful analogy. At the beginning of pregnancy, that mother's body immediately begins to put all kinds of different cells into exactly the right place. And by the time that 9-month period is over, that little fetus has got all of his little fingers, fingernails, the eyes and everything now complete. And isn't it amazing, as this author pointed out, that the body rarely makes a mistake by making one finger much longer than it should be or making toes longer. But everything stops its cell-making process at exactly the right time. And when it's all completed and that little baby is complete and the cell-making process stops, then what? Delivery!

Now the Church is the same way. God has been adding individual believers from all around the world; Chinese, Japanese, Russians, Burmans, French, British, Americans, Canadians, whatever. Believers are coming into the Body one at a time. But isn't it amazing, just like the fetus in the mother's womb, one day the Body of Christ is finally going to have the last person in place. We don't know where it will be, but one day the last person is going to be put into the Body of Christ - It's complete. Now what's God going to do? He's going to deliver it from it's confines here on earth and we're going to Raptured out, as we saw in our last program, and that then becomes the **"until"** of Romans 11:25. Because you see, as soon as God has completed His work with the Gentile Body of Christ, where is He going to turn to? The Jew! Now of course, the Jew is going to have to go through those seven years of Tribulation before he enjoys all the blessings of Christ's return.

Romans 11:25

"I do not want you to be ignorant of this mystery, brothers, so that you may not be conceited: Israel has experienced a hardening in part until the full number of the Gentiles has come in."

But nevertheless, we know from II Thessalonians Chapter 2, that as soon as the Church is gone, the Anti-christ is going to make his appearance and the world is going to go into that seven years, which is predominately the time that God starts dealing with Israel. And so that's when their blindness is going to fall away. As soon as the Church is gone and the Tribulation begins. Now at the same time, since we have the times or fulness of the Gentiles here in Romans 11, go back with me to Luke 21 and we have the other side of the coin, so far as Gentiles are concerned. And this of course is the unbelieving element. Now the fulness of the Gentiles here in Romans are the Church-Age believers, but Luke 21 speaks of another group of Gentiles who will be the unbelievers. The unsaved world of Gentiledom. Let's look at verse 23 and Jesus is speaking.

Luke 21:23

"But woe unto them that are with child, and to them that give suck, in those days! for there shall be great distress in the land and wrath upon this people."

Now he is speaking in Palestine, he's speaking to Jews, and so this is where all of this is going to take place, isn't it? But he's not talking about the end-time, He's talking about 70 AD here. He's talking about Titus' great invasion and destruction of the temple. We pick that up now in verse 24.

Luke 21:24

"And they (the Jews of Jerusalem) *shall fall by the edge of the sword, and shall be led away captive into all nations:* (now there's the clue that this is 70 AD and not the last of the Tribulation, because at the end of the Tribulation the Jews are not going to be led captive into all the nations. They're going to just survive until their Messiah appears. But here they were and we know they were. They were emptied out of the land and they were dispersed into every nation on the face of the earth.) *and Jerusalem shall be trodden down of the Gentiles,* (what's the next word?) *until* (there's your time word. How long is Jerusalem going to be under the boot of the Gentile armies?) *the time of the Gentiles is fulfilled."*

Now what are we talking about? Beginning way back here in 606 BC, way back at Nebuchadnezzar's invasion of Jerusalem, is the first time that Jerusalem falls under the complete control of a Gentile empire, Babylon. All the way up through human history. All the way to the time of the Cross and at that time it was the Romans. And even as you come on into modern history, Israel has been under the control of various Gentile nations; the Moors, the Turks, and lastly before Israel finally made her independence, was Great Britain, under mandate. Britain was in charge of the Nation of Israel. Now of course, they've had a semblance of sovereignty, but for the most part, Israel is under the heavy hand of the U.N. or all the other nations and so forth.

Ignorance! They didn't know Who He was. I've been telling my classes for 25 years, over and over, Israel should have known Who Jesus was. Israel could have known Who Jesus was because it was in the Old Testament. Why didn't they? They didn't bother to study. The priests knew it, and they knew the stuff on the surface, but they didn't get right down into the nitty-gritty of the Old Testament prophecies. When the wise men came to Herod and asked about the King of Israel, Herod calls up the big-wigs of Judaism, and they had to go search the Scriptures to see where He was to be born. Did they find it? Sure they did. They said "He was to be born in Bethlehem," so they could have known, but they didn't. And do you know America is no better right now today? Every last person in these 50 states should know that we are in the end times, that we are approaching the very coming of Christ, and the Tribulation, the appearance of the Anti-christ and world government, but do they? No. Most of them don't even know what you're talking about. Why? Because they chose to remain ignorant. They don't have to be, but they are. Paul is admonishing the believers at Rome, **"Don't be ignorant of this fact that God has literally dropped a spiritual blindness on the Nation of Israel."** Remember the individual Jew can still have his eyes opened and believe, but nationally they are blinded, in fact, here in this chapter look at verse 7.

Romans 11:7

"What then? Israel hath not obtained that which he seeketh for; *(What were they seeking? The King and the earthly Kingdom! How did they miss it? They were ignorant. How ignorant? Well, they were looking for a King Who would come in with pomp and power and circumstance, at least symbolically riding on a great white Arabian steed. Instead their King came riding in on a lowly donkey. And they missed it. Well, they were ignorant of Who He really was, and so Paul says, `that Israel did not obtain that which they were looking for,')* but the election *(Those few Jews who did believe)* hath obtained it, and the rest were blinded." *And that's the Nation of Israel to this very day. They are still blind to Who Jesus really was. Now coming back to verse 25, Paul says, "That we Gentiles are to understand that this spiritual blindness has fallen on the Nation of Israel, and it will remain on their spiritual eyes"*

Romans 11:25b

"...until the fulness of the Gentiles be come in."

Well, what's the fulness of the Gentiles? The Body of Christ, the Church. So when the Body of Christ is full then God will take us out of the way and He will start dealing again with the Nation of Israel. Now when I say that the Tribulation is primarily Jewish, here's where I have to go back with you to Jeremiah Chapter 30, and of course this is just one verse. There are many, many others. However this one is so plain that I think anybody can comprehend it.

FIRST FRUITS: GLEANINGS: OLD TESTAMENT SAINTS: RESURRECTION

Let's turn to 2 Thessalonians Chapter 2. Now, just for a little recap from the last lesson. I hope I didn't leave any questions unanswered. The first resurrection of believers of all ages is really broken down into the three categories as indicated by Israel's harvest of grain. That is, first there were the 'first fruits,' which was of course epitomized by Christ, and those that came out of the graves in Matthew 27.

We have the Main harvest that came from the Church Age and the great resurrection day at the Rapture, or the trumpet sound when Christ shall leave Heaven and meet us in the air. The Old Testament believers as well as the Tribulation Believers who will have been martyred and died, seemingly are represented by the gleanings and the corners that were left in the Jewish harvest, and they will be resurrected shortly after the kingdom has begun.

Then, I hardly had time to explain at the end of the lesson, **but you see this is why we have that picture in the parables, and in the Old Testament, that the Jewish believers will be the guests at the wedding feast**. We won't take time to look at that, but if you want to, you can pick that up in Psalms Chapter 45, I think. It's also alluded to in the Song of Solomon. Lots of people don't understand the Song of Solomon as being so typical of **Christ and His Bride**, the Church. Now on our Time Line we're coming to that next event. **The Church Age will have ended with the Rapture,** and then we know that the Tribulation will be ushered in next. It will be that seven years not associated with the Church - because the Church Age has ended - it's gone. Instead, we'll be coming back to God's dealing with the Jew once again. I'll never forget a little lady in one of my classes, all of a sudden she just happened to see it. Then she exclaimed, **"In other words God's going to pick up with the Jews where he left off."** She hit the nail on the head perfectly.

Now, he has taken this Old Testament program, as we saw back in Psalms Chapter 2. God's time table stopped when He turned to the Gentiles with the Gospel of Grace. When that period has ended you will find Grace and Law cannot mix. Israel is going to have the Temple, she's going to go back under the Law. If ever I have any argument that we will not go into the Tribulation, it's that one purpose right there. **You can not mix Law and Grace**. Therefore, Grace cannot go into the Jewish economy, as it will pick up again in that seven-year Tribulation period. It has to be removed, so they cannot be mixed.

Paul, here in 2 Thessalonians, is coming as close to prophecy, if you want to call it that, as he does in any portion of his writings. He is introducing us to this seven-year period of time which Jesus in Matthew 24 calls the time of Tribulation. Now in 2 Thessalonians Chapter 2 verse 1 Paul writes to the Thessalonians believers who, believe it or not, had gotten to the place with all

then the seven heads and ten horns and ten crowns - this again is a twofold picture I think, as Satan is often referred to as the seven heads and so forth, referring I think to his power and his authority. But usually we think of the seven heads and ten horns as the revived Roman Empire. It will be a consortium of ten nations coming out of the Old Roman Empire territory. And I think we are seeing it coming on the scene even tonight as the Common Market, or European Community. At the present time, I think there are twelve nations that make up the EC (it may go a little higher), but when the peace treaty is signed between the Anti-christ and the Nation of Israel there will be only 10. And we will be showing that as we come through our study of Revelation.

Back in verse 1 of Chapter 13, John "***stood upon the sand of the sea***." And remember that the sea here is the sea of humanity, the masses of people around the globe. The world is getting "global." That's the word you hear and see lately. So out of this mass of humanity will come this empire that has been dead since about 300 AD and will be headed up by this man of sin, the Anti-christ. Now verse 2:

Revelation 13:2
"And the beast which I saw was like unto a leopard, and his feet were as the feet of a bear, and his mouth as the mouth of a lion: and the dragon (Satan) *gave him his power, and his seat* (throne), *and great authority."*

Go back again to Daniel 7. When we studied Daniel several lessons ago I stressed then that when we studied Daniel we would have to study Revelation and Matthew 24 and 25. They just all fit together so nicely. You can't study one without the other two. Now that mandates a lot of repetition. But as I have learned over the years, repetition is one of the best tools of learning. Here, Daniel is describing a vision that he has had. Which, of course, is looking forward down through history, and he uses practically the same language.

Daniel 7:2,3
"Daniel spake and said, `I saw in my vision by night, and, behold, the four winds of the heaven strove upon the great sea." There's that symbolism again with the mass of humanity. And out of that sea of humanity the following happened:
"And four great beasts came up from the sea, diverse one from another." These were governments, not animals.

Daniel 7:4-7
"The first was like a lion (that was Babylon)... *And behold another beast, a second, like to a bear* (that was the Medes and Persians empire)... *After this I beheld, and lo another, like a leopard* (that was the Greek empire under Alexander the Great)... *After this I saw in the night visions, and behold a fourth beast* (or empire), *dreadful and terrible* (this was the Roman empire)..."

The Roman empire was noble in some aspects, but it was bestial in many others. It had no concern for the lower classes of people. They threw people to the lions and thought nothing of it. They also became grossly immoral, wicked and evil. And, consequently, the empire finally fell in on itself. If you compare this passage with Revelation 13, you will see that John doesn't list the Roman empire. He begins with the Greek, the leopard, because he is speaking at a time when the Roman empire is still on the scene. So he doesn't have to list that one. But out of this Roman Empire you are going to see the residue of the previous three great world empires. But here John lists the empires in reverse order. These four empires are the ones the Bible concerns itself with as the times of the Gentiles. We read about the Roman empire that faded off the scene, but now is coming back on the scene in verse 7:

Daniel 7:7
"After this I saw in the night visions, and behold a fourth beast, dreadful and terrible, and strong exceedingly; and it had great iron teeth: it devoured and brake in pieces, and stamped the residue with the feet of it: and it was diverse from all the beasts that were before it; and it had (what?) ten horns."

Now back to Revelation 13:3. Let's take this slowly so that we don't lose the overall picture. We have ancient Babylon, the ancient Medes and Persians, Greek, and Roman empires. Daniel sees all the residue of those empires coming back together in the revival of that fourth (Roman) empire that was dreadful and terrible:

Revelation 13:3
"And I saw one of his heads as it were wounded to death; and his deadly wound was healed: and all the world wondered after the beast (this empire).

Let's bring it right up to the present time. Western Europe is coming together more and more as the United States of Europe. Tonight, I think they are at the number twelve, and like I said, they may go to thirteen or more. But whatever transpires, we know they will drop back to ten. This is a revival of that empire that existed what - almost 2000 years ago? It was dead, and yet here it is coming back full force. And the world is amazed. How can this be. Just fifty years ago most of the great cities of Europe were in heaps of rubble, ravished by war. Their industries had been destroyed. Yet where are they tonight. They are almost looking down on us.

I've said for years, that it almost seems that there was a conspiracy to destroy our United States of America. I still think there is. Right after World War II, when we had utterly demolished our enemies, the Marshall Plan came on the scene and we just literally rebuilt Europe with American dollars. Since then we have seen our industries leaving. We have all the oil resources we will ever need, but where do we get our oil? Foreign suppliers. Our industries are farmed out to Japan, Europe, Mexico, and Third World countries. Our steel business is almost gone. So you can see it seems there is a conspiracy to just bleed our beloved America dry. And all of it to enhance this revival of the ancient Roman Empire, or what we call the 10 nations of the

when the right time comes. It may take an act of war or nature for the Mosque of Omar to be destroyed. But we do know that Israel will have Temple worship for the first 3 1/2 years, all with the approval of this man Anti-christ. So today, this is Israel's anticipation, that they will have their Messiah and their Temple worship. But remember, Israel is looking for their Messiah to come the first time, because they don't recognize that Jesus Christ was the Messiah.

Book 12 LESSON ONE * PART II

Revelation 13:5

"...and power was given unto him to continue (which means to carry on. How long?) forty and two months (or 3 1/2 years)."

So how far does this verse bring us? To the mid-point of the Tribulation. I'm going to stop there in this portion concerning the Anti-christ. Now let's drop down to verse 11. A couple of lessons ago I mentioned the fact that during the Tribulation there would be an unholy trinity. A counterfeit trinity, with Satan as the counterfeit of God the Father, with the Anti-christ as the counterfeit God the Son, and with the False Prophet, the religious leader as we will see here in verse 11, the counterfeit of the Holy Spirit. Not so much in his make-up, but in his operations.

Revelation 13:11

"And I beheld another beast (this also is a man, but it is also a system. Not a government but a religious system) coming up out of the earth; ..."

Stop a minute. The Anti-christ is described as coming up out of the sea, and since the Book of Revelation is dealing almost exclusively, or primarily with the Nation of Israel, it's God dealing with His Covenant people once again, in preparation for His return. Naturally all the Gentile nations are going to be affected by it, but it's Israel's seven-year treaty that concerns itself with the time factor and everything that is taking place here. Israel will be so quick to accept the Anti-christ and his treaty, his offers of protection, and the Temple worship. I don't say it to look down on the Jew in the least bit, but I feel that this man, Anti-christ, will be a Jew. An Apostate Jew to be sure. Otherwise I can't see Israel so readily accepting his offers that he will make to them.

Book 10 LESSON THREE * PART IV

Matthew 24:3-5

"And as he sat upon the Mount of Olives, the disciples came unto him privately, saying, `Tell us, when shall these things be? and what shall be the sign of thy coming (in other words, the setting up of your kingdom); and the end of the world (as we know it)?' And Jesus answered and said unto them, `Take heed that no man deceive you. For many shall come in my name, saying, I am Christ;...'"

Or "I am the Messiah." Now stop a minute. Are we already seeing that? Sure we are. But to no extent that it will after that seven years has begun. And remember that just as soon as the Anti-christ signs that seven-year treaty with the nation of Israel, this seven-year Tribulation period is going to tick off, month by month, and day by day. And it will end exactly at the end of the seven years. Now someone asked the question at break, "Well, what will the Anti-christ offer the nation of Israel, that they will sign the seven-year treaty?" Well, what is Israel most hungry for tonight? Peace. They want peace with their neighbors. They want to be accepted into the family of nations of the world. And they have to maintain their defense structure. They have to keep their people taxed to death just to keep their enemies at bay. So if this man comes in, and I think he'll come out of the European Community with the power of N.A.T.O. behind him. And I think he'll come in and offer the nation of Israel absolute protection and a sovereignty that no one can approach. He'll say, "I guarantee your borders. You can dismantle you armed forces. I'll protect you." And Israel is going to fall for that, hook, line and sinker. And on top of that, he's going to give them permission to have their Temple worship. And he's going to guarantee them freedom in that.

And so they're going to have no qualms about signing this seven-year treaty. Because like I said a few lessons ago, they'll almost think he's the Christ, if they don't indeed. But as we see Jesus unfold the events of the Tribulation, remember this: even though we are seeing the beginnings of it; we are seeing the great increase in earthquakes; we're already seeing the potential of famine; and we are seeing famine in some places. Yet it's nothing compared to what it will be when these seven years begin to unfold.

Book 11 LESSON TWO * PART IV

Matthew 24:3
"And as he sat upon the mount of Olives, the disciples came unto him privately (just the Twelve), *saying, `Tell us, when shall these things be? and what shall be the sign of thy coming* (remember in I Corinthians 1:22, the Jew requires a sign. They wanted to know when His Kingdom would be set up), *and of the end of the world?'"*

Jesus now begins to lay out the events of the seven years. It begins from the appearance of the white horse in Revelation 6 - the Man of Sin, the counterfeit christ, the Anti-christ.

Matthew 24:4,5
"And Jesus answered and said unto them, `Take heed that no man deceive you. For many shall come in my name, saying, `I am Christ;...'"

Do you see that? That's the white horse. He's will come on the scene and practically convince the world that he is Christ. He's what the world is looking for. And we are already seeing people

Revelation 17:17,18
"For God hath put in their hearts to fulfill his will, and to agree, and give their kingdom unto the beast (the Anti-christ), *until the words of God shall be fulfilled."* In other words, when the seven years will have finally come to its end. Then verse 18:
"And the woman which thou sawest is that great city, which reigneth over the kings of the earth." Now there is a lot of speculation as to what city that is. Personally, I think by this time it will be Jerusalem.

Book 14 LESSON THREE * PART II

Psalms 2:4
"He that sitteth in the heavens shall laugh: the Lord shall have them in derision."

That is where we are tonight. The nations think they are in control, but we know they're not. The world is falling apart completely, and I see no hope of the world returning to a stable condition. I'm not a pessimist, but rather an optimist; but on the other hand I see things that are going on in our beloved nation that we are no longer able to turn around. We are past that point of no return. So that tells me we are that much closer to the end and the calling out of the Body of Christ at the Rapture. I have a Jewish gentleman that lives in Hollywood, California, that watches the program, and we share with each other quite often. He's not a Christian Jew. He's an Orthodox Judaistic Jew. Anyway, he called so excited the other morning, and reported that He had just returned from a seminar of rabbis. He said the rabbis are all excited because they are convinced that we are right at the coming of the Messiah. He said they realized that they had some tough times ahead during the Tribulation. I always remind him that everything they are looking for in their Messiah coming the first time, is really the Anti-christ. And it is. The Jew is blind to that and they will accept Anti-christ. Remember Jesus said in *John 5:43, "I am come in my Father's name, and ye receive me not: if another shall come in his own name, him ye will receive."*

(7d) What mission will the two witnesses fulfill during the tribulation ?

Book 11 LESSON THREE * PART IV

REVELATION 6, CONTINUED
Let's turn to Revelation Chapter 11. And here is where you can pick up a time frame if you will just take time to study it. You will find here in verse 3, where God says:

Revelation 11:3
"And I will give power unto my two witnesses, and they shall prophesy (speak forth the Word. The word "prophesy" in Scripture can mean either one. To speak about the future or just speak forth the Word. They are His witnesses, and they are going to minister primarily to the Nation

of Israel and the area of Jerusalem.) *a thousand two hundred and threescore days, clothed in sackcloth."*

That is 3 $\frac{1}{2}$ years. We know that is not the last 3 $\frac{1}{2}$ years, because you see when you come to end of their ministry in verse 12.

Revelation 11:12a
"And they heard a great voice from heaven saying unto them, `Come up hither.' And they ascended up to heaven..." And then in verse 13:

Revelation 11:13a
"And the same hour was there a great earthquake,..."

This is at the middle of the Tribulation and not the end. These two witnesses will minister the first 3 $\frac{1}{2}$ years. That is why I've come to Chapter 11 (the middle of the Tribulation), after Chapter 6 (the beginning of the Tribulation) because again we are going to come right back to an event at the beginning of the Tribulation. It is the appearance of the two witnesses. I'll have to comment on who those two witnesses might be. We can't be dogmatic because the Scripture doesn't tell us. There's nothing in this verse that says that it's going to be so and so. But we can speculate. The one that I think is a little easier to decide on than the other, is Elijah. I think that it's very possible that one of these two witnesses will be Elijah, because Elijah was taken up without having died. And there is a good reason for that. Let's go to the Book of Malachi. It's the last book of your Old Testament. Malachi Chapter 4 and verse 5:

Malachi 4:5
"Behold (the prophet writes. God is speaking through the prophet)*, I will send you Elijah the prophet before the coming of the great and dreadful day of the LORD:"* That's plain English. I know it was originally in Hebrew, but for us it's in plain English. Before the great and terrible day of the Lord, Elijah will come.

Malachi 4:6
"And he (that is, Elijah) *shall turn the heart of the fathers to the children, and the heart of the children to their fathers, lest I come and smite the earth with a curse."*

Alright, flip back if you will to Matthew Chapter 11. Again, we are in Jesus' earthly ministry. Now in Chapter 11 he makes an unusual statement. Starting with verse 11. Jesus is speaking and he says:

Matthew 11:11,12
"Verily I say unto you, `Among them that are born of women there hath not risen a greater than John the Baptist: notwithstanding he that is least in the kingdom of heaven is greater than he.

And from the days of John the Baptist until now (and remember that this is during Christ's earthly ministry) *the kingdom of heaven suffereth violence, and the violent take it by force.'"*

Matthew 11:13,14a
"For all the prophets and the law prophesied (of the coming kingdom) *until John. And* (what's the next word?) *if* (a little word like that is so easy to gloss over. but it's loaded) *ye will receive it,...."*

Who is Jesus talking to? Jews. He's talking to the Nation of Israel. If they would receive what? The King and the Kingdom. That's what He's offering. He's their King and He's ready to set up the Kingdom, if Israel would accept the King and the Kingdom at this point and time. Remember that it's an offer. We know according to prophecy that it couldn't have happened because Christ had to die. But nevertheless, it was still a valid offer. They had the opportunity to accept Him as their King. So read it in that light.

Matthew 11:14a
"And if ye will receive it (the Kingdom then), *this is Elias,..."*

Who is? John the Baptist. Think about that for a minute. Jesus is offering the Kingdom to the Nation of Israel in fulfillment of those Old Testament Covenants. The Abrahamic and all the rest of them. The Old Testament said, **"that before the return of Christ or the setting up of the kingdom, Elijah had to come."** But Jesus said, **"If you accept the kingdom now, then what? John is the prophesied Elijah."** That's hard for us to comprehend, but that's what He's saying. But since Israel did not accept the King, and did not accept the Kingdom, what has to happen? **Elijah has to come.** Come back to Revelation Chapter 11. I have to feel that on the basis of those two scriptures, one of these two witnesses will quite likely be the Old Testament Elijah brought back on the scene. He was also at the Mount of Transfiguration. Back to Revelation 11:4:

Revelation 11:4
"These (the two witnesses) *are the two olive trees, and the two candlesticks standing before the God of the earth."*

In other words, they are God's messengers for that time. The candlestick refers to the light that a candlestick gives forth. In the midst of the Tribulation darkness and wickedness and iniquity, in the great cataclysmic events that are taking place, these two men will still be like a spiritual lighthouse. Now verse 5:

Revelation 11:5
"And if any man will hurt them (or try to), *fire proceedeth out of their mouth, and devoureth their enemies* (they're going to have a special power for their protection as they proclaim the Word of

God): *and if any man will hurt them, he must in this manner be killed."*

In other words, these two witnesses are going to have that kind of power. And then in verse 6, is another reason why so many people feel that one of these witnesses is going to be Elijah, because he's going to do the same thing that he did in his Old Testament experiences.

Revelation 11:6
"These have power to shut heaven, that it rain not in the days of their prophecy (or their speaking. Remember Elijah stopped the rain for three years back in the Old Testament.)*; and have power over waters to turn them to blood, and to smite the earth with all plagues, as often as they will."* Now that kind of language gives us an idea that it could be Moses. See? Now I never get dogmatic about this. Others say it has to be Enoch, because Enoch didn't die either. This isn't all that basic to our doctrine. All we have to do is believe that our Sovereign God is in control, and is going to bring these two men to the city of Jerusalem at the very onset of the seven years of Tribulation. Now verse 7:

Revelation 11:7
"And when they shall have finished their testimony (their 3 $\frac{1}{2}$ years), *the beast that ascendeth out of the bottomless pit* (I think the beast could either be the Roman Empire which is now the E.C. and is now back on the scene. Or the beast here could be in reference to the Anti-christ himself. I throw this out to get you to study. I remember years ago as our class was dismissed, a lady walked out the door and she had just been a visitor. She had come from another part of the country. And she said, "Well, I don't know that I agree with you, but I'll give you credit for one thing. I have already promised myself that starting tomorrow I'm going to study my Bible." And that is the only reason I teach. Then verse 7 winds up with this government that I think will be the Anti-christ or the revived Roman Empire) *shall make war against them* (They will try to destroy these two men. And they are going to succeed)*, and shall overcome them, and kill them."* So these two men will be put to death.

Revelation 11:8
"And their dead bodies shall lie in the street of the great city, which spiritually is called Sodom and Egypt, where also our Lord was crucified."

So that was what city? Jerusalem. So they are going to be killed and left to rot on the streets of Jerusalem. Just because of their mortal hatred for these two men. Verse 9:

Revelation 11:9
"And they of the people and kindreds and tongues and nations shall see their dead bodies three days and an half, and shall not suffer their dead bodies to be put in graves." They will just lie out in the hot sun for 3 $\frac{1}{2}$ days.

Revelation 11:10

"And they that dwell upon the earth (not just Israel, but the whole earth, from one end to the other) *shall rejoice over them, and make merry, and shall send gifts one to another; because these two prophets tormented them that dwelt on the earth."*

Well, how did they torment them? By simply pointing out their wickedness, and their iniquity. And the righteous judgment of God which is already to a certain degree upon them. And the world is going to hate them. But the amazing thing is that verse 11 says something that 50 or 60 years ago was almost hard to swallow, and the average Bible believers had problems with this. All you could say was that God in His wisdom knows how He is going to do it. And now you see it is so common. What is it?

Revelation 11:11

"And after three days and an half the Spirit of life from God entered into them (God brings them back to life)*, and they stood upon their feet; and great fear fell upon them which saw them."*

Who saw them? The whole world. How do they see them? Television. We do that everyday. It is very common now to see a news broadcast from the other side of the earth. I can remember when I was a kid, I would hear a preacher preach on this, and I can still hear mom and dad talk about, how that was going to be possible. How can the people of the world see two dead people lying on the streets of Jerusalem. Now, we just take that for granted. It will probably be on the 5:30 national news. And the whole world will see these two witnesses suddenly ascend.

Revelation 11:12

"And they heard a great voice from heaven saying unto them, `Come up hither.' And they ascended up to heaven in a cloud; and their enemies beheld them."

Right in view of the cameras up they go, and this is going to shake people up. But remember this will be the time of the supernatural and God isn't going to hide it. And when these two witnesses who have been put to death, are suddenly made alive, and ascend right out of the midst of Jerusalem, the whole world will witness it. Now these are Tribulation days. The days of Supernatural. Alright let's go on to verse 13:

Revelation 11:13a

"And the same hour (remember this is the mid-point of the Tribulation) *was there a great earthquake,..."* You have to remember that Jerusalem and especially the valley of the Jordan, and the Dead Sea, and the Sea of Galilee, are sitting right on a tremendous fault line. It's historical. In fact, that's probably why the Dead Sea is so deep and why it is so far below sea level (approximately 12-1400 feet below sea level). Because at times the fault has literally dropped the surface of the earth in that area. Remember the whole Jordan valley is below sea level. Even the Sea of

Galilee is 600 feet below sea level. So when the Bible speaks of great earthquakes in that part of the world it is not unusual.

So we know we are at the mid-point of the Tribulation. Remember I told you rather than go verse by verse chronologically, take Revelation by events. The beginning (the appearance of the Anti-christ and these two witnesses), and at the mid-point we have the end of these two witnesses and have a great earthquake. We studied earlier how the Anti-christ will come in and desecrate and defile the Temple at the mid-point. We will try to look at that in our next lesson. But for now let's look at Revelation Chapter 7. And here again is a portion of Scripture that has been so completely perverted that we have a lot of confusion and it doesn't have to be. It is so plain. Now since these two witnesses are beginning to proclaim Godly things, and I think again just like Jesus said, they are going to be proclaiming the King and the Kingdom is coming. Out of their preaching, almost immediately, they will have a response of their prophesying or speaking, by the 144,000 young Jewish men that we find in Chapter 7. Now let's read it:

Revelation 7:1
"And after these things I saw four angels standing on the four corners of the earth (remember this is supernatural experiences in a supernatural time)*, holding the four winds of the earth, that the wind should not blow on the earth, nor on the sea, nor on any tree."*

Revelation 7:2,3
"And I saw another angel ascending from the east, having the seal of the living God: and he cried with a loud voice to the four angels, to whom it was given to hurt (or judgment on) *the earth and the sea, Saying, 'Hurt not the earth, neither the sea, nor the trees, till we have sealed the servants of our God in their foreheads.'"*

Now isn't that easy to understand? These servants, I feel, have been listening to the two witnesses and so they are responding. Now look who they are in verse 4:

Revelation 7:4
"And I heard the number of them which were sealed (or designated or commissioned)*: and there were sealed an hundred and forty and four thousand* (now watch where they come from) *of all the tribes of the children of Israel."*

So that there are no mistakes, He names them in verse 5-8 except for one. And that question comes up often. Why aren't Dan and Ephraim mentioned in these 12 tribes? Remember, they moved up into the northern part of Israel, and what were the tribes guilty of? They were the first ones to go into idolatry. And, consequently, they are left out of these 12 tribes. So we have 12,000 from each of the other 12 tribes all sealed and they are given a particular mission.

(8d) What mission will the 144,000 Jewish men fulfill during the tribulation?

Book 11 LESSON THREE * PART IV

So we know we are at the mid-point of the Tribulation. Remember I told you rather than go verse by verse chronologically, take Revelation by events. The beginning (the appearance of the Anti-christ and these two witnesses), and at the mid-point we have the end of these two witnesses and have a great earthquake. We studied earlier how the Anti-christ will come in and desecrate and defile the Temple at the mid-point. We will try to look at that in our next lesson. But for now let's look at Revelation Chapter 7. And here again is a portion of Scripture that has been so completely perverted that we have a lot of confusion and it doesn't have to be. It is so plain. Now since these two witnesses are beginning to proclaim Godly things, and I think again just like Jesus said, they are going to be proclaiming the King and the Kingdom is coming. Out of their preaching, almost immediately, they will have a response of their prophesying or speaking, by the 144,000 young Jewish men that we find in Chapter 7. Now let's read it:

Revelation 7:1
"And after these things I saw four angels standing on the four corners of the earth (remember this is supernatural experiences in a supernatural time)*, holding the four winds of the earth, that the wind should not blow on the earth, nor on the sea, nor on any tree."*

Revelation 7:2,3
"And I saw another angel ascending from the east, having the seal of the living God: and he cried with a loud voice to the four angels, to whom it was given to hurt (or judgment on) *the earth and the sea, Saying, `Hurt not the earth, neither the sea, nor the trees, till we have sealed the servants of our God in their foreheads.'"*

Now isn't that easy to understand? These servants, I feel, have been listening to the two witnesses and so they are responding. Now look who they are in verse 4:

Revelation 7:4
"And I heard the number of them which were sealed (or designated or commissioned)*: and there were sealed an hundred and forty and four thousand* (now watch where they come from) *of all the tribes of the children of Israel."*

So that there are no mistakes, He names them in verse 5-8 except for one. And that question comes up often. Why isn't Dan and Ephraim mentioned in these 12 tribes? Remember, they moved up into the northern part of Israel, and what were the tribes guilty of? They were the first ones to go into idolatry. And, consequently, they are left out of these 12 tribes. So we have 12,000 from each of the other 12 tribes all sealed and they are given a particular mission. And here it comes in verse 9. As a result of their sealing:

Revelation 7:9

"After this I beheld, and, lo, a great multitude, which no man could number, of all nations (that indicates that the 144,000 will not limit their ministry to just the Nation of Israel), *and kindreds, and people, and tongues, stood before the throne, and before the Lamb, clothed with white robes, and palms in their hands;"*

Now remember back in Chapter 6 when we talked about that 5th seal, in verse 9-11 it reads:

Revelation 6:9-11

"And when he had opened the fifth seal, I saw under the altar the souls of them that were slain for the word of God, and for the testimony which they held: And they cried with a loud voice, saying, `How long, O Lord, holy and true, dost thou not judge and avenge our blood on them that dwell on the earth?' And white robes were given unto every one of them; and it was said unto them, that they should rest yet for a little season, until their fellowservants also and their brethren, that should be killed as they were, should be fulfilled."

This is where it all begins. These 144,000 young Jewish men will be encircling the globe in a miraculous way. They won't have to buy any airline tickets. I think they will be Spirit sent. They won't have to learn a language. They will know every language and dialect everywhere they go. And these 144,000 young Jews will circle the globe at least three or four years out of this seven. And here are the results of their ministry. Verse 13:

Revelation 7:13,14

"And one of the elders answered, saying unto me, `What are these which are arrayed in white robes? and whence came they?' And I said unto him, `Sir, thou knowest,' And he said to me, `These are they which came out of great tribulation, and have washed their robes, and made them white in the blood of the Lamb."

Now that is a vast number of people from every tribe and tongue and nation. And they will martyred almost as soon as they believe. But a few will survive. And we will pick them up in a later lesson. There will be some survivors, as we saw in the Book if Isaiah a couple of lessons ago. What I think we have here is sort of a compensation, or an evening out of what the Nation of Israel literally missed. They were originally going to be the vehicle to bring the pagan, Gentile world to a knowledge of their Jehovah. And they missed it. But the 144,000 will sort of make a compensation for that.

Book 12 LESSON ONE * PART I

ANTI-CHRIST - "FALSE PROPHET"

Turn to Revelation 7. The Book of Revelation primarily deals with those final seven years before the return of Christ at His Second Coming; then the setting up of His Kingdom upon the earth.

This seven years is primarily God dealing with the Nation of Israel; however, all the world will become involved. Remember Jeremiah 30:7?

Jeremiah 30:7
"Alas! for that day is great, so that none is like it: it is even the time of Jacob's trouble; but he shall be saved out of it."

We'll look at this verse more in detail later. It's God dealing with His Covenant people and for this reason they are still coming back to their homeland, getting ready for these final seven years.

The best way to study Revelation is not to try to take it chronologically, but find the events at the beginning, at the middle, and at the end of the Tribulation, and then fill in the gaps. Chronologically it won't make all that much sense to you. The past several lessons we have been looking at things at the beginning. **1. The appearance of the Anti-christ** when he will sign that seven-year peace treaty with the Nation of Israel, which will again kick God's time clock back in gear, as it has been stopped now all during the Church Age. **2. The appearance of those two witnesses.** They will come to the Nation of Israel in Jerusalem. And they will begin proclaiming God's Word to the Nation of Israel, and out of the ministry of these two... **3. God is going to seal and commission the 144,000 young Jewish men** whom God will use to circumvent the globe. They won't be preaching the Gospel of Grace as we know it, but, rather, they will be reverting back again to the Gospel of the Kingdom as it was being proclaimed at the time of Christ and Peter and the eleven.

There is a vast difference between the Gospel of Grace and the Gospel of the Kingdom. When you understand that, the Bible is much less confusing. At that time, the Age of Grace has ended and the Church is gone. A person will no longer have the opportunity to join a local congregation. But rather these 144,000 will be telling the world that the King is coming. After all, that was the message in Christ's earthly ministry. He Himself referred to it more than once as the Gospel of the Kingdom. The King and His Kingdom were about to come on the scene. Of course Israel rejected that, and the King was crucified. God raised Him from the dead, called Him back to heaven to sit at the Father's right hand until His enemies should be made His footstool. That `until' signifies the time when He will once again deal with His Covenant people of Israel.

We closed our last lesson with God sealing the 144,000 Jews (there were 12,000 from each of the twelve tribes). Remember, the reason that God set aside the Nation of Israel was to fulfill the promises of **Genesis 3:15, that the Seed of the woman would come to be the Redeemer of mankind.** In order to bring that to a fulfillment, He set aside the Nation of Israel, and promised Abraham that through that Nation of people would come the Messiah. So God begins to prepare the Nation of Israel for the roll of being the missionary to the nations. Exodus 19:6 says, *"And ye shall be unto me a Kingdom of Priests and an holy nation."* He put them under Law, I maintain, to prepare them for that tremendous role that would be theirs to carry out. But when the opportunity came and they could have had the King and the Kingdom, and they could have brought all the nations of the world to a knowledge of their God, they dropped the ball. In their unbelief they rejected the King and the Kingdom. They, in turn, were dispersed out into the world, lost their temple and worship, and God turned to the Gentiles through the Apostle Paul without using the Nation of Israel. Using that same analogy in order to get a sweet taste of some sort of a redeeming of themselves, God will let these 144,000 Jews at least get a taste of what the Nation of Israel missed. This 144,000 will see a multitude come to a knowledge of salvation through their ministry. Now verse 9:

Revelation 7:9,10
"After this I beheld, and, lo, a great multitude, which no man could number, of all nations, and kindreds, and people, and tongues, stood before throne, and before the Lamb, clothed with white robes, and palms in their hands; And cried with a loud voice, saying, `Salvation to our God which sitteth upon the throne, and unto the Lamb,'" In other words they had been martyred almost as fast as they had been converted throughout the Tribulation. Now verses 13 and 14. And after John sees this multitude of converted people.

Revelation 7:13,14
"And one of the elders answered, saying unto me, `What are these which are arrayed in white robes? and whence came they?' And I said unto him, `Sir, thou knowest.' And he said to me, `These are they which came out of (the) great tribulation, and have washed their robes, and made them white in the blood of the Lamb.'"

Book 13 LESSON TWO * PART IV

Revelation 7:3
"Saying, Hurt not the earth, neither the sea, nor the trees, till we have sealed the servants of our God in their foreheads."
That was like, I suppose, when God put a mark on Cain, that no one could take his life. And it's the same way with these 144,000. They were sealed so that they could not be killed. Suffer, yes, but they couldn't be killed. Reading on you will see that there were 12,000 sealed from each of the twelve tribes. To see how all of this fits with Matthew Chapter 25 come down to verse 16. These are the privations that Tribulation believers, as well as the 144,000, will suffer during this seven-year period.

Revelation 7:16
"They shall hunger no more, neither thirst any more;..."

Remember, if people don't take the mark of the beast during this time, they won't be able to buy or sell, and seven years is a long time if you can't buy groceries. Seven years is a long time if you can't make a house payment, buy gasoline, or pay a doctor bill. So they will end up hungry and thirsty, and naked. Come back to Matthew Chapter 25. So the 144,000 suffered these same privations during the Tribulation. They were thrown in prison and they're going to be hungry, and the only sustenance they had was from these believers. These believers, although they will have little to spare, will sacrifice to help these 144,000.

Editor's Note: More about the 144,000 and how their mission ties into chapter 25 of Matthew will be explained a few pages ahead under the question: "Will some people live through the tribulation?"

(9d) What will happen during the first 3 ½ years of the tribulation ?

Book 11 LESSON TWO * PART II

Revelation 5:1
"And I saw in the right hand of him that sat on the throne a book (or scroll is a better word. It was rolled up and sealed) *written within and on the backside, sealed with seven seals."*

Just picture a scroll rolled up and then sealed with seven seals. On the outside are written details. This is alluded to in the Old Testament economy, going back to Israel. They had every right to mortgage their property. Some may think mortgages are strictly twentieth century, but mortgages are not something new. Even at the time of Ruth and Boaz, they could mortgage their property. If they got in a bind and the mortgage was due, and they couldn't pay, they would either lose their property, or could go to a next of kin for help. If the next of kin had the funds, and wanted to, then the mortgage could be paid off. **There you have the three requirements for paying off a mortgage. Next of Kin, Able, and Willing.**

This was the whole idea in Israel, that the families would keep their inheritance. Now we have the same picture here of a mortgage. It says it was written inside as well as on the outside. The private details that were not for public scrutiny were written on the inside. But the things that needed to be made public were written on the outside – for example, who the property belonged to. We still do that at the court house today, so it's not that much different. The lesson here is, there is a mortgage involved, sealed with seven seals, but only One can open the scroll and pay it off.

Revelation 5:2,3
"And I saw a strong angel proclaiming with a loud voice, 'Who is worthy to open the book (or scroll), *and to loose the seals thereof?' And no man in heaven, nor in earth, neither under the earth, was able to open the book* (or scroll), *neither to look thereon."*

No one seemingly had the next of kinship, who had the wherewithal in wealth, and who was willing. And John says in verse 4:

Revelation 5:4

"And I wept much, because no man was found worthy to open and to read the book (or scroll), *neither to look thereon."* Look at verse 5:

Revelation 5:5

"And one of the elders saith unto me, 'Weep not: behold, the Lion of the tribe of Juda, the Root of David, hath prevailed to open the book, and to loose the seven seals thereof.'" And who is the Lion of the tribe of Juda? Christ.

Book 11 LESSON TWO * PART III

Revelation 5:13,14

"And every creature which is in heaven, and on the earth, and under the earth, and such as are in the sea, and all that are in them, heard I saying, 'Blessing, and honour, and glory, and power, be unto him that sitteth upon the throne, and unto the Lamb for ever and ever.' And the four beasts (creatures) *said, 'Amen (so be it).' And the four and twenty elders fell down and worshipped him that liveth for ever and ever."*

The stage is set. God the Son has taken the mortgage with the seven seals on it. And now He is going to open it and begin the process of paying it off. Now we come to Chapter 6, and the first thing we are introduced to is the four horsemen of the apocalypse; most have heard of it. They are very interesting. Verse 1:

Revelation 6:1a

"And I saw when the Lamb (God the Son) *opened one of the seals,..."*

He will take them off one at a time. And these seven seals are going to take us up to the mid-point of the Tribulation. Now the best way to understand the Book of Revelation is to realize that there are a whole series of sevens throughout the Book. The part we skipped was the seven letters to the seven churches. Now we will see the seven seals; the seven seal judgments. They will introduce the seven trumpet judgments. The seventh trumpet judgments will introduce the final seven bold judgments. Interspersed between, there are seven distinct persons, and seven woes.

The whole Book of Revelation is a breakdown of sevens. And seven is God's perfect number. The whole Book is not a book of myths and legends; it is a perfectly tuned Book that is definitely a part of the Word of God. What we have is the beginning of this final seven years. Several lessons ago from the Book of Daniel, we showed that this seven-year period of time, which we call Daniel's seventieth week, or the time of wrath and vexation, or primarily the Tribulation, will be opening when the Anti-christ signs that seven-year treaty with the Nation of Israel. That's back in Daniel Chapter 9. And when he signs that seven-year treaty, this is the beginning of the opening of the seals we see here in Revelation Chapter 6.

The first 3 $\frac{1}{2}$ years are not so much the wrath and vexation, although they will be bad enough. The last 3 $\frac{1}{2}$ years are going to be terrible for those who must go through it. Remember, as you study Revelation, that all through Scripture these seven years are divided 3 $\frac{1}{2}$ and 3 $\frac{1}{2}$; 42 months and 42 months; 1260 days and 1260 days

Book 11 LESSON TWO * PART IV

PROPHECY: THE WHITE HORSE OF REVELATION 6

Let's continue in Revelation Chapter 6. We left off in verse 2. Christ has taken the scroll from God the Father. And that scroll includes the mortgage that Satan is holding over the planet as a result of the curse. **And the curse is going to be lifted by the time all of this is over.** As we see the first seal of this mortgage removed, it's the appearance of a white horse. There are many who feel that, because it is a white horse, it has to be Christ. But I'm convinced it is the false christ, **because from Genesis Chapter 3, just as soon as man entered the scene, Satan came in as the master counterfeiter.**

Revelation 6:2
"...and he that sat on him had a bow;..."

"Bow" is hard to track down since it can be pronounced and mean different things. You can't really define this word from the Greek as to what is implied, so I'll have to follow in the tracks of men I've read, that most agree it's the bow that would shoot arrows. But, from our study of the Anti-christ out of Daniel, I trust I made it clear that Anti-christ is not coming in using power of military might or by fighting wars. How is he going to come in? Peaceably and with flattery. He is going to be a political maneuverer - a charismatic type individual. He doesn't have to use his ammunition, but may come with the threat of power behind him which he will have. Even Western Europe still has NATO. But he doesn't actually have the military power yet. He hasn't come that far along.

Revelation 6:2
"...and a crown was given unto him:..."

The world is going to recognize him as their leader. Remember, he will come up out of the Common Market of Europe. The European Community (EC). There will be 10 nations in all and he will come up and usurp the power. Look at Matthew 24. It's the perfect parallel of Revelation Chapter 6. So always compare the two. Note that Matthew 24 is all prophecy about the Tribulation. There is no Church Age doctrine in here whatsoever. This is strictly Tribulation ground.

Matthew 24:1,2

"And Jesus went out, and departed from the temple: and his disciples came to him for to shew him the buildings of the temple. And Jesus said unto them, `See ye not all these things? verily I say unto you, `There shall not be left here one stone upon another, that shall not be thrown down.'"

Jesus was looking toward the siege of the Roman armies under Titus. And that is just what the armies did. Once they got inside the city wall they devastated the city. Josephus recorded (and it's not Scripture), that the Roman soldiers had heard it rumored that between the very building stones of Herod's Temple, there was a lot of gold and other kinds of wealth. And soldiers being soldiers, tore it down stone by stone looking for that supposedly hidden wealth. But whatever the reason, we know that the Temple was destroyed just as Jesus said it would be. This Temple could not be destroyed by fire like King Nebuchadnezzar did to Solomon's Temple, but remember Solomon's Temple was built from the beautiful cedars of Lebanon. So it burned to a crisp. But Herod's Temple was predominately of stone and of course the precious gold and silver, etc. But anyway it was all destroyed except that little segment of the wall that is now known as the Wailing Wall.

Matthew 24:3

"And as he sat upon the mount of Olives, the disciples came unto him privately (just the Twelve), *saying, `Tell us, when shall these things be? and what shall be the sign of thy coming* (remember in I Corinthians 1:22, the Jew requires a sign. They wanted to know when His Kingdom would be set up), *and of the end of the world?'"*

Jesus now begins to lay out the events of the seven years. It begins from the appearance of the white horse in Revelation 6 - the Man of Sin, the counterfeit christ, the Anti-christ.

Matthew 24:4,5

"And Jesus answered and said unto them, `Take heed that no man deceive you. For many shall come in my name, saying, `I am Christ;...'"

Do you see that? That's the white horse. He's will come on the scene and practically convince the world that he is Christ. He's what the world is looking for. And we are already seeing people like that. Sigma Moon from Korea, about 15 years ago, tried to tell the world that he was the Christ. And we've had others, and we will have still more. But it's going to be culminated by the real counterfeiter, the real Anti-christ, and he's going to convince the world that he is the Christ and he shall deceive many. Going back to Revelation, stop at I John, Chapter 2 for a moment. This is the same writer who wrote the Book of Revelation. Now let's drop down to verse 18. And here again, as I have stressed before, is the one place where this Man of Sin is actually called the Anti-christ.

I John 2:18

"Little children, it is the last time (these writers of Scriptures had no idea there was going to be 1900 + years before this would happen. They thought it would be coming in a relatively short time)*: and as ye have heard that antichrist* (here John is speaking of the real Anti-christ) *shall come, even now are there many antichrists;..."*

Of course there are. But they can't hold a candle to the one that is coming. Now let's go back to Revelation Chapter 6. So we see this Man of Sin comes on the scene and he begins to conquer and overtake nations. He is setting up his power base.

Revelation 6:2b,3a

"... and he went forth conquering, and to conquer. And when he had opened the second seal,..."

Remember these seals are on that mortgage, that scroll. He signs the seven-year treaty with the Nation of Israel as we saw back in Daniel. The next event which may be within the first month or so after the seven years have begun, is another horse. This one is red.

Revelation 6:4a

"And there went out another horse that was red: and power was given to him that sat thereon (the red horse) *to take peace from the earth* (when you have the absence of peace, what do you have? War. I mean a real one. So this power entity, this rider of the red horse is going to bring war on the earth)*, and that they should kill one another:"* I want you to underline those last three words, because I think this indicates what I'm going to show is the rider of the red horse. We won't have time to take it all the way through during this lesson. But here we have the rider of the red horse, and his battle ground is going to be epitomized by not killing the enemy, but what are they going to do? They are going to kill each other. To whet your appetite, and as you are turning to Ezekiel, I want you to be thinking what great power on earth is associated with the color red? Russia. For over twenty years I've been teaching that I think the rider of the red horse will be the Russian invasion of Israel. Just as in Ezekiel 38 and 39. So in Chapter 38, and again, Ezekiel begins as he does so many times:

Ezekiel 38:1,2

"And the word of the LORD came unto me, saying, `Son of man, set thy face against Gog, the land of Magog, the chief prince of Meshech and Tubal, and prophesy against him,"

Most Bible scholars are convinced that Gog and Magog, Meshech and Tubal are Russia and her satellite nations. I have told my classes for quite some time not to believe for a minute that the Russian bear is dead. The Russian bear is alive and well. They may be crimped a little economically, and be a little cold and hungry, but the Russian army is sitting there east of the Ural Mountains just as intact as it has ever been. I read again in one of the major news magazines recently, that Russia has not cut one person from their staff of espionage. They are just as busy with their spying activity as they have always been. They have not slowed down the production of any of their war materials. They recently sent another rocket into space. How are they doing all of this if they are destitute and broke? Listen, they are just as alive as can be. And we know they have their problems, but one day soon the Communist will come back in and take over and Russia will be right back on track.

Editor's Note: The events of Revelation 6:4-8 and Ezekiel 39:1-9, which will also take place in the first 3 1/2 years of the tribulation, are covered under a separate question "What will happen to America during the tribulation?" a few pages ahead. Keep that in mind as we now move down a few verses from Revelation 6:4 to verse 9.

Book 11 LESSON THREE * PART III

REVELATION 6, CONTINUED

Let's go back to the horsemen of the Apocalypse in Revelation Chapter 6 for a quick review. First we have the appearance of the Anti-christ. He signs the seven-year treaty with Israel which gives them relative peace and safety. Then I feel you will have that great invasion of the red horde from the north, which in turn will precipitate a great demise in the food supply. That will trigger the famine (or the black horse in verses 5 and 6), as well as the pestilences. And remember that we showed you in Matthew 24 that Jesus foretold that these things were just the beginning of sorrow or travail. These are the beginning days of the Tribulation. It's going to be the most awful seven-year period in human history. We will be seeing that, as Jesus spoke of it in Matthew 24. But now, turn to Revelation Chapter 6. Remember, these horsemen were also seals, and we have four of the seals off (there were seven seals on the scroll to begin with). Now He opens the fifth seal. And John, in his visionary experience, of course:

Revelation 6:9
"And when he had opened the fifth seal, I saw under the altar the souls of those of them that were slain for the word of God, and for the testimony which they held:"

I have to feel he was making reference to the Tribulation martyrs. Later we're going to show that, yes indeed, there will be multitudes of non-Jews who will have a salvation experience during this turmoil. But they will not live very long to tell about it, because it's going to be a period of time where they are going to be martyred immediately. These are the ones I feel that John sees in a prophetic light, and these who have been martyred for their faith will cry:

Revelation 6:10
"And they cried with a loud voice, saying, `How long, O Lord, holy and true, dost thou not judge and avenge our blood on them that dwell on the earth?'" And, of course, we know that He's going to.

Revelation 6:11

"And white robes were given unto every one of them (that is, these that had been martyred for their faith)*; and it was said unto them, that they should rest yet for a little season, until their fellowservants also and their brethren, that should be killed as they were, should be fulfilled."*

That's all part of the fifth seal. Now we come to the sixth seal. Remember there's only seven that are holding this scroll together, and Christ is the One that is opening it in order to be able to read that mortgage and pay it off. Okay, we're coming back to that scroll that was in Revelation Chapter 5:

Revelation 6:12a

"And I beheld when he had opened the sixth seal, and , lo, there was a great earthquake;..."

In Matthew 24, that was one of the things that Jesus had mentioned, that there would be famine and pestilence and earthquakes in divers places. We're already seeing a tremendous increase in earthquake activity; thousands of percent in the last twenty or thirty years. There's so many earthquakes taking place every day that the media doesn't even bother to report them. I read recently in one of the daily papers there where three or four earthquakes; not huge, but 4.6 or 5 on the Richter scale. There was one in China, one in Southern Russia and one in Iran. They're taking place every day. This is contrary to history; it hasn't always been that way. In verse 12 we're approaching the mid-point of this seven years. We're about at the end of 3 $^1/2$ years as we get to the sixth seal.

Revelation 6:12b

"...and the sun became black as sackcloth of hair, and the moon became as blood;"

All you have to do is know the circumstances. When there's tremendous earthquakes, there's more than likely volcanic eruptions as well. As we know from the past, volcanoes can spew out so much dust that the sun can almost be blocked out. I think that's what we have here. It isn't that God all of a sudden is going to blacken the sun, per se. But as a result of all these activities on the planet, the sun will almost become like we've seen it at times, like a little red glow. And the moon became as blood, again because of all the pollution that has been blown into the atmosphere. Then verse 13. This is God dealing primarily with the Nation of Israel. Jeremiah said it was the time of Jacob's trouble. I've pointed out over the years, for those of you who have been following from Genesis on, that whenever God was dealing with Israel in the land, the supernatural was commonplace. Beginning when Moses went into Egypt, the plagues were supernatural events that were under God's control. The opening of the Red Sea was supernatural. The life and escapades of Samson were supernatural. And the appearance of the Angelic hosts at Christ's birth was supernatural. The opening of the prison, when Peter was in captivity, by the use of a earthquake - what was it? Supernatural. So this is what I'm talking about. When God is dealing with that Nation of Israel, as He will be in these seven years, we're dealing with the supernatural every day - things that are beyond the ordinary. In verse 13, we even have cosmic disturbances.

Revelation 6:13,14
"And the stars of heaven fell unto the earth, even as a fig tree casteth her untimely figs, when she is shaken of a mighty wind. And the heaven departed as a scroll when it is rolled together; and every mountain and island were moved out of their places."

In other words, tremendous earthquake activity. And this is only in the first half. The second half is going to be far worse. Even rulers and men in high places are getting shook up:

Revelation 6:15,16
"And the kings of the earth, and the great men, and the rich men, and the chief captains, and the mighty men, and every bondman, and every free man, hid themselves in the dens and in the rocks of the mountains (and they actually plead for death)*: And said to the mountains and rocks, `Fall on us, and hide us from the face of him that sitteth on the throne, and from the wrath of the Lamb:'"*

Do you see for the last 1900 plus years, mankind has not seen the wrath of God. Now we know there has been a lot of calamity. We know that there has already been a lot of earthquake activity, and wars and famine and so forth. But that has not been the wrath of God. I've always maintained that the things that come upon the human race, that plague us, are not acts of God's wrath. They are God permitting Satan to bring suffering and turmoil to God's creation. God is not in the business tonight of pouring out His wrath. He's a God of Grace, tonight. Paul says in Romans Chapter 5, that where sin abounded, what's always greater? **His grace** abounds even more. But, grace has ended here with the out-calling of the Body of Christ just before the Tribulation begins. We are seeing the wrath of the Lamb being poured out. Verse 17, and it's repeated twice in two verses:

Revelation 6:17
"For the great day of his wrath is come; and who shall be able to stand?"

Do you remember Psalms Chapter 2? We've used it so often coming up through the Old Testament. After mankind, Jew and Gentile, have rejected the King, they're going to go into a period of perplexity and derision - and that's where the world is tonight. They don't know where to turn. And then what does the next verse say in Psalms Chapter 2?

Psalms 2:5
"Then shall he speak unto them in his wrath, and vex them in his sore displeasure."

It's no longer the Age of Grace. All these events take us up to the mid-point of this seven years.

We've had the appearance of the Anti-christ. We've had the permission (if I may use that word) for Israel to go back into Temple worship. She's going to go back under the Law you might say. She's getting closer to that all the time. Now back again to Revelation 6. As we come to the end of the Chapter, let me repeat verse 17:

Revelation 6:17
"For the great day of his wrath is come: and who shall be able to stand?"

The Bible does not actually refer to the Tribulation as being the wrath of God until the last 3 ¹/2 years. The first 3 ¹/2 are going to be bad enough, but the last 3 ¹/2 years will be beyond human comprehension. Let's go to Matthew 24 once again. I've said before, you can't study Revelation without studying Matthew 24. Here Jesus is speaking of this very thing. Starting at verse 8, what does Jesus call all of these things that are taking place (the tremendous loss of life in that ¹/4 of world has died - and all the pestilences and famine)?

(10d) What is the mark of the beast ?

Book 12 LESSON ONE * PART III

Revelation 13:14,15
"And deceiveth them that dwell on the earth by the means of those miracles which he had power to do in the sight of the beast (the Anti-christ. Remember, he begins his power base in this revived Roman Empire, in the Mediterranean and Western Europe. By the time of the Tribulation, the Anti-christ's power will be world-wide. So this false prophet had power); *saying to them that dwell on the earth, that they should make an image to the beast."*
"And he (this false prophet) *had power to give life to the image of the beast,...."*

I previously have said that the Japanese have a technology to build a biological computer. In other words, it won't be just electronic, but will have living biological cells. Now what they are driving at, I don't know. But it will be a computer that will put the present day computers to shame. And I think that is just an indication of what we have here. That this image is going to be the brain of our technology so that it will actually be able to speak and think and give orders. One of our national news magazines a few weeks ago had a lead article on the electronic explosion that is about to come upon us. Where television will not only be the incoming of information, but also the outflow. The old TV set will just be the center of everything. This is being set up for just exactly this situation, where one world government will have their thumb on every home around the planet. Nobody will be left out. So this image was able to speak.

Revelation 13:15
"...that the image of the beast should both speak, and cause that as many as would not worship the image of the beast should be killed."

Again, I think it will come through the information of television. The powers that be will know all activity of every home. There will be no escaping it. I've told my classes that `they' know all about you. And more than once someone will say, **"And who are `they?'"** I don't know precisely, but I know it and you know it. We've all read articles about how they know where we spend our money and where we have it invested. They know our health. They know everything. **And so who are they? The powers that be**. Insurance companies, financial institutions, magazines. In farm magazines I can get a free subscription by completing a survey which asks how many cows I have, how many acres I have, etc. I quit filling them out. I'd rather pay for my subscription because they don't have to know. It is the same in every other occupation. They want to know everything about your business. It seems so innocent, but it isn't. It will come back to haunt people that someone out there knows everything about them. Once you are in someone's computer this information is kept and added to every time there is a transaction. They, who are they? Anyway, verse 16. So this great religious leader:

Revelation 13:16,17
"And he causeth all, both small and great, rich and poor, free and bond, to receive a mark in their right hand, or in their foreheads: And that no man (also women) *might buy or sell, save he that had the mark, or the name of the beast, or the number of his name.*

Revelation 13:18
"Here is wisdom. Let him that hath understanding count the number of the beast (the power, the political system, the religious system, etc.)*: for it is the number of a man* (and that is always 'six' in Scripture)*; and his number is Six hundred threescore and six."*

That's where we get the 666. Now let's clarify. You and I don't have to worry tonight about receiving the mark of the beast. This is a Tribulation event, and believers will not be here. Anyway, everybody isn't immediately going to accept this demand to have this mark placed on them. Just like Social Security would like everyone have direct deposit. But how slow are most people to accept it. They want to see that check in their hands and deposit it themselves. So there is foot-dragging, even though it's probably safer and faster. I use it. I'm not afraid of direct deposit. But it will be the same way with this mark of the beast. Multitudes of people will drag their feet. They won't take it right away, human nature being what it is. So it won't instantly take over. That will be a blessing in disguise, because anyone who has not taken that mark of the beast will have an opportunity of salvation as those 144,000 Jews will be proclaiming it. But if they have taken the mark, then they can preach their hearts out and that individual will have no chance for salvation. He's doomed the minute he takes the mark.

Now what is the mark of the beast? I said long before most of the big wheels began to realize it, that I was convinced that this mark of the beast is nothing more than an eighteen digit computer number. In other words, three sets of six numbers or digits. Most of you are acquainted with the little bars and lines on every product that you buy, especially in our supermarkets. What's it called? The universal product code. And the outside bars, and the very middle bar has a value of six. Now it's not on your boxes of cereals and so forth. Some of the other numbers are. You might see a 2 or 3 or 4, but remember, the outside and middle bars are valued at 6. Now all they have to do is expand this universal product code a little more and you will have eighteen digits. And that is sufficient to give everyone on the face of the earth a separate number. If they can keep track of products in a supermarket down to the last nitty-gritty, simply by running it over a scanner, then they won't have any problem keeping track of every human being. In fact the largest computer on earth is reported to be in Brussels, Belgium. And that thing is huge (I think I read it takes a city block just to house it). It is very capable of keeping track of every human being on earth. So just simply bring this whole mark of the beast down to something that is so common already. An eighteen digit number of 666, and you have the mark of the beast.

We also know that there have been places that have tried a cashless society. Can a community actually go for 30 or 60 days without ever using a checkbook or billfold? The only problems that they have is the check-out lines start backing up, because the people in this test area can never find their card in their purse. This secular article suggests that if there were some way of putting a mark on the flesh so that it can be scanned, it would speed up the check-out lines. It is all there, the technology is simply waiting to be implemented.

Believers don't have a fear of the 666. We have all the evidence of the world that the precursors of it are with us. You and I use it everyday. You can't go and get a drivers license without it, or file your taxes without it and what is it? Your social security number. It is not the mark of the beast, but it is the forerunner of it. And remember America is not the only nation with a social security system. I was surprised when I read a few months ago that even the small nations in what we call the third world have social security systems and all of their citizens have a number. Germany, years ago, began tattooing a number on the heels of newborn infants before they left the hospital. So we can see the world is getting ready for the fact that they can't do anything without a number. If it gets to the place where it is a completely cashless society, and if you haven't got that number, it will be impossible to do anything. So people without it will die for the lack of the necessities of life.

(11d) What will happen to America during the tribulation ?

Book 11 LESSON THREE * PART II

REVELATION 6, CONTINUED
As I have told you before, the only reason I teach is to help people better understand and enjoy their Bible. We have never attempted or intended to build a group or organization. We just like to teach the Word, and we have people taking it into their churches and Sunday schools and taking advantage of it.

Last lesson we were discussing the aspect of the red horse in Revelation Chapter 6. I like to tie it in with Ezekiel 38 be it right or wrong. I'm very comfortable putting this great invasion of Israel in the early stages of the Tribulation. Remember, after the Anti-christ signs that peace treaty of seven years with the Nation of Israel, she will suddenly drop her guard, thinking her borders are guaranteed with this treaty. So when you come to the language in Ezekiel 38, I think it is so appropriate that under those circumstances, with an outside power now guaranteeing their sovereignty and their safety, that it becomes what Ezekiel calls a land of unwalled villages.

When Ezekiel was writing, the walls of the city were the first line of defense. When you speak of a land of unwalled villages what does it tell you? Here is a land with no defense. They have been guaranteed safety by some outside political and military force, but for the nation itself, she is there with no real visible defense. This Northern confederation of nations, that we think will be headed up by Russia immediately takes advantage of this fact. Today, hardly anyone dares to attack the Nation of Israel because they know they will have a fight on their hands if they do. More than likely they'll get whipped. But here they now realize that Israel is complacent. Israel has finally gotten this almost Messiah-like atmosphere, that they no longer have to fear their enemies.

When we finally get into the Gospels, we will study about Zacharias, the father of John the Baptist, who suddenly had his speech given back to him. I always tell people to read what he had to say in Luke 1:67-71 and to read it carefully.

Luke 1:67-71
"And his father Zacharias was filled with the Holy Ghost, and prophesied, saying, `Blessed be the Lord God of Israel; for he hath visited and redeemed his people (Israel), And hath raised up an horn of salvation for us in the house of his servant David; As he spake by the mouth of his holy prophets, which have been since the world began: That we should be saved from our enemies, and from the hand of all that hate us;"

This is exactly what Israel is looking for today. That they could be safe from their enemies. It's not a spiritual thing. It's physical. And they will swallow what the Anti-christ will promise. Now picking up where we left off in the Book of Ezekiel. Chapter 38 and verse 9. God speaking through the prophet to the Northern Confederation, because it will involve more than just the Russians.

Ezekiel 38:9
"Thou shalt ascend and come like a storm, thou shalt be like a cloud to cover the land (not necessarily air power, but massive invasion armies.), thou, and all thy bands, and many people with thee." It will be a consortium of all these nations listed in verse 5 and 6.

Ezekiel 38:10

"Thus saith the Lord GOD; `It shall also come to pass, that at the same time shall things come into thy mind, and thou shalt think an evil thought:'"

Ezekiel 38:11,12a

"And thou shalt say, `I will go up to the land of unwalled villages (Israel is now sitting there relatively safe and secure. Now's the time for a surprise attack.)*; I will go to them that are at rest, that dwell safely, all of them dwelling without walls, and having neither bars nor gates,'"* Then to verse 12: *"To take a spoil, and to take a prey; to turn thine hand upon the desolate places that are now inhabited,..."*

What a perfect picture that is of Israel? It had been a no-man's land for years, and now since 1948, it has blossomed into a land of production. They are building highways; they're building apartments. It's almost like being in America. Their traffic patterns are much the same as any major city here. I had a gentlemen in my class when we were still in Iowa who's gone to be with the Lord now. He was stationed with an American group in Palestine during World War II. I can still remember his explaining the conditions. He said, **"Why in the world would anyone want that country? I just couldn't understand. There's nothing there."** Well that's not the case today. It's a vibrant country. It's producing. And they're just constantly coming up in production of agriculture, technology and medical. The Nation of Israel is at the forefront of all these things.

Ezekiel 38:12b

"...and upon the people that are gathered out of the nations (that's where the Jews have come from remember. Every nation on the globe.)*, which have gotten cattle and goods, that dwell in the midst of the land."*

Ezekiel 38:13a

"Sheba, and Dedan, and the merchants of Tarshish, with all the young lions thereof, shall say unto thee, `Art thou come to take a spoil?...'"

Tarshish, I think, either refers to Spain or Great Britain, and I would probably say Great Britain. Some of the other nations involved there in the NATO alliance, will be under the rule or control of the Anti-christ at this time. And all they're going to be able to say is, **"What do you think you're doing?"** Because this has caught them so by surprise, they won't have time to retaliate, militarily. And so all that they do I suppose, is tell the media at a press conference, **"Well, all we can say is, `What do they think they're doing' and there's nothing we can do about it."** Read on:

Ezekiel 38:13b

"...hast thou gathered thy company to take a prey (are you invading)*? to carry away silver and gold, to take away cattle and goods,..."*

In other words, to take a great spoil? That's about all the Western European nations are going to be able to do. But remember that God's going to intervene in short order.

Ezekiel 38:14,15a
"Therefore (God says to the prophet), *son of man, prophesy and say unto Gog, `Thus saith the Lord GOD; In that day* (when they invade Israel) *when my people of Israel dwelleth safely, shalt thou not know it? And thou shalt come from thy place out of the north parts,...'"* And that means everything from Lebanon, all the way, I think, to Moscow.

Ezekiel 38:16
"And thou shalt come up against my people of Israel, as a cloud to cover the land; it shall be in the latter days (that's the second time the word "latter" has been used. And that is why I have to feel that it will be in the Tribulation), *and I will bring thee against my land, that the heathen* (or the Gentiles) *may know me, when I shall be sanctified in thee, O Gog,..."*

In other words, when the rest of the world will see what a Sovereign God can do to a modern military force.

Ezekiel 38:18
"And it shall come to pass at the same time when Gog shall come against the land of Israel, saith the Lord GOD, that my fury shall come up in my face."

You need to remember that Russia has been anti-God for the past 70 years. And God hasn't forgotten. God is always just. And when He pours out His vengeance, He has a reason. I think that Russia still is going to have to answer for all the millions that the Communists put to death, and for their ill-treatment of the Jew. God says, **"My fury is coming up before me."**

Ezekiel 38:19
"For in my jealousy and in the fire of my wrath have I spoken, `Surely in that day there shall be a great shaking in the land of Israel;'"

As a result of this invasion. Now verse 21, and I want you to watch the language very carefully. God says:

Ezekiel 38:21a
"And I will call for a sword against him (that is, against these invaders) *throughout all my mountains,..."*

A lot of people don't realize that Israel is mountainous. In fact, I was reading an article just the other day, of someone who was speaking to one of our head government people (I think in the State Department). He didn't know that Israel was a mountainous country! I know that our younger generation hasn't been taught geography like I was. But there are people who are, seemingly, in places of high authority and they don't even know simple geography. But yes, Israel is mountainous. The very center of the country is just a string of mountains and valleys. Here is the very series of words that I tie with Revelation Chapter 6. And this is my reason for bringing it. I go by that basic rule of Bible study: Always go to the place of first mention. In other words, when something is mentioned in the Old Testament and then again in the New, see if they tie together. Now look at the language:

Ezekiel 38:21b
"...every man's sword shall be against his brother."

Do you see that? Now to those verses that we read in Revelation, Chapter 6, and I want you to see the comparison. Of course, I don't get dogmatic. If anyone says, "I can't see this," that's fine. This is the way I see it and I wouldn't teach it if I wasn't comfortable with it. Now back here now in Revelation:

Revelation 6:4a
"And there went out another horse that was red: and power was given to him that sat thereon to take peace from the earth, and that they (that is, the combatants) should kill (who?) one another:..."

Not the enemy but each other! That's what's so unique about this great invasion of Israel. Go back to Ezekiel and compare the words. The Sovereign God is going to fight this battle here on the hills of Israel. And of course it happened before. Do you remember Samaria had been encircled and was under siege, and they were starving to death. Then the Lord gave them a prophecy that by tomorrow night at this time, they would have more food than they would know what to do with. And you know the Syrian army was put into a route because in their confusion, they were killing each other. So it's happened before. Now look what Ezekiel then says again in comparison to the red horse statement in Revelation 6, that every man's sword should be against his brother. In other words, they're going to be annihilating themselves. God, Himself, of course, is going to come in with His own power.

Ezekiel 38:22,23
"And I will plead against him with pestilence and with blood; and I will rain upon him, and upon his bands, and upon the many people that are with him, an overflowing rain, and great hailstones, fire, and brimstone. (which of course is the same language of Sodom and Gomorrah, you'll remember) Thus will I magnify myself, and sanctify myself; and I will be known in the eyes of many nations, and they shall know that I am the LORD."

In other words, that Russian army or that Northern Confederation army will be defeated by not only its own confusion, but by a tremendous power of God. And it's going to be utterly destroyed there on the hills and mountains of Israel. Now we have to go into Chapter 39 because these two chapters tie together:

Ezekiel 39:1
"Therefore, thou son of man, prophesy against Gog, and say, `Thus saith the Lord GOD; `Behold, I am against thee,...'"

It would be awful to have God simply tell America for example, **"I'm against you."** I'm afraid the day is coming. But so far it hasn't happened. Now then, verse 2. He says to this invading force:

Ezekiel 39:2
"And I will turn thee back (God will. And remember that He brought them down. And this is the way God deals with nations when He judges them. He brought them into the Nation of Israel. He destroyed them there. And now He says, "I'll turn thee back"), *and leave but the sixth part of thee, and will cause thee to come up from the north parts, and will bring thee upon the mountains of Israel:"*

Ezekiel 39:3,4
"And I will smite thy bow out of the left hand, and will cause thine arrows to fall out of they right hand. Thou shalt fall upon the mountains of Israel, thou, and all thy bands, and the people that is with thee: I will give thee unto the ravenous birds of every sort, and to the beasts of the field to be devoured."

Now some people believe that this is Armageddon and I just can't agree with that. This is a separate war. A separate battle within the seven-year time frame. But it is not Armageddon.

Ezekiel 39:5
*"Thou shalt fall upon the open field: for I have spoken it, saith the Lord GOD (*and then look at verse 6. Underline it if you haven't before). *And* (God says) *I will send a fire on Magog, and among them that dwell carelessly in the isles:..."*

In other words, the homeland of Russia as well as the homeland of all these nations that have consorted against the Nation of Israel. The language is different than it is with the destruction of the army and Israel itself. Their (Israel's) God is going to do it by sending pestilence and hail and brimstone. That's God. But in Chapter 39 verse 6, I think God is using an outside force to destroy the Russian homeland. I'll comment on verse 6 in more detail, but first let's do verses 7-9 and pay particular attention to verse 9:

Ezekiel 39:7-9
"So will I make my holy name known in the midst of my people Israel; and I will not let them

pollute my holy name any more: and the heathen (or Gentile) *shall know that I am the LORD, the Holy One in Israel. Behold, it is come, and it is done, saith the Lord GOD; this is the day whereof I have spoken. And they that dwell in the cities of Israel shall go forth, and shall set on fire and burn the weapons, both the shields and the bucklers, the bows and the arrows, and the hand staves, and the spears* (remember Ezekiel is writing the language of his day. We would say today the tanks, armored personnel carriers and so forth), *and they shall burn them with fire seven years:"*

People will say, "**This can't be the Tribulation because there want be enough time for it.**" But if you will remember in Scripture a part of a year was counted a whole year. A good example was when a King would serve Israel for 10 years and 1 month, it would say he served for 11 years. So using that rule of thumb, an invasion of the Nation of Israel within the first 11 months for instance, after the seven-year treaty is signed, will still make this prophecy come true. I might also point out that back in the 1960's a Dutch scientist had perfected some sort of a process where he came up with a tank that was made with wood product that would actually repel shells and so forth. And the Russians bought a large quantity of them because they were so much more economical. Then after the war in 1967 in Israel, the Israelites captured some of these tanks and discovered that they burned like cardboard. Whether that is still the case, I don't know. But if it is, then you see again the Scripture is so accurate. The Jewish people will use this equipment as firewood if this is the case.

Now I want to finish commenting on verse 6 as I had promised. I'm going to speculate, and I want to make sure that people understand that this is only speculation. I can't prove it through Scripture, but I can certainly whet your thinking. And just consider the possibilities. Logically. Now I know that God doesn't have to work in the terms of logic. I know that. But many times He does. Logically then, I've put it before my classes over the years, and I've never had anyone ridicule the concept at all. Logically, if you were sitting in a place of authority, whether it's in the Kremlin or some other place in this Northern Confederation, and you were getting ready to invade the little Nation of Israel, I think that you would realize there's only one nation on earth that might oppose you. And who would that be? America. We are the only friend that Israel has in the world. And I think that the Russian leaders would understand that if they invaded Israel, America would probably come to her defense.

Now I mentioned in my last program, and Time magazine just stated it again a couple of weeks ago, that every missile that has ever been pointed at America before, is still sitting there. Still pointing at the American target. Speculate, project, that's all I can do. If you were the commanders, what would you do? I know what I would do. I would say, **"Let's unload everything that we have on North America. They're the only possible enemy that we have." And that's what I think will happen. I think the Russians will unload e**verything that they have and will utterly knock the Western Hemisphere out of the rest of prophecy. Because there's nothing for us in prophecy. Then, when it says that God will send a fire on the Russian homeland, we know that we have submarines all over the oceans of the world, loaded with ballistic missiles on board. So after we have suffered that initial attack, I think our military will still have enough left to give the command to unload all our submarines on the Russian homeland, which will destroy it.

I said that this is all speculation and I don't say it to cause fear or anything like that, because you want to remember that in the Tribulation, events are going to start taking place that are so beyond human understanding. And that's why I think it's so logical to teach it. That when America retaliates and knocks out the whole Russian homeland, then you see between those two annihilations, North America out of the picture for the most part. And the Russian homeland is also out of the picture. Now I want you to come back to Revelation once more. And you can stop again at Matthew 24, because I told you that Matthew 24 and Revelation 6 are direct parallels. So you might as well stop first at Matthew 24 verse 7. And remember, I stopped in the middle of verse 7 with regard to the red horse. Alright, let's go to the last part of verse 7. And this will tie us to the third horse of Revelation 6:

Matthew 24:7b
"...and there shall be famines, and pestilences, and earthquakes, in divers places." Now flip back to Revelation Chapter 6 verse 5:

Revelation 6:5,6a
"And when he had opened the third seal, I heard the third beast (or creature) *say, `Come and see.' And I beheld, and lo a black horse; and he that sat on him had a pair of balances in his hand. And I heard a voice in the midst of the four beasts* (or creatures) *say, `A measure of wheat for a penny, and three measures of barley for a penny;...'"*

What does that black horse indicate if you're going to have to ration the food supply? Famine. Alright, come back to my premise. Take, for example, the great production areas of the North American Continent; whether it's the great grain belt to the north, or the citrus growths in other areas such as California, that have vast food production. If you knock out the great food production area of Russia (the Ukraine), what does that do to the world's food supply? It almost annihilates it. So what will the rest of the world suddenly find itself in? A famine.
The language in this verse boils down to the average worker (a field worker for example) having to work a full day, sun-up to sun-down, just to earn enough money to buy bread for the next day. It's going to be runaway inflation caused by a shortage of goods. You're going to have a tremendous decrease in the production of food stuffs. And whenever you have famine and the amount of death as we've seen in Somalia and so forth, what accompanies it? Disease. It just goes hand in glove. Now, lest you think that I'm stretching the point, come down to the fourth horse in verse 7, because these all tie together now. The black horse spoke of famine. What comes as a result of the famine?

Revelation 6:7,8

"And when he had opened the fourth seal, I heard the voice of the fourth beast (or creature) *say, 'Come and see.' And I looked, and behold a pale horse: and his name that sat on him was Death, and Hell followed with him. And power was given unto them over the fourth part of the earth, to kill with sword, and with hunger, and with death, and with the beasts of the earth."*

The fourth horse is the pale one. As a result of the demise of two great power structures, he now sees this pale horse and on him was Death; and Hell followed with him. And power was given over them to kill with the sword. And what have you, what portion of the world? One fourth. Whether it's one fourth of the geographical area or one fourth of the population, either one. But this is the Tribulation. This is just the beginning.

Go back to Matthew 24 again. I guess you could just put a mark in it because we will be flipping back and forth. In Matthew 24, after these four horsemen have made their appearance (remember these are merely symbolisms. This isn't really someone riding on a horse and announcing that the world is going to have famine. They are symbolic of these events that are going to come on the planet) Jesus goes on to say in verse 8 that there would be famine and earthquakes and pestilence in divers places.

Matthew 24:8

"All these are the beginning of sorrows."

"Travail" is a better word. The King James uses "sorrow." Your newer translations may have the word **"Travail"** because Jesus is speaking in terms of a delivery. When we were back in Chapter 5 of Revelation, I spoke of a scroll, which was the paying off of a mortgage. It was also a delivery of the earth from the curse that was instituted back in the garden. This is what Jesus is referring to; all these events that are going to come on the planet, beginning with these horsemen of Revelation. This is just a beginning. This is like the mother who is about to deliver. Her birth pains are relatively mild and far apart. That's what we have here. As great as this is going to be, it is mild compared to what it is going to be at the end. And so he says, **"These things are just the beginning of Travail."** This is the beginning of the delivery process. Look at one verse in the Book of Jeremiah Chapter 30:

Jeremiah 30:7

"Alas! for that day is great (that is, this Tribulation), *so that none is like it: it is even the time of* (who's trouble?) *Jacob's trouble* (the Nation of Israel); *but he shall be saved out of it."*
So these things will have their vortex upon the Nation of Israel.

(12d) What will happen during the second 3 ½ years of the tribulation ?

Book 12 LESSON TWO * PART IV

Revelation 12:12
"Therefore rejoice, ye heavens, and ye that dwell in them. Woe to the inhabiters of the earth and of the sea! for the devil is come down unto you, having great wrath, because he knoweth that he hath but a short time."

Now think about that. At the mid-point, after Satan has been cast down from heaven, he will indwell the man Anti-christ, even as he did Judas. And as we saw in our last lesson, he's going to turn his wrath particularly upon the 144,000 Jews, but all the people of the world are suddenly going to feel the wrath of Satan. But not only of Satan, we are also going to have the wrath of God. Now what does that tell you. No wonder Jesus said that it was going to be worse than anytime in human history. People will say, **"Now wait a minute, God is a God of love."** Oh, He still is today. But once this day comes, His Grace ends, and He becomes a God of judgment, and a God of wrath. Let's go back to the Book of Psalms, Chapter 2 for a moment. We must overcome this theology that God is just a God of love. You see, that's another reason that people think that He couldn't possible dream up something like an eternal Hell, or the lake of fire. Here, we have to qualify. He was a God of love when He sent Christ to the Cross, that's for sure. And He has loved the human race ever since. He has poured out His Grace upon humanity. But what has humanity done with it? They have walked it under foot. And so now He finally gets to the place where His love and Grace is withdrawn and it's His wrath that has come in. Psalms Chapter 2 verse 5. This is taking us into the Tribulation:

Psalms 2:5
"Then shall he speak unto them (the people of the world) *in his wrath* (not His Love), *and vex them in his sore displeasure."*

Now you know what vex means. He is literally going to torment them. And He is going to do it righteously with all fairness and justice because you see, He has so patiently poured out His love to toward the human race and they continue to react in unbelief. And that is the worse sin possible. Unbelief is the sin that sends all mankind to doom. It's just the opposite of faith. And when you have faith, then you are pleasing unto God. That is, faith in His Word. And when you have faith in His Word you are obedient to it. And when we are obedient to the Word, then we become exactly what God want us to be. Now come back to the last part of Revelation 12:12 again. The Devil is literally kicked out of heaven. He comes down to his domain on the earth. He comes to Jerusalem to join the Anti-christ:

Revelation 12:12
"...having great wrath, because he knoweth that he hath but a short time."

And how long does he have? 3 1/2 years. And he will pull out all the stops. He will use things he has never used before. I know the average person will say, **"Now why would Satan do that? They are in his pocket."** I've given the illustration before, but it's worth repeating. If some underworld organization can't get a business man to knuckle under their demands because he's too strong in himself, who will they threaten? His family. His wife and children, because he knows that if that father sees them suffer, then he will react. Now Satan does the same thing to God. Satan feels that when he torments and brings all of these things upon the human race, who does he really get at? The heart of God. Now God's wrath is going to be coupled with it, and that will make that final 3 1/2 years what it is. If you don't think that last 3 1/2 years is going to be awesome come back with me to Revelation Chapter 8.

We have come through six seals during our study. The sixth seal was the great earthquake which triggers the mid-point of the Tribulation. Now when you come to Chapter 8 we come to the seventh seal. The seventh seal will open up the scroll and the paying off of that mortgage that's within. The seventh seal in itself is not an event, but it triggers the seven trumpets. So out of the seventh seal comes the first of the trumpet judgments, and there will be seven of those. When we first started our study in Revelation, I put it on the board that the events of the Tribulation are like a mother approaching her day of delivery. First comes a light birth pang. Just enough to know that your time is at hand. And maybe an hour or two later comes a little harsher one. And it just keeps increasing in intensity as well as in closeness. And so it will be that way in the Tribulation. It will start out rather mild, but as it moves to the end it's going to crescendo. Until finally the last day comes and Christ returns. As we start to read, remember we are still at the mid-point, and this is what follows.

Revelation 8:1
"And when he had opened the seventh seal, there was (what?) *silence in heaven* (there is not an angelic voice, an instrument, a note of music, a shout, or trumpet, but absolute silence in heaven. Now that is sobering! Why? Because of the awful things that are about to happen on the earth) *about the space of half an hour."* I don't think we can get the drama of it. Everyone in heaven is so aware of the awful things that are about to happen. Now verse 2:

Revelation 8:2
"And I saw the seven angels which stood before God; and to them were given seven trumpets." These trumpets will simply announce the next event:

Revelation 8:3,4
"And another angel came and stood at the altar, having a golden censer; and there was given unto him much incense, that he should offer it with the prayers of all saints upon the golden altar which was before the throne. And the smoke of the incense, which came with the prayers of the saints, ascended up before God out of the angel's hand."

Now what was the purpose of the incense in the tabernacle? What's the purpose of incense anytime? To give a sweet aroma. That holiness of worship and righteousness. Now for God, the sweetest incense that could ever come up to His nostrils is the prayers of the saints. That's how much emphasis God puts on prayer. He wants us to pray. We are commanded to pray. So now we have the beginnings of the trumpet judgments.

Revelation 8:5

"And the angel took the censer, and filled it with fire of the altar, and cast it into the earth: and there were voices, and thunderings, and lightnings, and an earthquake."

When you read of thunderings, and lightnings, and voices again, flash all the way back to Exodus. When God came down on Mount Sinai, what did you have? Thunderings, and lightnings, the voice of God; so it's just a constant replay, except on a totally grander scale.

Revelation 8:6,7

"And the seven angels which had the seven trumpets prepared themselves to sound. The first angel sounded, and there followed hail and fire mingled with blood, and they were cast upon the earth (and as a result)*: and the third part of trees was burnt up, and all green grass was burnt up."*

We won't take time now to go back to Exodus, but if we did, what was one of the plagues? This very same thing. Fire running along the ground, and hail. I imagine it was a very traumatic thing. I always think of it this way. Even though the events in themselves will probably bring a lot of death and destruction, there will also be a lot of psychological warfare, if you want to call it that. These things are just going to lambaste the very mental part of people. It's going to be beyond our comprehension to see these things happening one right after the other. Now to the next one. Verse 8:

Revelation 8:8

"And the second angel sounded (this won't be a matter of hours, but it probably will be a matter of days and weeks)*, and as it were a great mountain burning with fire was cast into the sea: and the third part of the sea became blood;"*

Here again, if we had time we could go back into the Old Testament, and prophecy tells us there will be great disturbance in the cosmos. In other words, I think there is going to be great meteorites coming down and hitting the earth. A good example are the ones that hit the planet Jupiter not long ago. Our scientists are trying to dream up a nuclear device to explode on any meteorite that might be heading for the earth and try to deflect it. So we know that this particular one will land in the ocean, and the third part of the sea became blood.

Revelation 8:9

"And the third part of the creatures which were in the sea, and had life, died; and the third part of the ships were destroyed." It will be in an area where there are shipping lanes and lots of ships will be destroyed in this one event.

Revelation 8:10

"And the third angel sounded, and there fell a great star from heaven, burning as it were a lamp, and it fell upon the third part of the rivers, and upon the fountains of waters;"

In other words, it's going to attack the fresh water. Again go back to Egypt, and remember when Moses caused the river Nile to turn to blood? And it was normally their source of drinking water. So what did the Egyptians quickly do? They dug wells for fresh water. And then God affected even the well water. So God will constantly be one step ahead of them. Now verse 11 is very interesting:

Revelation 8:11

"And the name of the star is called Wormwood: and the third part of the waters became wormwood; and many men died of the waters, because they were made bitter,"

Now this is just an interesting thought, and I don't know if it has any impact on this verse at all. But what does the word Chernobyl (where they had the nuclear disaster in Russia) mean? Wormwood! So that might be just a little indication of things that may be used of God, to brings these things to pass. Well it looks like we have time for one more trumpet in this lesson. And that will be the fourth one in verse 12:

Revelation 8:12,13

"And the fourth angel sounded, and the third part of the sun was smitten, and the third part of the moon, and the third part of the stars; so as the third part of them was darkened, and the day shone not for a third part of it, and the night likewise. And I beheld, and heard an angel flying through the midst of heaven, saying with a loud voice, `Woe, Woe, Woe, to the inhabiters of the earth by reason of the other voices of the trumpet of the three angels, which are yet to sound!'"

There has already been a tremendous loss of life, both man and creatures, and it's all coming under the wrath of God. And yet the angel says, ***"It's nothing compared to what is still future for the inhabitants of the earth."***

LESSON THREE * PART I

TRUMPET & BOWL JUDGMENTS: BATTLE OF ARMAGEDDON

The best way to understand the Book of Revelation is to determine all the things that take place at the beginning of the Tribulation, the things at the mid-point, and the whole host of events at the end, which of course, will be at the time of Christ's Second Coming. And then He will set up the Kingdom. **I know there are folks and groups who just cringe at my teachings that the Kingdom will be here on the earth at the end of the Tribulation. And I make no apologies for teaching that. Because this Book is full of it. That's what it talks about from cover to cover - the coming of this Kingdom on earth. Which in reality is where heaven will be also.** And that is another concept that a lot of people can't understand, that heaven will be on the earth. When this earth is destroyed at the end of that initial 1000 years, of course, and you get into the last two chapters of Revelation, what do you have? A new heaven and a new earth. Even the eternal abode is going to be on an earth-type situation, and not up in the regions beyond in a heaven of an ethereal, and all the foggy notions that people have about heaven. But nevertheless, it's going to be a viable, social existence on planet earth.

Another thing I would like to share is that the Church Age we are in at the present time, will someday end, and I've always emphasized that the Church Age is indeterminate in time, for we don't know when it will end. It began back here in the Book of Acts, especially as Paul, the apostle of the Gentiles, began preaching the Gospel of the Grace of God, and calling out what he refers to as the Body of Christ. I've always told folks in my classes that it's not so important what congregation you are a member of. But are you a member of the Body of Christ? **You can be any denomination you want to, but unless you are a member of the Body of Christ, you are eternally lost. The Scripture is so plain. But once we have entered into God's salvation and the Holy Spirit's work of placing you into the Body of Christ, then we have what the Bible refers to as eternal life, eternal salvation, the hope of glory.**

I got a letter from a gentlemen from Indiana, who said, **"Les, I just thrill at all you are teaching, but I've still got some questions about the Rapture of the Church."** I'm sure he was wondering if the Church going to go into the Tribulation. I've made the statement more than once, that I could stand here for an hour or two and give you references that prove beyond a shadow of doubt that the Church will not go into the Tribulation. **And mostly because this whole concept of the Body of Christ is a revelation only given to the Apostle Paul, you will never find it mentioned in the Old Testament or the four Gospels. It is strictly a Pauline revelation. Paul maintains that this Body of Christ, which is all wrapped up in another word that is predominately Pauline, is "the mystery." Now the mystery is the revelation that God is now doing something different in these last 1900 + years of time, after the revelation of these mysteries. He is calling out the Body of Christ, not under Law, not associated with the Nation of Israel, not associated with Judaism, or the Temple. It is totally the operation of the Grace of God, based upon the finished work of the Cross, His death, burial and Resurrection.**

And this is so totally removed from Law, which will again come in during the Tribulation, because Israel will again have her temple worship. And you can not mix Law and Grace. We couldn't mix it during the Church Age and it won't mix in the Tribulation. The Church would be as out of place as a fish out of water in the Tribulation. It just wouldn't fit. It is not part of the Jewish program. It is completely insulated from all of God's dealing with Israel. Whereas in the Tribulation, God is primarily dealing with Israel. So as the Church Age is completed then, it must be taken out of the way so God can once again pick up where He left off with Israel.

Why is it that the world is always so concerned about peace in the Middle East? Every United States President, at least since President Kennedy, has almost made it their prerogative to some-how or other be the one that could bring peace to the Middle East. Yet, look at all the other areas of the world that need peace. They are not that concerned about those. But they are hung up on the Middle East and peace for them. Well again, it comes back to the Scriptures. What do the Scriptures say about Jerusalem? **It will be a stone of stumbling.** And isn't that exactly what it is. Every President has stubbed their toe on Jerusalem. They are so intent on bringing peace to the Middle East. And that's why the Anti-christ will finally be the one to do it. He will bring a seven-year treaty of peace to Israel and the Middle East. Seemingly the world is going to think that he is the mastermind and so forth. So the very fact he signs that treaty will begin God's clock ticking again, and the seven years of Tribulation will begin.

Then as we noticed in previous lessons, we have the introduction of the two witnesses who will proclaim the Word of God again to the Nation of Israel. Out of them will come the 144,000 young Jews who will be sealed and commissioned of God. We have also discussed the Great Russian invasion of Israel sometime after the Tribulation has begun. And then we have the various judgments of God begin to fall. When we get to the mid-point of the Tribulation, the Anti-christ at that time will go in and defile the temple, and immediately stop temple worship. He will demand that He himself be worshiped as God. That will trigger this final 3 1/2 years.

This is where we are now in this study. We have seen the sixth seal removed and the trumpet judgments begin. And again, I like to make the analogy that Jesus made in Matthew 24. These Tribulation judgments are a perfect parallel of a young lady approaching delivery of her little one. And when the birth pangs begin they are rather mild and far apart. But as she gets closer and closer to the delivery hour, everything will crescendo. So, as we have come past the mid-point and the trumpet judgments are taking place, they also will keep getting a little closer together. They keep getting worse and worse until finally we get to the last seven judgments and they are called the Bowl judgments. In the King James they are called `vials.' I prefer to use the word `bowl' and I'll tell you why in a little bit.

In our last lesson we finished Revelation Chapter 8 with the end of the fourth trumpet judgment. Now let's go into Chapter 9, where we come to the 5th trumpet judgment. These trumpets are merely God's way of indicating that it is now time for the next judgment to fall. This won't be isolated to the Middle East, but will be world-wide. Many of the plagues that will take place in the Tribulation are a repetition of what took place in Egypt under Moses.

Another thing to remember, all the way up through the Old Testament the supernatural was rather commonplace. All you have to do is reflect back and all of them had to do with the Nation of Israel, and we don't have a problem with that. But as soon as you get into the Book of Revelation and start talking about these supernatural things that take place, a lot of people think you've got to be a weird person to believe them. They say, **"This isn't really going to happen."** But yes it is, because most of them have happened before and the Book says it will. I'm not a prophet of doom, neither am I one to sensationalize. Those of you who have heard me teach over the years know that. We just simply teach it because the Book says it.

Revelation 9:1

"And the fifth angel sounded, and I saw a star fall from heaven unto the earth (now here is how you learn to study your Bible. You will notice in the next statement that this star is given a pronoun. What's the pronoun? Him. We don't know what angel it is, but it's a personality. It's a person of some sort. I think it's an angel and I don't know which one it is. But nevertheless it's not just a body from outer space falling): *and to him was given the key of the bottomless pit,"* Now the bottomless pit is not Hell, or the lake of fire. It is a unique place that God has reserved.

Revelation 9:2,3

"And he opened the bottomless pit; and there arose a smoke out of the pit, as the smoke of a great furnace; and the sun and the air were darkened by reason of the smoke of the pit. And there came out of the smoke locusts upon the earth: and unto them was given power, as the scorpions of the earth have power."

If you have ever been stung by a scorpion, you know it has a unique sting to it. Their sting burns and lasts for quite a while. Now these locusts are going to have a psychological effect on humanity as much as anything, by their appearance and their ability to sting.

Revelation 9:4

"And it was commanded them (Notice God has complete control of them. This is God's wrath being poured out upon God-rejecting mankind. We will see shortly that everything He does is fair and just.) *that they should not hurt the grass of the earth, neither any green thing, neither any tree; but only those men which have not the seal of God in their foreheads."* Who are those (which do have the seal of God in their foreheads)? The 144,000. Remember back in Chapter 7, verse 3, where the angel is instructed:

Revelation 7:3

"Saying, hurt not the earth, neither the sea, nor the trees, till we have sealed the servants of our God in their foreheads." Then are listed the twelve tribes from which come the 144,000 young Jews. These are referred to in Chapter 9, verse 4. These locust will not be able to touch the 144,000. Now verse 5 of Revelation 9:

Revelation 9:5

"And to them (the locusts) *it was given that they should not kill them, but that they* (that is man-kind) *should be tormented five months;"*

I know the first thing that comes to mind is, "How can a God of love do something like this to His created beings." Well, you must remember the big picture. For thousands of years God has been nothing but gracious, kind, loving, and patient. But back to Psalms Chapter 2, all of a sudden we break into a period of time that is going to be the wrath and vexation of God. When He has finally run out of His patience and said, "I've had enough." In the day that you and I are living and have seen the fabric of the world society just rot at the seam (even in these last 15 to 20 years), don't you often ask yourself, **"How long will God put up with it?"** You look at what men and women are doing today and you just have to ask yourself that question. Well it won't be much longer! And when He does stop being gracious, His wrath is going to be beyond our comprehension. And as the Scripture tells us, it is fair and just. He will torment the human race with the stings of these locust, and instead of hurting for an hour or two it's going to sting for 5 months. The 5 months refer to the length of the result of that sting.

Revelation 9:5-7

"...and their torment was as the torment of a scorpion, when he striketh a man. And in those days (remember, here we are in the last half of the Tribulation) *shall men seek death, and shall not find it ; and shall desire to die, and death shall flee from them."* In other words, people won't even be able to commit suicide. Because a Sovereign God is going to take even that from them. Then verse 7:

"And the shapes of the locusts were like unto horses prepared unto battle;..."

I know for years I looked at that and couldn't figure anything out. Then one day I was catching grasshoppers for my wife to fish with, and it had never struck me before. Have you ever looked real close at the head of a big grasshopper? What does it look like? A horse's head. And then I read soon after, that in Germany there is a species of grasshopper that they call the Horse-headed Locust. And so there is something for thought. It's not way out in left field. These locusts will also be psychologically frightening. It will also attack the human race mentally.

Revelation 9:8,9

"And they had hair as the hair of women, and their teeth were as the teeth of lions. And they had breastplates, as it were breastplates of iron; and the sound of their wings was as the sound of chariots of many horses running to battle."

We here in America have never had to come under the attack of swarms and clouds of locust. But in the Middle East, when locust can all of a sudden come up and literally cloud out the sun, it is indeed a roar that can be heard in their coming. These things are going to be so numerous and huge, that the sound of their wings will sound like many chariots.

Revelation 9:10

"And they had tails like unto scorpions, and there were stings in their tails, and their power was to hurt men five months." It's beyond our comprehension isn't it?

Revelation 9:11

"And they had a king over them, which is the angel of the bottomless pit, whose name in the Hebrew tongue is Abaddon, but in the Greek tongue hath his name Apollyon." Which really means the "Destroyer." Beyond that, we don't know who this angel is. It's not Satan I'm quite sure. But it could be one of his lieutenants. Now verse 12 says:

Revelation 9:12

"One woe is past; and, behold, there come two woes more hereafter." If this isn't bad enough, there are still 2/3 of it left.

Revelation 9:13,14

"And the sixth angel sounded, and I heard a voice from the four horns of the golden altar which is before God. Saying to the sixth angel which had the trumpet, `Loose the four angels which are bound in the great rive Euphrates.'"

Why the Euphrates? If you remember back in Genesis Chapter 11, what took place on the Euphrates River? The Tower of Babel. And as I have stressed over the years, all pagan religions were instituted there. Every pagan, mystical religion that you read about or research has its roots at the Tower of Babel on the Euphrates River. Now evidently at the time that God scattered the human race or even later after Babylon fell to the Medes and Persians, and some of the high priests of these pagan religions fled - I think somewhere back there God confined four of these powerful demonic beings who had been under Satan's rule, and they were bound in the area of the Euphrates River. Another thing I like to point out about the Euphrates is that the Euphrates River is the boundary between East and West. Have you ever thought of it that way? Religiously and you know I don't like that word, but religiously it's the same way. East of the Euphrates has always been predominantly your pagan, idolatrous religion. West of the Euphrates you have some of the other religions - like Judaism, even Mohammedism, and of course Christianity. So the Euphrates River is like the dividing line. These four angels now have been confined in that boundary area. And now verse 15, then we will have to continue in our next lesson.

Revelation 9:15

"And the four angels were loosed, which were prepared for an hour, and a day, and a month, and a year, for to slay the third part of men."

In other words, God has kept them waiting for a particular hour of a particular day, of a particular month.

Now I read something the other day (and I'm always stressing how God is meticulous in His timing), about how the temple that was built by Solomon, was destroyed on the same day and month (naturally in a different year) by the Babylonians.

LESSON THREE * PART II

TRUMPET & BOWL JUDGMENTS: BATTLE OF ARMAGEDDON

In the last lesson, we were on verse 15 of Revelation Chapter 9. These are events that are going to happen. The Book of Revelation is totally different than any other portion of Scripture. When we taught the Book of Genesis, we just went verse by verse and chapter by chapter. You can do the same thing in the New Testament, but when you get to the Book of Revelation you can't do that. **It would make absolutely no sense to just simply take the Book of Revelation and go verse by verse and chapter by chapter. But you must isolate the events into the beginning, middle, and end of the Tribulation. And why the Lord has seen fit to do this, I don't know. Except maybe to make us study. I can't see any other reason for it. He just wants to make sure that it's not so simple that we don't have to study it.** We have been jumping around a lot purposely so we can keep the continuity of the events rather than the chapter and verse. So in Chapter 9 verse 15, we have been following the trumpet judgment, I don't know how far apart the events are at this point in time, maybe within 6 months, but they will keep getting closer together.

When we get to final seven bowl judgments, there will be, I dare say, every month a new one striking the human race. Now in verse 15 where we left off, these angelic beings that God has confined in the area of the Euphrates River are now released. They were prepared for a specific role. Their role is to slay the third part of men. I was thinking the other day, how many million people lost their lives as a result of World War II. 50 million. That is civilian, and military combined. But that's just a drop in the bucket compared to what's going to happen here. Today, we have between 5 and 5 1/2 billion on the earth. Do you remember back in the sealed judgments when we first opened the Tribulation, by the end of the disease and pestilence, 1/4 of the population will be gone. That's over a billion people in a matter of two or three years. Within a matter of months the human race will lose 1/3 of the worlds population. And people can just go on their way and think nothing of being caught in these events. I wouldn't be able to sleep at night. Anyway, it's coming. I think the way these people are put to death is in the next verse.

Revelation 9:16

"And the number of the army of the horsemen were two hundred thousand thousand: and I heard the number of them."

Those of you who know your math, how many is that? Well, that's 200,000,000. Remember there is only one power on earth that brags about being able to put 200 million men on the field of battle, and that is China. They have over a billion people. I have to feel that this is what is referred to. I feel that this 200 million men army will be the Chinese along with probably a few of the other Orientals. And they are going to be making their way westward toward the Middle East. Also remember we will be in a period of time when God is again doing the supernatural. And we will see God's Sovereignty causing the Chinese authorities to send that army westward. As they do, I feel they will be like Sherman's march to the sea in the Civil War. What did he do? He destroyed everything in their path. I think this Chinese horde is just going to literally murder and mutilate and ravage the countryside as they move to the Middle East. And at this time there is still one great natural barrier. And that is the Euphrates River. The various bridges across that river today couldn't move that many men across it. So we will see in a future chapter that God will dry up the Euphrates River so that they won't need bridges, but simply walk across. Now verse 17:

Revelation 9:17
"And thus I saw the horses in the vision, and them that sat on them, having breastplates of fire, and of jacinth, and brimstone: and the heads of the horses were as the heads of lions; and out of their mouths issued fire and smoke and brimstone."

This is probably ancient language for tanks and all of their fire power. So this is probably the modern warfare of today. Then these 200 million men and the weapons of war will kill many:

Revelation 9:18
"By these three (fire, smoke and brimstone) *was the third part of men killed, by the fire, and by the smoke, and by the brimstone, which issued out of their mouths."*

Also remember, take things scripturally, and many times it's spiritual. But on the other hand, many times it's logical. What percent of the population of this planet lives in the Orient? A good part of it. I've already mentioned that China alone has 1/4 of the population of the world. And India with it's masses and millions. Japan also has millions. So if this great army is indeed just killing as they go, you can see easily see where a third part of mankind will be killed.

Revelation 9:19
"For their power is in their mouth, and in their tails: for their tails were like unto serpents, and had heads, and with them they do hurt." And again, take this language as modern warfare.

Revelation 9:20
"And the rest of the men which were not killed by these plagues yet repented not of the works of their hands, that they should not worship devils, and idols of gold, and silver, and brass, and stone, and of wood: which neither can see, nor hear, nor walk:" And here again, this is unique to the Orient. You have more idol worshippers in the Orient today than any other place on earth. All the areas of the east are still under idolatry.

Revelation 9:21
"Neither repented they of their murders, nor of their sorceries, nor of their fornication, nor of their thefts."

There is an interesting little word buried in this verse that very few people catch. And it's unfortunate that the King James translator haven't caught it. And that word is `*sorceries.*' And it is from the Greek word Pharmakeia. Now think for a minute. What is the English word that comes from Pharmakeia? Pharmacy. And the main role of a pharmacy? Drugs. Now read it in that light:

Revelation 9:21
*"Neither repented they of their murders, their **drugs**, their immorality, or thefts."*
What do you have in that verse? The drug culture. You have the typical drug culture. Because wherever you have drugs, as we are seeing in our inner cities, what do you have? Murder. Along with murder comes theft, because they have to rob and steal in order to support their habit. And as soon as people become involved in that kind of a wicked culture then morality means nothing. So their immorality gets more gross by the day. I'm in favor of the so called **"War on Drugs,"** but it is a losing battle. The world is headed more and more toward that end. The drug culture and demon worship many times go hand in hand. You can hardly separate them. Drugs muddle the mind. Demon worship muddles the mind. So it is an interesting verse and you can see how readily it fits into our society already, but it will be even worse during this time. The world will be completely saturated with drugs and all the evils that go with it.

Now that is the sixth trumpet, and we need to skip over to Chapter 11 and verse 15 to pick up the seventh. Do you see why you can't take it verse by verse. We have to follow the events and then come back to pick up what we had to skip:

Revelation 11:15
"And the seventh angel sounded: and there were great voices in heaven, saying, `The kingdoms of this world are become the kingdoms of our Lord, and of his Christ; and he shall reign for ever and ever.'"

Now put that all together in one thought. What is Christ going to reign over? The Kingdoms of this world are going to become the Kingdom of Christ. And again, it comes right back to what we showed in our last lesson. **As you come out of the Tribulation it is the paying off of the curse; it's going to deliver the world from the curse. The earth is going to revert back as it was in the Garden of Eden.** And in comes the Kingdom. The thing that is amazing is the reference in Matthew Chapter 4. We know Satan is powerful and cunning, but on the other hand you wonder how he can be so ignorant as to think he can still overcome The Christ. But he will never give up until his doom is sealed. Let's look at it in Matthew. This is the temptation of Jesus, after 40 days of fasting. You all know the account:

Matthew 4:8

"Again, the devil taketh him up into an exceeding high mountain, and sheweth him all the (what?) *kingdoms of the world, and the glory of them:"*

We are not talking about something out there that is ethereal or invisible. We are talking about the Kingdoms of this world. Now from this point in history, when Satan is dealing here with Jesus during the time of His earthly ministry, what great kingdoms have already come and gone? Some of the great Pharaohs of Egypt. And then the Babylonian Empire. And then the great Medes' and Persians' Empire. The great and glorious Empire of Greece. And now we are at the very epitome of Rome. And all of these great empires flourished. And Satan says, "Look back at the centuries of time and look ahead. All these Kingdoms are mine. I'll give them to you on one condition." And what was that condition? If Jesus would fall down and worship him. Now isn't that something? Evidently, Satan at that point in time did not understand or comprehend that Christ was going to have those Kingdoms. They are going to be His, and He is going to one day just obliterate them from view, and they will blow away like the dust of the summer threshing floor as Daniel says. And He will set up His own Kingdom. A glorious Kingdom. Can you imagine what this world would be like if it was totally ruled and reigned over by Satan, as it will one day be ruled by Christ! Satan is still held in check by God's checks and balances. Satan can only do so much. But never lose sight that he is the god of this world. He is in control, but is still under the Sovereign God. But when Christ sets up His Kingdom, His power is going to be absolute and total and it will be glorious. Back to Revelation Chapter 11. Since we are fast approaching the return of Christ to set up His Kingdom, here is the language again.

Revelation 11:15

"...The kingdoms of this world are become the kingdoms of our Lord, and of his Christ; and he shall reign for ever and ever."

I feel that this thousand years of Christ, which is delineated in Revelation as a thousand years, will just simply be the introduction to the eternal. In other words, when the thousand years of Kingdom rule has run it's course on the planet as we now know it back in the Garden of Eden situation, it too will be destroyed. It will be burned up by fire at the end of the millennium reign.

And then as I have mentioned before in Chapter 21 and 22 we have a new heaven and a new earth. But that new earth will again be the abode of those who have believed unto eternal life. I think it will be just an extension of the Kingdom economy. It will be an earth of tremendous production and activity. We won't be just sitting around getting bored or strumming on a harp. To me that wouldn't be heaven. Or just sitting around shouting `Alleluia,' although that will be part and parcel. I feel we will be intensely busy. Remember, God didn't create us to be idle. Did He? Why no! So when His Kingdom comes and He rules and reigns, yes it will be limited to the thousand years. But like I said, it will be interrupted for a little while, when the Great White

Throne Judgment for the lost is conducted and then we will go into the eternal, I think based on that same pattern. Now verse 16:

Revelation 11:16,17
"And the four and twenty elders, which sat before God on their seats, fell upon their faces, and worshipped God," We have made reference to these 24 elders before in earlier lessons.
"Saying, `We give thee thanks, O Lord God Almighty, which art, and wast, and art to come; because thou hast taken to thee thy great power, and hast reigned.'" And here it comes again.

Revelation 11:18
"And the nations were angry (in their rebellion), *and thy wrath is come* (it's no longer love, mercy, and Grace), *and the time of the dead* (I think that's the spiritual dead), *that they should be judged, and that thou shouldest give reward unto thy servants the prophets, and to the saints, and them that fear thy name, small and great; and shouldest destroy them which destroy the earth."* In other words, God is going to deal with rebellious mankind. Now verse 19. These 24 elders are declaring that God is over all and will destroy those who have rebelled against Him. And it's coming close to the end of this seven-year period.

Revelation 11:19
"And the temple of God was opened in heaven, and there was seen in his temple the ark of his testament (or the ark of His Covenant)*: and there were lightnings, and voices, and thunderings, and an earthquake, and great hail."*

Come back with me to the Book of Exodus Chapter 25. Remember here, Moses has just brought the Children of Israel out of Egypt and they are gathered around Mount Sinai. And now God is going to give them instructions for building their little place of worship, the tabernacle. Here the Lord is speaking to Moses.

Exodus 25:8,9
"And let them (the Children of Israel) *make me a sanctuary; that I may dwell among them. According to all that I shew thee, after* (or according to) *the pattern of the tabernacle, and the pattern of all the instruments thereof, even so shall ye make it."*

A pattern is always from an original. So where is the original? It has to be in heaven. Now come back to the Book of Hebrews Chapter 9. The blueprint that God gave to Moses and Aaron was simply a pattern or a blue print patterned after the original which is in heaven. And it's the one in heaven we are going to see opened up in these closing days of the Tribulation in Revelation Chapter 11:19. But for now, Hebrews Chapter 9:

Hebrews 9:11
"But Christ being come an high priest of good things to come, by a greater and more perfect

tabernacle, not made with hands, that is to say, not of this building (or creation); This tabernacle not built with human hands is in heaven. So now back to Revelation 11:19 and this is what we see. Reading the verse again.

Revelation 11:19
"And the temple of God was opened in heaven, and there was seen in his temple the ark of his testament (or Covenant)*: and there were lightnings, and voices, and thunderings, and an earthquake, and great hail."*

As God continues His wrath upon mankind, that's the end of the seven trumpets. We have had all seven of them unfold after the mid-point of the Tribulation. Now we are probably within a year of the very end of the Tribulation. We need to come all the way over to Chapter 15 where we are introduced to the final seven judgments, called the vials in the King James Version, or the bowl judgments. Now the reason they are referred to as bowl judgments is this. Picture a soup bowl rather shallow, as compared to a Coke bottle. Now if you were going to pour out the contents of that soup bowl, what would be the time element compared to pouring out the contents of a narrow-necked Coke bottle? It's instantaneous! So these bowl judgments are not going to be dribbled out. But literally, the whole planet will receive this whole bowl judgment as one quick strike.

LESSON THREE * PART III

TRUMPET & BOWL JUDGMENTS: BATTLE OF ARMAGEDDON
Now let's again turn to Revelation Chapter 15, where we pick up the bowl judgments. And remember as we are nearing that last year of the Tribulation, these judgments will become more severe, and closer and closer together.

Revelation 15:1
"And I saw another sign in heaven, great and marvelous, seven angels having the seven last plagues (this is the wind down)*; for in them is filled up* (or is consummated, or finished) *the wrath of God."*

This is constantly emphasized. This is truly the wrath of God. There is no love here. And it is so refreshing to know that, as believers of the Gospel of Grace, we won't be here. We will be taken out before these things begin. We can read these things and not have to worry about having to endure them. He tells us that we have not been saved to His wrath! We have been saved from it.

And for any of you who know not the Lord, who have never experienced salvation, this is written for you as an instigation to get right with the Lord, because this is going to be a terrible time. We know that eternal Hell will be worse than this, because it will be without end, but nevertheless, these folks will have to go through all of this with the physical and emotional pain and suffering and no hope of escaping it. So it is written as a warning for the unbeliever to yet consider God's offer of salvation while the time is still available. Now in verse 2 we have a vision in heaven:

Revelation 15:2

"And I saw as it were a sea of glass mingled with fire: and them that had gotten the victory over the beast (here we see the martyred Tribulation saints already present with the Lord in glory), *and over his image, and over his mark, and over the number of his name, stand on the sea of glass, having the harps of God."*

It's a verse like this where people get the idea that all we will do when we get to heaven is strum a harp. That may be part of it. But it will be far more than that! Now an interesting verse:

Revelation 15:3

"And they sing the song of Moses the servant of God, and the song of the Lamb,..."

Now those are two separate songs. Let's go back to the song of Moses. Turn to the Book of Exodus Chapter 15. Remember that Israel has just come through the Red Sea. They've looked back and seen the residue of all the floating Egyptian horsemen, chariots and everything else. From all practical aspects it wasn't a very pretty picture. But when Israel could look back on their years of slavery and mistreatment and sufferings, and then be able to see what had happened to their enemies, no wonder they could sing. So this is the song of Moses. And again this is (as I have made the analogy over and over as we have studied Revelation) such a repeat of that Exodus experience and dealing with the Pharaoh and the plagues, only on a far grander and greater scale. And here is another parallel. These Tribulation saints, who are now removed from their suffering and are in the presence of the Lord, they too will sing the song of Moses and the song of the Lamb. We won't read it all because it's too long, but here is the gist of it. Verse 1:

Exodus 15:1

"Then sang Moses and the children of Israel this song unto the LORD, and spake, saying, `I will sing unto the LORD (I remember when I was teaching up in Iowa, I had a class of young people on Saturday night, and the kids would bring their guitars and we would always sing songs before I would teach. And one of their favorite songs was based on the song of Moses), *for he hath triumphed gloriously: the horse and his rider hath he thrown into the sea.'"* And they continue on in their singing:

Exodus 15:2-4

"The LORD is my strength and song, and he is become my salvation: he is my God, and I will prepare him an habitation: my father's God, and I will exalt him. The LORD is a man of war: the LORD is his name. Pharaoh's chariots and his host hath he cast into the sea: his chosen captains also are drowned in the Red Sea." Now that is only a part of the song of Moses. Now come on down to verse 11, continuing the song:

Exodus 15:11-13

"Who is like unto thee, O LORD, among the gods? who is like thee, glorious in holiness, fearful in praises, doing wonders? Thou stretchedst out thy right hand, the earth swallowed them. Thou in thy mercy hast led forth the people which thou hast redeemed: thou hast guided them in thy strength unto thy holy habitation."

Do you get the picture? They are singing that song of deliverance of redemption. That is the song of Moses. Now I would like for you to stop at Psalms Chapter 22. Here is a song of David, and David could also put his thoughts into songs. Which were always to God's glory. Words of praise and worship. This chapter is the chapter of the Crucifixion and Resurrection. Come on down to verse 22:

Psalms 22:22,23

"I will declare thy name unto my brethren: in the midst of the congregation will I praise thee. Ye that fear the LORD, praise him; all ye the seed of Jacob, glorify him: and fear him, all ye the seed of Israel."

Now turn on over to Psalms 86 and you will see more or less that same theme of worship and praise. This, of course, will be so appropriate for those in the very throne room of heaven, having come out of that horrible Tribulation experience.

Psalms 86:8

"Among the gods (that is the gods of this world) *there is none like unto thee, O Lord; neither are there any works like unto thy works."*

Psalms 86:9

"All nations whom thou hast made shall come and worship before thee,..."

This song is being sung in Revelation just before the Lord returns to set up His Kingdom. Do you see how appropriate all of this is? We will study about that when we get a little further into the Second Coming of Christ and the setting up of His Kingdom.

Psalms 86:9-13

"...O Lord: and shall glorify thy name. For thou art great, and doest wondrous things: thou art God alone. Teach me thy way, O LORD; I will walk in thy truth: unite my heart to fear thy name. I will praise thee, O Lord my God, with all my heart: and I will glorify thy name for evermore. For great is thy mercy toward me: and thou hast delivered my soul from the lowest hell,"

Do you see the praise and exalting of that song? Now back to Revelation and this is exactly what they are going to be singing and proclaiming here in the very presence of God. Now verse 3:

Revelation 15:3

"And they sing the song of Moses the servant of God, and the song of the Lamb, saying, `Great and marvellous are thy works, Lord God Almighty; just and true are thy ways* (remember I've told you that God isn't being unfair), *thou King of saints.'"

Revelation 15:4

"Who shall not fear thee, O Lord, and glorify thy name? for thou only art holy: for all nations shall come and worship before thee* (it has never happened yet, but it will!)*: for thy judgments are made manifest."

Revelation 15:5

"And after that I* (John) *looked, and , behold, the temple of the tabernacle of the testimony in heaven was opened:"* We saw that happen before back in Chapter 11.

Revelation 15:6

"And the seven angels came out of the temple, having the seven plagues* (now here is your final bowl judgments), *clothed in pure and white linen, and having their breasts girded with golden girdles."

Revelation 15:7

"And one of the four beasts* (or creatures. We referred to them early in the Book of Revelation. They are angelic beings) *gave unto the seven angels seven golden vials* (or bowls) *full of the wrath of God, who liveth for ever and ever."* This is a symbolic picture again of how this wrath will be poured out.

Revelation 15:8

"And the temple was filled with smoke from the glory of God, and from his power; and no man was able to enter into the temple, till the seven plagues of the seven angels were fulfilled."

Now here they come, one right after the other. Each one will be more severe then the previous one, leading up to the very battle of Armageddon. And the bringing of the nations to the Middle East. But first, Chapter 16, verse 1:

Revelation 16:1,2

"And I heard a great voice out of the temple saying to the seven angels, Go your ways, and pour out the vials* (or bowls) *of the wrath of God upon the earth. And the first* (angel) *went, and poured out his vial* (bowl) *upon the earth; and there fell a noisome and grievous sore* (or boil, remember Egypt) *upon the men which had the mark of the beast, and upon them which worshipped his image."

Now remember the mark of the beast (and we talked about in an earlier lesson), this is where people cannot buy or sell or do any kind of business unless they have the mark in their right hand or forehead. So just about the whole world will come under this plague of miserable boils. Now verse 3:

Revelation 16:3
"And the second angel poured out his vial (bowl) *upon the sea* (I think this is possibly the oceans as we know them)*; and it became as* (liken unto) *the blood of a dead man; and every living soul* (creatures and fish) *died in the sea."* Can you imagine what that does to the shores and ocean? We talk about pollution. We know nothing of pollution as it's going to be here.

Revelation 16:4
"And the third angel poured out his vial (bowl) *upon the rivers and fountains of waters; and they became blood."*

This is literal blood. Remember again, the Egyptians had to dig fresh water wells and tried to get fresh water that way. Here, God is going to turn all drinkable water into blood. Why blood? Again look at the human race tonight. They are blood-thirsty. I've always put it this way: God created Adam a human being, but as soon as Adam became a sin creature, he became inhuman. And all you have to do is look at your newspaper tonight, and what has mankind become? He has, I think, become an inhuman being. There is not another species on earth that misuses their own species as man does. You don't see anything in the wild kingdom that torments its own. Only man. I suppose according to the Jerusalem Post that the Syrians are the masterminds on torture. They can dream up things that no one else can dream up. We use to think that Iraq was the best at this, but the Syrian puts them in the shade in torturing people. Man has intrinsic ability to somehow be blood thirsty. So God is saying here, **"Alright, you've been blood thirsty now for 6000 years, now drink it."** And it becomes a plague.

Revelation 16:5,6
"And I heard the angel of the waters say, `Thou art righteous (Even the angels will never come back and say, "God, why are you doing this." Instead they say, "You are righteous God. They are getting exactly what they deserve.")*, O Lord, which art, and wast, and shalt be, because thou hast judged thus.'"* Now here is what we are talking about:
"For they have shed the blood of saints and prophets, and thou hast given them blood to drink; for they are worthy."

History tells us that during the dark ages (that period of time between about 500 to 1500 AD - that period before the reformation), in that thousand years of human history, it is estimated that at least 50 million Christians were put to death. Many of them horrible deaths. We can't even imagine, and yet they did it gladly for their faith. Bring it up to recent history. Again, during the seventy years that communism reigned and ruled Russia, also about 50 million people were put to death. By their own government! Indeed, they have shed the blood of saints.

Revelation 16:7
"And I heard another out of the altar say, `Even so, Lord God Almighty, true and righteous are thy judgments.'"
Do you see the emphasis here? I know the first thing that we humanly think is, God isn't being fair. After all, why does this one generation have to come under such terrible cataclysmic events? It's this generation that is just simply bringing to a head everything that the previous generations have been sowing the seed of. And God has always done that. Remember the verse that contains the Ten Commandments? **"And I will visit down to the third and fourth generation."** That's the way God does things. Now verse 8:

Revelation 16:8
"And the fourth angel poured out his vial (bowl) *upon the sun; and power was given unto him to scorch men with fire* (or intense heat).*"*

Go back for a moment to Isaiah Chapter 13. Because I always like to help people realize, that there are some groups who think that Revelation shouldn't even be in our Bible. But always remember, it still fits with all the rest of the Old Testament. Let's start at verse 9:

Isaiah 13:9
"Behold, the day of the LORD cometh, cruel both with wrath and fierce anger, (now this is Isaiah written approximately 700 years before Christ)*, to lay the land desolate: and he shall destroy the sinners thereof out of it."* Now here it comes in verse 10:

Isaiah 13:10,11
"For the stars of heaven and the constellations thereof shall not give their light: the sun shall be darkened in his going forth, and the moon shall not cause her light to shine. And I will punish the world for their evil, and the wicked for their iniquity; and I will cause the arrogancy of the proud to cease, and will lay low the haughtiness of the terrible."

And in another place, the earth will be moved in and out of its orbit. And our scientists tells us if the earth was to tilt just two degrees off of what is normal, the earth would either burn up with heat, or would freeze up in the cold. So during that time the weather will be almost out of control. We are already seeing just a little bit of it, the bizarre weather around the world. Let's come back to Revelation. I would like to finish the sixth bowl judgment and then be ready for the battle of Armageddon in our next lesson. So now let's look at verse 10:

Revelation 16:10
*"And the fifth angel poured out his vial (*bowl) *upon the seat of the beast* (Anti-christ in the city of Jerusalem)*; and his kingdom* (world-wide) *was full of darkness* (don't forget this also happened

in Egypt); *and they gnawed their tongues for pain,"*

Revelation 16:11,12
"And blasphemed the God of heaven because of their pains and their sores, and repented not of their deeds. And the sixth angel poured out his vial upon the great river Euphrates; and the water thereof was dried up (why?), *that the way of the kings of the east might be prepared."*
So the Euphrates River will be as dry as a bone. And that last obstacle will be removed for the 200 million-man army to come to Jerusalem.

Editor's Note: Next comes the Battle of Armageddon at the end of the seven year tribulation. It will be discussed just a few pages ahead under the question, "What will happen during the Battle of Armageddon?"

(13d) What will happen to churches and religion during the tribulation ?

Book 11 LESSON TWO * PART IV

Let's come back to Revelation again. In Chapter 6, we don't have any of the descriptions that are equal to Revelation 19, so this has to be the counterfeit. The counterfeit christ is the Anti-christ. As we come into this seven-year period of Tribulation, 3 1/2 years and 3 1/2 years, we are going to find ourselves confronted with an unholy trinity all through the Book of Revelation. Satan is the counterfeit of the Father. The counterfeit of the Son will be the Anti-christ. And the counterfeit of the Holy Spirit and His works will be what we refer to in the Book of Revelation as the false prophet. I think Revelation Chapter 19 is the only place where he is named. This is at the end of the Tribulation, and all the horrible judgments have all ready happened. And it's time for the King and the Kingdom to come on the scene.

Revelation 19:20
"And the beast (Anti-christ) *was taken, and with him the false prophet* (here he is named. The rest of the time he's referred to as a personality. Revelation 13 refers to him as the lamb with two horns) *that wrought miracles before him, with which he deceived them that had received the mark of the beast, and them that worshipped his image. These both were cast alive into a lake of fire burning with brimstone."*

They go into the lake of fire without benefit of the Great White Throne Judgment. They are the very first ones to inhabit the eternal doom of the wicked, the lake of fire. All the other lost are going to stand before the Great White Throne and at least have their moment of time, and I guess they can put up an argument if they feel like it. Because Jesus said in that day, and He was referring to the Great White Throne, they will say unto Me: **"But Lord, didn't we cast out demons in your name?"** And what's His answer going to be? "Depart from me I never knew you." So there will be a time of rebuttal or whatever you want to call it. But not for the false prophet and

Anti-christ. These two humans who are part of this unholy trinity will go to their doom.

Satan is going to go there as well, but he will join them sometime later. As we come through the Book of Revelation, be aware that Satan and the Anti-christ and the false prophet are working in unison, much like the Holy Trinity. The Holy Spirit today in the Age of Grace points people to God, the Son. This is the work of the Holy Spirit, to point lost people to the Son. For we believers, it's the Holy Spirit's work to teach and encourage and reprove us, so that we might in turn bring honor and glory to the Son. Now the false prophet is going to do the same thing during the Tribulation. He is going to cause people to worship the Anti-christ. Consequently, he fulfills a counterfeit role of the Holy Spirit. Both of these will be under the power of Satan.

Book 12 LESSON ONE * PART IV

ANTI-CHRIST - "FALSE PROPHET"

Now let's come back to where we left off in Revelation 17. In verse 3 remember we are talking about this great religious system that is going to come on the world. We are already seeing all the seeds of it. Which particular religious system ends up heading it up I don't know. There is a lot of speculation. There are a lot of world-wide huge religious organizations on the scene tonight who have tremendous wealth, and political power. They have for the most part been persecutors of true believers. It has always been that way, even back in the Old Testament the pagan idolatrous world was always making life miserable for the true people of God. Even on this side of the Cross, I have always said that most, if not all, of the world's conflicts (and you look around the planet tonight and it stills bears it out), most of the conflicts have been precipitated by religionists trying to force somebody either out of their area or under their thumb. You just think about that. For example, that whole situation in Yugoslavia is exactly that.

So as this great religious system comes on the scene, it will of course be satanic. Just because it's a religion doesn't mean it's Godly. It will be a satanically inspired organization under the guise of religion, which will be headed up by this one-world religious leader, the false prophet, who could very easily be an apostate Jew. I was reading a few weeks ago about this famous Jew who was a Moslem. So it's not unusual for Jews to embrace something other than Judaism. But we do know that it's going to have tremendous power over the everyday individual. We will also see in a moment that it is supported by the government of the Anti-christ. Now that isn't new. Even today, you go into certain nations in Europe and the government actually subsidizes and supports some of the large denominations. One of the reasons our forefathers left Europe was the separation of church and state. That was going on over there in their generation. That didn't mean that they didn't want God in government. That is where it has been twisted all around. They didn't want God out of government, but they didn't want government to run their church. And that is as it should be. But in verse 4 let's look at the language:

Revelation 17:4

*"And the woman was arrayed in purple and scarlet colour, and decked with gold and precious stones and pearls, having a golden cup in her hand (*that speaks of wealth. And again look at some of the large religions of the world. Their subjects are as poor as church mice, but the wealth is in the hands of the hierarchy. And this will be the same thing. Remember all the religions of the world will come under this one. It will be satanic, demonic because you see in her hand is this golden cup) *full of abominations and filthiness of her fornication:"* Not so much the physical immorality, but the spiritual. Verse 5. We will come to the point where she is carried by the government in verse 7.

Revelation 17:5

"And upon her forehead was a name written, MYSTERY (from which we get the word `secret'), *BABYLON THE GREAT, THE MOTHER OF HARLOTS AND ABOMINATIONS OF THE EARTH."*

When we were studying back in Genesis, where several years after the flood, the Tower of Babel was built which started all pagan idolatrous religions. Any cult today, if they are a true cult, even though they may use a certain amount of scriptures, takes parts of their doctrine that will put their roots right back in the Tower of Babel. And so all the religions of the world have their roots at Babel. That's where it all began. And that is what the Apostle Paul meant when he wrote in II Thessalonians.

II Thessalonians 1:7

"For the mystery of iniquity doth already work:..."

It's been working since God scattered them from the Tower of Babel. And it has been a constant adversary of the true worship of Jehovah God. What was Israel's problem all through their early history? Going into idolatry. And on this side of the Cross you have the Apostle Paul going out into the Gentile world. What was he confronted with? Turn to the Book of Acts, and this is just one example. As Paul is now taking the Gospel of the Grace of God to the Gentile world, and as he and Barnabas have come into Ephesus, multitudes of those pagans are being converted. As they were being converted to Paul's Gospel, what were they doing with their idols? They were throwing them away. Now that in turn caused the ire of the men who made the idols, the silversmiths. Look what happens when Christianity begins to make inroads into idolatrous worship of these pagan religions. It's no different today.

Acts 19:23

"And the same time there arose no small stir about that way." What way? Paul's way. The Gospel of Grace.

Acts 19:24,25

"For a certain man named Demetrius, a silversmith, which made silver shrines for Diana (a female goddess), *brought no small gain unto the craftsmen* (the silversmiths); *Whom he called together with the workmen of like occupation, and said, `Sirs, ye know that by this craft* (making silver shrines of Diana) *we have our wealth.'"*

And after all, what is the engine of economy? Greed. It's that constantly wanting more and more. And that's what fuels it. I'm certainly not in favor of sitting back and saying, "I'm not going to do anything." But on the other hand there has to be a tempering. So greed is what prompted the silversmiths to rise up against Paul's ministry and against Christianity.

Acts 19:26,27

"Moreover ye see and hear, that not alone at Ephesus , but almost throughout all Asia (that is Asia Minor, that would be Turkey), *this Paul hath persuaded and turned away much people, saying that they be no gods, which are made with hands; So that not only this our craft is in danger to be set at nought; but also that the temple of the great goddess Diana should be despised, and her magnificence should be destroyed, whom all Asia and the world worshippeth."*

Now that is what idolatry does. Idolatry just feeds on the baser instincts of humanity. Come back to Revelation Chapter 17. Here we have this great religious system. Verse 5 again takes us all the way back to ancient Babylon, the Tower of Babel. And it's been the adversary of the truth of God ever since. But it's going to crescendo during this last seven years. It will suddenly come to a peak.

Even though idolatry is basically dealing in the realm of the dark side of the spiritual, yet idolatry is dealing with man's desire to worship something. But when you get into a study of pagan worship, especially at the time of the Apostle Paul, remember that part and parcel of their worship was gross immorality. Because most of their places of worship, like the one mentioned in Acts 19, where nothing more than glorified houses of prostitution. All in the name of their religion. And those pagan priests would conscript young ladies from across the countryside and force them into prostitution. This is what God is finally referring to. Now verse 6.

Revelation 17:6

"And I saw the woman (the religious system) *drunken with the blood of the saints* (who has been the persecutor of true believers? Religion of one sort are another), *and with the blood of the martyrs of Jesus: and when I saw her, I wondered with great admiration."* I suppose that John marveled at wealth, and pomp and circumstance and power.

Revelation 17:7

"And the angel said unto me, `Wherefore didst thou marvel? I will tell thee the mystery of the

woman, and of the beast that carrieth her, which hath the seven heads and ten horns.'" The Anti-christ.

What does that tell you? If you've got a beast of burden carrying something, then it's support-ing it. What you really have here is this revived Roman Empire; this great political world-wide system headed up by the man Anti-christ is going to subsidize, and support this world church. Do you see that? And the church is riding upon it.

Revelation 17:8
"The beast that thou sawest was (and again I'm holding to the fact that this is the Roman Empire. It was, then it faded off the scene), *and is not; and shall ascend out of the bottomless pit, and go into perdition: and they that dwell on the earth shall wonder, whose names were not written in the book of life from the foundation of the world* (so we have the unbelieving element of the world who are going to be part and parcel of this great religious system), *when they behold the beast that was, and is not, and yet is."* In other words, when the ancient Roman political, economical system as well as the pagan religious system are all going to culminate.

Revelation 17:9-11
"And here is the mind which hath wisdom. The seven heads are seven mountains (Kingdoms or nations), *on which the woman sitteth."* In other words she has rule. Now verse 10. Again I'll come back to the Nations of Western Europe who will be the core of all of this.
"And there are seven kings (remember we started with ten)*: five are fallen, and one is, and the other is not yet come* (in other words there is one to come on the scene)*; and when he cometh, he must continue a short space."* Not for a very long period of time. Now in verse 11 we come to the rise of the Anti-christ.
"And the beast that was, and is not, even he is the eighth, and is of the seven, and goeth into perdition."

In other words, the Lord is going to destroy it at His coming. Here you start out with ten nations. Three of them will lose their identity rather shortly. But each of their kings or prime ministers will stay in the picture. But the sovereignty of their nation will be lost. So the ten will be down to seven. Out of the seven will come the Anti-christ who will take over complete control and the others will fade off the scene. And he then is the eighth. Verse 12:

Revelation 17:12,13
"And the ten horns which thou sawest are ten kings (do you see how plain that is? There's no gimmick here), *which have received no kingdom as yet* (they don't have the power and political clout that the Anti-christ will have)*; but receive power as kings one hour with the beast."* Or Anti-christ and his empire. Here is what they will do:
"These have one mind, and shall give their power and strength unto the beast."
The Anti-christ. Now that is what he has been working for. He came in with peace and prosperity

and flatteries, not with civil war. He's going to manipulate. He's going to be very smooth. And all of a sudden he's going to have the pre-eminence. **Now leaping to the end of the seven years in verse 14:**

Revelation 17:14-16
"These (all these nations under the headship of the Anti-christ and the false prophet) *shall make war with the Lamb* (Christ), *and the Lamb shall overcome them* (at Christ's Second Coming)*: for he is Lord of lords, and King of kings: and they that are with him are called, and chosen, and faithful."* You and I are the ones that will be coming with him.

"And he saith unto me, 'The waters which thou sawest, where the whore sitteth (in other words, where this great religious system is operating), *are peoples, and multitudes, and nations, and tongues,...'"* It's a world wide religious system. Verse 16:

"And the ten horns which thou sawest upon the beast, these (now all of a sudden you have a change in language so watch it. Remember in verse 7 this religious system is riding on the back of the beast but now) *shall hate the whore* (or religious system)*, and shall make her desolate and naked, and shall eat her flesh, and burn her with fire."*

That again is symbolic language. What is the Anti-christ going to do with the religious system? He's going to destroy it. Why? We must come back to II Thessalonians as we must compare Scripture with Scripture. We can also go all the way back to the Book of Daniel.

II Thessalonians 2:4
"Who (the Anti-christ) *opposeth and exalteth himself above all that is called God, or that is worshipped; so that he as God sitteth in the temple of God, shewing himself that he is God."*
He's going to set himself up as God and won't let the world religion have anything to do with him anymore. He's going to take absolute control himself. And since he is going to sit in the temple of God, we know that Israel will rebuild her temple and it will be in Jerusalem. In Daniel Chapter 9 we find out what this fellow will do at the mid-point of the Tribulation. We find he's going to move into the temple in Jerusalem. He then will defile it. Verse 27, where the prince that shall come in verse 26 shall:

Daniel 9:27
"And he shall confirm the covenant with many (the Jews) *for one week;* (seven years) *and in the midst of the week* (at the end of 3 1/2 years) *he shall cause the sacrifice and the oblation to cease,..."*

(14d) Will some people live through the tribulation ?

Book 13 LESSON TWO * PART III

Matthew 19:27
"Then answered Peter and said unto him (Jesus), *Behold, we have forsaken all* (their occupations), *and followed thee; what shall we have therefore?*

Peter wasn't talking about his salvation, he knew he had that. He had already believed that Jesus was the Christ. So what's he talking about? He wanted to know what their reward would be for following Jesus (leaving everything else behind). Look at Jesus' answer:

Matthew 19:28
"And Jesus said unto them, Verily I say unto you, `That ye which have followed me (the twelve, but we must leave Judas out), *in the regeneration* (that's when you restore something back like it was. The earth back like it was in the Garden of Eden) *when the Son of man shall sit in the throne of his glory* (and according to Psalms Chapter 2, it will be in Jerusalem), *ye* (the twelve, we will have Matthias in the Book of Acts) *also shall sit upon twelve thrones, judging* (or ruling) *the twelve tribes of Israel.'"*

Now isn't that so plain? When the Kingdom is set up and the Nation is now under their King, under The King will be twelve original Apostles each ruling the twelve tribes, there in Jerusalem. There in the land of Israel. Let's look at another verse or two. This comes back to the closing days of the Tribulation, but that is all tied to the beginning of the Kingdom.

Luke 21:25,26
"And there shall be signs in the sun, and in the moon, and in the stars; and upon the earth distress of nations, with perplexity; the sea and the waves roaring; Men's hearts failing them for fear, and for looking after those things which are coming on the earth: for the powers of heaven shall be shaken." Now that's the end of the Tribulation. Look at what the next verse says:

Luke 21:27
"And then shall they (the Jews. What's the next word?) *see* (lock that word in for I'll come back and make a point with it) *the Son of man coming in a cloud with power and great glory."*

Luke 21:28
"And when these things begin to come to pass, then look up, and lift up your heads; for your redemption draweth nigh." Remember, He is addressing the Nation of Israel.

Luke 21:29-31
"And he spake to them a parable; Behold the fig tree, and all the trees; When they now shoot forth,

ye see and know of your own selves that summer is now nigh at hand. So likewise ye, when ye see these things come to pass, know ye that the (what's the next word?) *kingdom of God is nigh at hand."*

Now come on over to the Book of Acts Chapter 1. Of course, the Crucifixion has come and gone. Christ has been raised from the dead. He has spent forty days with the eleven. And now verse 3:

Acts 1:3

"To whom also he shewed himself alive after his passion by many infallible proofs, being seen of them forty days (they saw Him. How? With their eyes), *and speaking of the things pertaining to the kingdom of God:"* Now verses 6 and 7:

Acts 1:6,7

"When they therefore were come together (Jesus and the eleven, on the Mount of Olives), *they asked of him, saying, Lord, wilt thou at this time restore again the kingdom of Israel?"* Notice He didn't tell them there wouldn't be a Kingdom, but rather:
"And he said unto them, `It is not for you to know the times or the seasons, which the Father hath put in his own power.'"

Don't think Peter had forgotten about the promise of both him and the others sitting on the twelve thrones we read about earlier.

I just had a thought. I'm going to give you something to look for. I want you to search the four Gospel accounts, and see if you can find a single time that the twelve referred to the Lord as **"Jesus."** I think you will have an eye-opener.

So the Kingdom has been the theme throughout all of Scripture. That this Kingdom is going to come on the earth where Christ will be the absolute King of Kings and Lord of Lords. Satan, as we have seen, is going to be bound and there will be no sin. But the question is, "Who is going to go into the Kingdom?" There are qualifications, of course. Come back to John's Gospel Chapter 3. A portion you all know forward and backward. And you have heard dozens of sermons on it. And here we have Nicodemus in verse 2:

John 3:2

"This same came to Jesus by night, and said unto him, Rabbi, we know that thou art a teacher come from God: for no man can do these miracles that thou doest, except God be with him."
Notice Nicodemus was head and shoulders ahead of most of the Jews of that day. He recognized that these miracles were telling him something. And he knew that Jesus was Someone special.

John 3:3

"Jesus answered and said unto him, `Verily, verily, I say unto thee, Except (or unless) *a man be*

born again (or born from above)*, he cannot see the kingdom of God.'"* Now what does that tell you. Who can go into the Kingdom? ONLY BELIEVERS!

There will be no unbelievers in the Kingdom. Come back to Matthew 24. Several lessons ago, I had my timeline on the board showing the seven years of Tribulation. And at the mid-point of the Tribulation we see the Anti-christ coming in and defiling the temple at Jerusalem? Matthew 24 verses 15a and 16:

Matthew 24:15a,16
"When ye therefore shall see the abomination of desolation, spoken of by Daniel the prophet,... Then let them which be in Judaea flee into the mountains:"

I call this the escaping remnant of Israel. They go down to the mountains to the southeast of Jerusalem. They won't be the whole nation but as I taught you before, only the remnant. And in those mountains God is going to protect them for the last 3 1/2 years. Then as this remnant of Israel who have gone out to the mountains in unbelief (in that they have never recognized Christ as their Messiah), when they **see** Christ coming with glory and power at His Second Coming they will believe. So they, too, will get to go into the Kingdom.

Let's look at this remnant as they see Him coming from the view of Zechariah. Remember, I told you earlier in the lesson in Luke 21:27 to remember that word `see' - in that they would see Him:

Zechariah 12:10
"And I will pour upon the house of David, and upon the inhabitants of Jerusalem, the spirit of grace and of supplications (remember this is the house of David, no Gentiles are there)*: and they shall look upon me whom they have pierced* (His Crucifixion),...*"*

They will suddenly not only have their physical eyes opened but also their spiritual eyes. And they will recognize that this coming manifestation of The Christ, The Messiah is the One Who died back there on that Roman Cross. Let's look at one more verse in this lesson:

Zechariah 13:6
"And one (this remnant of Israel) *shall say unto him, `What are these wounds in thine hands?' Then he shall answer, `Those with which I was wounded in the house of my friends,'"*

Then this remnant of Israel will experience that new birth that Nicodemus was told he had to have in order to go into the Kingdom. This remnant, by far, will be the largest number of people to survive the Tribulation. This then will be the seed stock of the Nation of Israel as they come into the Kingdom. All twelve tribes will be represented here. Isaiah tells us, ***"Will a nation be born in a day."***

LESSON TWO * PART IV

FIRST RESURRECTION - "WHO GOES INTO KINGDOM:"
GENTILE BELIEVERS

Turn in your Bible to Isaiah 24. We continue our study on who goes into the earthly Kingdom after the Tribulation. Remember at that time the earth will be restored back to the way it was in the Garden of Eden before sin entered. It will be glorious and beautiful. As we saw last lesson, the remnant of Israel that God had protected all during the last 3 1/2 years of the Tribulation will believe when they **see** Christ coming with power and great glory at His Second Coming. They will see the nail prints in His hands, the wound in His side and by sight, believe and know that He was and is their Messiah. They then will go into the Kingdom. Also remember this remnant is a mixed group of Jews we saw in Matthew 24 as they fled Jerusalem. They will then become the seed stock for the Nation of Israel. They are not the 144,000 Jewish men who preached during the Tribulation.

They will also, by far, be the largest nation in numbers to go into the Kingdom. So now we have the Nation of Israel established. Now let's pick up the Gentiles whom God hasn't forgotten. Even though the Age of Grace was primarily to the Gentiles yet even in the Tribulation, God has been preparing Gentiles to go into the Kingdom in ordinary flesh and blood bodies. Remember the Kingdom is going to see a tremendous population explosion. So by the end of that thousand years when Satan will be released for a little season to test those born during this Kingdom Age, there will be probably as many people on earth then as there are now. So in Isaiah Chapter 24 we will pick up these Gentiles. We will begin at verse 1, and again, it's a graphic description of the Tribulation as we have been studying it for the last several lessons.

Isaiah 24:1,2
"BEHOLD, the LORD maketh the earth empty, and maketh it waste, and turneth it upside down, and scattereth abroad the inhabitants thereof." We have been talking about all the cataclysmic events that will be taking place during the Tribulation.
"And it shall be, as with the people, so with the priest; as with the servant, so with his master; as with the maid, so with her mistress; as with the buyer, so with the seller; as with the lender, so with the borrower; as with the taker of usury, so with the giver of usury to him." In other words, everyone is going to come under this tremendous cataclysmic seven-year period of events.

Isaiah 24:3,4
"The land shall be utterly emptied, and utterly spoiled: for the LORD hath spoken this word. The earth mourneth and fadeth away (under these judgments), *the world languisheth and fadeth away, the haughty people of the earth do languish."* Even their wealth is not going to protect them.

Isaiah 24:5,6

"The earth also is defiled under the inhabitants thereof; because they have transgressed the laws (the basic laws of morality laid down back in the Ten Commandments)*, changed the ordinance, broken the everlasting covenant."* In other words, they have been totally disobedient to everything that God has instructed.

"Therefore hath the curse (that began with Adam) *devoured the earth* (it's because of sin that all of these things take place)*, and they that dwell therein are desolate: therefore the inhabitants of the earth are burned* (yes there could be tremendous amounts of nuclear energy released)*, and few men left."*

And despite all the cataclysmic events that happen, there will be survivors in just about any catastrophe that happens. There are normally some survivors. When we dropped the bomb on Hiroshima, there were people who survived that blast and they were at ground zero. When there are terrible earthquakes, where there's a building collapse and it doesn't look possible for any one to be alive, they always find survivors. And so it will be at the end of the Tribulation. They will be scattered around the planet from every nation that you can think of.

Now let's try to figure out in the statement of verse 6, *"and few men left."* How many is a few? You can use any percentage you wish to figure a few. We have tonight in the world around 5 1/2 billion people. But for sake of easy mathematics let's round it off to 5 billion. I think 10 percent is too high for a few. When I think of a few I think of something less then 5 percent. So what would be 5 percent of 5 billion people? 250 million people. Let's bring it down to 1 percent and you still have 50 million. That is still a lot of people.

Don't forget the fact that at the beginning of the Tribulation God sealed 144,000 young Jews who will preach the Gospel of the Kingdom. Their main message will be, during almost all of the Tribulation, **"The King is coming to set up His Kingdom."** Many people will believe and be martyred. However some people will believe and survive. Then some people who won't believe survive. So all of survivors combined are the, *"few men left"* we read about here in Isaiah. Let's go to the Book of Matthew and pick these survivors up again and see what happens to them. Remember, no unbelievers can go into the Kingdom. Because Satan is going to be locked up, and we will start out with a generation of parents who are believers. In Matthew Chapter 25 we have the perfect description of how God is going to do it. Here we will be dealing with a point in time where the supernatural will be almost common-place. And so Christ is going to bring supernaturally all of the **survivors**, from all over the world, to Jerusalem. So, beginning in verse 31, this is Jesus speaking:

Matthew 25:31

"When the Son of Man shall come in his glory (now watch the language here)*, and all the holy angels with him* (that includes you and I; this is at His Second Coming)*, then shall he sat upon the throne of his glory* (His Kingdom rule in Jerusalem)*."*

Matthew 25:32

"And before him shall be gathered all nations (the biggest percentages of the population of the nations have been killed, as this is at the end of the Tribulation. But we still have the survivors, who are representative of their nations)*: and he* (The King) *shall separate them one from another, as a shepherd divideth his sheep from the goats."* Here Christ the King will separate the believers from the unbelievers.

Matthew 25:33

"And he shall set the sheep on his right hand, but the goats on the left."

Matthew 25:34

"Then shall the (what's the next word) *King* (notice He is already on the throne here ready to start ruling over the Kingdom) *say unto them on his right hand* (believers), `Come, ye blessed of my Father, inherit the* (what?) *kingdom prepared for you from the foundation of the world:'"*

That is nothing new to you is it? What does Ephesians Chapter 1 tell us? When were we chosen and in the mind of God? Before the foundation of the world. God in His foreknowledge knew exactly which one of these Gentiles would hear the Gospel of the Kingdom from the 144,000 and believe. Now in verse 35, the following is not what saved them but what distinguished them as believers:

Matthew 25:35,36

"For I was an hungred, and ye gave me meat (food)*: I was thirsty, and ye gave me drink: I was a stranger, and ye took me in: Naked, and ye clothed me: I was sick, and ye visited me: I was in prison, and ye came unto me."*

Matthew 25:37-40

"Then shall the righteous (these surviving believers) *answer him, saying, `Lord, when saw we thee an hungred, and fed thee? or thirsty, and gave thee drink? When saw we thee a stranger, and took thee in? or naked, and clothed thee? Or when saw we thee sick, or in prison, and came unto thee?' And the King shall answer and say unto them, `Verily I say unto you, Inasmuch as ye have done it unto one of the least of these my brethren,...'"*

That word `brethren' is the secret here. Jesus was a Jew so His brethren were Jews. So who is He referring to? The 144,000 that had preached the Gospel of the Kingdom during the Tribulation. It wasn't their good deeds that saved them. It is never good works that save anyone. They were saved by their faith in this message that was preached unto them. And as soon as they were saved what were they willing to do? **Help these people who had brought this saving message to them.**

Remember during World War II, who helped and hid the Jewish people from the Nazis? Christians. Why? Because it's a Christians' nature to do things like this. So here, Jesus is showing that these 144,000 are going to suffer privation all through their ministry. Go back to Revelation Chapter 7 for a moment, where the angel says:

Revelation 7:3
"Saying, Hurt not the earth, neither the sea, nor the trees, till we have sealed the servants of our God in their foreheads."

That was like, I suppose, when God put a mark on Cain, that no one could take his life. And it's the same way with these 144,000. They were sealed so that they could not be killed. Suffer, yes, but they couldn't be killed. Reading on you will see that there were 12,000 sealed from each of the twelve tribes. To see how all of this fits with Matthew Chapter 25 come down to verse 16. These are the privations that Tribulation believers, as well as the 144,000, will suffer during this seven-year period.

Revelation 7:16
"They shall hunger no more, neither thirst any more;..."

Remember, if people don't take the mark of the beast during this time, they won't be able to buy or sell, and seven years is a long time if you can't buy groceries. Seven years is a long time if you can't make a house payment, buy gasoline, or pay a doctor bill. So they will end up hungry and thirsty, and naked. Come back to Matthew Chapter 25. So the 144,000 suffered these same privations during the Tribulation. They were thrown in prison and they're going to be hungry, and the only sustenance they had was from these believers. These believers, although they will have little to spare, will sacrifice to help these 144,000. Then Jesus said:

Matthew 25:40
"...Inasmuch as ye have done it unto one of the least of these my brethren, ye have done it unto me." This is the only setting in which this text fits. You can't put it into anything else. It's simply the response of these believers who have survived awful events of the Tribulation. Then in verse 41 Jesus addresses the goats or unbelievers.

Matthew 25:41-45
"Then shall he (Christ) *say also unto them on the left hand, `Depart from me, ye cursed, into everlasting fire, prepared for the devil and his angels* (and they will ask why)*: For I was an hungred, and ye gave me not meat* (food)*: I was thirsty, and ye gave me no drink: I was a stranger, and ye took me not in: naked, and ye clothed me not: sick, and in prison, and ye visited me not. Then shall they also answer him, saying, `Lord, when saw we thee an hungred, or athirst, or a stranger, or naked, or sick, or in prison, and did not minister unto thee?'* (and look at the Lord's reply)*: Then shall he answer them, saying, `verily I say unto you, Inasmuch as ye did it not to one of the least of these* (the 144,000)*, ye did it not to me:'"* And now He

gives each group what they deserve in verse 46:

Matthew 25:46

"And these shall go away into everlasting punishment: but the righteous into life eternal." And although the Kingdom is stipulated a thousand years it is still the beginning of eternity.

I had a gentleman call the other night who said, "Les, I have problems with what takes place in the Kingdom and what takes place in eternity. What's the difference?" I told him there were a lot of great theologians who debate the issue in their books as to what's in the Kingdom Age and what's in eternity. I can just simplify that by saying, "Always remember that all the situations concerning the Kingdom are an introduction to the eternal." Now that's the way I see it. It will be interrupted, by a new heaven and a new earth, but I think eternity will be based on pretty much the same set of circumstances that we have in the thousand years. So when Jesus tells these people that are going into the Kingdom that they are going into eternal life, indeed they are! Let's look at a few more of the attributes of the Kingdom. Turn to Isaiah Chapter 11:

Isaiah 11:1,2

"And there shall come forth a rod out of the stem of Jesse, and a Branch shall grow out of his roots:" Jesse was the father of David and Christ is always considered the Son of David. So we are speaking of the Branch here as the Messiah, the Christ.

"And the spirit of the LORD shall rest upon him, the spirit of wisdom and understanding, the spirit of counsel and might, the spirit of knowledge and of the fear of the LORD:" Those are all attributes of the Spirit and also indicative of the Christ.

Isaiah 11:3,4

"And shall make him of quick understanding in the fear of the LORD: and he shall not judge after the sight of his eyes, neither reprove after the hearing of his ears: But with righteousness shall he judge the poor, and reprove with equity for the meek of the earth (this is where the Beatitudes come into play, and become the constitution of the Kingdom)*: and he shall smite the earth with the rod of his mouth, and with the breath of his lips shall he slay the wicked* (He did that at Armageddon)*."* And in verse 5 we come back again into the Kingdom.

Isaiah 11:5,6

"And righteousness shall be the girdle of his loins, and faithfulness the girdle of his reins." This is all on the earth.

(15d) Can people that hear the Gospel during the Age of Grace and refuse it, be saved during the tribulation?

Book 12 LESSON ONE * PART I

Go back to II Thessalonians, because I think the following thought should immediately come to any student of Scripture: **If people have missed being saved during this Age of Grace or Church Age, are they going to get a second chance? No.** Here we see Paul (inspired by the Holy Spirit in II Thessalonians Chapter 2) identify those who cannot be saved with the message of the 144,000 during the Tribulation. Paul is not associated with prophecy per se. He's associated with the doctrines of Grace and with mysteries. Nevertheless he connects the end of the Church Age with the Tribulation by a description of what will take place as the Anti-christ comes on the scene here in II Thessalonians Chapter 2:

II Thessalonians 2:3
"Let no man deceive you by any means: for that day shall not come, except there come a falling away first (the Church being raptured), *and that man of sin be revealed, the son of perdition;* "

II Thessalonians 2:7,8
"For the mystery of iniquity doth already work (that goes back to the tower of Babel): *only he who now letteth* (hindereth) *will let,* (continue to hinder) *until he be taken out of the way."* I always teach it's the Holy Spirit who is the hindering force in the person of the believer, until he's taken out of the way, which would be in the departure when the Church is removed in verse 3:
"And then (when the Church is gone, and the Holy Spirit in His role as indwelling the believer has ended. Of course the Holy Spirit will be back on the earth as the Omnipresence of God) *shall that Wicked* (one) *be revealed, whom the Lord shall consume with the spirit of his mouth* (at the end of the seven years), *and shall destroy with the brightness of his coming;"*

II Thessalonians 2:9,10
"Even him (Anti-christ), *whose coming is after the working of Satan with all power and signs and lying wonders, And with all deceivableness of unrighteousness in them that perish* (unbelievers); *because they received not the love of the truth, that they might be saved."*
Now get the picture. Those who will be ready to accept the coming of the Anti-christ will be those who had the opportunity to hear the Gospel, the truth of the Word of God, but they loved their unrighteousness and they spurned God's offer of salvation. Now verse 11:

II Thessalonians 2:11a
"And for this cause..."

As we are entering into the Tribulation in this verse, we are entering in with God dealing in the supernatural. Today, we are fairly unaccustomed to that. God still works in miraculous ways, but we're not living where the supernatural takes place commonly.

II Thessalonians 2:11
"And for this cause (because this group of people have heard the Gospel and rejected it and so it is for that cause) *God shall send them strong delusion, that they should believe a* (and again I like to use the article `the') *lie:"*

337

There has been one lie all through Scripture. And I call it `the' lie. That is when Satan tells a person, **"You can be God."** They are going to believe it. God is going to send these people *"strong delusion"* who have heard the Gospel and rejected it. And these will be the very first people who will proclaim the Anti-christ as the god of this world, the one they have been looking for. **But the ones who have never heard the True Gospel will have a chance in the Tribulation by the preaching of the 144,000.** And now verse 12:

II Thessalonians 2:12
"That they all might be damned (or condemned) *who believed not the truth, but had pleasure in unrighteousness."*

Go back to the Book of Ephesians Chapter 1, because we have almost the same kind of language (so that you will know what the Apostle Paul is talking about). As we come down to the appearance of the Anti-christ and the Church has been removed, what should they, the unrighteous that were left behind, believe?

Ephesians 1:13
"In whom ye also trusted (Paul writes to believers only)*, after that ye heard the word of truth, the gospel of your salvation: in whom also after that ye believed, ye were sealed with that holy Spirit of promise."*

Let's take time to look at the Gospel again in I Corinthians Chapter 15, especially as we look at the awful things that are about to come upon the earth. I think there is nothing wrong with the whole concept of literally being scared out of our boots. And maybe fear will prompt someone to seek God's saving Grace in order to escape some of these things. I think that is one of the reasons it is put in here. Now I don't subscribe to the fear concept, but on the other hand, when the Scripture makes it so plain that these terrible days are coming on the earth, and we can escape it by simply partaking of God's salvation, then why not. Why be foolish and spurn so great a salvation only to end up in the horrors that are coming upon the earth. Now I Corinthians 15:1-4, and here is the most explicit definition of the Gospel that you can find.

I Corinthians 15:1-4
"Moreover, brethren, I declare unto you the gospel which I preached unto you, which also ye have received, and wherein ye stand (positionally)*; By which also ye are saved, if ye keep in memory what I preached unto you, unless ye have believed in vain."* You must know what you believed. Here it is in verses 3 and 4. This is our Gospel:
"For I delivered unto you first of all that which I also received (from our ascended Lord)*, how that Christ died for our sins according to the scriptures; And that he was buried and that he rose again the third day according to the scriptures:"* That's what the Book of Ephesians calls the truth of the Gospel. This is what Paul is referring to in II Thessalonians Chapter 2:10:

II Thessalonians 2:10

"And with all deceivableness of unrighteousness in them that perish; because they received not the love of the truth...."

What is the love of the truth? The Gospel. And what's the Gospel? That Christ died for my sins, was buried, and that He arose from the dead. Those of you who have been in my classes over the years know that I do not ascribe to just an easy-believism. In other words, just saying that, yes, I believe that Christ lived, and that He died, and I believe that He rose from the dead; that's not what the Bible is talking about. The Bible is talking about a concerted faith and trust in that very act of God. That God Himself paid the penalty for all our sins. I have told my classes many times (and I like to put it this way): if you or I had been the only person living, Christ would have still gone to the Cross to purchase our redemption. When you have that kind of faith, that you can say that I believe that with all my heart, and can say that you know He is alive, I know that His Word is true; **then God sees that faith as salvation. Romans 4 makes it so clear. It wasn't by works that Abraham was saved, but by faith. What was Abraham's faith? He believed God! And God counted it unto him as righteousness. He was a believer.**

Folks who have heard this Gospel, and have been convicted by the Holy Spirit that they need this Gospel and reject it. They are the ones that will have no further chance at salvation and will be blinded from the truth. But there are literally billions of people upon the face of the earth tonight who have never heard the Gospel. I always maintain in every city that I teach, that there are multitudes who have never heard the Gospel. Now I know that is hard for us to believe. But listen, there are people who may walk into a place of business and there may be a preacher on the radio or television preaching the Gospel in all of it's truth and sincerity. But they don't hear it. They don't pay any attention to it. So I maintain they are going to still be candidates for the preaching of the 144,000.

I feel that the only ones who will be completely condemned are the ones we have talked about, who have completely heard, understood, were convicted by it and said, **"No thank you"** or, **"I'll do it later,"** or whatever. We even have church people who have been in my classes, who have come and said, **"Les, we have never heard the Gospel before."** And they had been in church all their life. That is a sad commentary I know, but it's still the truth. So as these 144,000 Jews go out around the world, there's no one being saved as a second chance. But only those who have never heard the True Gospel. The ones who have rejected and are doomed will also be the first to take the mark of the beast, the 666. For us believers tonight we don't have that to fear as we will be gone when that comes on the scene for the Tribulation people. But they will accept that mark of the beast at the drop of a hat for they have already been completely deluded by a Sovereign act of God, that the Anti-christ is the man the world is looking for.

(16d) What will happen during the battle of Armageddon ?

Book 11 LESSON THREE * PART I

Always remember that prophetically there are only three areas of the world that are involved in those last days of the Tribulation or the battle of Armageddon. And that is Western Europe, the Orient, and parts of Africa. There is nothing at the very end that concerns Russia, or the Western Hemisphere. There is nothing in prophecy that would involve those two great areas in that last great battle.

Book 12 LESSON THREE * PART IV

TRUMPET & BOWL JUDGMENTS: BATTLE OF ARMAGEDDON

Now to Revelation 16. We studied the last 6 terrible judgments that will be coming upon the earth. I'm going to stop before we get to number 7 for a reason. After the sixth bowl had been poured out, which was the drying up of the Euphrates River so the armies can come into the Middle East from the Far East, John says in verse 13:

Revelation 16:13

"And I saw three unclean spirits like frogs come out of the mouth (communications) *of the dragon, and out of the mouth of the beast, and out of the mouth of the false prophet."*
Satan, who is now indwelling the Anti-christ, will make contact probably by phone with all the national leaders still in place. He will ask for their armies to come to the Middle East to get rid of the real problem of mankind, the Jew (what Hitler called the final solution). I look at this final gathering of the nations at Armageddon as Satan's attempt once and for all to annihilate the Jewish people. But it's really going to end up, Satan against The Christ.

Revelation 16:14

"For they are the spirits of devils, working miracles, which go forth unto the kings of the earth and of the whole world, to gather them to the battle of that great day of God Almighty."
When President Bush was putting together the nations in Desert Storm, the papers said he would just pick up the phone and call the leaders of the various nations. Using only phone calls, he was literally getting these leaders convinced they should unify against Iraq. That was just a little tiny preview of what we have right here. Now verse 15, and The Sovereign God is behind it:

Revelation 16:15,16

"Behold, I come as a thief. Blessed is he that watcheth, and keepeth his garments, lest he walk naked, and they see his shame." In other words, the Lord is reminding us that it is time for His appearance at the Second Coming, but before He does that:
"And he gathered them together (this is the power of a Sovereign God working through, of

340

course, the mind set of the Anti-christ who puts out the call to the nations to come to Jerusalem) *in a place called in the Hebrew tongue, Armageddon."*

From which the word Megiddo comes. Another word is Esdraelon. And if you go to Israel as we did last spring, that is one of the tourist attractions. You will see the archaeological digs of the ancient city of Megiddo. When you stand on the hills of Megiddo amongst all the ruins of that ancient city, you can look off to the northeast and there is that beautiful flat valley. The Nation of Israel is predominately mountainous. You have these valley areas between the mountain ranges. The reason I'm pointing this out is that when God brings the armies of the world to Israel, naturally they will put their encampments on those valley floors. And this area of the valley of Esdraelon has been a battlefield throughout time. The place had great strategic importance, since it commanded the pass through the mountains between the plains of Sharon and Esdraelon. There have been hundreds of battles fought here. So he will bring the nations of the world to the Middle East. Now I know there is not a bit of military intelligence connected to it, but you must remember we are dealing with a Sovereign God and He is going to cause those generals to pack their troops into these valleys, beyond description. They will be in there like sardines in a can, because a Sovereign God is forcing the issue. Now let's come back a couple of chapters to Revelation 14, and we have a tremendous symbolic picture of all of this.

Revelation 14:14-16
"And I looked, and behold a white cloud, and upon the cloud one sat like unto the Son of man, having on his head a golden crown, and in his hand a sharp sickle." I feel this is an allusion to Christ. He is the One who is about to reap this harvest.
"And another angel came out of the temple, crying with a loud voice to him that sat on the cloud, `Thrust in thy sickle (they used to use the sickle to harvest the grain), *and reap: for the time is come for thee to reap; for the harvest of the earth is ripe.'"* Remember the communication is between the angel and Christ.
"And he that sat on the cloud thrust in his sickle on the earth; and the earth was reaped." Chapter 16 shows the call going to all nations to come to the Middle East. That's the reaping A Sovereign God is bringing about.

Revelation 14:18
"And another angel came out from the altar, which had power over fire; and cried with a loud cry to him that had the sharp sickle, saying, Thrust in thy sharp sickle, and gather the cluster of the vine of the earth: for her grapes are fully ripe."

The word `fully' in the Greek means `over-ripe.' It's past harvest time. Here is the symbolism again. The grapes were gathered and put into a wine vat, where they could be crushed; the juice taken out of them and made into wine. The juice was squeezed out of the grapes by walking on them in the wine vat. They would put two or three people in a vat and they would walk until all the juice would run out. That is the allusion here, that this is exactly what God is doing with the peoples of the world. Now come back to the Book of Isaiah Chapter 63, and you will get the beautiful analogy. And again, I do this so you can see that all of Scripture fits together.

Isaiah 63:1,2

"Who is this that cometh from Edom, with dyed garments from Bozrah? this that is glorious in his apparel, travelling in the greatness of his strength? I that speak in righteousness, mighty to save." Who do you suppose he is referring to? Christ! This is a picture of His returning and bringing forth judgment upon these gathering armies. *"Wherefore art thou red in thine apparel, and thy garments like him that treadeth in the winefat."* Don't lose that analogy. The grape harvest was put in the wine vat, and it was trampled by individuals. Naturally, the grape juice would spurt and juice would get all over them. The prophet sees Christ also covered with this red apparel. And he says, **"Why are you this way?"** Look at the answer in verse 3. And again, Christ is speaking:

Isaiah 63:3,4

"I have trodden the winepress alone (in Revelation Chapter 5, God the Father had a scroll. No one was worthy to open that scroll except the Son of God and He came and took the scroll. Here it comes to its fruition. He alone was worthy, and no one else was worthy of bringing on this particular judgment) *and of the people there was none with me: for I will tread them in mine anger, (do you see that) and trample them in my fury; and their blood* (He's not speaking of His own Blood here) *shall be sprinkled upon my garments, and I will stain all my raiment."* As He more or less tramples the people in the wine vat. Now verse 4:
For the day of vengeance is in mine heart (this isn't the God of Grace now. This is a God of wrath!), *and the year of my redeemed is come."* Let's hold all of this together. Revelation Chapter 19:

Revelation 19:11

"And I saw heaven opened, and behold a white horse; and he that sat upon him was called Faithful and True (it's the Christ), *and in righteousness he doth judge and make war."*
Because after all, what kind of people does he have in the wine vat? Military. It's the armies of the world that have come to the Middle East. Supposedly to annihilate the Nation of Israel. Don't forget those 200 million coming from the East. They will be packed into that little geographical area. And I think it will also include every valley in the Nation of Israel where these troops will be packed in. And as I said before, it will be contrary to all military strategy. But it's the Sovereign God who has reaped the earth, and has placed them in what the Scriptures call His wine vat. But remember, it's in righteousness. Now verse 12:

Revelation 19:12-14

"His eyes were as (He doesn't say they are flames, but **as**) *a flame of fire, and on his head were many crowns; and he had a name written, that no man knew, be he himself."* And here it is now. This is in complete accord with the Book of Isaiah:

"And he was clothed with a vesture dipped in blood (not His, but His victims), *and his name is called the Word of God."*

"And the armies which were in heaven (that will be the saints, as this is His Second Coming. The saints have been with him for seven years because they have been raptured out ahead of time. That includes you and I as believers. Now they are coming back with him) *followed him upon white horses, clothed in fine linen, white and clean."* That is also in verse 8 of this Chapter, where the fine linen is the righteousness of the saints.

Revelation 19:15

"And out of his mouth goeth a sharp sword (what is the sharp sword? The Word of God. Remember Hebrews 4:12 says, *"For the Word of God is quick, and powerful, and sharper than any two-edged sword"*), *that with it he should smite the nations* (how will He destroy them? With the spoken word)*: and he shall rule them* (the nations, Believers only) *with a rod of iron* (benevolence, but absolute rule, there will be no funny business in His Kingdom. A good example is the Beatitudes. What are Beatitudes? Well the constitution of His government. That's when the Beatitudes will come into their full definition, *"Blessed are the meek..." "Blessed are the poor..."* That doesn't fit in the Church Age. You talk to a poor person today and I don't believe that he feels blessed. Do you? The Lord may provide and get them through, but they are not happy as such. But in the Kingdom there will be no unhappiness)*: and he treadeth the winepress of the fierceness and wrath of Almighty God."*

What's His winepress? The valleys of Israel, wherein all these millions of troops will be packed, and He will destroy them with one fell swoop. It's hard for us to understand. Let's read on in Verse 16:

Revelation 19:16

"And He hath on His vesture and on his thigh a name written, KING OF KINGS, AND LORD OF LORDS."

Remember, I purposely stopped just before we came to the seventh bowl judgment back in Chapter 16. I left off after the sixth judgment because I wanted to leave the seventh one till now:

Revelation 16:17,18

"And the seventh angel (we've covered six of them. We're bringing you right up close to the end of the Tribulation) *poured out his vial* (bowl) *into the air; and there came a great voice out of the temple of heaven, from the throne, saying, 'It is done.'"* This is the finale:

"And there were voices, and thunders and lightnings; and there was a great earthquake, such as was not since men were upon the earth, so mighty an earthquake, and so great."

And again, I don't feel that this is an isolated one. I think the whole planet is going to come under these convulsions. Although the epitome of all of this is going to be in Jerusalem in the area of Israel. Let's go on:

Revelation 16:19

"And the great city (Jerusalem) *was divided into three parts, and the cities of the nations fell: and great Babylon came in remembrance before God, to give unto her the cup of the wine of the fierceness of his wrath."*

Now I have to stop again. The Babylon in Revelation is not the ancient city, because the Old Testament says it will **never** be rebuilt. It will always be a habitation of nothing but wild animals and birds of prey. But the Babylon of Revelation is the **whole world wide-system** as we see it coming together today. The **whole one world concept**. Where Tokyo and Berlin and London and Rome and New York are just like one little tightly knit group. When I picture these end time events, I like to think that when Babylon falls, it won't be just one city. It will be all the cities of the world, who will in one hour fall into nothingness, by the spoken word of God. Now remember that. The Babylon here is **all the world**. I just read an interesting article in our daily paper that some junior high student had just won a great essay contest. What do you suppose the title of her essay was? **"The Great New One World."** That's what people love to hear tonight. They love to hear about the great one-world that's coming. And it is! It's getting smaller and smaller. But you see, it's going to suddenly evaporate.

Revelation 16:20,21

"And every island fled away and the mountains were not found. And there fell upon men a great hail out of heaven, every stone about the weight of a talent (most of your Bibles tell you what that is. It's 100 pounds. We talk about golf ball-sized hail and softball-sized hail, but these are hundred pound chunks of ice!)*: and men blasphemed God because of the plague of the hail; for the plague thereof was exceeding great."*

Now to Revelation 14, where we finish that analogy of the grape vat. Can you hold all of this together? Just like the vineyard keepers put all of their grapes into the vat and they had some-body trample them, so God has brought all the armies of the world to the Middle East. How is He going to trample them? With this final plague of the hailstones. Picture all of the millions of troops out there in nothing more then tents to protect them from the elements. Can that stop a hundred pound hailstone? **NO!** So they will be literally squashed, even as the grapes in the vat. I know this verse has been a verse hard to swallow over the years, but I'll make it real easy to swallow.

Revelation 14:20

"And the winepress was trodden, without the city (indeed, these valleys are all to the north of Jerusalem)*, and blood came out of the winepress* (out of these valleys)*, even unto the horse bridles* (a river of water, and blood three to four feet deep)*, by the space of a thousand and six hundred furlongs* (about 180 Miles)*."*

As that melting hail, which has crushed these millions of troops, begins to melt in that Middle

Eastern heat, do you see how fast you're going to have a literal river of blood flowing as deep as a horse's bridle? That's not hard to believe. In fact, I always remind my classes that during World War II, during one of the battles on one of the islands in the Pacific, so many men were lost as they were coming ashore, that the ocean was red for about 5 miles out with the blood of our marines.

(17d) What will take place during the 1000 year Kingdom Age ?

Book 13 LESSON TWO * PART III

FIRST RESURRECTION - "WHO GOES INTO KINGDOM:" GENTILE BELIEVERS

I don't claim to have any special revelations, and I don't think I teach The Bible that much different than a lot of men who are far more important and educated than I am. But I trust that I am able to make it a little easier to understand. We have been talking about the Kingdom the past few lessons. Christ has returned, the Tribulation has run its course, and I think the questions that come into everybody's mind are, "Who is going to go into the Kingdom? Are they going to be flesh and blood? Will they be having families? Will they be reproducing?" And the answer to all these question is, absolutely! This Kingdom will be on the earth, and will be `Utopia,' (that's the word the secular world likes to use). So let's take a few references out of the Old Testament to show that this Kingdom idea has been on God's mind from the very onset of the Book it-self, but especially after the call of Abraham.

I stressed many months ago that the Abrahamic Covenant you see was the Covenant between God and the Nation of Israel. He would make them a special, separated nation of people. He would put them in a geographic area of land and then, at the appropriate time, He would come to be their King, and set up the government. That comprises the Kingdom that everything is looking forward to.

Book 13 LESSON TWO * PART II

Revelation 20:6
"Blessed and holy is he that hath part in the first resurrection:... but they shall be priests of God and of Christ, and shall reign with him a thousand years."

Now the question came up in our last coffee break. That in verse 4, it sounds like just Tribulation people will reign and rule with Christ, and I was glad that someone caught that. Because that is probably true, but again you have to take Scripture with Scripture, and you can't make a doctrine, or identify anything with just one verse. Come back to Revelation Chapter 5, and here we have a verse that I would say includes all of us believers in verse 10.

Revelation 5:10

"And hast made us unto our God kings and priests: and (what) *we* (an all inclusive word) *shall reign on the earth* (with Christ)." We can also look at Chapter 19 verse 7:

Revelation 19:7

"Let us be glad and rejoice, and give honour to him: for the marriage of the Lamb (remember the Lamb is to married to the Body of Christ) *is come, and his wife hath made herself ready."*

Revelation 19:8

"And to her was granted that she (the Body of Christ, the Church) *should be arrayed in fine linen, clean and white: for the fine linen is the righteousness of saints."*
Go over to verse 14 in this same Chapter. Here we are now included in this army that is coming with Christ at His Second Coming.

Revelation 19:14

"And the armies (Heavenly congregation) *which were in heaven followed him upon white horses, clothed in fine linen, white and clean."*

Now can you tie all of that together? Not only are the Tribulation saints going to be included in that reigning and ruling with Christ for a thousand years but we are also included. Since we are talking about the Church Age believer in the Kingdom as this Kingdom will come on earth, come back to the Book of Colossians. Now Paul the Apostle to the Gentiles does not dwell a lot on the Kingdom, not nearly as much as the Old Testament does, and the Gospels as they pertain to Israel. But nevertheless we are involved in the Kingdom. Don't think for a moment that we won't be. In Colossians Chapter 1 (and again I'm going to run out of time in the middle of a subject). But if the Lord tarries there will be another lesson, and if He doesn't, we won't need it. Here in this passage Paul has been praying for the Colossi Gentile believers.

Colossians 1:12

"Giving thanks unto the Father, which hath made us meet (or prepared us) *to be partakers of the inheritance of the saints in light: Who hath delivered us from the power of darkness, and hath (past tense) translated us* (you and I as believers) *into* (what?) *the kingdom of his dear Son:"*

We are already members of the Kingdom. But always remember, where is the Kingdom tonight? In heaven, in the Person of Christ. When He was on the earth John the Baptist approached Jesus and what did He say? *"The Kingdom of heaven is at hand."* Why? Because the King was at hand. So when the King went back to glory, then the Kingdom is again in heaven (and we don't refer to Him as the King in the Church Age, but as Savior and Lord.)

But always remember the Kingdom won't stay in heaven, but will come back to the earth, and Paul says, **"We will be with Him. Part and Parcel of that Kingdom."** So we are indeed a part of this coming Kingdom, which will then be on the earth.

Book 13 LESSON THREE * PART I

BEMA SEAT: GREAT WHITE THRONE:
NEW HEAVEN AND EARTH

Let's recap our last lesson for a moment about who will go into the Kingdom. First we will have the remnant of Jews that God is going to protect during the last 3 1/2 years of the Tribulation. They will be Jews that we read about in Matthew 24 that were escaping to the mountains at the mid-point of the Tribulation. They were a cross-section of the population of Jerusalem, from children and young pregnant women to retired older people. They will be the seed stock to repopulate the Nation of Israel. Second, there will be the survivors that believed the Gospel of the Kingdom as presented by the 144,000 that survive the Tribulation. They too will be a cross-section of society. This group will be Gentiles and will be the seed stock to repopulate all the nations, except the Nation of Israel. This Kingdom Age will last a thousand years and there will be only believers in this Kingdom. Satan will be locked up, the earth will be like the Garden of Eden. There will be no sin there. And Christ will be the absolute Ruler, a benevolent Dictator if you want to call Him that. It's going to be a glorious time. There will be no sin, sickness, or death, and you will have a population explosion that the world has never seen before. We also know that since the curse has been lifted, there will be no more pain in childbirth, which I think will encourage large families.

Regarding other aspects of the Kingdom, I've had many people ask me if they will see their dog or cat again in heaven (they want me to say yes)? But I have to say, "Not the one you had here." But there will be animals in the Kingdom. I'm sure that among those animals, people will have pets. I'm a dog lover myself, and have loved dogs ever since I was a kid. I had one for 15 years and I sure got attached to her. But I know I won't see that little black dog in the Kingdom economy. But there will be animals. That is why I had you turn to Isaiah Chapter 11. We touched on this in the last lesson, so let's just review a little. I like to show everything from Scripture. If I can't show it from Scripture then it's just my own idea. But when you can, I trust you will read it and believe it as this is the inspired Word of God. I take it literally. When you take the Scriptures literally you satisfy a lot of questions (and why not take it literally). If you read the account of Washington and his men crossing the Delaware on that cruel winter day, back there in the early days of our nation, do you spiritualize that and try to dream up something totally different? Of course not. You take it literally, and you take it so literally that you can almost feel the cold and pain they went through. And you need to do the same thing with Scripture. Don't read and then try to dream up something that it must have meant. Just say, ***"This is what it says, and I believe*** *it."* So looking at the animal part of the Kingdom again, let's go to verse 6:

Isaiah 11:6
"The wolf also shall dwell with the lamb, and the leopard shall lie down with the kid (baby goat)*; and the calf and the young lion and the fatling together; and a little child shall lead them."*

Can you picture all of that? Just take it literally. The animal kingdom as we know it today would be in total opposition. That lion would eat that little calf in a second. But here they are lying down together. Do you see the difference? I'm always trying to get people to read their Bibles carefully. Don't just read it to be reading it. Here we have wild animals all of a sudden cohabiting with domestic animals! And unbelievable as it may seem, who is in the midst of them? A little child. Immediately you should ask yourself, "Where does this child come from?" Well, like the children today it came from parents, a father and a mother. Let's read on:

Isaiah 11:7
"And the cow and the bear shall feed (together)*; their young ones shall lie down together: and* (now here is the secret of the whole thing) *the lion shall eat straw like the ox."*

Now let's compare Scripture with Scripture. Come back to Genesis Chapter 1. This is why I say the Kingdom will be a reversion back to the Garden of Eden, before the curse came in. Now the comparison. Isaiah says the day is coming when these wild meat-eating animals are going to eat the same diet of grasses that cattle do today. In Genesis 1:28-30 we read (here God is speaking to Adam):

Genesis 1:28-30
"And God blessed them, and God said unto them, `Be fruitful, and multiply, and replenish the earth, and subdue it: and have dominion over the fish of the sea, and over the fowl of the air, and over every living thing that moveth upon the earth.' And God said, `Behold, I have given you every herb bearing seed, which is upon the face of all the earth, and every tree, in the which is the fruit of a tree yielding seed; to you it shall be for meat (or food).'" Now verse 30:
"And to every beast of the earth (that also includes the animals we read about in Isaiah)*, and to every fowl of the air, and to every thing that creepeth upon the earth, wherein there is life, I have given every green herb for meat:* (or food) *and it was so."*

You won't see God give permission (I don't think even to the animal kingdom) to kill and eat meat for food until after the flood. Noah was then instructed that he could kill and eat the meat of these animals. But definitely before Adam sinned, none of the animals could eat meat, only green herbs. So that is what is here in Isaiah 11. The whole animal kingdom, including the most ferocious, carnivorous meat-eating species are going to change their diets and live peaceably with animals they once would have eaten.

Isaiah 11:8

"And the sucking (or nursing) *child shall play on the hole of the asp,* (which of course was a very poisonous serpent) *and the weaned child shall put his hand on the cockatrice's* (adder's) *den."*

Here we have had three children mentioned in just two verses. The inspired Word of God tells us that when this Kingdom is set up there will be human beings coming in at the front end of the Kingdom who are going to reproduce. They have to. We know by the time we get to the end of the thousand years, there are multitudes of people on the earth. We will be looking at that in a later lesson. Where did they come from? They came from believing parents who started at the beginning of the Kingdom.

Coming out of the Old Testament we came to the time of the Cross, and now we are in that undetermined period of time known as the Church Age. It will end when the Church is Raptured, or called out. And then began that seven-year period of time called the Tribulation. After Christ returns at the end of the Tribulation we come into this thousand years of what we call the Kingdom Age. It will be on earth in which these things will take place that we are reading about. All through this period of human history everything has been under the curse, and we have no question about wild animals and their behavior, and children should never play with them. And then at the end of the last lesson and I recapped at the beginning of this lesson who would be going into the Kingdom. All of these people I showed you will be different than you and I. We will have our new resurrected bodies, flesh and bone. These believing survivors of the Tribulation will have the same bodies that they had before - flesh and blood. They will then be the parents of these children we just read about with the wild animals in verse 6 and 8 of Isaiah Chapter 11. Let's look at verse 9:

Isaiah 11:9

"They shall not hurt nor destroy in all my holy mountain (a mountain in Scripture, especially in the Old Testament, is a Kingdom. Always look at the text)*: for the earth shall be full of the knowledge of the LORD, as the waters cover the sea."*

Let's look at some more Old Testament references of the earthly Kingdom. Go to the Book of Amos Chapter 9 (in our next lesson I'm going to explain the **opposition** to this line of teaching about a literal earthly Kingdom that will come on the earth. We call this opposition Amillenialism). Hopefully we'll show you that we are not throwing you a bunch of smoke, but that we can rest assuredly that even in the very early days of Christianity they all held to this view of an earthly Kingdom that someday would be on the scene. We have a lot of people who watch and are in my classes, who are handed books that are in opposition of the earthly Kingdom, the Book of Revelation and so forth. Now look at Amos 9:11,12:

Amos 9:11,12

"In that day (in other words when Christ is setting up His Kingdom) *will I raise up the tabernacle*

of David that is fallen, and close up the breaches thereof; and I will raise up his ruins, and I will build it as in the days of old: That they (Israel) *may possess the remnant of Edom, and of all the heathen* (Gentiles), *which are called by my name, saith the LORD that doeth this.”* In verse 13, Here it is:

Amos 9:13

“Behold, the days come (when this Kingdom is finally set up), *saith* (Who?) *the LORD, that the plowman shall overtake the reaper* (what does that mean? Intense reproduction, remember there will be no curse, so they won't have to put up with weeds and insects, fungus and moles, and pests and all the things that hinder good crop production), *and the treader of grapes him that soweth seed; and the mountains shall drop sweet wine, and all the hills shall melt.”* And God goes on to say that with His dealing with His people Israel, as we have here in the Old Testament:

Amos 9:15

“And I will plant them upon their land, and they shall no more be pulled up out of their land which I have given them, saith the LORD thy God.” Go to the Book of Zechariah, Chapter 14 verse 8:

Zechariah 14:8

“And it shall be in that day (when the Kingdom is in operation), *that living waters shall go out from Jerusalem: half of them toward the former sea* (the Mediterranean sea), *and half of them toward the hinder sea* (Dead Sea): *in summer and in winter shall it be.”* In order to pick up on this you have to go back to Ezekiel Chapter 47. Ezekiel sees this same river, beginning in verse 1:

Ezekiel 47:1

“AFTERWARD he brought me again unto the door of the house; and, behold, waters issued out from under the threshold of the house eastward: for the forefront of the house stood toward the east, and the waters came down from under from the right side of the house, at the south side of the altar,” Notice this river has it source under the temple in Jerusalem. Now verse 8:

Ezekiel 47:8-10

“Then said he unto me, These waters issue out toward the east country, and go down into the desert, and go into the sea (that is the Dead Sea): *which* (when these waters) *being brought forth into the* (Dead) *sea, the waters shall be healed,”*
“And it shall come to pass, that every thing that liveth, which moveth, whithersoever the rivers shall come, shall live: and there shall be a very great multitude of fish, because these waters shall come thither (from the temple area): *for they* (the waters of the Dead Sea) *shall be healed; and every thing shall live whither the river cometh.”* Now look at verse 10:
“And it shall come to pass, that the fishers shall stand upon it (this is the Dead Sea, and we know

that from the term Engedi) *from Engedi even unto Eneglaim; they shall be a place to spread forth nets; their fish shall be according to their kinds, as the fish of the great sea* (the Mediterranean), *exceeding many."*

When we were in Israel, we stopped at the oasis of Engedi at the Dead Sea and some of our group went swimming. Someday, this will again be fresh water. In Matthew Chapter 19, here again is the promise of this coming Kingdom when Peter says to the Lord:

Matthew 19:27,28
"...Behold, we have forsaken all, and followed thee; what shall we have therefore? And Jesus said unto them, `Verily I say unto you, that ye which have followed me, in the regeneration when the Son of Man shall sit in the throne of his glory, ye also shall sit upon twelve thrones, judging the twelve tribes of Israel.'"

Part E – Answers from the Quarterly Newsletters

(1e) PRETERISM --- DON'T YOU BELIEVE IT !

Preterism is the theory that all future prophecies were nullified by the "fulfillment" (their word) of Matthew 24:34 where Jesus says, *"Verily I say unto you, This generation shall not pass, till all these things be fulfilled."* In other words, preterists try to tell us that 70 AD fulfilled every-thing. There is nothing left but? - they really don't say. But if that is the case, how do they explain present day Israel back in the land being prepared for their Messiah.

They claim to be letter perfect in their interpretation of Matthew 23:34, and then proceed to expel or twist all the prophetic things that are still awaiting a future fulfillment. If all future events were fulfilled by Titus in 70 AD, then what do they do with the following scriptures? Did any of these things take place before, and up to, 70 AD? An ounce of common sense says, "No." But if the Preterists' premise is true, then what do they do with all of these things that have not happened yet?

Acts 1:11 - "...this same Jesus which is taken up from you into heaven shall so come in like manner as ye have seen him go into heaven." - (Bodily, head first, from the Mt. of Olives)

Romans 11:12 - "Now if the fall of them (Israel) be the riches of the world (our gospel of Grace), and the diminishing of them the riches of the Gentiles (our age of Grace); how much more their fulness?" (Israel's future blessing)

Romans 11:23 - "And they also, if they abide not still in unbelief, shall be graffed in: for God is able to graft them in again."
Romans 11:24 - "...how much more shall these, which be the natural branches (Israel), be graffed into their own olive tree?"

Romans 11:25 - "For I would not, brethren, that ye should be ignorant of this mystery (secret), lest ye should be wise in your own conceits; that blindness in part (for a while) is happened to Israel, until the fulness of the Gentiles (the Body) be come in."

II Thess. 2:3,4 - "Let no man deceive you by any means: for that day (the Day of the Lord - the Tribulation) shall not come, except there come a falling away (or a departure) first, and that man of sin be revealed, the son of perdition; Who opposeth and exalteth himself above all that is called God, or that is worshipped; so that he as God sitteth in the temple of God, shewing himself that he is God."(Compare this with Daniel 11)

II Thess. 2:8 - "And then shall that Wicked (the Anti-christ) be revealed, whom the Lord shall consume with the spirit of his mouth, and shall destroy with the brightness of his coming."
Jude verses 14 and 15a - "And Enoch also, the seventh from Adam, prophesied of these, saying, Behold, the Lord cometh with ten thousands of his saints, To execute judgment upon all,...."

Now, here are more verses from the Old Testament - Keep asking - "Have/Did these things happen before 70 AD?"

Deut. 30:1,2a - "And it shall come to pass, when all these things are come upon thee, the blessing and the curse, which I have set before thee, and thou shalt call them to mind among all the nations, wither the Lord thy God hath driven thee, And shalt return unto the Lord thy God, and shalt obey his voice...."

Ezek. 37:1-10, 12- (the vision of the dry bones) "Therefore prophesy and say unto them (the whole house of Israel), Thus saith the Lord God; Behold, O my people, I will open your graves, and cause you to come up out of your graves (the Gentile nations), ...and bring you to the land of Israel."

Ezek. 37:21, 22, 23- "And I will make them one nation in the land upon the mountains of Israel; and one king shall be king to them all: and they shall be no more two nations, neither shall they be divided into two kingdoms any more at all: Neither shall they defile themselves any more with their idols, nor with their detestable things, nor with any of their transgressions: but I will save them out of all their dwellingplaces, wherein they have sinned, and will cleanse them: so shall they be my people, and I will be their God."

Ezek. 47:9- "And it shall come to pass, that every thing that liveth, which moveth, whithersoever the rivers shall come, shall live: and there shall be a very great multitude of fish, because these waters shall come thither: for they shall be healed; and every thing shall live whither the river cometh."

Ezek. 47:10- "And it shall come to pass, that the fishers shall stand upon it from En-gedi (now a resort on the West shores of the Dead Sea) even unto En-eglaim; they shall be a place to spread forth nets; their fish shall be according to their kinds, as the fish of the great sea (Mediterranean), exceeding many."

Daniel 9:27- "And he (the Prince-the Anti-christ) shall confirm the covenant with many for one week (7 years): and in the midst of the week he shall cause the sacrifice and the oblation to cease, and for the overspreading of abominations he shall make it desolate, even until the consummation, and that determined shall be poured upon the desolate." (the desolator, the Anti-christ)- (This is the verse Jesus referred to in Matthew 24:15)

Joel 3:2- "I will also gather all nations, and will bring them down into the valley of Jehoshaphat, and will plead with them there for my people and for my heritage Israel, whom they have scattered among the nations, and parted my land."

Joel 3:15, 16- "The sun and the moon shall be darkened, and the stars shall withdraw their shining. The Lord also shall roar out of Zion, and utter his voice from Jerusalem; and the heavens and the earth shall shake: but the Lord will be the hope of his people, and the strength of the children of Israel."

Amos 9:15- "And I will plant them (Israel) upon their land, and they shall no more be pulled up out of their land which I have given them, saith the Lord thy God."

Zech. 14:4a- "And his feet (the Lord's-see verse 3) shall stand in that day upon the mount of Olives, which is before Jerusalem on the east...." (Compare that with previously quoted Acts 1:11 - He left head first - He returns feet first.)

Zech. 14:8- "And it shall be in that day, that living waters shall go out from Jerusalem; half of them toward the former sea, and half toward the hinder sea (Dead Sea): in summer and in winter shall it be." (Compare with previously quoted Ezek. 47:9 and 10.)

Zech. 14:9- "And the Lord shall be king over all the earth: in that day shall there be one Lord, and his name one."

These are just a few of the scriptures that refer to future events that could not have taken place before 70 AD.

So, what do Preterists do with all this? They simply throw them out or twist them so completely that they change their meaning. And what does Scripture say about people who twist Scripture? **II Peter 3:16**- "As also in all his epistles, speaking in them of these things; in which are some things hard to be understood, which they that are unlearned and unstable wrest, as they do also the other scriptures, unto their own **destruction**."

(2e) Why do you use the word Palestine, when it is not even in the Bible?

Answer -- It is in the Bible. Exodus 15:14, Isaiah 14:28 & 31, and Joel 3:4. They all are in reference to the strip of land between the Eastern Mediterranean Sea coast and the Jordan Valley. In Antiquity, this was inhabited by the Philistines, from which Palestine is derived. I use the word sparingly, and only because it is the term quite readily understood by even the Biblically ignorant. But, I much prefer to use the term "Israel," especially since the Jews once again, according to prophecy (Deut. 30:1 & 2 and Ezekiel 37:12-14) have made it their Sovereign homeland.

Actually, to call the Arabs now living in Israel "Palestinians" is a misnomer. Palestine, or Israel as we now know it, was the homeland of the Jewish people from Joshua, about 1400 BC, until, by God's Sovereign design, they were expelled and scattered into every nation on earth by the Roman destruction of the temple and Jerusalem in 70 AD From that time until the early 1900's it was primarily a wasteland under the occupying boots of several different empires. Little by little, Jews started settling the land by way of Kibbutzes.

After World War II, they escaped Europe and their numbers grew until the War of Independence. They were declared a Sovereign State. But, by a United Nations supervised cease-fire, the borders were established that left the Arabs in what we have come to know as the West Bank. I do not like to call present day Israel the Promised Land, because the Promised Land goes all the way out to the Euphrates River and back to the River of Egypt in the West. The Jews have never occupied much of that except a small area east of Galilee during Solomon's reign.

But, when Christ returns and sets up His Kingdom, ruling from Jerusalem, Israel will finally enjoy all the real estate promised to Abraham in Gen. 15:18. And, it will not be desert. It will be as the Garden of Eden was. Isaiah 51:3 - "For our Lord shall comfort Zion; He will comfort all her waste places; He will make her wilderness like Eden and her desert like the garden of the Lord; joy and gladness shall be found therein, thanksgiving and the voice of melody.

(3e) Question about Tithing and keeping Saturday Sabbath

We continue to get questions concerning tithing and keeping Saturday Sabbath. It must be the end time deception that we are warned to avoid. When I show clearly from the letters of Paul that we are not under the law but under Grace, I get a response like, "But the Saturday Sabbath goes back to Genesis 2 when God rested."

Abraham gave titles of all in Genesis 14. He began circumcision in Genesis 17. Now, all three of these were incorporated into the Mosaic Law. Consequently, all 3 were set aside when God opened the windows of Grace and set us free from the Law. So, the early church moved the day of rest and worship to the resurrection day. Not the day of the Sun as some foolish arguments try to put it.

When the Church, which is His Body, is complete, God takes it out of the way by calling it up to meet Him in the air, and with the advent of the 7-year Tribulation the law will once again be in effect. Matthew 24:14, Revelation 12:17. Compare Romans 6:14b.

Relevant Scriptures:
SABBATH: **Romans 14:5** - One man esteemeth one day above another: another esteemeth every day alike. Let every man be fully persuaded in his own mind. **I Corinthians 16:1 & 2** - Now concerning the collection for the Saints, as I have given order to the churches of Galatia, even so do ye. Upon the first day of the week let every one of you lay by him in store as God hath prospered him, that there be no gatherings when I come. **Colossians 2:16** - Let no man therefore judge you in meat, or in drink, or in respect of an Holy day, or of the New moon or of the Sabbath days. **Acts 20:7** - And upon the first day of the week, when the disciples came together to break bread, Paul preached unto them, ready to depart on the morrow, and continued

his speech until midnight.

TITHING: **II Corinthians 8:12** - For if there be first a willing mind, it is accepted according to that a man hath, and not according to that he hath not. **II Corinthians 9:7** - Every man according as he purposeth in his heart, so let him give; not grudgingly, or of necessity: for God loveth a cheerful giver.

Paul never uses the words Sabbath (except in Colossians 2:16, above) or Tithe in any of his Epistles.

(4e) Malachi 1:2 says, "Jacob have I loved and Esau have I hated." Was God being unfair?

Answer: First, the term 'hate' in Scripture is a comparative term. In other words, God's love for Jacob was so much greater that comparatively speaking, He hated Esau. Why did God have such a low esteem for Esau? Because, Esau was destitute of Faith. He had none! Hebrews 11:6, without faith it is impossible to please Him. Esau showed his total lack of faith when he gladly exchanged His Birthright, which was Spiritual, for a bowl of bean soup. He showed it again, when he married Canaanite wives and still again when he went and married a daughter of Ishmael. Everything in Esau's life showed a complete absence of faith. Nothing God said counted in Esau's thinking.

(5e) What does I Timothy 4:10 mean? "For therefore we both labor and suffer reproach because we trust in the living God who is the Savior of all men, specially of those who believe."

ANSWER: This goes back to what we have said on the program over and over. When Christ finished the work of the Cross, God forgave all men all their sin. It is a done deal. He also reconciled every one to Himself. But, each individual has to appropriate that forgiveness and place of reconciliation by faith. The moment we believe it, God says you are forgiven. That is Grace!

(6e) Genesis 49:10, we read, "The scepter shall not depart from Judah, nor a lawgiver from between his feet until Shiloh come," Who is Shiloh?

ANSWER: Shiloh is another Old Testament term or title of Christ. In accordance with all other Scripture, the Nation of Israel will not disappear until Christ returns to the Mount of Olives. Zechariah 14:4, and His feet shall stand in that day upon the Mount of Olives which is before Jerusalem on the east. Compare with Acts 1:11 - "Ye men of Galilee, why stand ye gazing up into heaven? This same Jesus, which is taken up from you into heaven, shall so come in like manner as you have seen Him go into Heaven.

(7e) In the light of Isaiah 65:17, do you think we will know each other in Heaven?

ANSWER: I would say yes based on II Samuel 12:23, where King David is mourning over the dead child born of his adultery with Bathsheba. He finally consoled himself with, "But now he is dead, wherefore should I fast? Can I bring him back again? I shall go to him, but he shall not return to me." Also, on the mount of transfiguration, Matthew 17:1-4, Peter, James and John immediately recognized Moses and Elijah.

(8e) Then what about loved ones who are not there?

ANSWER: I am sure our memories of them will be erased. It will be as if we never knew them. Otherwise, Heaven would be a place of intense sorrow. And it will not be.

(9e) For whom was Matthew 24 written?

ANSWER: Matthew 24 was spoken by the Lord Himself to the 12 as representatives of Israel. Consequently, Matthew 24 is all tribulation. Now that the Jews are back in the land, we can see everything being prepared for the final seven years of Daniel's prophecy -Daniel 9:27.

(10e) Why did Mary Magdalene not recognize Jesus in John 19?

ANSWER: Consider, first, the physical suffering and abuse at the hands of the Romans. He was scourged, his beard torn from His face, the crown of thorns forced upon His Head, plus other acts of violence against Him. But, most of all, because on Him were laid the total sins of the human race from Adam until the end of time.

This is beyond our understanding. For all these reasons, Isaiah 52 prophesied that His visage or appearance was more marred than anyone had ever been. That was the last mental picture of Jesus that Mary had. Also, she, nor any of the other followers of Jesus, including the 12, had any idea that He would be raised from the dead. Luke 18:31 & 32, John 19:9.

No wonder Mary, on first impression, did not think of seeing Jesus in a glorious, resurrected body with only the nail prints and the spear wound as evidence of His suffering. She recognized Him primarily by His voice.

(11e) Then, why did He refuse her touching or embracing Him ?

ANSWER: Back in Genesis 14, we were first introduced to Melchizedek, the priest of the Most High God, a term of deity not restricted to Israel. Hebrews 7, then, throws more light on Melchizedek and that Christ is the fulfillment of that Priesthood.

The first step of preparing the High Priest after Aaron's priesthood was wash, wash in water. The typology of that was fulfilled at Christ's baptism. Then, in the purity of His resurrected Body, He was now ready to present His blood in the Holy of Holies in Heaven, according to Hebrews 9: 11 & 12. He then returned and presented Himself to the 11 and invited them to see and feel the nail print proofs of His death, burial and resurrection.

That, then, is the Glorious Body after which we will be fashioned in eternity. Philippians 3:21.

(12e) I have heard you speak of the 7 "I AM's" in the Old Testament and the 7 in John's Gospel. What are they?

ANSWER: Old Testament:
1, Genesis 22:13 & 14 Jehovah Jireh I AM your Provider.
2. Exodus 15:26 Jehovah Rapha I AM your Healing.
3. Exodus 17:8 15 Jehovah Nissi I AM your Banner.
4. Judges 6:24 Jehovah Shalom I AM your Peace.
5. Psalms 23:1 Jehovah Ra-ah I AM your Shepherd.
6. Jeremiah 23:6 Jehovah Tsidkenu I AM your Righteousness.
7. Ezekiel 48:35 Jehovah Shammah I AM Present (with you).

————————

New Testament: Before John 8:48-58 - Before Abraham was I AM
1. John 6:48 I AM the Bread of Life.
2. John 8:12 I AM the Light of the World.
3. John 9:5 I AM the Light of the World.
4. John10:11 I AM the Good Shepherd.
5. John 11:25 I AM the Resurrection and the Life.
6. John 14:6 I AM the Way, the Truth and the Life.
7. John 15:5 I AM the Vine.
8th - New Beginning Revelation 22:16 I AM the Bright and Morning Star.
When does the morning star appear? At the end of night and the beginning of a new day!
ETERNITY!

(13e) Are we a covenant people?

ANSWER:
No. Ephesians 2:12 is very plain. Our Gentile forefathers were strangers from the covenants of Promise, without hope and without God in this world. But, the flip-side, now in Christ Jesus we are made nigh, not by covenants, but by the Blood of Christ. By the finished work of the Cross, we are now in a greater relationship than even the covenants, we are joint-heirs with Christ, Romans 8:1417. The covenants were directed only to the nation of Israel. In order for the covenants to be fulfilled, Christ had to accomplish the atonement, His sacrifice of Himself.

But, by His Grace that was extended beyond the covenants, and opened the windows of heaven's salvation to the whole race; beyond Human comprehension; the unsearchable riches. No wonder it can only be appropriated by Faith.

(14e) Will the Body of Christ will go into or even through the tribulation ?

In Matthew 24:3, the disciples asked about signs of the end. Jesus' direct answer in verse four was, let no man deceive you. Or, in other words, one of the signs is deception or confusion. Now, Matthew 24 is totally tribulation ground, but the world has to be prepared for even that. So, even though we are not seeing the super-natural events of the tribulation which are truly prophesied (i.e. the 2 witnesses of Revelation 11), common sense tells us the world cannot be made ready for the appearance of the Anti-christ and the False Prophet over night. So, we are naturally witnessing all the preparations. I have often likened it to getting the stage ready before the curtain goes up. Therefore, when Jesus warned of deceivers, it follows that we can see that happen before the tribulation begins.

One of the many deceptions cascading on the Christian community like an avalanche, is the claim that the Body of Christ will go into or even through the tribulation.

The one cord that binds all these deceivers together is the rejection of Paul's Apostleship. For Paul alone reveals the Doctrines, Practices and the end of the Body on earth. For example, Paul alone reveals a salvation based on faith and faith alone in the finished work of the Cross. How Christ died for the sins of the whole world. How that His shed Blood and our faith in it brings justification. How the Power of His resurrection is imparted to us when we believe. Paul alone gives instruction for the Communion service, Paul alone gives instructions concerning Deacons (no one else uses the term) and alone gave instructions for the local church. So, also, Paul alone teaches us the end of the Body of Christ on earth. Consequently, Paul alone gives us the Scriptures concerning what many now ridicule - the rapture or the catching up of the Church which is His Body. The language of I Corinthians 15:51-54, I Thessalonians 4:13-18, II Thessalonians 2:1-3 can not be found anywhere else in our Bible.

Every book that listeners send me advocating a later out-calling mixes these verses with all other verses that apply only to the Second Coming when Christ will stand on the Mount of Olives. If you mix Paul's doctrine concerning the rapture of the Church with the Second Coming, then you can mix law and Grace. And, when you mix law and Grace, Satan smiles and God is grieved.

In II Timothy, Paul paints a vivid picture of America today. But, in Titus 2:13, he gives us the Blessed Hope of the believer - the glorious appearing of the great God and our Savior Jesus Christ. I have to believe we are getting close. I trust none of you will be "left behind."

15e) Why didn't Jesus write any of the books of the Bible ?

ANSWER:
II Timothy 3:16 - All Scripture is given by inspiration of God and is profitable.... Hebrews 12:2 - Looking unto Jesus the author and finisher of our faith. II Peter 1:21 - For the prophecy (the Word) came not in old time by will of man, but holy men of God spake as they were moved (inspired) by the Holy Spirit.

In actuality, then, Christ wrote, through human instruments, the whole Bible from cover to cover. Our Lord is the visible manifestation of the invisible God (Godhead) - Colossians 1:15. So, He personifies all three Persons. When Acts 16 says the Lord opened Lydia's heart, we know it was actually by the Holy Spirit. When Peter is told in Matthew 16, flesh and blood had not revealed it, but your Father in heaven, it too was by the Holy Spirit. To understand the workings of the Trinity is beyond human understanding, so we take it by Faith. Slowly digest Isaiah 9:6 - For unto us (Israel) a child is born, unto us a son is given and the government shall be upon his shoulder (King of Kings) and his name shall be called Wonderful, Counselor, the Mighty God, the Everlasting Father, the Prince of Peace. Remember whom it is talking about in the first part of the verse - the Son.

(16e) If all are called and few are chosen, and none can come unless called - why are we to testify and witness?

ANSWER:
Because God in His Wisdom has seen fit to communicate to the human race by empowering believers with the Holy Spirit to proclaim God's Word to our fellow humans. For example, the Lord opened Lydia's heart in Acts 16:14 , but Paul spoke the words she needed to hear. Isaiah 6 is another good example. The Lord said "whom shall I send, who will go (to the nation of Israel) for us?" Isaiah answered "send me." Romans 10: 14,15 & 17 - How shall they call on him in whom they have not believed? And, how shall they believe in him of whom they have not heard? How shall they hear without a proclaimer? How shall they proclaim except they be sent? (Remember Isaiah?) So then, Faith cometh by hearing and hearing by the word of God. The call to salvation is extended to everyone. But, salvation comes only to those who are willing to believe.

(17e) Did Jesus go down to Hell the three days and three nights He was in the tomb?

ANSWER:
No and Yes. He did not go into Hell as we usually define the word. Hell, Hades or Sheol all mean the same thing. The place of the dead during the first 4,000 years of human history. Animals blood could not take away or atone for sin, so, even believers such as Abel, David,

Isaiah and all, except Enoch and Elijah (remember, God is Sovereign and He can make exceptions) went down into Sheol.

But, Sheol was divided by a great gulf fixed (Luke 16:26) into torments and Paradise. That Jesus did not go into torments is attested to by the remark to the thief on the Cross, "Today thou shalt be with me in Paradise, not torments.

That He went down is obvious from His own words in Matthew 12:40 and Paul's in Ephesians 4:8-10. Peter also refers to His going down to the Paradise side of Hell or Hades and proclaimed to those Old Testament Saints that now the atoning Blood has been shed; now, they are ready for entrance into God's Heaven. And so, at His resurrection, Paradise was removed from the Center of the Earth up to Heaven. Now, Paul teaches that believers go immediately, at death, in soul and spirit up to Paradise (or the Lord's presence), II Corinthians 5:8; waiting for the Great Resurrection Day, I Thessalonians 4.

For your own personal study, refer to these Scriptures, Matthew 12:38-40, Luke 16:19-26, Ephesians 4:8-10, I Peter 3:18 & 19, I Thessalonians 4:13-18, and I Corinthians 15:51-52. As for the unbelievers, they continue to go down to torments waiting for their resurrection to the Great White Throne Judgement. Since Paradise was removed, it has all now become Hell as we use the term (Isaiah 5:14).

(18e) "Is the Day of the Lord and the Day of God in II Peter 3:10-15 the same?"

ANSWER:
"Yes. The Day of the Lord or the Day of God begins with the opening of the final seven years of tribulation and, though interrupted by the 1,000 year reign, it continues in the destruction of the Kingdom inhabitants who follow Satan in rebellion against Christ the King. It then goes on to the destruction of the present heavens and earth according to the above Scripture and continues on to the Great White Throne judgment of Revelation 20. Then, with that finished, we, according to Revelation 21:1, will go to Eternity. A new heaven and a new earth.

The Day of Christ on the other hand is what the Body of Christ is anticipating - the Rapture and meeting our Lord in the air.

(19e) "Does the believer have two natures?"

ANSWER:
"Yes. Everyone born into the human race has the nature or personality they inherited from Adam.

"It is a nature that is in total rebellion to the things of God. Romans 8 calls it an enemy of God. It is subject to the ruler of this world, Satan (II Corinthians 4:4).

"Even though many good people have refined this old sin nature and kept it under control, it is still the personality that Paul describes in Romans 1 and Ephesians 2. But, that personality has to die the death of crucifixion (Galatians 2:20 and Romans 6).

Though God reckons it as dead, in our experience, he, the old Adam, is still alive and operates opposite the New Divine nature of Person, which God created in us the moment we believe the Gospel. Hence, the Christian is in a constant battle. The old nature leading us into rebellion and the new nature leading us into obedience to Christ.

The old nature can do nothing good, and the new nature cannot sin. So, which one has the upper hand in our daily life? The one we feed the best. Feed the old Adam and you will be a defeated, miserable Christian. Feed the new, or Spiritual, and you will be victorious and joyful.

NOTES

NOTES

NOTES

NOTES

NOTES

NOTES